ATLANTIS OF THE NORTH

ATLANTIS
OF THE NORTH

JÜRGEN SPANUTH

SIDGWICK & JACKSON
LONDON

First published in Great Britain by
Sidgwick and Jackson Limited 1979

First published in Germany by
Grabert-Verlag
Originally published as **Die Atlanter**
by Grabert-Verlag

Copyright © 1976 by Grabert-Verlag, 74 Tübingen
English translation © 1979 by
Sidgwick and Jackson Limited

ISBN 0 283 98495 3

Typesetting by
Rainbow Graphics, Liverpool
and Printed in Great Britain by
R. J. Acford Limited, Chichester, Sussex,
for Sidgwick and Jackson Limited,
Tavistock Chambers, Bloomsbury Way,
London, WC1A 2S6

CONTENTS

LIST OF ILLUSTRATIONS

INTRODUCTION

I have received several thousand letters since the appearance in 1965 of my book *Atlantis*. The sentiments of many of my correspondents are summarized in the words of one of them, Professor Schmied-Kowarzik:

> You have earned our most heartfelt thanks for rescuing for German history a most ancient and yet living narrative, from before the Cimbrian and Teutonic migrations, before Tacitus's *Germania*, before Pytheas – from the thirteenth century BC. Scholarship now has a great task before it. . . . Humbly but joyfully we must now follow up your pioneering discovery.

Atlantis was a lengthy and comprehensive work and many letters asked me to publish a shorter version without the full scholarly apparatus of references to my sources. I was anxious to publish new material which I had assembled since 1965, and to treat certain aspects of the Atlantis narrative in more detail. The present volume, therefore, restates the conclusions of my earlier researches and adds the new evidence that has accumulated over more than a decade. However, I could not state my conclusions without the scholarly apparatus of references and quotations. My solution to the 'riddle of Atlantis' is so novel and startling that I should lay myself open to accusations of merely peddling fantasy if I did not support every assertion with evidence from the researches of experts in the relevant subjects.

As not all readers of the present book will know my *Atlantis*, or have it available, I have had to repeat much of what I wrote in 1965. However, I hope that readers of my earlier publication will read this new one with interest and profit, and that those who do not yet know my work will allow themselves to be convinced by the results of my researches.

The 'riddle of Atlantis' is often described as 'the greatest enigma of world history'. It is no such thing. The only riddle is why nobody until now has tackled the questions of the date at which Atlantis must have existed, and the site of its empire and island capital, by the usual methods of historical research; that is to say, by looking for the *original documents* from which Solon derived the account that he brought back from Egypt.

It is also something of a riddle that men who claim to value their professional integrity as scholars should produce falsifications of my statements, or those of others, or even of their own, and moreover refuse even to read my book and assert that they have no idea of the archaeological questions with which it deals.

In the words of Professor Schmied-Kowarzik: 'Scholarship now has a great task before it.' It will only be able to fulfil this task if it lays to heart the advice of Plato – who after all wrote down the Atlantis narrative – 'We must pursue the truth with our entire souls.'

CHAPTER 1

THE KEY TO THE RIDDLE
OF ATLANTIS

The historical foundations

The real 'riddle of Atlantis' is not where the realm of Atlantis lay, nor when its island capital sank beneath the sea. It is rather the fact that not one of the many writers who have commented on the Atlantis narrative has found, or even looked for, the key which the text of the tale itself repeatedly offers. Again and again it asserts that the story which Solon, 'the wisest of the seven wise men' *Ti.* 20*, brought back to Athens from his stay in Egypt in 570–560 BC was *derived from original records* contained in ancient Egyptian temple inscriptions and papyrus texts.

Solon was the great Greek statesman who gave the Athenians the first democratic constitution the world has known, to replace the harsh dictatorial Draconian code. He then made the Athenians swear to rule their city-state according to this constitution for ten years without altering it. In the meanwhile he wished to travel to Egypt in order to study the lore of ancient times.

He could not have chosen a more suitable country for such studies, for the Egyptian priests of that period, which the Egyptologist Breasted has rightly named 'a time of restoration', had already been busy for about a century collecting, copying and arranging the old inscriptions and manuscripts of their country. They had at their disposal, therefore, an extensive body of historical knowledge, which they willingly shared with Solon. About a hundred years later Herodotus, the 'father of history', was also in Egypt, and he likewise brought back much historical information which the priests there gave him.

Nor could Solon have chosen a better moment in time for his enquiries, for this was the reign of King Amasis (sometimes known as l'ahmases II, or Amose (570–526 BC) who 'belonged to and was

---

* *Ti.* = Timaeus, *Criti.* = *Critias* – the dialogues by Plato which contain the Atlantis narrative. They are reproduced in the Appendix.

largely a product of the Greek world' (Breasted 1954, p. 316).

Solon 'was highly honoured' in Egypt (*Ti.* 21e). In the ten years of his residence there he heard and saw much, but what interested him most was the story that is known as the Atlantis narrative, since it told of an outstandingly heroic action of his native city, Athens.

The Egyptian priests, among them Sonchis of Thebes and Psenophis of Heliopolis, 'who were most knowledgeable on the subject' (*Ti.* 22) showed Solon temple inscriptions and papyrus scrolls which told of his native city and of the heroic stand that the Athenians had made alone against the armies of the island realm of Atlantis which had campaigned through Europe into Greece.

As Solon could not read the hieroglyphic writing of the old texts, he 'eagerly begged the priests to describe to him in detail the doings of these citizens of the past' and one of them replied, 'I will gladly do so, Solon, both for your sake and your city's' (*Ti.* 23d).

The priest then recounted to Solon the old Egyptian story, consulting the records to refresh his memory (*Ti.* 24a). Solon wrote down the story and brought it back to Athens. He had wished, as he once said, to compose a great epic on the subject, but unhappily was obliged 'because of the class struggles and other evils he found . . . on his return' (*Ti.* 21c) to postpone the project. He died a year later and so his epic of Atlantis and Athens was never written. Critias the Elder, who inherited Solon's manuscript, said that he did not think 'any poet, even Homer or Hesiod, would have been more famous' (*Ti.* 21d) if Solon had written his poem.

During one of the discussions which Socrates held with his pupils, Plato, Timaeus, Critias the Younger and Hermocrates, one of the company spoke of the 'true history' of the ancestors of the Athenians and their preservation in war and peace. The speaker was Critias· the Younger, who explained that he had inherited from his grandfather, Critias the Elder, the original writing that Solon had brought with him from Egypt. 'My father had his [Solon's] manuscript, which is still in my possession, and I studied it often as a child' (*Criti.* 113b). He asked for leave until their next meeting, to refresh his memory, and next day he passed on to Socrates and his fellow pupils the narrative that Solon had brought back from Egypt. Plato incorporated it into his dialogues *Timaeus* and *Critias*, and so preserved it for posterity.

At one point it is said that the account is 'not a fiction but *true history*' (*Ti.* 26e), at another that Solon 'vouched for its truth' (*Ti.* 20d), and at another that it is an 'unrecorded yet authentic achievement of our city' (*Ti.* 21a).

The Viennese classical scholar, W. Brandenstein, who has published a detailed study of the Atlantis narrative, has rightly said: 'The theory that Plato simply invented the Egyptian derivation, while at the same

time showing an extensive knowledge of sources, and constantly reaffir-
ming that it was all pure truth, *cannot be sustained'* (1951, p. 61).

To sum up: the Atlantis narrative is derived from ancient Egyptian
temple inscriptions and papyrus texts.

It is clear, therefore, that the only key to unlock all the problems
raised by the narrative – which unfortunately breaks off in mid-
sentence – must be contained in those same inscriptions and texts. To go
ad fontes, to the sources, the original texts, has always been considered the
fundamental principle of all historical research. Yet in Atlantis studies it
has not even been tried. That is the true 'riddle of Atlantis': It will only
be possible to find answers to the many questions raised by Solon's
narrative if we first seek and find the ancient Egyptian temple inscriptions and papyrus texts.

The date of the Atlantis narrative

In order to find the ancient Egyptian originals of the Atlantis narrative it
is first necessary to ascertain the *period* from which this 'true history'
derives. But here is a major problem, for the priests told Solon that
everything they recounted to him had happened eight or nine *thousand
years* earlier.

This is a quite impossible date, for it is certain that eight or nine
thousand years before Solon's stay in Egypt, none of the things mentioned in the Atlantis narrative existed. In Egypt there was no Egyptian
state, no temples with inscriptions, no papyrus texts. The Nile valley was
then uninhabited – the first few remains in the area date from the fifth to
sixth millennia BC and were found on the heights nearby. There were no
Libyans either in western Egypt; they appear for the first time in the
records of Merneptah in about 1227 BC.

In Greece there was at that date no city of Athens, no citadel on the
Acropolis, no temple to Athena and Hephaestus, no city wall. There
were no Greek states and no Greek armies. Nowhere on earth at that
time was there any people who wielded weapons of bronze and iron,
had at their disposal a fleet of warships, and could send chariots and
cavalry into battle. Yet the Atlantis narrative mentions all these things,
and many others which certainly did not exist in the ninth to tenth
millennia BC.

Anyone, therefore, who takes literally the date given by the Egyptian priests is bound to dismiss the entire Atlantis story as an 'unhistorical myth'. Realizing that it cannot be correct, many researchers
have tried to assign a period of their own to the events of the story and in
the attempt have come up with some quite absurd dates.

Rudolf Steiner asserted that the narrative referred to events 'eighty

thousand years ago' (1928, p. 14) and that the Atlanteans of that time
'knew how to put the germinal energy of organisms into the service of
their technology. . . . Plants were cultivated in the Atlantean period not
merely to use as foodstuffs but also in order to make the energy dormant
in them available to commerce and industry. . . . The vehicles of the
Atlanteans, which floated a short distance above the ground, were
moved in this way.'

It is hardly necessary to point out that statements like this have
nothing whatever to do with the Atlantis narrative, and that
archaeology has found not the slightest trace of the manufactures and
the marvellous flying machines which Steiner ascribed to these 80,000-
year-old Atlanteans.

Among innumerable other attempts, the Hamburg scholar Adolf
Schulten suggested one of the latest datings for Solon's story. According
to him, the events of which it tells occurred about 500 BC. A similar date
was given by H. Diller, a classicist from Kiel. In his opinion the Atlantis
narrative is a 'fictional parallel to the Persian wars, projected backwards
into prehistory, and set on the opposite front'. The wars between Persia
and Greece took place in 500–449 BC.

The answer to this attempt at explanation must be that Solon, 'the
wisest of the seven wise men', was on the one hand not so wise that he
could describe an event which only began fifty-nine years *after* his own
death and on the other hand was too wise to invent a 'fictional parallel'
to the Persian wars without a single parallel feature but with many
divergences.

Some of these divergences may be enumerated here.

The capital city of Atlantis lay on an island, in the estuary of great
rivers, had three harbours and was surrounded by a fruitful countryside.
It had its origin in the mists of antiquity, when 'there were still no ships
or sailing'. The capital of the Persians, Persepolis, lay in semi-desert, far
from the sea or any navigable harbours, far from all rivers and canals. It
was founded by Darius I in 517 BC, some time after Solon's death.

The royal city of Atlantis was 'swallowed up by the sea and vanished'
(*Ti.* 25d) long before Solon's day. Persepolis remained a large and
flourishing city until 330 BC when Alexander the Great destroyed it. Its
ruins are still there to admire. In 1973 kings and presidents attended a
great festival to commemorate its foundation.

The people of the island realm of Atlantis were notable seafarers and
had at their disposal a fleet of 1200 warships. The Persians were an
inland people and the ships for their fleet had to be provided by their
allies and subject peoples.

In the course of their invasion the Atlanteans conquered all the
Greek states and found serious resistance only at Athens. The Persians
captured Athens without opposition, because the Athenians had fled to

the Peloponnese. The Atlanteans were unable to capture the Athenian Acropolis. The Persians took it by storm and destroyed it.

The Atlanteans had conquered 'Libya up to the borders of Egypt and Europe as far as Tyrrhenia' (*Ti.* 25b). The Persians never overcame nor ruled over these lands. The Atlanteans were repulsed when they tried to conquer Egypt (*Ti.* 25c). The Persians overcame Egypt in 485 BC and their rule there lasted until Alexander the Great ended it in 322 BC.

There are numerous other divergences between the Persian wars and the account given in the Atlantis narrative. Even Diller could cite only differences – 'projected backwards and set on the opposite front'.

No, Solon was not such a fool as to invent a 'fictional parallel' without parallels!

So all, or nearly all, the attempts to assign a period to the Atlantis narrative fall to the ground. Only one researcher, Wilhelm Brandenstein, after a long exchange of letters with myself, arrived at the solution: 'What the Egyptian priests told Solon, drawing on the past history of their country, was the story of the terrible invasion by the Sea Peoples of the North, which was repulsed by King Ramses III (1200–1168 BC)' (1951, p. 60).

The Acroplis of Athens. In the foreground, the earliest wall mentioned in the Atlantis document (Criti. 112b)

Indeed, both the statements in the Atlantis narrative itself and all the other relevant data indicate that the events described are those of the decades just before and after 1200 BC. From the many pieces of evidence that could be cited, I will mention only the following.

In Athens at that time 'the military class lived by itself round the temple of Athena and Hephaestus, surrounded by a single wall like the garden of a single house. On the northern side they built their common dwelling-houses' (*Criti.* 112a).

The archaeologists E. Kirsten and W. Kraiker wrote of this first and oldest wall on the Athenian Acropolis:

> In the second half of the thirteenth century BC the entire summit was surrounded by a great ring-wall of huge unhewn limestone blocks, from 4 to 6 m in thickness and at least 10 m in height. It was constructed on the same plan and by the same technique as the contemporary citadel wall of Mycenae, and contained a larger area (35,000 square metres compared with 30,000 square metres at Mycenae and 20,000 at Tiryns). (1956, p. 40.)

The archaeologist F. Dirlmeier published a detailed study of this oldest wall on the Acropolis, which is known as the 'Pelasgic' or 'Cyclopean' wall. 'We may see this Pelasgic wall as the mighty fortification of a place of refuge, built in a moment of extreme danger. The Americans conjecture "an early stage of the Dorian invasions".' (Dirlmeier 1940a, p. 42.)

The Atlantis narrative further states: 'There was a single spring in the area of the present Acropolis, which was subsequently choked by the earthquakes and survives only in a few small trickles in the vicinity; in those days there was an ample supply of good water both in winter and summer' (*Criti.* 112d).

In 1938 this fountain was rediscovered and excavated, in precisely the spot described, 'in the area of the present Acropolis', 'on the northern side'. There, in a natural shaft in the limestone cliff, were found man-made steps which led down 'on the northern side' of the Acropolis, inside the Cyclopean wall to a spring which rises at a depth of about 40 m. The upper part of this staircase was accessible up to modern times, 'The lower part was destroyed and already forgotten in the classical era' (Broneer 1948, p. 111 ff.; Franke 1972, p. 282). At the bottom of the shaft a deep well had been dug, in late Mycenaean times, in which the water of the spring collected.

The archaeologist F. Matz (1958) summarized the excavation results as follows:

> According to Broneer, the stairway leading to the spring on the north side of the Acropolis was constructed at this period [the end of the thirteenth century BC]. The potsherds, which, as is clear from the position in which they were found, belong to the time of its construction, date from the

transition period from Mycenaean IIIb to Mycenaean IIIc. In the opinion of the excavators, the stairway was only used for twenty to twenty-five years. The pottery found in the ruins of the steps dates from that interval. . . . It is connected, indirectly but convincingly, with the known date of the catastrophe in the Peloponnese.

Broneer conjectured that severe earth tremors ruined the site of the spring and so made it inaccessible up to modern times. The remains lend support to this conjecture. In the lower part of the well-shaft were found the skull of a child and the remains of the skeleton of a woman. The inference would seem to be that a woman and child were just fetching water when the earthquake shattered the well. Evidence of a severe earthquake which destroyed the buildings of the Acropolis has been found elsewhere. Just by the entrance to the well, ruined houses have been found, which had been neither burnt nor plundered. Moreover the inhabitants must have fled so suddenly that they could not take their household goods, some of which were found undisturbed in their places. 'In one room . . . a cooking pot on three feet was discovered standing in the ashes of the fire over which presumably the last meal had been cooked when the occupants suddenly had to rush away without taking time to salvage their household goods' (Broneer 1948, p. 112).

Many houses, fortresses and palaces in the eastern Mediterranean have been found in the same state. They had undoubtedly been destroyed at the same time – 'the end of the thirteenth century BC' – by a major earthquake.

So the statement in the Atlantis narrative that the spring 'was subsequently choked by the earthquakes' may be taken as historically correct.

The other statements in the narrative concerning 'the layout of the city in those days' are undoubtedly true. A. Franke made a thorough investigation of these texts and concluded: 'If we compare with this description the results of the research on Mycenaean Athens carried out during the various excavations organized by the Greek, American and German institutes in the early and mid-twentieth century, we find amazing correspondences' (1972, p. 279).

A help towards the dating of the Atlantis narrative is its statement that these catastrophes spared 'none but the unlettered and uncultured' whereas all those who could read and write perished (*Ti*. 23a–b).

Until a few decades ago it was generally assumed that the inhabitants of Greece in the Mycenaean age were illiterate, and that the art of writing only became known in Greece some time in the eighth century BC. Then Sir Arthur Evans found in the ruins of Knossos quantities of clay tablets covered in script, dating from *before* the destruction of the palace in 1200 BC. Subsequently, similar inscribed tablets were found at Pylos, Mycenae, Orchomenus, Thebes, Eleusis,

Tiryns, Melos, Thera, Cydonia and Dendra Midea. The script used was named 'Linear B'. Since it became known, tablets and potsherds with the same writing have been found at practically every excavation which has uncovered Mycenaean strata.

In the opinion of J. Chadwick, who with Michael Ventris deciphered them in 1956, the tablets with Linear B inscriptions found at Knossos and Pylos were incised on the damp clay by thirty to forty different hands. The numerous finds of this script show that in the thirteenth century BC, the period from which all the tablets derive, writing was known all over Greece and practised by many scribes.

Linear B writing must have been used in Greece over a long period. Yet all the tablets that have been preserved date from the same time. There is a reason for this. The script was impressed on soft, unfired clay tablets which naturally had only a short life. All those that have been preserved have been baked hard by the terrible outbreaks of fire which visited all the Mycenaean and Minoan palaces. Then the buildings were thrown down by fearful earthquakes, covering the tablets with thick layers of debris, impervious to air and water. In this way they were preserved up to our own day. Chadwick cites many additional indications that 'all the tablets from each site are contemporary within narrow limits' (1967, p. 127).

When all the palaces of the Greek mainland and Crete were thus destroyed, naturally most of the scribes were killed and only those ignorant of writing were left. Linear B died out suddenly all over Greece and Crete, and was never written again. Only in the eighth century did Greece acquire another script, which had nothing to do with the older one.

So during the 'Dark Ages' after 1200 BC there was no writing in Greece and these were centuries of great poverty and need. This too was accurately described by the Egyptian priest: 'For many generations they and their children were short of bare necessities, and their minds and thoughts were occupied with providing for them, to the neglect of earlier history and tradition' (*Criti.* 110a).

'How did things seem during the Dark Ages? The Aegean culture had been wiped out. Its heirs, mixed with their conquerors [i.e. the Atlanteans] forgot the old script. They could no longer read and write. They even forgot small useful contrivances, such as oil-lamps.' (Kahl-Furthmann 1967, p. 11.)

It is true that oil-lamps, which are common in Mycenaean strata, are absent in the post-Mycenaean ones. Not, however, because the later inhabitants of Greece had forgotten their use, but because in their former home they had used nothing but pine torches.

So here too the Atlantis narrative has transmitted historically accurate facts: about 1200 BC the Linear B script suddenly ceased to be used. 'In Solon's or Plato's time no memory whatever of Linear B survived, and no inscriptions in it were extant' (Franke 1972, p. 272). From where then could Solon or Plato have learned this historical reality, if not from Egypt? Only there did writing survive, even in the Dark Ages. But in Greece, as the Atlantis narrative truly says, 'many succeeding generations left no record in writing' (*Ti.* 23c). So Solon was right when he admitted to the Egyptian priests 'that both he and all his countrymen were almost entirely ignorant about antiquity' (*Ti.* 22a).

Many other features of the narrative show that the events it records belong to the period around 1200 BC. Among them are the statements about the severe natural catastrophes which visited the world in the second half of the thirteenth century BC, the change of climate which began at that time, the great invasion of the Atlanteans up to the Egyptian frontiers, the heroic and successful resistance of the Athenians and the information that the Atlanteans had, even at that date, the use of iron weapons. (The first iron weapons appear with the invasion of the North and Sea Peoples, who at the end of the thirteenth century BC broke like a hurricane on the Mediterranean lands, as W. Witter, the expert on prehistoric metallurgy, explained in an exhaustive study (1941, p. 223 f.; 1942).)

Moreover the repeated mention of Libya and the Libyans shows that the narrative deals with events of this date. The names 'Libya' and 'Libyans' appear for the first time in Egyptian texts in inscriptions of the time of Merneptah, about 1227 BC. The wars against the Libyans and the North and Sea Peoples, which the Atlantis narrative mentions, took place about 1200 BC. The use of cavalry, which is also ascribed to the Atlanteans, occurred for the first time in the Mediterranean region at about this same date (Wiesner 1943, p. 110).

Even the assertion of the Egyptian priests that these events took place eight thousand or nine thousand years before, shows that the account does indeed come from Egypt, and that in fact the thirteenth century BC is meant. This paradox is easily explained. Egyptian priests gave similar, totally impossible dates to Herodotus during his stay in Egypt, and to the historian Manetho (third century BC). So, for example, we read in Herodotus that from the time of the Egyptian Heracles (a god-king of the past) up to the reign of Amasis (died 526 BC) 17,000 years had passed (*History* 2.143). Or, 'One gets a total of 11,340 years, during the whole of which time, they say, no god ever assumed mortal form' (2.143). Or, 'They declare that 341 generations separate the first king of Egypt from the last' (*ibid.*). Or, 'Dionysus . . . appeared, they say, 15,000 years before Amasis' (2.145).

Greek historians soon recognized that these dates were impossible. Eudoxus of Cnidos (c. 408–355 BC), like Plutarch four centuries later, gave the explanation: 'The Egyptians reckon a month as a year.'

Diodorus Siculus (fl. 60–30 BC) wrote of the Egyptians: 'Some men would maintain that in early times, before the movement of the sun had as yet been recognized, it was customary to reckon the year by the lunar cycle. Consequently, since the year consisted of thirty days, it was not impossible that some men lived 1200 years.' (1.26.)

Even in our own time, ex-King Farouk wrote in his memoirs: 'Our calendar reckons by the moon, and not, like the Gregorian calendar of most Western countries, in years of 365 days. So our "year" is shorter.' (*Stern*, 1952, 43, p. 13).

Now if the 9000 or 8000 'years' of the Atlantis story are converted into the moon-months of the Egyptian calendar – a year has 13 moons – then we arrive at the period between 1252 and 1175 BC, precisely the time during which all those events of which the Egyptian priests told Solon did in fact occur. For there can be no doubt, from all those statements in the Atlantis narrative to which a date can be assigned, that the events it describes are those of the decades just before and after 1200 BC.

Ancient Egyptian temple inscriptions and papyrus texts
c. 1200 BC

The fullest extant ancient Egyptian inscriptions and papyrus scrolls date from precisely the period about 1200 BC. Of the temple inscriptions, the most important, apart from those of the time of Merneptah, are the ones from the palace-temple of Ramses III at Medinet Habu.

Ramses III, who came to the throne at the age of forty in 1200 BC*, had, like every other Pharaoh, to mark his accession by beginning two buildings: a temple and a tomb. Work would continue on them throughout the Pharaoh's reign and they would be completed only at his death. The magnificent palace-temple of Ramses III was excavated between 1927 and 1936 by the Oriental Institute of the University of Chicago. About 10,000 square metres of inscriptions and mural reliefs were discovered, still clearly visible, though a large part had been destroyed. The inscriptions have been translated into English and published, together with exact copies of the original murals, by the American Egyptologists J.H. Breasted, W.F. Edgerton and J. Wilson. Twelve large volumes have been published to date.

> On the Western plain of Thebes, at the point now called Medinet Habu, he [Ramses III] built a large and splendid temple to Amon which he began early in his reign. As the temple was enlarged and extended from rear to

---

* The choice of dates for events in Egyptian history is explained on page 158.

Captive North Sea warriors in chains (Medinet Habu, 2nd courtyard, photo Spanuth)

front the annals of his campaigns found place on the walls through successive
years following the growth of the building until the whole edifice became a
vast record of the king's achievements in war which the modern visitor may
read... Here he may see the hordes of the North in battle with Ramses'
Sherdan mercenaries... the first naval battle on salt water, of which we
know anything, is here depicted, and in these reliefs we may study the
armour, clothing, weapons, warships and equipment of these Northern
peoples with whose advent Europe for the first time emerges upon the stage
of the early world. (Breasted 1954, p. 366.)

The German Egyptologist F. Bilabel called these documents 'texts of
the greatest historical value' (1927, p. 213) and 'the most interesting
records that have come down to us' (1927, p. 259). The translators
themselves call them 'most directly historical'.

In addition to the Medinēt Habu texts and murals, a kind of report
on the reign of Ramses III has survived in the 'Harris papyrus'. This is a
papyrus scroll, 39 m long, which Breasted has called 'one of the most
remarkable documents' and 'the largest document which has descended
to us from the early Orient' (1954, p. 271).

From the same period – the end of the thirteenth century BC – dates
also the 'Ipuwer papyrus'. This was discovered in Memphis and
acquired in 1828 by the Museum of Leiden in the Netherlands, where it
is still preserved. Its close verbal correspondence with the texts from
Medinet Habu has led the Egyptologists S. Morenz, J. Leiden and C.
Baux to date the composition of this papyrus to the time between 1220
and 1205 BC.

Other papyri are, for example, the 'Golenischeff papyrus' (or
papyrus Hermitage 1116B), which speaks among other things of the
erection of a fortress to block the advance of the North and Sea Peoples.
It dates from the second half of the thirteenth century. Another is in the
collection of the Archduke Rainer in Vienna. It is a copy made in the
third century BC of a thirteenth-century (BC) original.

A sarcophagus which was preserved in the museum of Ismailia up to
the outbreak of the last Israeli-Egyptian war has on it an account of the
downfall of the Pharaoh who, about 1220 BC, was drowned in the 'Jam
Suf', the 'Sea of Reeds', in pursuit of the Children of Israel.

So there is available a large body of inscriptions, mural reliefs and
papyrus texts dating from the period to which the events of the Atlantis
story have been shown to belong. They will help to answer the question
whether Solon, in describing these events, was following reliable
sources. The answer must be yes, for all the main statements in
the Atlantis narrative are confirmed and completed by these
documents.

Two Northmen with horned helmets on board a Northern ship (Medinet Habu, photo Spanuth)

Dying North Sea warrior with 'rayed crown' (Medinet Habu, photo Spanuth)

The home of the Atlanteans

The problem of the location of Atlantis has been considered in a thousand books. It can be finally answered with the help of the ancient Egyptian originals of the Atlantis narrative.

In the texts of Medinet Habu it is said of the peoples who attacked Egypt in about 1200 BC from Amurru (approximately the modern Palestine), from the sea and from the West in alliance with the Libyans and Tyrrhenians (as the Atlantis narrative also says), that they came from 'the islands and coastlands of the Ocean, in the farthest North'.

As W. Helck rightly said, 'The place of origin is named as "the islands in the Ocean, that lie in the North".' (1962, p. 242.) In this context it must be emphasized that the Egyptians understood by the *sin wur* – the 'great water-circle', 'ocean', – *not* the Mediterranean but always the outer water or encircling stream which in their cosmology surrounded the disc of the earth. As a collective term for the various tribes and peoples who came from 'the islands in the Ocean, that lie in the North', the name 'Haunebu' or 'Haunebut' is used in the Medinet Habu texts. According to R. Eisler (1928, p. 2), 'The name of this foreign people is not Egyptian' – and so is possibly one which they applied to themselves.

The 'Haunebu' appear in quite early Egyptian texts. The amber which from about 2400 BC on is found in Egyptian tombs or mentioned in inscriptions is said to come from the Haunebu. From the Haunebu, who are described as 'all the northern lands from the ends of the earth', there came in the reign of Thutmose III (c. 1500 BC) an embassy bringing 8943 pounds of amber to the Pharaoh. They are mentioned in the oldest pyramid texts; for example: 'Behold you are great and round in (your name of) Ocean; behold, you are circular and round as the circle which surrounds the Haunebut' (Faulkner 1969, utterance 366; also G. Roeder 1919, p. 195; Grapow, p. 52). The list of peoples of Edfu has: 'Haunebut is the name of the islands of the great water-circle, and the northern lands that live from the water of the stream'. (Bilabel 1927, p. 395). In an inscription from the New Kingdom is: 'All the lands of the Haunebu, the foreigners from the Great Ocean' (Grapow, p. 52; Dunichen, *Historische Inschriften*, 2, 47d).

On the pylon of Horemheb (1335–1310 BC) is: 'The Haunebu come from the great water-circle at the end of the world' (Grapow, *loc. cit.*). In an inscription from Phylae it says: 'the stream of the great water-circle, that leads to the Haunebu'.

There can be no question, then, that the Egyptians placed the homeland of the Haunebu in the 'great water-circle', the northern

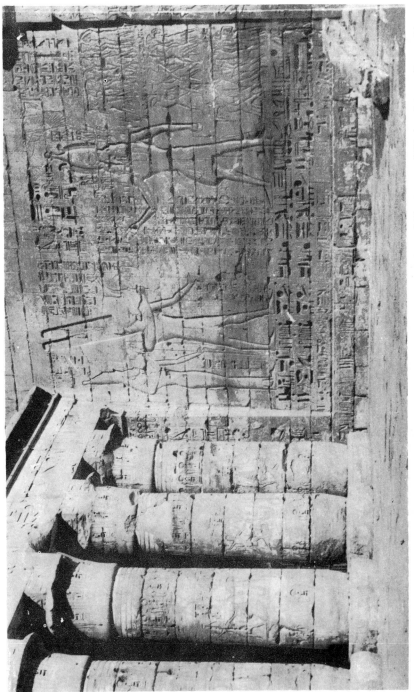

Medinet Habu, left of courtyard. Ramses III leads captured North Sea People before the god No-Amun of Thebes (photo, Spanuth)

ocean, and *not* in the Mediterranean, which never counted as part of the 'water-circle'.

This is *not* contradicted by the fact that on the Rosetta Stone the word 'Haunebu' is translated as *Hellenikos* (= Greek). The famous stone dates from the time of Cleopatra (69–30 BC), who is mentioned on it. At that period the Haunebu or North Sea Peoples had been settled in Greece for more than a thousand years, since the time of their great migration.

The phrase 'peoples from the islands and coastlands of the Ocean, in the farthest North' has been translated in many books as 'North and Sea Peoples'. This is inexact; it leads the reader to look for their home around the Mediterranean and to think in terms of two different groups – the 'North People' and the 'Sea People'. Helck's translation, 'the islands in the Ocean, that lie in the North', is much better. For short, one could translate the phrase as 'Northern Ocean Peoples' or, as I shall say from here on, 'North Sea Peoples'.

In other texts these tribes are referred to as 'peoples from the ends of the earth'. This also means people from the extreme north of the inhabited world, as the Egyptians knew it. In innumerable places Egyptian, Hebrew, Babylonian, Greek and Latin writings refer to the most northerly lands as 'the ends of the earth'.

Other sections of the Medinet Habu text say of the North Sea Peoples, 'They come from the pillars of heaven.' The Egyptians, like all the ancient peoples, believed that the sky rested on one or more pillars, upon whose apex or apices it revolved. Now since the pole star appears to be the only fixed point in the sky, all ancient peoples believed that the pillar(s) of heaven stood below this – and consequently were in the extreme north. As E. Tièche has shown with numerous supporting quotations in his work, *Atlas als Personifikation der Weltachse*, the Greeks regarded Atlas, the heaven bearer, as the 'personification of the world-axis' – the axis of the earth – which stands in the north reaching up to the pole of heaven.

Yet another description of the home of these North Sea Peoples says, 'They come from the distant darkness' or 'midnight'. The Egyptians believed that in the north eternal darkness (*duat*) reigned. For instance, they said, 'The sun rests in the sixth hour of the night (midnight) in the depths of the darkness,' and, 'The sun leaves the thick darkness at the twelfth hour of the night (six in the morning)' (Sethe 1928, p. 261 f.). In the Old Testament one finds that 'north' (*ha sa poni*) is described as 'the midnight' (Josh. 11:2; 13:3; 15:5; 15:8; 16:6; 17:10; 18:5; 18:12; 16–19 *passim*).

Even more precise is the description in the Medinet Habu texts: 'people from the ninth bow'. The Egyptians saw the world as divided into nine 'bows' which correspond roughly to the modern concept of meridians of latitude. The term for the entire earth is 'all the nine bows'. The Graeco-Roman world took over the conception; the 'bows' are called *paralelloi* in Greek and *circuli* in Latin. Pliny the Elder, for example, said that the ninth division of the world goes 'across the Hyperboreans' (i.e. the Cimbrian peninsula, present-day Jutland) 'with a seventeen-hour day' (at its longest). F.A. Ukert pointed out long ago that this method of dividing the world was taken from the Egyptians and that the 'ninth bow' corresponds to the area between latitudes 52 and 57 (1816–46, Bd 1, T12, p. 187; Bd 3, T1 2, p. 396 ff. and elsewhere). Between those latitudes lie north Germany, Denmark and southern Scandinavia.

Therefore it is in this region that the homeland of the peoples 'from the ninth bow', 'from the pillars of heaven', 'from the islands in the Ocean, that lie in the North', must be sought.

The Egyptian world picture about 1200 BC. The 'circle of the earth' is surrounded by the 'great water-circle' *(sin wur,* Greek *Okeanos).* The circle of the earth is divided into 'nine bows'; hence the whole world can be described as 'all the nine bows'. The ninth bow lies 'at the ends of the earth in the furthest North'. The Greeks called the 'heaven-pillar' *stele boreios =* the north pillar, and the heaven bearer, 'Atlas'. For this reason alone the 'holy island' of the Atlanteans, on which stood the 'pillars of Atlas' can only be in northern Europe

These indications correspond with those given in the Atlantis narrative. There too we read that the war expedition of the Atlanteans had its starting point in the 'Atlantic sea' (*Ti.* 24e), whose name is explained as follows. 'He [the god Poseidon] gave them all names. The eldest, the King, he gave a name from which the whole island and the surrounding ocean took their designation of "Atlantic", deriving it from Atlas the first King.' (*Criti.* 114a.)

It is a basic fault in historical method, but an extremely common one, to attribute to ancient peoples modern geographical knowledge and conceptions, and to equate the names and phrases used by the ancients with those of modern geographers. This mistake is constantly made in translating the phrase 'Atlantic sea' in this narrative; in many books it is identified with the 'Atlantic Ocean' of today. But to the ancients it did *not* mean our 'Atlantic' but the North Sea – or rather, the North Sea together with the Baltic, which they conceived as one sea.

The 'pillars of heaven' stood – as I have shown – under the pole star. The god of these world-pillars was known to the Egyptians as 'Tat', to the Greeks as 'Atlas', and to the Germanic peoples as 'Irmin' (who is called Iormun in the *Eddas**). All these peoples believed that the heaven-bearing god stood in the far north. This is why the Egyptians said of him: 'I am Tat, son of Tat, born in the distant darkness.' The Greeks said of Atlas:

> . . . And here stand the terrible houses
> of dark Night,
> . . . Before them
> Atlas, son of Iapetos, stands
>   staunchly upholding
> the wide heaven upon his head
>   and with arms unwearying
> sustains it. . .

Hesiod *Theogony*, 746 f.

Since the ancients placed the heaven bearer in the extreme north, the north pole was called the 'Atlantic pole' or 'the pole held up by Atlas' (Tièche 1945, p. 70–85). Apollodorus wrote, 'Atlas (stands) among the Hyperboreans' (Apollodorus 2.5.11). The 'Hyperboreans' means the tribes living on the Cimbrian peninsula (Jutland).

Hecataeus said: 'The land of the Hyperboreans lies on the Atlantic sea, opposite the land of the Celts' (Jacoby, *Fragmente der Griechischen Historiker*, 2.386). This, and many other passages from ancient authors quoted by Tièche, shows that Atlas the heaven bearer was imagined as standing in the north, and the 'Atlantic sea' was the North Sea (together with the Baltic).

So the statements in the Atlantis narrative that the Atlanteans came from 'the Atlantic sea' and that their kings there 'ruled over many islands and parts of the mainland' correspond exactly with those of the

---

* The *Eddas* are works of old Scandinavian traditional lore, recorded in writing in medieval Iceland. The *Elder* or *Poetic Edda* is a collection of traditional poems, written down *c.* AD 1200 but deriving from much earlier times. The *Younger* or *Prose Edda* consists of two treatises on mythology by Snorri Sturluson (1179–1241).

Medinet Habu texts that 'they come from the islands and coastlands of the Ocean, in the farthest North', or 'they come from the pillars of heaven'.

The Atlantis narrative is also correct when it states that the country and the sea were called after a King 'Atlas' (*Criti.* 114). In the *Eddas** the northlands are called 'Atalland' (*Thule,* 23.74) and the sea 'Atle's path' (20.320). Gustav Neckel explained the name Atal or Atle as that of a sea king. The same king, it would seem, who ruled over the sea, and from whom 'the whole island and the surrounding ocean took their designation of "Atlantic"'. The names 'Atland', 'Adalland' and 'Oatland' occur frequently in old records as names for districts in various countries around the North Sea (see Föstemann, *Altdeutsches Namenbuch,* under these headings).

Did those invading peoples who, as the texts from Ramses III's reign and the Atlantis narrative both agree, penetrated as far as the frontiers of Egypt, indeed come from northern Europe? The pictures in the murals of Medinet Habu leave no doubt of it. Here the ancient Egyptian artists, in their typical naturalistic style, have preserved the likenesses of many hundreds of North Sea warriors, with the horned helmets, rayed crowns, flange-hilted swords, types of ship and racial characteristics typical of the people who inhabited northern Europe at that time.

Bronze helmets from about 1200 BC. Danish National Museum, Copenhagen (photo from the Museum)

God of the North Sea Peoples. Bronze statuette from Enkomi, Cyprus (from Schaeffer 1966)

The only known Bronze Age horned helmets come from north Europe. Warriors with horned helmets are depicted on many Scandinavian rock scribings and on decorated razors; and a few original helmets of this type have been found in Denmark.

In the course of their great migration, the North Sea Peoples occupied Cyprus among other places, as the Medinet Habu texts confirm. There they built a large settlement at Enkomi which has been excavated by the French archaeologist Claude Schaeffer. There he found 'undisturbed, securely dateable material for the study of the "Sea Peoples" . . . including bronze statuettes, graffiti representing ships and battles, weapons and tools, jewellery and seals. All . . . entirely different from the late Mycenaean finds . . . which occur in the strata below them, sealed in by a burnt layer,' (1966, p. 60 .) The most important finds in the present context are the statuettes of men in horned helmets. One holds a small round shield in his left and a spear in his right hand, with a horned helmet on his head. Another bronze statuette wears a sort of cap covered with knots or curls, looking rather like astrakhan, out of which emerge two bull's horns.

Germanic flange-hilted swords were found in the same stratum and so Schaeffer considers this statuette to be a representation of the 'horned Apollo', the god whom the North Sea Peoples brought with them to the Mediterranean.

Head-dresses made of knotted fabric are known only from northern Europe. G. Schwantes called them 'a characteristically Nordic garment' (1953, p. 27). Karl Schlabow discussed these 'thick, felted caps with an astrakhan-like surface' in an exhaustive article (1943). Since this type of head-dress was made from a layer of felt a centimetre thick, sewn all over with hundreds of knots, it was naturally very warm, and only used among the peoples of northern Europe, not those of the Mediterranean. Several well preserved examples are in the National Museum in Copenhagen.

Claude Schaeffer, in a letter to me (22 June 1966), agreed with the theory that the 'North and Sea Peoples' originated in northern Europe, and most generously presented me with a copy of his work, 'Götter der Nord- und Inselvölker auf Zypern' ('Gods of the North and Sea Peoples on Cyprus').

Of the statuettes of gods with horned helmets that have been found on Schonen and on the island of Zealand, Denmark, Schwantes said: 'We are almost certainly dealing with the representation of a sky god, with the horned helmet, symbol of the sun bull, as he so often appears in Scandinavian rock scribings' (1939, p. 522).

At Medinet Habu, many of the North Sea warriors are shown with 'rayed crowns'. These paintings have caused some confusion; R. Herbig described the head-dresses as 'reed crowns' because he had only inaccurate reproductions of the murals. However, a thorough examination of the paintings themselves shows that they cannot possibly represent reeds. The tufts that project from the warriors' headbands are of exactly the same yellow colour as their hair, and from their shape could be made neither from reeds nor from feathers.

> Rays, headband and chinstrap form a single unit; the 'rays' are not the hair of the warriors. . . In these pictures the 'rays' are ranged thickly side by side, and stand up to a height equal to about a third that of the owner's head. Pliable human hair could not be dressed upright in this way. Finally, human hair can give no protection to the head. We must remember that one section of the North Sea warriors are shown wearing solid horned helmets; it is hardly realistic to imagine the remainder going into battle with no equivalent protection. (H. Vinke, letter to the author, 1 March 1974.)

Vinke conjectured that the 'rays' must consist of tufts of horse-hair, which could give good protection to the head. 'If one strikes with one's hand the bristles of a clothes-brush, it is remarkable with what strength and elasticity the bristles take the blow.'

A. Fichtel has put forward a theory of the origin of these long, yellow bristles. His starting point is the fact that during the Second World War a breed of horses, thought to have been extinct, was rediscovered – the 'Norwegian fjord horse'. He wrote: 'In the course of my research on the fjord horses, I came to realize the great antiquity of this strain, which has been preserved almost unmixed in the west of Norway for as long as human memory reaches.' The distinguishing marks of the breed are 'a stiff, upright-standing mane', a characteristic head form and an unusually strong, stocky build. It is very hardy and resistant. The pure-bred fjord ponies are yellow in colour, and their stiff manes are also yellow. Fichtel called this breed 'the horse of the far North', and observed that it first came to Greece with the migration there of the Northern peoples. Frescoes from Mycenaean times always show the long-maned and slender-limbed 'Cilician horse', but on later vase paintings in the geometrical style (which grew up under the influence of the North Sea Peoples) the 'northern stiff-maned horse' is found. On the Parthenon frieze 'only stiff-maned horses are shown'.

In the wall-paintings of Medinet Habu similar 'fjord horses' are shown, as well as the longer-maned variety. Evidently the former are shown as booty captured from the North Sea Peoples.

Interestingly enough, these horses are described in Egyptian, Hebrew and Greek texts as 'mules' (Baranski 1903, p. 105). In Ezek. 27:14, it says: 'They of the house of Togarmah traded in thy fairs with horses and horsemen and mules.' Ezek. 38:5 mentions Togarmah 'of the north quarters'. In Genesis there is mention of Japheth, undoubtedly the

Iapetus of the Greeks. His eldest son is called Gomer, whose descendant was Togarmah. The people of Gomer are called 'the eldest people' and in the cuneiform writings are named 'Gimirai', in Homer *Kimmerioi* (*Od.* 11.31 ff.) (known as 'Cimmerians' in English) who live 'at the furthest end of land and sea' (*Il.* 8.478). I will show on page 223 that they are identical with the people later known as Cimbri, who inhabited the Cimbrian peninsula (present-day Jutland). E. König wrote: 'The context in which "Gomer" occurs in Ezek. 38:6 clearly indicates the extreme North and suggests that the name is related to the "Cimmerians" of the Greeks' (1919; on Gen. 10:1 ff.)

So 'Togarmah' is the name of a Northern tribe who brought 'mules' to market. Homer too called the Northern horses 'mules'; he spoke for instance of 'the lands of the Eneti, from which the wild mules come' (*Il.* 2.852). The Eneti of Homer are identical with the Eneti whom Scymnus described as living in the neighbourhood of the Celts and the northern pillar 'which rears its head high over the sea' (see page 99) and so are another Northern people. If Homer's 'mules' of the Eneti are 'wild', they cannot be genuine mules, which are sterile and could not breed and exist in the wild state. Homer must be referring to a breed of horses which resemble mules in their build and stiff manes.

I will show later (page 233) that Homer also called horses 'mules' in a passage specifically relating to the Atlanteans.

This 'Norwegian fjord-horse' was highly valued in ancient times. This is shown by the unbelievable sum of 100,000 talents, which Alexander the Great paid for a 'stiff-maned horse', his famous Bucephalus. Contemporary writers reported that Alexander, after he had ridden all night in pursuit of Darius and found the latter's camp abandoned, rode another hundred uninterrupted kilometres on this horse before he finally found the king, murdered by his followers, on the banks of the Caspian (Lartéguy 1964, p. 123). It is no wonder that horses of such toughness and stamina were highly valued.

In a letter to me (8 May 1969), Fichtel wrote of the hair tufts in the 'rayed crowns', 'Only the fjord-horses have hair suitable for such a purpose, since human hair is far too soft. It is the finest decoration of this ancient people, and so handsome, that one might well think of setting it in a helmet. Horses' manes have also been used to make natural necklaces.'

Warriors with 'rayed crowns' are repeatedly shown on Scandinavian rock scribings and Bronze Age razors. A comb from a Bronze Age grave shows a face, with eye and nose, above which rises a rayed crown. This kind of head-dress seems to have remained popular for a long time. A German unit in the Roman army wore it. On a Frankish carved stone at Niederollendorf (seventh century AD) a warrior is seen wearing one. A coin of the Emperor Konrad II shows a portrait of him with a crown of this type. The line of development from the 'rayed crown' to the Imperial Crown can be followed without a break.

In the Medinet Habu murals, many of the warriors are shown with swords which correspond in every detail with the common Germanic flange-hilted sword of about 1200 BC. Sprockhoff, who has been described by Schwantes as 'the greatest expert' on this type of sword, published in 1936 a study of the subject in which he concluded that the spread of the Germanic flange-hilted sword may be taken as marking the extent of German territory. He referred to the 'enormous number of swords found in the North' and of the moulds for casting the bronze that have been found in that area. This shows, according to Sprockhoff, that 'it may be taken as evident that these swords originated in the Nordic culture area'.

M. Burchardt has written a description of five Germanic flange-hilted swords that were discovered in Egypt. Among them is one carrying the seal of Sethos II (who died just before 1200 BC), of which Burchardt wrote, 'This sword is certainly of north European origin' (1912, p. 61). The Danish prehistorian H.C. Broholm wrote of this sword that 'It is so close in form to the Nordic pieces that it could as well have been found in Jutland' (1944, p. 218). Many other scholars, among them C. Schuchhardt, F. Behn and G. Schwantes, have stated that the flange-hilted swords discovered in Egypt originated in northern Europe.

In the course of their great migration the North Sea Peoples left swords in the graves of their dead, or lost them in battle, and so it is possible to trace by these finds the whole course of their journey as far as the frontiers of Egypt. So these swords are not only marks of the extent of the territory of the Germanic peoples, but an indication of the routes they took in their wanderings.

The style of ship with which the fleet of the North Sea People fights in the sea-battle depicted on the walls of Medinet Habu is also very indicative. These vessels have a steep stem at bow and stern, decorated with a swan's head. Ships like this are often represented in northern Europe in Bronze Age rock scribings, on bronze shields, cauldrons, razors and sword-blades.

R. Herbig called these ships in the murals of Medinet Habu 'foreign to the Mediterranean – something brought from elsewhere' and described their 'non-Mediterranean, rather Nordic mode of construction' (1940, p. 61; 1947, p. 7f.). Bronze Age ship-graves in Sweden and Denmark show in stone the same form of ship, with tall stems at bow and stern, as at Medinet Habu.

The French archaeologist J.G. Février has published a study (1949) on the navigation and shipbuilding techniques of the Phoenicians. About the year 1200, he says, 'a thoroughly mysterious change in shipbuilding' began. Clay models and pictorial representations of the

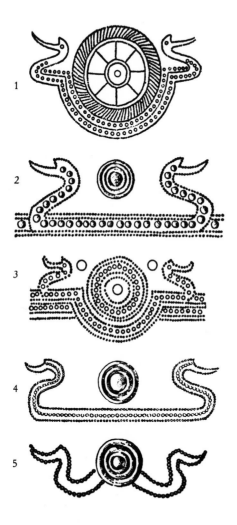

Ships from Scandinavian rock scribings of the Bronze Age, (From Reinerth, Vol. 1.)

new type of Phoenician ship 'recall the Viking ships of later times'.

Dimitri Baramki, curator of the archaeological museum in Beirut, has established that the Canaanites, who migrated in the twelfth century BC from the interior of Arabia to the Syrian coast, 'entirely lacked that nautical and technical expertise without which navigation on the open sea is quite impossible'. This knowledge was only brought 'by the mysterious invaders who entered the lands of the Near East about 1200 BC, the "Sea Peoples".' (Herm 1973, p. 74.)

These 'Sea Peoples' (our 'North Sea Peoples', i.e. Atlanteans) who also attacked part of Libya, later mingled with the Canaanites and were absorbed by them. This mixture, in which the strangers contributed their seamen's skills, was the origin of the Phoenician nation. 'Baramki considers that this conclusion follows by a most inescapable logic', and he emphasizes that many of his colleagues agree, or have arrived separately at very similar conclusions (*ibid.*).

The round shields, too, that the warriors of the North Sea Peoples are shown bearing in the Medinet Habu murals, are often found on the Bronze Age rock scribings of Scandinavia. A few round bronze shields have been found in northern Europe. At that time the Mycenaean Achaeans carried a large shield in the form of a figure eight; the Hittites were equipped with a smaller one of the same shape; and in Egypt an oblong shield was used. But in the Medinet Habu murals, the Northern warriors carry round shields with precisely the same circular decoration found on the examples from northern Europe.

On the racial characteristics of the warriors shown on the murals, the Viennese archaeologist F. Schachermeyr wrote: 'What we know of the physical appearance of the Philistines [the leading tribe of the North Sea Peoples] from Egyptian reliefs and from the Old Testament, points to a European, indeed a Nordic, type' (1929, p. 245). The archaeologists R. Herbig and J. Wiesner have expressed the same opinion.

The origin of these peoples in northern Europe is also shown by all the archaeological finds that have been made along their migration route – flange-hilted swords, shield bosses (the wooden shield itself having vanished), spear-heads and brooches of north European manufacture.

I began by asking: did the North Sea warriors of the texts of Ramses III, whom I have identified as the Atlanteans of Plato, come from northern Europe? The question has been answered, with the help of ancient Egyptian texts and pictures, and abundant archaeological material. These people, from all that can be discovered about them, indeed came from the north European area, from the 'ninth bow', the 'pillars of heaven', the 'ends of the earth', the 'islands and coastlands of the Ocean, in the farthest North'.

The site of the royal island

If, then, it is accepted that the North Sea Peoples = Atlanteans came from northern Europe, it becomes a simple matter to discover the site of their island capital.

In the Medinet Habu texts it is not mentioned. The evidence may have been recorded on papyrus scrolls, now lost, or on those parts of the Medinet Habu inscriptions that have been destroyed. Today the only legible statement remaining is, 'The head of their cities is sunk in the sea.'

But the information that the Egyptian priest gave Solon was so precise, that it may be assumed to be derived from the statements of captured North Sea warriors.

The Atlantis narrative includes the following clues:

1 The royal island, also called 'Basileia' = the royal one, lay at the mouths of several large rivers (*Criti.* 118d).

2 Immediately in front of the royal island lay cliffs which 'rose precipitously from the sea' (*Criti.* 118a). These cliffs consisted of white, black and red stone (*Criti.* 116b).

3 From these mountains 'were mined both solid materials and metals' (*Criti.* 114e); elsewhere (*Criti.* 116b) this metal is identified as *chalcos* = copper ore.

4. Behind the mountains lay 'a plain, said to be the most beautiful and fertile of all plains' (*Criti.* 113c).

5 In the middle of this plain, 50 stades (i.e. 9.2 km) from the sea, lay 'a hill of no great size (*Criti.* 113c). On this hill stood the chief citadel and most sacred shrine of the Atlanteans, on account of which it was also called *nesos hiera* = the sacred island (*Criti.* 115b).

6 On this island, 'One metal which survives today only in name, ... was then mined in quantities in a number of localities ... orichalc, in those days the most valuable metal except gold' (*Criti.* 114e).

7 After the sinking of the island of Basileia, the whole area of sea in which it lay became an impassable mass of mud-banks. The passage reads: 'At a later time there were earthquakes and floods of extraordinary violence, and in a single dreadful day and night all your [i.e. Athenean] fighting men were swallowed up by the sea and vanished; this is why the sea in that area is to this day (*kai nyn*) impassable to navigation, which is hindered by thick mud, the remains of the sunken island.' (*Ti.* 25d.)

8 'It was subsequently overwhelmed by earthquakes and is now (*nyn de*) the source of the impenetrable mud which prevents the free passage of those who sail to the sea beyond' (*Criti.* 108e).

In the whole of northern Europe, indeed on the whole surface of the
globe, there is no other spot which fulfils all these conditions so precisely
as the area between Heligoland and the mainland at Eiderstedt.

The great rivers which flowed into the sea near Basileia are the
Weser, the Elbe, the Eider and the Hever. (The last has now disappeared
under the sea, which according to the researches of Andreas Busch (1936,
p. 11–71) flowed from north to south and entered the Eider estuary about
20 km west of Heligoland.)

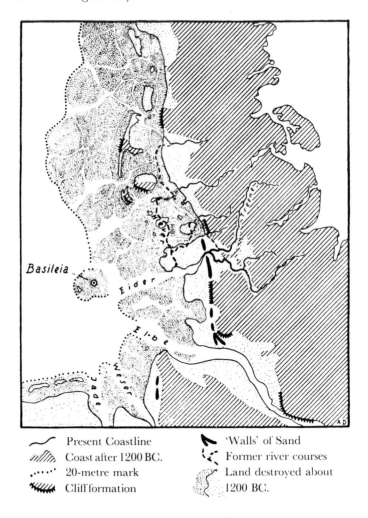

⌒ Present Coastline	➤ 'Walls' of Sand
∥∥∥ Coast after 1200 BC.	⸙ Former river courses
⋯⋯ 20-metre mark	⸰ Land destroyed about
⥿⥿ Cliff formation	1200 BC.

The scale of the catastrophe of 1200 BC. The sea overflowed the islands and coastal
area between the present 20-metre mark and the 'central ridge' of Schleswig-Holstein,
and threw up walls of sand and cliffs

As the researches of several geologists have shown, during the Stone Age and Bronze Age there was an area of marshland here which stretched far out into the North Sea. At that time all these rivers flowed into the sea via a common broad estuary just south of Heligoland. They had dug their beds so deep in the subsoil that their old courses and the estuary itself can still be recognized on sea charts.

Immediately east of Heligoland, in the shelter of the cliffs, lay an island which, after being flooded over about 1200 BC, partly reappeared during the retreat of the sea in the Iron Age. According to the most reliable experts in geology, oceanography and archaeology, and the testimony of witnesses of the period, it still existed in the eleventh to thirteenth centuries AD and was only finally submerged in the terrible floods of the thirteenth and fourteenth centuries (Heimreich 1666, p. 41).

The red cliffs

The mountains or cliffs which lay before the island, and 'rose precipitously' from the sea are the rock massif of Heligoland. According to O. Pratje, the present-day size of this massif is 0.35 cubic kilometres, but its former size was 18 cubic kilometres.

Years of observation have shown that the sea carries away about 10 metres from the massif every hundred years. Consequently 3000 years ago it was at least 300 metres longer on all sides than today. It consisted then of red, white and black stone. The red stone ('new red sandstone') is what is seen today. The white cliffs were of chalk and gypsum, and as late as 1637 still stood 'as high as the upper land (i.e. the top of the present massif)' (Johannes Mejer's map, 1639). They stood in the area of the present-day 'Düne' (the sandy strip now separated from the rest of Heligoland by an arm of the sea), whose basis consists of chalk and gypsum. The name 'Wittes Kliff' which the area still bears preserves the memory of those cliffs, whose 'shining whiteness' was praised by six-teenth-century writers.

The black rock remains in the form of a kilometre-long reef to the north of the Düne. It consists of sandstone very richly impregnated with cupric carbonate, to which it owes its blue-black coloration (Bolton 1891, p. 276f.). This too once towered over the sea.

Copper ore on Basileia

The copper ore that, according to the Atlantis narrative, was mined in the mountains, is found in a copper-bearing layer between the upper and the lower, somewhat darker, sandstone. This layer is inclined at an angle of 20–23 degrees, climbing from east to west. Today this stratum emerges about 8–10 metres below the upper surface of the rock massif. It is obvious that 3000 years ago, when the west coast lay about 300 metres

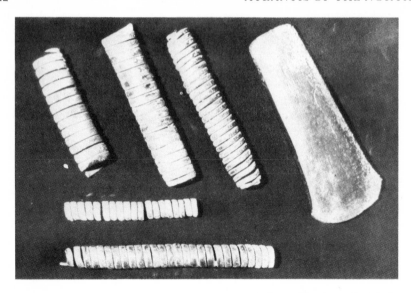

The cartouche (seal) of Pharaoh Sethos II on a Germanic flange-hilted sword made from
Heligoland copper ore (photo Spanuth)

Copper objects found at Riesebusch, district of Eutin, made from Heligoland copper ore,
Neolithic period (photo Spanuth)

further out, the copper-bearing stratum would have reached up to the then ground surface, and could have been easily mined.

Spectrum analyses and investigations of chemical composition and smelting techniques, carried out by experts in Germany, Austria, Switzerland and France, have led to the conclusion that the Heligoland copper ore was being mined, worked and widely distributed as early as the Neolithic period (Spanuth 1965, p. 361ff.). (It was presumably traded along with the amber – see page 47.)

This stratum, which according to Bolton 'leaps to the eye', would undoubtedly have been noticed by the people of the Neolithic culture whose remains have been discovered on Heligoland. At first, they probably threw the nuggets of native copper which occur in it onto their fires and noticed that they melted in the heat of the embers. So the working of this ore began even in those early times.

The researches of the Kiel prehistorian O. Olshausen have demonstrated that it was also worked later on, in the Bronze Age. He discovered while excavating a Bronze Age burial mound, that it was full 'from top to bottom' with charcoal and slag (1893, p. 516). Copper plaques – 'blanks' or 'rough forgings' – which have been found by divers on the sea-bed off Heligoland have been shown by spectrum analysis to be smelted from the same ore. In one case, the ore has been poured round a mussel, and pieces of mussel-shell can be seen sticking in its upper surface. The inference is that the liquid metal was poured into rough moulds made of sea sand (Hundt and Weber 17 December 1974).

The fruitful hinterland

The fertile plain, which lay behind the mountains and surrounded the city mound, was the Neolithic/Bronze Age marshland. This still survives in a few places, for example behind the embankment of Lunden; its soil is several metres deep. As recently as fifteen years ago, local farmers thought it worthwhile to dig up soil from it to spread over their fields, since it is more fertile – mainly because of its high lime content – than the 'new marsh' which has only been deposited by the sea during the last seven or eight centuries.

The sacred island

The circular island of Basileia, which had a radius of 50 stades (9.2 km) and consequently a diameter of 100 stades (18.4 km), fits precisely into the gap between the rock massif of Heligoland and the old course of the river Hever. And moreover there was indeed 'near the middle of this plain, about 50 stades inland' a 'hill of no great size'. This is the rise in the present sea-bed known today as the 'Steingrund'. Upon this hill must have stood the chief citadel and the most sacred shrine of the Atlanteans.

Underwater photograph showing pavement of fitted flint slabs on the 'Steingrund'
(photo Spanuth)

In the year 1943, the prehistorian Peter Wiepert, honorary member of Kiel University and holder of the rarely awarded Kiel University Medal, together with divers belonging to the then German Navy, discovered on the Steingrund 'the remains of a Germanic royal fortress', and sent me a detailed report on it.

In the course of five subsequent diving expeditions that have been made on the Steingrund since 1953, under the author's direction, remains of settlement have also been discovered. These include the outlines of walls, hewn stones, and flat pieces of flint. The latter, according to investigations made by archaeologists, mineralogists and geologists, are of human workmanship. The divers report that they 'had been knocked out of place', and lay with the smooth side up and the rough side down, flat on the Steingrund. Mineralogical tests (Professor H. Rose, test report, 10 July 1953) have shown that these flints come from a quarry on a hill near Ålborg, which was in use in the Neolithic period but went out of operation at the end of the Bronze Age. The Danish archaeologist Johannes Bröndsted wrote of these flint mines: 'In this hill were discovered five deep shafts, with galleries and floors where the flint was worked. They provide conclusive evidence that there was a flint-mining industry in this area, a centre of trade and export' in the copper-dagger period (according to Bröndsted about 1800–1500 BC) (1960, v.1, p. 334).

Divers from the Heligoland Institute of Marine Biology have also found these flat flints on the Steingrund; they call them 'Atlantis stones' (P. Lippens 1974; *Husumer Nachrichten,* 10 September 1974).

Similar flints were found by Olshausen and von Aschen in a Bronze Age grave on the Heligoland plateau (Olshausen 1893, p. 500). K. Kersten has found flint tiling on the walls of several Bronze Age graves on the island of Sylt (1935, p. 164 ff.). Professor H. Rose stated in his mineralogical report on the flints from the Steingrund, 'The Atlanteans must have obtained them from Denmark': that is, 400 km over land and sea, since this is the distance between the Ålborg flint mines and Heligoland.

This island, which lay in the shelter of the high rock mass of Heligoland, was flooded over in the natural cataclysms at the end of the Bronze Age. During the recession of the North Sea which occurred in the Iron Age it partly reappeared; a common enough event on the Schleswig-Holstein coast. The Greek geographer Marcellus said of this re-emergence, citing 'the oldest historians', who had reported the event: 'The inhabitants of these islands, have preserved the memory, handed down from their ancestors, of the great island of Atlantis, which once existed in this area, and during many centuries ruled over all the islands of the outer sea, and was sacred to Poseidon. The island of Atlantis was, they say, flooded over by the sea and lost. Where it once lay, there are now seven smaller and three larger islands, of which the greatest is still sacred to Poseidon.' (Marcellus, *Aethiopica*, quoted in Proclus *In Platonis Timaeum commentarii.*)

On this island the Christian missionaries, Wulfram (AD 689), Willibrord (in 690), and Liudger (in 780–785), preached the Gospel. They called it 'Fositesland,' because on it stood the principal shrine of the Frisian god Fosite.

Alcuin, the teacher of Charlemagne, wrote in his *Vita Willibrordi* (ch. 10):

> Now while [Willibrord] was pursuing his journey, he came to a certain island on the boundary between the Frisians and the Danes, which the people of those parts call Fositesland, after a god named Fosite, whom they worship and whose temples stand there. This place was held by the pagans in such great awe that none of the natives would venture to meddle with any of the cattle that fed there nor with anything else, nor would they dare draw water from the spring that bubbled up there except in complete silence.

Adam of Bremen described the site of this island precisely.

> The archbishop [Adalbert of Bremen] consecrated from among his own clerics Rudolf for Schleswig, Wilhelm for Zealand, Eilbert for Fyn. Eilbert, a convert from piracy, is said to have been the first to find the island of Farria, which lies hidden in a deep recess of the ocean in the mouth of the Elbe river, and, having built a monastery there, to have made it habitable. This island lies across from Hadeln. It is barely eight miles long by four miles wide, and its people use straw and the wreckage of ships for fuel... This island produces crops in the greatest abundance and is an exceedingly rich foster-mother for birds and cattle. On it there is but one hill and not a single tree. It is hemmed in on all sides by very precipitous crags that prohibit access except in one place, where also the water is sweet. All sailors hold the place in awe, especially, however, pirates. Hence it got the name by which it is called, 'Heiligland'. From the *Vita* of Saint Willibrord we learned that it was called Fositesland and that it is situated on the boundary between the Danes and the Frisians.' (Adam of Bremen 4.3.)

So this island was given various names: 'Fositesland', 'Heiligland', and 'Farria'. This latter name is derived by some writers from the old word *farre* = a bull; by others from the Frisian word *feer* – infertile or dry. However the latter meaning contradicts Adam of Bremen's statement: 'This island produces crops in the greatest abundance.' So we may translate 'Farria' as 'bull island'.

Since Adam of Bremen used the Roman mile, which is equivalent to 1.481 km, the island in his time must have been about 11.8 by 8.8 km. A twelfth-century scholiast or commentator on his text wrote as a note to this passage: 'The island of Farria or Heiligland lies two or three days' journey from England, near to the land of the Frisians, and our Wirrahe

[Weser]. It is visible from an island in the mouth of the river Egidore
[Eider]. From the island of Uthulmo [Utholm] it lies within sailing
distance.'

From these accounts it is evident that the names 'Fositesland',
'Heiligland' and 'Farria' cannot possibly refer to the rock massif of
Heligoland, which Adam of Bremen rightly describes as having 'very
steep cliffs'. The rock massif was certainly not 11.8 by 8.8 km in size in
Adam's time, nor was it ever 'exceedingly fertile', and the complete
absence of human remains from the period shows it was uninhabited
between 1200 BC and AD 1200. We are told that Liudger destroyed 'all
the shrines' (omnia fana) on Fositesland, while Eilbert built a monastery
there. No trace of any pagan shrines, monastery, or dwellings of the
population have been found on the Heligoland plateau. The
archaeological evidence indicates a considerable population on
Heligoland up to the thirteenth century BC and then nothing until the
island's reoccupation in 1200 AD. The Frisian chronicler Antonius
Heimreich, who recorded many now forgotten traditions in his North
Frisian Chronicle in 1666, was right when he wrote 'Near the southern coast
at Eiderstedt lies Heiligland, which in 1030 had nine parishes, which in
the floods of 1216 were washed away, so that by 1300 two churches only
remained.'

'Orichalc' = amber

The 'orichalc' which, according to the Egyptian priest, 'was then
mined in quantities in a number of localities' on Basileia, has been the
subject of much confusion, since the name 'orichalc' was given to an
artificial alloy of gold, silver and copper, which obviously could never
have been 'mined'.

The Egyptian priest did not know what the material was which was
named in his sources. This was why he called it a 'metal which survives
today only in name, but . . . in those days the most valuable metal except
gold' (Criti. 114e). However, he described this unknown metal as
'gleaming like fire' and said that the Atlanteans covered the walls of
their temple with it and that the sacred pillar in the middle of the shrine
was adorned with it.

All these indications fit only one substance, namely amber. Amber
could be 'mined' in many places in the area between Heligoland and
Eiderstedt, for just here was the 'amber country of the ancient world'
(K. Andrée 1937, p. 17).

It was indeed thought for a long time that the amber country
mentioned in the ancient authors was the coasts of the Baltic, chiefly the
east Prussian peninsula of Samland. But this is disproved by the ancient
sources themselves. These speak of the 'Elektrides' or 'Glaesari', the
'amber islands', and the principal amber island, 'Basileia' or 'Abalus', as

lying at the mouth of the Eridanus river, which carried great quantities of amber to the coast of Basileia, especially in the spring. All the ancient authors agreed, too, that the Eridanus flowed into the Northern Ocean; but the Baltic was never called the 'Ocean', and there are no amber islands there.

This shows that the Eridanus of the ancients is in fact the Eider and that the amber islands of the ancients should be sought on the west coast of their Cimbrian peninsula – the present-day Jutland. It was the ancient historian K. Lohmayer who first recognized this in 1872. Then the Kiel prehistorian O. Olshausen proved overwhelmingly that 'the amber of the Bronze Age came from the west coast of Jutland' (1890, p. 270 ff.). This was in any case evident from the fact that the amber trade-routes of pre-Christian times without exception led to the North Sea coast. Montelius 1911, p. 276 ff.; Hennig 1941a, p. 93; Andrée 1951, p. 88 f.; etc.)

To this day amber is often washed up on the west coast of Jutland, especially to the west of Eiderstedt. Pieces of amber have been found – pendants, animal figures, beads – 'that were evidently worked with primitive implements, and perhaps thousands of years ago adorned some Stone Age or Bronze Age beauty' (*Husumer Nachrichten*, 30 December 1965; 4 June 1968; also Neitzel 1969, p. 88).

During dredging operations in the Eiderstedt area, large masses of amber are regularly brought up with the sludge. When in 1968 the north coast of Eiderstedt was being dredged of sand, quantities of amber were found. Dr H. Steinert reported: 'The "gold of the North" is being gathered by the hundredweight on the north coast of the Eiderstedt peninsula, on the banks of the river Hever. Amber was until last year a rarity on these coasts. Now suddenly since the dyke construction a veritable "gold rush" has broken out.'

'Lumps as big as babies' heads were found; many people made 3000 or 4000 DM from their finds. . . . The largest piece, weighing more than 2 kg, found by a boy from the village of Oldenswort, sold for well over 2000 DM.' (*Husumer Nachrichten*, 10 December 1968.)

The dredging operations on the coast of Eiderstedt, and more recently on the coast off Pellworm, have shown that the dredger had reached a stratum which contained 'nests of amber, or a rich layer of it' (Steinert). This explains why fishermen who sink their nets between Heligoland and Eiderstedt have often 'fished' pieces of amber, which had been washed by the water out of that layer.

The Atlantis narrative is therefore correct when it says that on the island of Basileia amber was 'mined in quantities in a number of localities'.

It is also correct in asserting that amber was 'in those days the most valuable "metal" except gold'. The archaeologist E. d'Aulaire states:

'In the Greek states and in Rome amber was literally worth its weight in gold' (1975, p. 147). Pliny said that amber was so expensive that 'A very diminutive effigy, made of amber, has been known to sell at a higher price than living men' (*Natural History*, 37.12).

It cannot have been otherwise in Egypt. This is shown, for example, by the fact that amber was worked there together with gold into costly necklaces, which clearly shows that its value was near to that of gold. For example, the breast ornament of solid gold worn by the Pharaoh Tutankhamen (died 1352 BC) contains a large amber drop (Neitzel 1969, p. 90).

From at least the time of Thutmose III (about 1500 BC) the Egyptians knew that amber came from the remote north. In a tomb inscription from that period it says that, 'An embassy from the Haunebu from the northern lands at the end of the earth brought with them 8943 pounds of amber.' This amber was used, as we learn from inscriptions, chiefly for the decoration of temples and obelisks. This use of the substance on sacred buildings or sacred pillars is probably accounted for by the belief that: 'Amber is the fruit of the eye of Ra [the sun god]; the gods live in its sweet scent; its colour is like gold' (quoted in Baranski 1903, p. 64).

The Greeks too believed that amber was 'The many tears that Apollo shed for his son Asclepius when he visited the sacred people of the North' (Apollonius Rhodius *Argonautica* 4.611). Here too, therefore, amber was used for the decoration of temples. Homer for example said that the hall of Menelaus 'gleams with copper and gold, amber and silver and ivory' (*Od.* 4.73).

'Lavish quantities of amber' have been found in shaft-graves of the Mycenaean culture (Kossinna 1928, p. 244). In Cretan graves too, amber beads were placed with the dead from early Minoan times (about 2000 BC) on. A gold-bound amber disc from a grave at Knossos, dated about 1425 BC, resembles those 'great curved amber discs' that have often been found in Schleswig-Holstein, Denmark and England (Schwantes 1939, p. 234; Childe 1957). Similarly, an amber necklace which was found in a tholos tomb at Kakovatos in western Greece resembles those from northern Europe or England (Childe 1957).

An 'immense wealth' of offerings of gold, silver, amber and cornelian was found in the inner-Anatolian chieftains' tombs, which Bittel has dated to the period 2500–2200 BC. Amber beads were found under the temple tower of Assur, in the most ancient strata (La Baume 1924). The Assyrians too knew that amber came from the North Sea. A cuneiform inscription from Assur, now in the British Museum, mentions caravans that were sent from 'the island of Kaptara, where the pole star stands at the zenith, and amber [literally "saffron that attracts"] is fished out of the sea'.

Amber, worked into beads, miniature double-axes, or small pendants, is frequently found in the graves of the Megalithic culture which spread along the coasts of Europe and the islands in the Neolithic period. La Baume published in 1924 a long list of amber finds from Megalithic tombs, which could be filled out with many more discovered in the fifty years since. La Baume conjectured, mainly on account of the many axe- and hammer-shaped pieces, that amber 'played an important part as a protective charm' and 'was credited with apotropaic powers on account of its magnetic properties'. It is probable that the superstition, common to this day in Lower Saxony and Schleswig-Holstein, that amber is a protection against sickness and evil spirits, has its roots in pre-Christian religious ideas. Even Martin Luther, otherwise so hostile to all superstition, wore a piece of white amber which Duke Albrecht had given him, 'in order that this good stone should drive out the bad one' – Luther suffered from gallstones (Neitzel 1969, p. 47).

'The health-giving and protective power ascribed to amber, which presumably derives from its magnetic property, gives it its name *electron* from *aleco* = I protect' (Andrée 1951, p. 83).

Other scholars are of the opinion that the Greek name for amber, *electron* (which became 'electrum' in English), means 'shining stone', from the name of the sun god Elector (Ukert 1838, p. 427 and elsewhere; Usener 1899, p. 186; Andrée 1951, p. 82). This view was put forward by Pliny, who wrote: 'It is called electrum, for the sun also is called Elector, as many poets tell' (*Natural History* 37.11).

One can readily understand then that amber, thought of as the tears of Apollo or of the Heliades, and as having healing and protective powers, and perhaps also because of its wonderful 'electric' power, was held in high esteem by the ancients, and that they gave gold in exchange for it.

All prehistorians agree, that the 'extraordinarily large quantities of gold that the Northern farmers of the Bronze Age possessed' (Schwantes) came into the Cimbrian peninsula and the nearby islands through the amber trade.

'Not without reason is amber called "the parent of the Cimbrian trade", for as a valuable currency it made possible the far-flung exchanges of the Bronze Age. That the North Sea amber was exchanged for, and valued in gold is one of the reasons for its name of "gold of the North".' (Nietzel 1969, p. 90); the other reason was its colour.

Indeed, by means of the 'extremely large grave-mounds, which experience shows often contain particularly richly furnished graves', a 'gold route' has been reconstructed, which leads from the west coast of the Cimbrian peninsula, north-east and south (Ahrens 1966, p. 175, p. 177, p. 245). Ahrens concluded from these prehistoric pointers, 'that the chief amber island, Abalus, lay between Heligoland and Eiderstedt, and that we may ascribe to this island an important part of the early Bronze Age amber trade'.

Rudolf Much in his work on the god Balder said: 'A land where so precious a product could simply be picked up off the ground seemed indeed no ordinary place, and it could easily become connected with ideas of a supernatural other-world' (p. 103). I will show in Chapter 3 that the chief amber island, Basileia, was from the most ancient times the sacred island and highest assembly-place of the far-flung Atlantean cultural and religious community.

Even today the red cliffs of Heligoland exercise a strange charm over all those who see them rising out of the blue sea. H. Prigge called it 'a natural formation unique in northern Europe, wonderful, mysterious, wayward in its colours and shapes, and altogether magical'. But 3000 years ago, besides the red sandstone cliffs – which were themselves then 100 metres higher – there also towered the shining white cliffs of chalk and gypsum where now the Düne lies; and to the north of those the black cliffs. In the red sandstone the precious copper was mined, and on the sacred island sheltered by these cliffs, costly amber was dug out of the earth, and washed up on the shore by the river Eridanus/Eider. Was it not to be expected that this place, with its magical colours and shapes, its precious deposits, and its unique site, should have a central religious, political and economic significance?

The statement of the Egyptian priests to Solon, that orichalc 'survives today [i.e. about 560 BC] only in name' is also correct.

For this precious material, the object of a trade network which reached as far as Egypt, vanished suddenly and totally from the market after 1200 BC, and was not known again for centuries. That amber was exported in great quantities to the Mediterranean lands during the Neolithic and Bronze ages, is shown by the 'amber routes' that have been reconstructed right across Europe by means of archaeological finds, especially those hoards which were deliberately buried for safe-keeping – 'underground amber stores', as Andrée calls them. In such hoards there have often been found 'up to twelve hundredweight of raw amber, with only a few worked pieces' (Andrée 1951, p. 87).

'This amber route began in the amber-rich Dithmarschen, at the mouth of the Eider' (Andrée 1951, p. 89). It then led either across Westphalia (Helweg) to Asciburgium (present-day Duisburg) on the Rhine, then up the river, through the Burgundian gap and down the Rhône to Marseille; or through Lower Saxony up the Elbe to the Danube. Here the route split in two. One way led up the Inn and across the Brenner into Italy to the mouth of the Po. Another went down the Danube and through the valley of the Morava and the Vardar to Greece.

During the Bronze Age, as I have said, great masses of amber passed down these routes into the Mediterranean countries. With the submergence of Basileia this traffic abruptly ceased.

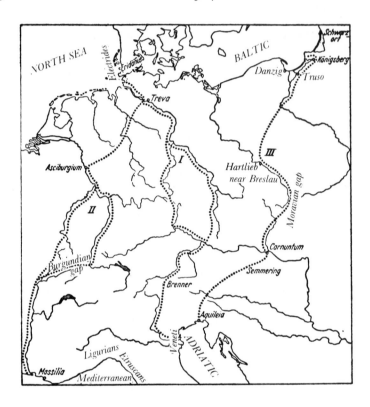

Amber routes of antiquity. I, route used in the Early Bronze Age. II, route used from the Middle Bronze Age. III, route used from the time of the Emperor Nero (AD. 54–68). Pliny (*Natural History* 37.11) reported that the amber of the Samland coast was 'newly discovered' (*nuper percognitum*) at that time

'This lively north-south trade continues all through the northern Bronze Age, only to break off suddenly' (Behn 1948, p. 161).

The author of the article on amber ('*Bernstein*') in *Pauly-Wissowas Realenzyklopädie* (1899) spoke of a 'centuries-long stoppage in the amber supply' to the Mediterranean lands.

The Hungarian archaeologist Pál Patay said of the time between 1200 and 500 BC: 'Even the economically very important amber trade from the North Sea through the western part of Hungary to Greece was then interrupted' (in E.B. Thomas 1956, p. 14).

S. Gutenbrunner considered that the interruption of this traffic is to be explained by the invasion of the Celts, and wrote, 'Together with the change in the climate, this explains the impoverishment of the Germanic peoples at the time of the transition to Iron Age culture' (1939, p. 31).

So when the Egyptian priest gave the Atlantis narrative to Solon in about 560 BC, there had been no amber coming into Egypt for more than 600 years. The priest had no knowledge of the substance, and could not understand what precious stuff it was that his sources referred to. He chose the translation 'oreichalcon' – a word which suggested itself because it is formed from the words 'oros' = mountain and 'chalcos', which as R. Eisler has shown originally meant 'belonging to heaven' or 'coming from heaven' (1928, p. 24). That amber came from heaven, as the tears of the sun god, or 'as moisture from the sun's rays' (so Nicias, quoted by Pliny *Natural History* 37.11; see also Tacitus *Germania*, ch. 45) was a very widespread idea. If this 'heaven-born' stuff, 'shining gift of the gods' (*Od.* 7, 132), could be 'mined' in many places on the island of Atlantis, then the naming of this fabulous substance as 'oreichalcon' was an obvious choice.

Besides this, the words 'oreichalcon' and 'electron' were frequently confused with each other (Mitchel 1955). H.W. Pfannmüller, too, is of the opinion that 'oreichalcon' in the Atlantis narrative should be translated as 'amber' (1970b, p. 72).

After an interruption, lasting several centuries, in the supply of amber to Mediterranean countries, it was once again imported in very large quantities at the time of the Roman Empire. Then, however, the greater part of the 'shining stuff' probably came from Samland and the Baltic coast. Pliny (died 79 AD) said that 'Sarmatian amber was newly discovered (*nuper percognitum*)' (*Natural History* 37.11). He also said that at the time of the Emperor Nero (died 68 AD), a Roman knight brought with him to Rome so much amber that 'the nets, which were used for protecting the podium (at the circus) against the wild beasts, were studded with amber' and that 'the arms, the litters, and all the other apparatus, were for one day decorated with nothing but amber. . . . The largest piece of amber that this personage brought to Rome was thirteen librae in weight.' (*Natural History* 37.35ff.) So in Roman times an eastern amber route was in use, which had its starting-point on the East Prussian coast.

It is possible that the Atlantis narrative is also correct when it says that on the royal island amber was 'laid in oil' on the temple walls, and that the sacred pillar in the middle of the shrine was adorned with it. I have already said that Egyptian temples and stelae were adorned richly with amber and that the hall of Menelaus 'gleamed with copper and gold, amber and silver and ivory' (Homer). The same must have been

true of the principal shrine of the far-flung Atlantean cultural community, the chief amber island of prehistory.

Local folklore asserts that near Heligoland a temple with 'glass walls'
sank into the sea; or that a 'city of gold' once stood on the Steingrund
(Hansen 1865, p. 87). And folk-tales from all the coasts of the North Sea
tell of a sunken '*Glasburg*', '*Glasturm*' (glass tower), '*Glasheim*' (glass land),
or '*Glasberg*' (glass mountain). The words themselves show that these are
stories from the Germanic area; for the Old High German *glass*,
latinized as *glaesum*, was the old term for amber. Pliny said: 'It is well
established that amber comes from the islands in the Northern Ocean,
and is called by the Germans *glaesum*' (*Natural History* 37.11).

In Irish legends the *Glasberg* is called 'Glastonbury' or 'Avalon', or
'Insula pomonum', and is said to be sunk 'in the North Sea'. O. Huth
compares the name 'Avalon' with 'Abalus', Pliny's other name for
Basileia. The word means 'island of apples' (E. Krause 1891, p. 122;
Gutenbrunner 1939, p. 71; Huth 1955, p. 15 and elsewhere). These
names recall the story of the apples that the goddess Idun guarded in
Asgard, 'which the gods must taste whensoever they grow old; and then
they all become young' (*Gylfaginning*, ch. 36; *Skáldskaparmál*, ch. 22).
This myth of the youth-giving apples is certainly very ancient, for
Euripides also sang of:

> . . . that shore planted with apple-trees
> Where the daughters of evening sing,
> Where the sea-lord of the dark shallows
> Permits to sailors no further passage,
> Establishing the solemn frontier of heaven
> Which Atlas guards. . .
>
> *Hippolytus*, 732 ff.

Apollodorus too (second century BC) said explicitly that Heracles
fetched the golden apples of the Hesperides (the 'daughters of evening')
not from Libya but from the land of the Hyperboreans. He next had to
fight with the Libyan king Kyknos (= swan), before he could reach the
Eridanus, where Atlas stood. There, among the Hyperboreans, Atlas
gave him the pillars of heaven to hold, not in the West (2.5.11).

These stories would seem to indicate that on the amber island
Abalus/Avalon/Abalonia, in a temple of amber, were kept golden
apples which were credited with special powers.

Perhaps the statement that on the walls of the temple on Basileia,
amber was 'laid in oil' (*Criti.* 116b), can be explained by the following
observations. Amber can be heated in oil, or melted, at temperatures
between 290 and 385°C. It then produces either amber-lacquer or
amber-resin (Andrée 1951, p. 9). Now as far back as memory goes,

pieces of resin have floated ashore on the shores of Eiderstedt and Dithmarschen. The local people say that a ship with a cargo of resin once sank off the coast and these pieces come from it. A piece of this material as big as a man's hand has been analysed by Professor Andrée, who stated: 'It is undoubtedly amber-resin' (report, 19 July 1954). Is this the by-product of the manufacture of amber-lacquer? Or was it made when 'the inhabitants [of Abalonia] use this amber by way of fuel' as Pliny said (*Natural History* 37.35)? W. Splieth, the pioneer of the prehistory of Schleswig-Holstein, wrote in his work on the gathering of amber on the coast: 'The black pieces are not used for trade, but used by poor people to light their fires' (1900, p. 18).

The ancient Germanic peoples knew how to melt amber: this is shown by, among other things, the 'ring of pure cast amber' which was dug up on the island of Sylt (Handelmann 1882, p. 31). Tacitus also mentioned the melting of amber (*Germania*, ch. 45), and Pliny said that it was cooked in the grease of a sucking-pig and coloured artificially (*Natural History* 37.35).

So the amber-resin that is washed up on the north-west coast of Europe can be explained in a number of ways. When amber is burnt it gives off an aromatic scent, and consequently, up to recent times, it was worked into fumigation-candles, powder, or sticks, in Eiderstedt (Neitzel 1969, p. 89). This is also a most ancient practice, which is mentioned by Pliny. The Greeks also called amber *thyion* from *thuein* = to smoke. The ancient Egyptian text quoted above, 'the gods live in its sweet scent', probably refers to the use of amber as a burnt offering.

Amazingly, the assertion has been made that the area between Heligoland and Eiderstedt has been under the sea for 6000 years; and that consequently the island Abalus/Basileia/Farria/Fositesland could never have lain there (Gripp 1953). This is contradicted by the researches of all genuine experts in the geology and oceanography of this area, whose results may now be summarized.

The Kiel geologist E. Wasmund placed the amber island 'off the coast of Eiderstedt, where tertiary clays overlay amber- and carbon-bearing sands' (1937, p. 36). The geologists W. Wolff and H.C. Reck, also from Kiel, wrote: 'One may well accept that somewhere between Heligoland and Eiderstedt lies the ancient amber land . . . so it is also probable that in this area lies the island Abalus of the ancients' (1922, p. 360). O. Pratje, one of the greatest experts on the geology of Heligoland, wrote: 'But Heligoland remained joined on the east side to the mainland, from which it projected as a peninsula. Its submersion did not occur all at once, but piecemeal; this can be seen from the series of underwater terraces, the remains of former shorelines. . . The Stone Age and Bronze Age people, whose remains have been found on Heligoland, must have reached here dryshod, without having to cross any wide sea inlets. For at that time the island was joined to the mainland'. (1953, p. 57f.) C. Delf, an outstanding expert on the history of North Frisia, wrote that the island of Abalus/Basileia lay 'east of Heligoland, but 15-20 km west of St Peter' (1936, p. 126).

R. Hennig looked for the island, on the evidence of the ancient authors, 'halfway between Heligoland and the mainland' (1941, p. 955). Finally, the prehistorian C. Ahrens has stated on the evidence of many geological, oceanographic and archaeological investigations: 'At all events some particularly high-standing parts of the south ridge must have remained as islands, whose traces can still be recognized on the Steingrund, the 'Loreley bank', and near Oldenswort – today part of the mainland of Eiderstedt.' He further stated that, 'This chain of islands resisted the attacks of the sea for a considerable time, in places perhaps to the frontier of historic times' (1966, p. 38-9).

But there is more. There is reliable evidence to show that this island was *still inhabited* up to medieval times. I have already described how, after the catastrophic flooding of 1220 BC, the island re-surfaced when the sea retreated during the Iron Age. It will be shown below (page 250) that it was visited by Pytheas of Massilia in about 350 BC and its position precisely described. I have also described the reports of the early Christian missionaries, and of Adam of Bremen.

In papal documents from the period 1065-1158, 'Farria' is mentioned as a bishop's see (Carstens 1965, p. 52ff.). Eilbert, for example, is described as '*Farriensis Episcopus*'. In the year 1065, Pope Alexander wrote to the bishops of Denmark, mentioning that Archbishop Adalbert of Hamburg had complained of Bishop Eilbertus, '*Farriensis Episcopus*', who had failed to appear at synods for three years and had committed various offences. At the same time Adalbert wrote to King Sweyn (or Svein) II of Denmark, to ask him to break off all communication with Eilbert of Farria and to take over the collection of church revenues (*Diplomatarium Danicum*, 1963, No. 5).

The island of Farria is also mentioned later. About 1193, a Bishop Orm '*Faroensis*' is named next to Bishop Hermann of Schleswig (*Diplomatarium Danicum*, 1963, No. 77). The Emperor Frederick Barbarossa declared in a deed of 1158 that the privileges which were accorded to the bishop of Hamburg were to be extended and Hamburg was to be the metropolitan see for Farria also. In the documents of the time, 'Farria' and 'Frisia' alternate.

Laur has given it as his opinion that 'Farria' is to be understood as the Faeroes (1951, p. 416ff.). But this is impossible. The Faeroes do not lie 'in the mouth of the Elbe', 'across from Hadeln', as Adam of Bremen described the site of Farria. They have never been inhabited by Frisians, nor are they 'on the boundary between the Frisians and the Danes', nor (as the scholiast stated) 'visible from an island at the mouth of the Eider'. Besides, the history of the bishops of the Faeroes is perfectly well known. The first one was called Gudemund; he died in 1116; his successor Matthew in 1157. And the missionaries Wulfram, Willibrord and Liudger were never on the Faeroes.

So we have evidence from Papal and Imperial documents from the eleventh and twelfth centuries that the island of Farria/Heiligland existed at that time and had by no means sunk into the sea 6000 years previously.

It is most probable that Heimreich used older documents now lost for his *North Frisian Chronicle* of 1666 when, in the passage I have already quoted (page 47), he stated that on 'Südstrand' or 'Heiligland' (which he elsewhere calls 'Heiligland or Farria insula') there were nine parishes '*anno* 1030', but that after the great floods of 1202 and 1216 'but two churches remained'. According to Heimreich these last two churches finally disappeared after the 'great deluge' of 1362. It appears from a letter of indulgence of the Council of Basle in the year 1442, that during the preceding period on the west coast of Schleswig no fewer than sixty churches had been flooded over (Peters 1929, p. 542). At that time (1362) according to the Dithmarsch chronicler Neocorus, who was preacher in Büsum from 1590 to 1624, 'between flood and ebb-tide 200,000 folk were drowned' (1.313).

On the oldest extant map of Heligoland, we find written to the east of it, 'Here is a stone-work that stretches one and a half miles into the sea, where in past time, they say, seven churches stood. They can still be seen at low water.' The 'mile' here is the Danish mile of 7.42 km. So in 1570 ruins could still be seen at low water 11–12 km east of Heligoland. W. Stephe, who studied this map (1930, p. 96) remarked that the tradition of the seven churches is found also in Rantzau and other sixteenth-century writers. Caspar Danckwerth, the learned doctor and Burgomaster of Husum, whose work describing the country was 'unequalled in its time for scope and accuracy' (Hedemann 1926, p. 878) confirmed these reports, and said that even at high water one could walk eastwards from Heligoland 'for a mile [7.42 km] on the sand'.

In King Waldemar II's 'Earth Book' of 1231, we find: 'Eydersteth and Lundebiarghaereth, whence the King is used to cross over to Utland'. So Utland, or Südstrand, between Eiderstedt and Heligoland, must have been large enough in 1231 for King Waldemar to find accommodation there for a whole army.

In the *Eiderstedt Chronicle,* which records many events from the period between 1103 and 1547, we read under the year 1338: 'Here began Utland first to break in two, and all the dykes to break up' (Peters 1929, p. 581). There is an old map which must have been drawn before 1634 because it shows the island of 'Strand' which was destroyed in that year.

On it is written: '*Universa haec regio Frisica Septentrionalis olim fuit terra . . . in tot partes disrupta*' ('This whole region of North Frisia was once land, but has been broken up into many parts'). Johannes Petrejus, 'whose notes are fully confirmed by documents in the Royal Archives at Copenhagen' (Panten 1976), reported in the year 1597 that in an old missal of the church of St Peter, the island was 'called Süderstrand', but that it had 'now disappeared'. These and many other pieces of evidence show that in the early Middle Ages, an island or a chain of islands still lay between Heligoland and Eiderstedt, 'of which part was of old called Utland or Süderstrand, that once reached as far as Heligoland' (Heimreich 166b, 80).

The last remains of these islands must, as Heimreich says, have sunk in the 'great deluge' of 1362, which is mentioned not only by Neocorus but by the *Eiderstedt Chronicle: 'Anno* 1362 at midnight there came the greatest of floods; then were drowned most of the folk of Utland' (Peters 1929, p. 581).

A fatal ignorance of these and many other historical and geological researches is shown in Gripp's assertion that the 'Area around Heligoland sank slowly into the sea about 5000 BC. The Neolithic remains that have been found on Heligoland are simply the remains of hunting expeditions, for it was only visited from time to time by hunters. A Bronze Age settlement there is not indicated.' In answer I refer him to the many Bronze Age finds, and the thirteen Bronze Age grave-mounds, which 'show the existence of a considerable settlement on Heligoland up to the period 1550–1300 BC' (Zylman 1952, p. 39; Ahrens 1966, p. 244).

Equally imbecile – in the face of the many catastrophic floods of which we have not only documentary evidence but traces in the shape of finds from drowned woods and settlements – are Wetzel's assertion that 'our geological evidence indicates gradual, on the whole disturbance-free, processes', and his talk of 'Spanuth's outdated catastrophe-theory'; and the appeals to 'special researches' whose results are not available and which in spite of repeated invitations he cannot produce.

These two gentlemen know nothing of the 'Steingrund', about which they asked, and nothing about the undersea ridge between Heligoland and Eiderstedt, which was formerly known as the 'Süderstrand'. This underwater ridge is still clearly visible on the isobath chart of the sea between Heligoland and Eiderstedt.

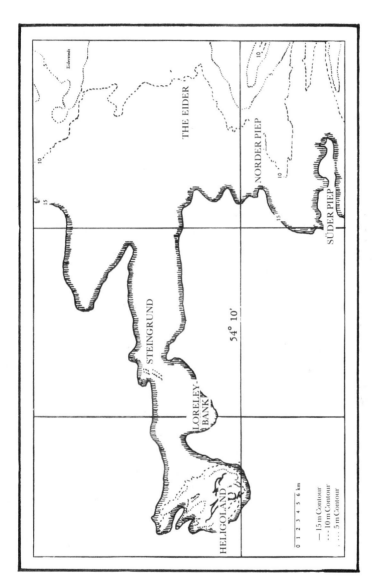

Heligoland as a peninsula of Schleswig-Holstein (15 m depth contour)

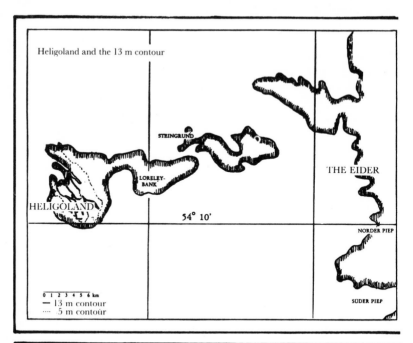

Heligoland and the 13 m contour

STEINGRUND

LORELEY-
BANK

THE EIDER

HELIGOLAND

54° 10'

NORDER PIEP

0 1 2 3 4 5 6 km
— 13 m contour
···· 5 m contour

SÜDER PIEP

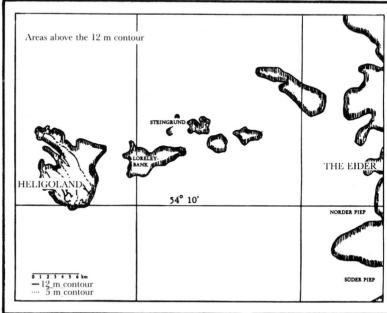

Areas above the 12 m contour

STEINGRUND

LORELEY-
BANK

HELIGOLAND

THE EIDER

54° 10'

NORDER PIEP

0 1 2 3 4 5 6 km
—12 m contour
···· 5 m contour

SÜDER PIEP

The sea of mud

After the sinking of Basileia, there remained where it had been a very thick and impassable sea of mud, which faced whoever wished to sail into the sea beyond with an impenetrable barrier. Twice in the Atlantis narrative it is emphasized that it is so 'to this day' – i.e. at the time at which the Egyptian priest told the story to Solon.

It is not hard to recognize in this thick sea of 'impenetrable mud' the shallows and sandbanks off the west coast of Schleswig-Holstein. This area would be 'to this day' impossible to navigate if it were not for the 600 or so floating navigational aids, eighty buoys and numerous lighthouses which today guide shipping through the navigable channels. Because the muddy shallows and sandbanks, and with them the channels, continually change their positions, these navigational aids continually have to be moved to new places.

The Husum cartographer Johannes Meyer in 1651 measured this sandbank area, and published a chart of the region, from which it can be seen that at that time quite a large stretch of sandbanks lay to the east of Heligoland. Caspar Danckwerth, a highly educated man, who in 1633 won his doctor's hat in Basle, published Meyer's chart in his *Neuen Landesbeschreibung* ('New description of the country') of 1652. In the note accompanying the chart he wrote that one could then even at high water walk 'a mile on the sand' from Heligoland. Since at that time the Danish mile of 7.42 km was used, there was to the east of Heligoland a sandbank of this size. Von der Decken reported that 'in the year 1809 many Heligolanders, without having read any history of their island, could point out at ebb tide those places where there had once been heathen temples, the monastery, churches, castles.' Friedrich Oetker tells in his book on Heligoland, published in 1855, that the inhabitants had told him that north-east of the rock massif had lain an island, with a wood, to which the people used to go to pray.

There is no doubt that there were sandbanks east of Heligoland as late as the seventeenth century. On them could be seen, even at high tide, the ruins of large buildings. On the oldest map, which dates from 1570, these ruins are marked 'churches' (Stephan 1930). The Frisian chronicler Antonius Heimreich reported that in that area, which in his time was still a sandbank, in heathen times a temple and castle had stood, and that 'there was the residence of the first king of the land'.

As we have seen, this 'holy island' had risen out of the sea during the Iron Age recession of the North Sea, which seems to have been by about 3 metres. The experts are not agreed whether the sea-level sank by 3 metres, or whether the land rose by the corresponding amount. Whichever we accept, the result is the same. From our point of view what counts is that the island reappeared, and all the genuine experts on the area are agreed on this.

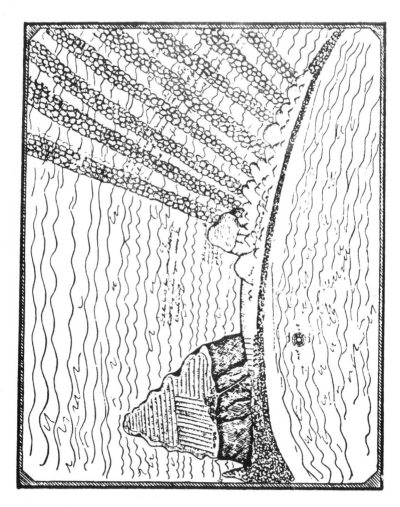

Copy of the oldest known map of Heligoland, dating from about 1570 (Schleswig Museum)

Consequently Pytheas of Massilia on his famous voyage of exploration in about 350 BC (see below page 250) could visit Basileia and give a precise description of it. He reported that there was 'no longer either land properly so-called, or sea, or air, but a kind of substance concreted from all these elements, resembling a sea-lungs – a thing in which the earth, the sea, and all the elements are held in suspension; and this is a sort of band to hold all together, which you can neither walk nor sail upon' (quoted by Strabo in his *Geography* 2.4.1).

The reports of this sea of mud in the North occur frequently in Greek and Roman authors. In the Orphic *Argonautica* which dates from the sixth century BC, it is said that the Argonauts, when they came to the coast of the Cimmerian land that 'lies under the pole in the furthest water of Tethys', and to the 'holy island of Electris', 'sprang onto the muddy bank of the congealed sea' (quoted in Müller 1844). Among the oldest tales of the Greeks are those which describe the land of the Hyperboreans. These tell that the sea on their coast is 'passable neither by ship nor on foot' (Pindar *Pytheas* 10.42). The 'Hyperborean ocean' was also known as the *pepygia thalatta, okeanos pepegos, mare amalchium, mare concretum,* all of which mean the thick, viscous, or muddy sea. It is also called *aestuarium* = sand banks, *mare piger* = lazy sea, or the *mare mortuum, okeanos nekron, marimarusa* (in Celtic), all of which mean 'sea of the dead' – this last perhaps a memory of the many who lost their lives in the terrible flood of 1220 BC.

When Drusus Germanicus wished to discover the 'pillars of Hercules' in the North Sea (see Chapter 3), the fleet stuck fast in the thick mud (*sidere limo*) and the 'lazy waves' (*pigrae undae*). Albinovanus Pedo, a Roman officer who formed part of the expedition, closed his poem on the subject with these words: 'But the gods cry "Back!" It is not permitted for mortal eyes to see the limits of the earth. Why do our rudders trouble the strange seas, the peaceful seat of the gods?' (The poem is preserved in the *Suasoriae* of the elder Seneca (died c. AD 40), 1.15.)

Similarly, Wulfram's ship stuck in the mud on the way to Fositesland when he went to meet Willibrord, and only got free at high tide (*Vita Wulframni*, ch. 8). It seems that the passage to Fositesland was hindered by the then existing sandbanks. This agrees with the statement of Adam of Bremen, that there was no entrance but one. He cannot be referring to the Heligoland cliffs, for until the destruction of the chalk cliffs in the area of the present 'Düne' there lay between them and the red sandstone cliffs the 'north harbour' and the 'south harbour', which had clear access at both high and low water.

The closed access to the sea beyond

The statement that after the sinking of Basileia 'an area of impenetrable mud bars the way to any one who tries to sail to the sea beyond' (*Criti.* 108e) corresponds exactly with the local facts.

In prehistoric and early historical times it was possible to sail from the North Sea to the 'sea beyond', i.e. the Baltic, by way of the rivers Eider and Schlei. This shipping route was frequently used during the Bronze Age, as is shown by the many finds and Bronze Age burials on the banks of both rivers.

It is not known for certain whether in the Bronze Age there was still a direct connection between the two rivers, or whether they were already separated by a small neck of land. The Kiel geographer Maack was convinced that at that time 'the Eider in the west was joined to the Schlei of the eastern sea'. He pointed out that the soil of the present isthmus between the two rivers was still known locally as 'bottomless', and only sixty years before had marsh flora growing in it (1869, p. 94). Other writers consider that the connection between them, 'through which for thousands of years water flowed from the Baltic into the North Sea' no longer existed at that time.

The question need not be decided here. Scandinavian rock scribings show that the men of the Bronze Age knew how to draw ships overland with horses. The low, narrow neck of land between Eider and Schlei could easily have been crossed in this way. The Vikings used to cross it by means of a 'North Sea – Baltic Canal on rollers' (P. Herrmann 1952, p. 58). In the Bronze Age, to be sure, this system of rollers and slides did not exist; they must have simply pulled the ships over the narrow watershed. But then, in the terrible natural catastrophes of about 1220 BC, the 25 km long 'Brandungswall' (literally, surf embankment) was thrown up right across the Eider valley and made the old shipping route impassable.

'By means of the "Lunduner Nehrung" [*Nehrung* = spit] (so the Brandungswall is known today), and the "Strandwall" [literally, shore embankment] which joins it in the north, the Eider estuary was turned into a closed bay, and the foundations laid for the problems which now confront our hydraulic engineers. Behind the embankments, sedgy swamps and fens began to build up.' (Schott 1930, p. 6.)

Many centuries later – the precise date is unknown – the Eider broke through the Brandungswall and tried to regain its old bed.

To summarize: all the eight indications which we have for the locality of the amber island Basileia fit with great exactitude the area between Heligoland and the mainland. There is on the surface of our planet no other spot of which this can be said. Two statements alone, that in the mountains of Basileia copper is mined, and that there orichalc = amber is taken from the ground, show unambiguously that the royal island of the Atlanteans/North Sea Peoples lay in this area, since copper and amber occur together nowhere else.

This amazingly accurate information must clearly have come from someone who knew that area. It cannot all be simply the invention of an Egyptian priest, or of Solon, or indeed of Plato. We must suppose that these correct geographical details go back to the account given by some captured North Sea warrior.

This assumption is supported by the statement that the Egyptians 'translated the originals into their own language' (*Criti.* 113a), which shows that the original Atlantis narrative was in a non-Egyptian language; presumably that of the Atlanteans/North Sea Peoples; and was first translated by those. Egyptians who wrote it all down to begin with.

CHAPTER 2

THE GOLDEN AGE

In Greece and northern Europe

The Atlantis narrative tells of an age of benign climate, which was later brought to an end by terrible natural catastrophes (*Criti.* 109-112). Before these catastrophes Greece had been rich and fertile:

> In those days the damage had not taken place, the hills had high crests, the rocky plain of Phelleus was covered with rich soil, and the mountains were covered by thick woods, of which there are some traces today. For some mountains which today will only support bees produced not so long ago trees which when cut provided roof beams for huge buildings whose roofs are still standing. And there were a lot of tall cultivated trees which bore unlimited quantities of fodder for beasts. The soil benefited from an annual rainfall which did not run to waste off the bare earth as it does today, but was absorbed in large quantities and stored in retentive layers of clay, so that what was drunk down by the higher regions flowed downwards into the valleys and appeared everywhere in a multitude of rivers and springs. And the shrines which still survive at these former springs are proof of the truth of our present account of the country. (*Criti.* 111b-e.)

The population enjoyed 'an excellent soil, an abundant water supply, and a well balanced climate' (*Criti.* 111e).

This account corresponds to the circumstances in the most flourishing period of Mycenaean culture, which the Greeks knew as the 'Golden Age'. We know of the fertility, the wooded landscape, the prosperity and high culture, and the abundant population of Greece during this period from the Homeric epics, and from numerous archaeological finds.

Hesiod in the eighth century BC sang of the 'Golden Age' when men were 'prosperous in flocks' and when,

> ... The fruitful grainland
> yielded its harvest to them
> of its own accord; this was great and abundant,

Works and Days, 116f.

During this period, on the Greek mainland, on Crete, and on many other islands in the Ionian and Aegean seas, settlements blossomed into populous cities, and many imposing castles and palaces were built. In the 'catalogue of the ships' in the second book of the *Iliad,* Homer names many cities which sent more than 1200 ships each, with numerous warriors, to the Trojan War. That this is a true account of the state of Greece in the heyday of Mycenaean culture has been overwhelmingly proved by Viktor Burr in his interesting article '*Neon Katalogos*'.

The English scholar H.D.F. Kitto quoted the passage from the Atlantis narrative given above, and added: 'Hence, no doubt, the startling difference between the Homeric and the classical Greek diet; in Homer, the heroes eat an ox every two or three hundred verses, and to eat fish is a token of extreme destitution; in classical times fish was a luxury, and meat almost unknown' (1957, p. 34).

The Homeric epics show too how well forested Greece was. When Homer spoke of Parnassus, Ithaca, Zacynthus, Crete and the mountains of Ida, he called these and other parts of Greece 'well wooded', 'murmuring with woods', or 'tree-covered'. Parnassus had 'wooded slopes and valleys'. Ithaca was 'thick with trees and murmuring with woods', and so on.

The inscriptions from the Linear B tablets mention 'woodcutter' and 'fire-burner' (which according to Chadwick (1967, p.119) may mean 'charcoal burner') so often that Chadwick has concluded that Mycenaean Greece must have been much more thickly wooded than Greece of later times. 'Today four-fifths of Greece is barren; in early times . . . the mountain-slopes were well forested, a rich source both of timber and of game, large and small' (Kitto 1957, p.37).

The reference in the Atlantis narrative to 'trees which when cut provided roof beams for huge buildings whose roofs are still standing' also corresponds to the facts. The excavation of Mycenaean buildings has shown to the surprise of archaeologists, that they 'made use of large quantities of timber, and even masonry walls were tied together by a system of timber baulks, rather like medieval timbering in structure' (Chadwick 1967, p.15). H. Sulze published a study of the carpentry of Mycenaean buildings in which he wrote that 'in Greece in those times great forests rustled . . . building in wood was the first type of construction, and the model for later styles' (1958, p. 394f.). The numbers of ships that were built then also show that there was no shortage of wood.

On Crete and the Ionian and Aegean islands conditions were similar. According to Homer they were thickly wooded, fruitful, and inhabited by a numerous and prosperous population. Homer called Crete 'a rich and lovely land . . . densely peopled and boasting ninety cities' (*Od.* 19, 172 f.). In the *Iliad* he spoke of 'fine cities . . . in Crète of the hundred towns' and mentioned by name many cities, several of which were no longer inhabited in his day (*Il.* 2, 645 ff.).

On the island of Talos, as Thera/Santorin was known in Mycenaean times, ruled – according to Homer – King Mecisteus, who sent his son Euryalus with ships and men on the Trojan expedition (*Il.* 2. 565f.) – an indication that the height of the Mycenaean culture was before the terrible volcanic eruption, which destroyed all life and covered Thera with a layer of lava and ash sixty metres thick.

The Atlantis narrative, then, describes accurately the conditions that prevailed in the Golden Age.

The same is true of its description of the kingdom of the eldest son of Poseidon, Atlas – that is, of the home of the Atlantean/North Sea Peoples, which I have shown lay in northern Europe between latitudes 52 and 57.

This too enjoyed a most beneficent climate during the Bronze Age, with warmth and heavy rainfall which resulted in great fertility and heavy forestation. The *Eddas* – which as I will show have preserved accurate memories of this time – called this the 'Age of Gold' (*Gylfaginning*, ch. 14).

The snow-line during the Bronze Age lay 1900 metres above sea-level (Schwarzbach 1961, p.178). It has never been as high at any other time since the last ice-age. At that time Scandinavia was covered with warmth-loving deciduous trees up to the Arctic circle (Oxenstierna 1957, p.18; Suball 1958, p.76; Andersson 1914). Oxenstierna has written of the 'long-lost Bronze Age, bathed in warmth and light, when there were none of the coniferous forests so typical of Scandinavia today, but only mixed deciduous woods'. Impressions from grape and wheat seeds in pottery vessels from the Mälor valley north-west of Stockholm show that wine and wheat were cultivated there from the early Bronze Age on (Florin 1943, p.89).

The Atlantis narrative is therefore correct when it says, after enumerating the most varied fruits and plants 'all these were produced by that sacred island, then still beneath the sun, in wonderful quality and profusion' (*Criti.* 115b).

During this favoured epoch, the population of northern Europe increased steeply. Several hundred thousand grave-mounds and a profusion of archaeological finds testify to the dense settlement of the area. H. Schilling said that in 'certain regions, above all in west Jutland, there was alarming over-population' (1940, p. 317). On the quite small islands of Sylt, Föhr and Amrum alone, prehistorians have identified 1100 grave-mounds dating from the Bronze Age. Another archaeologist, L. Meyn, said there was 'extremely dense settlement on Sylt, which shows that here lived a rich, ruling people' (1937, p. 16). On the Heligoland plateau, which today is only 0.35 square kilometres in area, thirty tombs of the period have been found, which is a very large number for such a small piece of ground (Ahrens 1966, p. 244).

So it is understandable that the Atlantis narrative says: 'there was an unlimited supply of men in the mountains and other parts of the country' (*Criti.* 119a).

I have shown that prehistoric research indicates that Heligoland, or rather Basileia/Abalus, played a major part in the Bronze Age amber trade. Research also shows that there was a brisk trade between the north-west coast of Europe and England and one can see how this fits with the following statement of the Atlantis narrative about Basileia:

> Finally, there were dockyards full of triremes and their equipment, all in good shape . . . Beyond the three outer harbours there was a wall, beginning at the sea and running right round in a circle, at a uniform distance of fifty stades from the largest ring and harbour and returning on itself at the mouth of the canal to the sea. This wall was densely built up all round with houses and the canal and large harbour were crowded with vast numbers of merchant ships from all quarters, from which rose a constant din of shouting and noise day and night. (*Criti.* 117d–e.)

It is well established by prehistoric research that the Atlantean/North Sea Peoples did in fact possess large fleets and knew how to navigate on the high seas. Indeed H. W. Brogger, the director of the Norwegian Museum in Oslo, has even thought it likely that these seafaring Northerners had, by the Bronze Age, discovered the sea route to North America, since 'at that time the art of seafaring was at its height' (1934). A. Koester called the North Sea Peoples, who about 1200 BC sailed into the mouths of the Nile, 'the most experienced sailors of their day' (1923, p.42).

Social organization in the Nordic culture area, and in the kingdom of Atlantis

The territory of the Nordic culture area in the Bronze Age was, as researches into legal history have shown, extremely well organized. The whole territory was divided into lots; 100 lots made up a district, under an overseer. The name for these districts of 100 lots was therefore 'hundred': *hundari* in Swedish, *haeret* in Danish, *harde* in Frisian.

For a long time it was assumed that the ancient Germanic organization of the army into hundreds meant that each district had to contribute 100 men for military service. But recent research has shown that this idea is untenable. The 'hundreds' were not military but economic units. The term does not mean that the district contributed 100 men but that it consisted of 100 units of land. Each 'hundred' contributed only twenty men to the army; six hundreds together formed a kind of military unit of 120 men. This is the famous 'Germanic long hundred'. Scandinavian historians have frequently pointed out that 'a hundred was a band of 120 men' (Rietschel 1907, p.31; Stemann 1871, p.65 ff; Steenstrup 1974, p.18 f.; Matzen 1893, vol.1, p.15).

The legal historians Siegfried Rietschel and Claudius von Schwerin have produced a quantity of evidence that 'this division of the land and organization of the army is original, and must go back to the time of the earliest settlement'. Rietschel summarized his researches in the following words: 'If it is possible to find among any people a political division which has all the marks of antiquity and clearly shows its origin in prehistory, then that is the case with the "*hundari*".' He went on to say that 'unanimity reigns' on the extreme antiquity of this form of organization (1907, p.368, 399). Schwerin confirmed and amplified his findings, and called this division of land and army 'a product of the Germanic settlement' (1907, p.214).

Now the 'settlement period' of the Germanic peoples was, in southern Sweden, the Bronze Age, and in Denmark and Schleswig-Holstein, the Neolithic. So it may be assumed that in the thirteenth century BC the whole territory of the Germanic culture area was uniformly ordered, and that army and fleet were organized on the system described above.

Having seen the close agreement of the geographical and historical information in the Atlantis narrative with the actual geography and history of this area it is hardly surprising that it also describes precisely the organization of the country and ordering of the army that historians have found in Germanic territory in the Bronze Age.

Criti. 119 states:

The distribution of manpower was as follows: each allotment of land [our 'hundred'] was under obligation to furnish one leader of a military detachment. Each allotment was ten square stades in size and there were in all 60,000 allotments; there was an unlimited supply of men in the mountains and other parts of the country and they were assigned by district and village to the leaders of the allotments. The leader was bound to provide a sixth part of the equipment of a war chariot, up to a total complement of 10,000, with two horses and riders; and in addition a pair of horses without a chariot, a charioteer to drive them, and a combatant with light shield to ride with him, two hoplites, two archers and two slingers, three light-armed stone throwers and three javelin men, and four sailors as part of the complement of 1200 ships.

If one adds up the number of warriors who had to be produced by the leader of a district (hundred), the result is twenty men. Consequently six districts must have sent 120 men – the 'long hundred' mentioned above.

There is evidence for this form of organization in England also. Rietschel said of England that 'all the evidence points to this arrangement going back to the time of the original settlement . . . this antiquity is attested by the similarity between the Anglo-Saxon and the Scandinavian "hundred", which can best be explained, not by either having borrowed from the other, but their common ancient Germanic origin' (1907, p. 78 f.). However, this kind of organization does not occur in Norway or Iceland, which according to prehistorians did not belong to the Bronze Age Germanic culture area.

This Germanic, also called 'Nordic', culture area of the Bronze Age is characterized not only by a most ancient form of organization of the land and army, but by its own particular types of weapons, jewellery, pottery, graves, etc. The typical weapon of the area is the 'Germanic flange-hilted sword', also called 'common Germanic', since it was borne by all the Germanic tribes. Sprockhoff (see page 36) spoke of the 'enormous quantity of swords found in the North' and said that the distribution of such swords 'may serve as markers for the extent of Germanic territory' (1936, p. 257). They were most common in southern Sweden, Denmark, Schleswig-Holstein, Mecklenburg as far as the Oder, and Lower Saxony as far as the Weser. This, then, was the 'Nordic culture area', the 'Germanic realm of the Bronze Age', between latitudes 52 and 57 north – the 'ninth bow' of the Egyptian cosmology.

The size of this heartland is given as follows: 'three thousand stades [555 km] in length and at its mid-point two thousand stades [370 km] in breadth' (*Criti.* 118a).

This corresponds exactly with the size of the 'Germanic realm' in the Bronze Age. Three thousand stades or 555 km amounts to the distance between latitudes 52 and 57. Two thousand stades or 370 km corresponds to the distance between the mouth of the Weser and the Oder, or between the west coast of Jutland and a line from the Oder estuary to the southern part of lake Vättern, which at that time formed the eastern frontier of Germanic territory.

This heartland is described as a 'plain', in which however there were 'mountains', since 'the rivers which flowed down from the mountains' emptied into the canal which had been dug on the island of Basileia and they used the canal 'to float timber down from the mountains' (*Criti.* 118e). The description of the area as a plain is correct, however the 'mountains' in this region are rarely higher than 100–200 metres.

This plain was sheltered against the north wind by mountains which were 'celebrated as being more numerous, higher and more beautiful than any which exist today' (*Criti.* 118b). Here one may think of the mountains of Norway, which this description fits. Occasional finds of Germanic flange-hilted swords on the Norwegian coast show that seafarers from the Germanic settlement area had been there too.

In this context one point must be clearly understood. The name 'Atlantis', is used in the *Timaeus* and the *Critias* in three distinct senses, to refer to: (1) the royal island of Basileia, which had a radius of fifty stades (9.2 km), (2) the heartland – the kingdom of Atlas, which was 3000 by 2000 stades in size, and (3) the entire culture area, i.e. the regions ruled over by the other brothers of Atlas.

'Plato uses the term "Atlantis" as we, for example, use "Rome". We can say "Rome lies on the Tiber", and "the frontiers of Rome reached as far as the Danube" and "the architecture of the Sassanids shows the influence of Rome". "Rome" here means (a) the city, (b) the Empire, and (c) the cultural area of influence.' (Franke 1976, p. 4.)

When the submerging of the island of Atlantis is described, only the royal island, Basileia, is being referred to. This is the place where, as we are told immediately before, 'had arisen a powerful and remarkable dynasty of kings' (*Ti.* 25a). The whole kingdom of Atlas, which covered 'many islands and parts of the mainland' is not involved here. The 'parts of the mainland' were not submerged. Neither was the whole great culture area, which included 'Libya up to the borders of Egypt', 'Europe as far as Tyrrhenia' and many lands 'outside the pillars of Heracles', which was 'larger than Libya and Asia [i.e. Asia Minor] combined' and was 'ruled over by the kings of the island of Atlantis'. This whole region was not submerged; for example, it is stated that the kingdom of Gadirus, the younger brother of Atlas, was still called by his name.

Kingship among the ancient Germanic peoples

The oldest extant written record of the institution of kingship among the ancient Germanic peoples comes from the Roman historian Tacitus (about AD 55–120). In his *Germania* (ch. 7) he wrote: 'The power even of the kings is not absolute or arbitrary. The commanders rely on example rather than on the authority of their rank.' From later times there are repeated statements that kings were accountable to an assembly, a '*thing*'. Indeed, in the *Heimskringla* (Snorri Sturluson's history of the kings of Norway) the lawman Thorgnyr says to King Olaf Ericsson (eleventh century AD), 'If you do not abide by our decisions, we will kill you, for we will tolerate no bullying and lawlessness. Our ancestors did so; they drowned five kings in a single well at the Mora-*thing*.'

The Germanic kings, then, were not god-kings or absolute monarchs. They received no divine honours, stood *under* the law, and

had at regular intervals (in Iceland, every fifth and sixth year alternately) to answer to a *thing*.

We have no written evidence for the institution *before* the time of
Tacitus's *Germania*, but evidently this type of kingship goes back to the
Bronze Age, for in the Atlantis narrative there is the following about the
rule of the kings:

> Their rule and their community were governed by the injunctions of
> Poseidon, enshrined in the law and engraved by the first kings on an orichalc
> pillar in the temple of Poseidon in the middle of the island. Here they
> assembled alternately every fifth and sixth year (thereby showing equal
> respect to both odd and even numbers), consulted on matters of mutual
> interest and inquired into and gave judgement on any wrong committed by
> any of them. And before any prospective judgement they exchanged mutual
> pledges in the following ceremony. [Here follows the description of the bull
> sacrifice, which will be discussed on page 93] . . . then when darkness fell
> and the sacrificial fire had died down they all put on the most splendid dark
> blue ceremonial robes and sat on the ground by the embers of the sacrificial
> fire, in the dark, all glimmer of fire in the sanctuary being extinguished. And
> thus they gave and submitted to judgement on any complaints of wrong
> made against them; and afterwards, when it was light, wrote the terms of the
> judgement on gold plates which they dedicated together with their robes as a
> record. And among many other special laws governing the privileges of the
> kings the most important were that they should never make war on each
> other, but come to each other's help if any of them were threatened with a
> dissulution of the power of the royal house in his state; in that case, they
> should follow the custom of their predecessors and consult mutually about
> policy for war and other matters, recognizing the suzerainty of the house of
> Atlas. But the king of that house should have no authority to put any of his
> fellows to death without the consent of a majority of the ten. (*Criti.*
> 119c–120d.)

This account has been described as an 'unhistorical fairy-tale', but in
several ways it does correspond with what is known about the ancient
Germanic culture area. To begin with, Ramses III in the Medinet Habu
text speaks of 'the ten' who led the North Sea Peoples (Breasted 1906–7,
vol. 4, p. 38). Poseidon, the father of Atlas and ancestor of the royal
twins, is one of 'those gods whom the Greeks brought with them [to
Greece] from their original home in the North', according to the
Swedish scholar Martin Nilsson (1938, p. 294). He is identical in both
name and nature with the high god of the Frisians, Fosite, after whom
'Fositesland' was named. It was customary for Germanic kings to trace
their descent from a god, just as the narrative tells us of the ten kings of
Atlantis.

As will be shown later (see page 197) it appears from the 'Wen-Amun
papyrus' (11th century BC) that a tribe of North Sea Peoples settled on
the coast of the present-day Lebanon. They were the 'Sakar'. The king

of the Sakar was no god-king with absolute power, like those of Egypt or the Achaean realm; he had to sit in council with his nobles and bow to their opinions. Among the Dorians – who were related by blood and tribal affiliation to the Sakar and to the 'Phrs', i.e. Philistines, of the texts – the kings similarly were under the law and the '*apella*', the council of nobles. Among them, too, Poseidon was said to be the ancestor of the royal house.

The custom of honouring pairs of divine twins was also widespread in the Germanic culture area. This is shown by the many representations of pairs of identical figures, rightly interpreted as twins, on the rock scribings or on razors of the time. Particularly noteworthy is the picture of a pair of divine twins with rayed crowns on a razor from Voel.

According to ancient Greek tradition, the divine twins Castor and Pollux came from the land of the Hyperboreans, the amber country in the North. H. Lüdemann said: 'The twin Tyndarides perhaps derive from an old Nordic twin godhead' (1939, p. 37).

The Romans too honoured the twins Castor and Pollux; Hauer (1940, p. 14) noted that 'this goes back to Indo-Germanic antiquity.' Tacitus said of the Germanic tribes: 'In the traditional songs which form their only record of the past [they] celebrate an earth-born god called Tuisto. His son Mannus is said to be the fountain-head of their race.' (*Germania*, ch. 2). Hauer and others have translated 'Tuisto' as 'twin'. In the *Völuspá* it says 'And the sons of the brothers of Tveggi abide / In Vindheim now'. Tacitus (*Germania*, ch. 43) noted that the Germanic tribe of the Naharvali worshipped a pair of twin gods, the Alci.

Many Indo-Germanic peoples have the remarkable institution of 'double kingship' and associate it with descent from an original pair of divine twins.

So the description of the five pairs of twins who held their assembly every fifth and sixth year alternately on Poseidon's holy island is a description of Germanic kings who held their *thing* on Fositesland.

The Atlantis narrative mentions the 'most splendid dark blue ceremonial robes' which the ten royal twins wore at their assembly. The Greek text has: *kallisten kyanen stolen;* a *stole* was a long draped cloak or robe, worn in particular by kings.

It is a remarkable coincidence that just such a blue royal robe, though dating from a much later period, the third century AD, has been found in an old Nordic sacred place, the marsh of Thorsburg in Schleswig-Holstein. An expert on prehistoric textiles, K. Schlabow, has made a detailed study of it. He has pointed out that the 'technical marvel' of this mantle is not so much its original length, which was at least 2.36 metres, as the fact that it combines two different weaves, which must have demanded 'a highly developed type of weaving apparatus'.

Schlabow has adduced proof that this highly sophisticated type of loom had been in use in the North since long before the Thorsburg mantle was made on it; in fact 'as early as the Bronze Age', 3500 years before.

The colour of the mantle was once blue, in various shades. Infra-red photography has revealed that 'The yarn for the twill was not of one shade, but appears as a range of dark, medium, and light tones. . . We are dealing in fact not with a plain blue robe, but one in which the blue background is picked out with a regular chequered design, a fact which justifies the title of "ceremonial robe".' Schlabow also said that 'the style appears in royal robes of later centuries' (1951, p. 176).

The precious blue 'star mantle' of the Emperor Henry II (died 1024) is well known. It is preserved today in the diocesan museum at Bamberg. It has its name because of the figures of the sun, moon and stars which are embroidered on it in gold on the blue silk. G. Hofmann, the director of the Bavarian State Library, has written: 'The wearing of a star-embroidered robe by the Ruler of the World – the heavenly sphere serving as a symbol of the earthly one – is a custom that can be traced back to the sixth century BC, and was widespread in Antiquity. The Diadochi [Macedonian generals among whom the empire of Alexander the Great was divided after his death] wore it, as did the kings of Ancient Rome and Julius Caesar, Augustus and the Roman Emperors.' (1950, p. 93.) In the Atlantis narrative we have the earliest written reference to these 'most splendid dark blue ceremonial robes' which the five pairs of royal twins wore at their assembly – forerunners of later dark blue royal robes.

The North Sea Peoples, during their great migration to the frontiers of Egypt, left along their route many tombs with their complement of grave gods. Among them is a grave in Kličevač (Yugoslavia) in which were found earthenware statuettes showing the 'Hyperborean Apollo' in a chariot drawn by swans. The god wears, on his neck and breast, yellow figures of the sun and stars; on his head is a rayed crown with a headband which has a zigzag pattern. His robe, which reaches to the ground, is, as the remains of paint show, dark blue with yellow designs. A similar model from Dupljaja near Belgrade shows the same god on a cart drawn by swans. The figure wears a floor-length robe, with neck- and arm-rings with spiral terminals, which 'must be compared with our Nordic period IV' (Sprockhoff 1954, p. 70f.). Sprockhoff recalls, apropos of these statuettes, a fragment of a hymn by the Greek lyric poet Alcaeus (about 600 BC), in which he sang of the journey of the god Apollo to the land of the Hyperboreans; 'O King Apollo, son of great Zeus, whom thy father did furnish forth at thy birth with golden headband and lyre of shell, and giving thee moreover a swan-drawn chariot to drive, would have thee go to Delphi. . . But nevertheless, once mounted, thou badest thy swans fly to the land of the Hyperboreans'. Sprockhoff commented,

'A more exact description of the chariot of Dupljaja one could not find' and continued, 'Clearly, when he travels to the Hyperboreans, he is going to his old home, to the place from which he started his journey to Greece.' So here, from the period about 1200 BC, is the earliest representation of the Hyperborean Apollo, in a long blue robe.

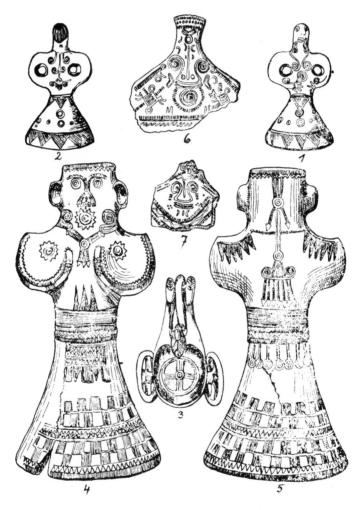

Apollo on the swan-chariot from Dupljaja (1) front view (2) back view. The statuette from Kličevač (3) view of the chariot from above (4) front view (5) back view. (6) Fragment of an earthenware idol from Orsova. (7) Fragment of an earthenware idol from Kubin.

Note the 'rayed crown' represented by the zigzag pattern on (4) and (5), and the stylized 'heaven-pillar' on (6) and (7). (From Kossack 1954)

Statuette from Dupljaja: Apollo on the swan-chariot

It may be noted that Odin, the greatest of the Aesir, the gods of the Norsemen, wore the blue heaven-mantle (Hauer 1940, p. 151).

When the Atlantis narrative says that the royal twins 'gave and submitted to judgement' *by night*, this concurs with Tacitus's remark that among the Germanic tribes the most serious cases were debated by night, for 'They do not reckon time by days, as we do, but by nights. All their engagements and appointments are made on this system. Night is regarded as ushering in the day.' (*Germania*, ch. 11.) This counting by the night is a consequence of reckoning time by the changes of the moon. It is still recalled by expressions like the German *Fastnacht*, *Weihnacht*, or the English 'fortnight', 'twelfth night'.

The golden tablets which are mentioned in the Atlantis narrative are probably also no fairy-tale. Euhemerus of Messene (about 300 BC) said in his 'Sacred Scripture' (*Hiera anagraphe*) that in the Northern Ocean on an island an ancient shrine stands, in which are preserved golden tablets with the histories of the kings of the place inscribed upon them. The kings were called Uranus, Cronus and Zeus (Wide 1910, p. 245). Aeschines (4th century BC), a pupil of Socrates, said that the Hyperborean maidens Arge and Opis brought with them to Delphi 'brazen tablets with written memorials' (*Axiochos* 371).

According to Herodotus, 'Arge and Opis came to the island at the same time as Apollo and Artemis' (who were said to be twins); they died at Delphi and were buried there; their tomb stood 'behind the temple of Artemis, facing east, close to the banqueting-hall of the Ceians', where it was on view in Herodotus's own day (*History* 4.35).

In the *Völuspá*, which contains traditions transmitted from the 'Golden Age' (see Chapter 6), it says that the earth, after the terrible cataclysm known as 'Ragnarök', rises again from the sea:

> In wondrous beauty   once again
> Shall the gold tablets   stand mid the grass
> Which the gods had owned   in the days of old

Völuspá 61

In the *Gylfaginning* it is told how after Ragnarök the Aesir 'shall sit down together and hold speech with one another, and call to mind their secret wisdom and speak of those happenings which have been before. . . Then they shall find in the grass those golden chess-pieces* which the Aesir had had' (53).

So here we have a Germanic tradition which, independently of the Atlantis narrative or the ancient Greek authors, speaks of the 'golden tablets' which the Aesir used in the most ancient times.

---

* The Old Icelandic word *tafl*, translated above as 'tablet', means a piece in a game similar to chess. (Translator's note.)

Was there a Bronze Age runic alphabet?

A much harder question is posed by the statement of the Atlantis narrative that the kings 'wrote the terms of the judgement on gold plates'. The question is whether a system of writing existed in the Nordic culture area in the thirteenth century BC. According to the *Eddas*, the Aesir 'remember their secret wisdom'; the word for 'secret wisdom' is *runar*, which also means 'runes'. But was there a runic script in the North, before the great catastrophe of Ragnarök?

The question is almost always answered in the negative. The Germanic peoples of the Bronze Age are held to have been illiterate, just as not so long ago the Mycenaean Greeks were held to have been illiterate, before the discovery of the thousands of Linear B tablets. Yet there are indications that the Germanic peoples of that time may have known how to write.

F. Altheir and E. Trautmann have published Bronze Age rock scribings which they consider to be similar to runes. On their route south, which led them over the Brenner Pass, the North Sea Peoples came to the Val Camonica, where they left many thousands of rock scribings. There, among other designs, are those 'pre-runic ideographs of Nordic origin' which Altheir and Trautmann have compared with similar inscriptions from Scandinavia. They summed up their results as follows:

> The resemblances which we have assembled cannot be coincidental. It can no longer be doubted that the ideographic writing of the North Germans (Scandinavians) leads directly to the carvings of the Val Camonica. This result is no surprise. We have tried to show from the beginning that the rock art of this Alpine valley can only be explained if it is derived from the Scandinavian. The correspondence of the forms and motifs is overwhelming. In the context of the sun and seasonal cult, they can be followed in unbroken continuity. Here the correspondences show themselves most clearly. This system of ideographic writing, like the art of the Val Camonica as a whole, is of Nordic origin. . . . In the Val Camonica we encounter, alongside the north Italian alphabet in its various stages of development, an older, ideographic script. It shows a thorough-going correspondence with the pre-runic ideographs of the Germanic North, and must be derived from it. (1941, pp. 57, 62.)

These two researchers therefore posit a pre-runic ideographic system of writing, which was known in the Bronze Age in northern Europe.

In view of the striking similarity between the runic letters and those of the Italic and Greek alphabets, students of the history of writing have often spoken of a direct connection between the two systems, and put forward the theory that the Greek alphabet, originally borrowed from the Phoenicians, was passed on in its turn to appear in altered forms in the Italic and the Northern runic letters. They could call for support on a statement in Herodotus: 'The Phoenicians . . . introduced into Greece . . . a number of accomplishments, of which the most important was writing, an art till then, I think, unknown to the Greeks' (5.58).

Who were the Phoenicians?

This question has only recently been answered. About 1200 BC the North Sea Peoples possessed the west coast of Syria and Palestine. They had discovered a territory thoroughly devastated and depopulated by the severe natural catastrophes of the second half of the thirteenth century BC. They established kingdoms there; in Lebanon that of the Sakar, and on the coast of Palestine that of the Phrs or Philistines. The Wen-Amun papyrus tells of these kingdoms, from the beginning of the eleventh century BC, and so do various books of the Old Testament.

In about the eleventh or tenth century BC, a people calling themselves the Canaanites moved out from the interior. These Canaanites became mixed with the North Sea Peoples, i.e. in Lebanon with the Sakar, and from this union the Phoenicians derived.

Now it is very likely that the Canaanites, who until then had no system of writing, learned from the 'Sea Peoples' not only the arts of shipbuilding and navigation on the high seas, but also their runic writing; and that the striking likenesses between the Phoenician, Greek and Italic alphabets, and the Nordic runic signs, are to be explained in this way.

Did the 'Sea Peoples', in this case the Sakar of the Lebanon, have a writing system? In the Wen-Amun papyrus (which deals only with the Sakar, their chieftains and ships, in the Lebanon, and says nothing about Canaanites or Phoenicians) it states that the King of Sakar had fetched out the records of his father and grandfather, in which were recorded precisely how much cedar wood the latter had exported to Egypt. In other words, in the twelfth century BC, the grandfather of the Sakar chieftain knew how to write and keep his accounts. Of course we do not know what script he used for the purpose. The Hittite script, like Linear B, was lost in the natural catastrophes of the previous century. He could hardly have learnt Egyptian hieroglyphics. The Sakar and the Philistines, who had been settled since about the year 1200 on that coast, were not among those North Sea tribes who were captured by the Egyptians and made to labour for them. Nor was the chief's grandfather likely to have learnt the cuneiform writing which was used in the thirteenth century in Ugarit and Assyria. Ugarit had been completely ruined in the catastrophes, and the North Sea Peoples never went to

Assyria. So at present it is not known what script a Sakar chieftain could have used in the twelfth century BC. But the possibility remains that he could have used that runic script from which later on, in the tenth century, the 'Phoenician alphabet' arose.

So it is not altogether impossible that the kings of Atlantis could have written 'the terms of the judgement on gold plates'.

The opinion of Herodotus that the Phoenicians had invented writing and brought it to Greece was denied even in antiquity. Diodorus, who drew his knowledge from very ancient sources, said that the Thracian singer Linus and his pupil Orpheus brought the art of writing from the North to Greece, and there adapted it to the Greek language. It was called 'Phoenician' after the story of Cadmus, who brought it from Phoenicia; but according to an old Cretan tradition, the Phoenicians had not invented it, but merely altered the form of the letters (Diodorus Siculus, 3.67 and 5.74). Tacitus too probably came near the truth when, questioning its invention by the Phoenicians, he said, 'The Phoenicians gained the reputation of inventing a form of writing, which they merely received' (*Annals*, 11.14).

Behn has pointed out that:

> The most important find of inscribed signs from the culture of the final stages of the Ice Age comes from the cave of Mas d'Azil in France. Here there are several hundred pebbles bearing designs in red paint. The picture content – if there ever was one – is no longer recognizable; they are purely conventional signs . . . which show an astonishing similarity with later Greek and Latin letters. It is easy to construct a line of development directly from the Ice Age to early historical times, and hail the pebbles of Mas d'Azil as the oldest known ancestors of our writing system. The strikingly large number of these pebbles has prompted the bold hypothesis that the cave was a schoolroom in which the children of the Ice Age learnt their letters. . .
>
> In the Neolithic cultural stage we find on the walls of megalithic monuments very similar signs, which bear such a strong resemblance to those of the Ice Age that they must be derived from them. Most of these come from Brittany, a few from other parts of France and West Germany.' (Behn 1948, p. 172.)

In the Megalithic tombs of Portugal, offerings of small stones have been found with inscriptions on them, which bear 'the most striking similarity' to the runes (Kossina 1933, p. 17). On the Canary Islands, too, where 'We certainly have before us the remains of the West European and Nordic Megalithic culture' (Huth 1939, p. 133), inscriptions have been found which, according to D. Wölfel, show four different kinds of script. Wölfel wrote of the 'kinship of the old Libian alphabet [as he called the Canarian inscriptions] with the Iberian and Sinai alphabets, and perhaps also with the runes' (1941/42, p. 131).

The peoples who inhabited the islands and coasts of the North Sea and the Baltic in the Neolithic period possessed remarkable astronomical and mathematical knowledge (see page 141). Professor R. Müller has written:

> These learned men [of the Neolithic and Bronze Ages] handed on their knowledge from one generation to the next. How they managed to keep 'notebooks' of their observations we do not know. But one thing seems to me certain: that they must have needed aids to memory in order to make observations of the heavens over years, even decades; and also that they could not have transmitted the knowledge, which had thus been revealed to them, to the younger generation, by word of mouth alone. If they made notch marks on wood or bone, then in the intervening thousand years all trace of them has been lost. (1970, p. 70.)

The same author has also described various signs inscribed on stone found in the dwelling sites of the Stone Age, whose meaning alas can only be guessed.

CHAPTER 3

CULT AND RELIGION
ON ATLANTIS

A 'troy town' on Atlantis

Among the monuments bequeathed to us by the Megalithic culture, which flourished at the end of the Neolithic period, are the often gigantic circles of stones to be found on the islands and coastlands of north-western Europe, on the Canary Islands and in North Africa. These stones, erected sometimes in the shape of concentric circles, sometimes in spiral patterns, are known in Germany as *Trojaburgen*, or *Walburgen*, and in England as 'troy towns', in Sweden as *trojeborg* or *trelleborg*. It is the unanimous opinion of archaeologists that they represent very ancient sun temples. Often there is a traditional story connected with these troy towns, that a virgin is held prisoner within them. This story is an old sun myth. The imprisoned virgin, it is held, represents the sun. The concentric, or in later times spiral, circles represent the sun's path through the heavens. The sun, in the form of a young woman, is bound within these circles, and so compelled to keep to her life-giving course. The names 'troy town', *Trojaburg*, etc., are derived from the old verb which appears in Middle English as *throwen*, in Old High German as *draja*, in Gothic as *thruaian*, in Celtic as *troian*; meaning to turn, twist – from the many twists and turns of these circles or spirals.

Everywhere that these ancient sites are found, traditions have been preserved in connection with them, of sacred dances or rounds, which must have been meant to represent the course of the sun, or even to influence it. This dance is transmitted in stories and customs of the Swedish, Danish, North German and English troy towns; we may include here the 'Troy dance' of the Romans, and the labyrinth dance of Crete and Delos.

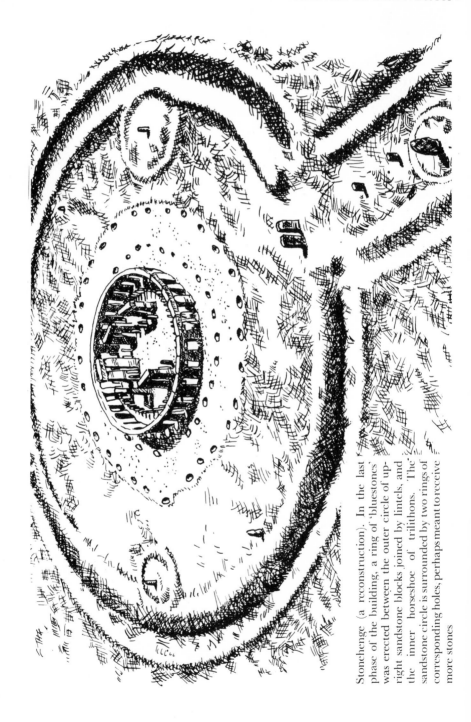

Stonehenge (a reconstruction). In the last phase of the building, a ring of 'bluestones' was erected between the outer circle of upright sandstone blocks joined by lintels, and the inner horseshoe of trilithons. The sandstone circle is surrounded by two rings of corresponding holes, perhaps meant to receive more stones

The most famous of these sites is Stonehenge, in southern England. This magnificent monument was erected, as archaeological research has shown, in three distinct phases. The first consisted merely of a circular bank and ditch; in the second, two concentric rings of 'bluestones' with connecting lintels were erected. This phase was, as associated finds of pottery show, the work of people of the 'beaker' culture.

Rudolf Ströbel in his book *England und der Kontinent in vor – und frühge-schichtlicher Zeit* ('England and the Continent in prehistoric and early historic times') (1940), assembled many proofs that at the time of this second building phase 'colonists from Jutland' inhabited a large part of England. The types of battleaxe, the lancet-shaped flint daggers, the pottery forms, the method of burying the dead, and the grave deposits, often rich in amber, all come from Jutland. 'Germanic bronze articles, especially swords, were very popular in England. There is much evidence that "Vikings" were travelling to England even at this early date.' (p. 167 f.) Ströbel points to close connections between the Nordic Megalithic area, with its stone circles, and the Megalithic monuments and stone circles of Britain, including Stonehenge.

The third phase of the building of Stonehenge also owes its origin to 'colonists from Jutland', or to their descendants. In this phase, which is dated about 1500 BC, the 'rich and powerful lords of the Beaker Folk from Jutland' had Stonehenge II entirely rebuilt. First the 'bluestones' were moved away, then from the mid-point of the enclosure (where a hole marking the spot has been discovered), a circle of 29.5 metres was measured and on it thirty stone uprights were erected. The stones varied in length, but they were set into holes of different depths, so that their tops were even. Smaller stones were rammed into these holes, to provide a firm foundation. 'While this was going on, other stonemasons chipped out the slightly curved forms of the lintels. Each one was 3.25 metres long, 1 metre broad, and 450 mm thick, and had a mortice and groove, so that each could fit tightly into its neighbour.' (Maisel 1961, p. 65 ff.)

These lintels were laid on the stone uprights so that they formed a closed ring. Then the bluestones were re-erected where they have remained to this day, in a circle inside the stone colonnade, and in a horseshoe shape inside the great horseshoe of five sandstone 'trilithons', which itself had been placed within the main circle. Inside the two horseshoes, a 5 metre long altar stone was placed. The five trilithons are the twin symbol which also appears on Scandinavian rock scribings and which was used in Greece as a symbol of the Dioscuri. Most probably these five trilithons represented five pairs of twins.

Outside, beyond an outer circular bank, stands the so-called 'heel stone', from which a broad avenue led to the mid-point of the whole enclosure. Astronomical calculations have shown that viewed from the 'altar stone', the sun rises over the 'heel stone' on the longest day of the

Stonehenge as it is today (photo Spanuth)

year; or did so in about 1800 BC. So the phase II monument must already have been built by that date. Phase I was a mere 'cattle pen', put up by the people of the native 'Dorchester culture'. They had no sun cult, and did not know how to transport and work such huge stones – the average weight of the pillars of the inner circle is 26,600 kg.

The land of the Hyperboreans

Many English scholars have supposed that Stonehenge is the temple of the Hyperboreans. Diodorus Siculus described an account of this by Hecataeus (about 500 BC):

> In the regions beyond the land of the Celts there lies in the ocean an island no smaller than Sicily. This island, the account [i.e. Hecataeus's] continues, is situated in the North and is inhabited by the Hyperboreans, who are called by that name because they are beyond the point where the north wind (Boreas) blows; and the island is both fertile and productive of every crop, and since it has an unusually temperate climate, it produces two harvests each year. Moreover the following legend is told concerning it: Leto was born on this island, and for that reason Apollo is honoured among them above all other gods; and the inhabitants are looked upon as priests of Apollo, after a manner, since daily they praise this god continuously in song and honour him exceedingly. And there is also on the island both a magnificent sacred precinct of Apollo and a notable temple which is adorned with many votive offerings and is built after the pattern of the spheres [*sphairoeide to schemati* – see below]. Furthermore, a city is there which is sacred to this god, and the majority of its inhabitants are players on the cithara; and these continually play on this instrument in the temple and sing hymns of praise to the god, glorifying his deeds.
>
> The Hyperboreans also have a language, we are informed, which is peculiar to them, and are most amiably disposed towards the Greeks, and especially towards the Athenians and the Delians, who have inherited this goodwill from most ancient times. The myth also relates that certain Greeks visited the Hyperboreans and left behind them there costly votive offerings bearing inscriptions in Greek letters. And in the same way Abaris, a Hyperborean, came to Greece in ancient times and renewed the goodwill and friendship of his people towards the Delians. They say also that the moon, as viewed from this island, appears to be but a little distance from the earth, and to have upon it prominences, like those of the earth, which are visible to the eye. The account is also that the god visits the island every nineteen years, the period in which the return of the stars to the same place in the heavens is accomplished; and for this reason the nineteen-year period is called by the Greeks 'the year of Meton'. (Diodorus Siculus 2.47.)

The expression *'sphairoeide to schemati'* – 'in the pattern of the spheres' – has often been wrongly translated as 'spherical'. This, however, is not the correct meaning. The expression refers rather to early astronomical ideas.

According to very primitive conceptions, the sky is a dome or inverted bowl, upon which the stars are fixed, and which turns about the earth once every day. However, as observation advanced people became more aware of the *movement of the planets*. This needed an explanation. One was supplied by the idea that in the space between the earth and the sky dome there were several transparent shells, or *spheres*, each with its separate individual motion. Outside the shells or spheres on which the sun and moon were fixed, there were those of the various planets, and finally that of the fixed stars. Since the evidence of their eyes showed that the same constellations returned each day, men supposed that the spheres continued under the earth. These spheres were represented diagrammatically by a series of concentric circles. 'In the pattern of the spheres' does not therefore mean simply that the temple of the Hyperboreans was round, but that in it the scheme of the heavenly spheres was represented by large circles.

It was thus an enclosure like those of the 'troy towns' described above. Here it may be mentioned that in the *Prose Edda* it is said of the greatest sanctuary, Asgard, that 'men call it Troy' (*Gylfaginning* 9). The temple of the Hyperboreans and Asgard, then, were built as 'troy towns'.

But the shrine of the Hyperboreans cannot simply be identified as Stonehenge, as is often done. For the account says explicitly that the temple stands in the land of the Hyperboreans, that the Hyperboreans live there, and that from there the Hyperborean Abaris came to Greece.

The land of the Hyperboreans is not England but the Cimbrian peninsula or, as it is called today, Jutland. The earliest extant accounts of the Hyperborean land connect it with the amber river Eridanus, with Apollo, and with Phaethon, who fell into the mouth of the Eridanus. It is also reported in early accounts that on the coast of the land of the Hyperboreans stretched a sea of mud. The 'holy island of Electris', which the Greek authors also called 'Helixoia', lay at the mouth of the Eridanus. Pliny said explicitly that the ninth circle goes 'across the Hyperboreans and Britain, with a seventeen-hour day' (*Natural History* 6.219). So Pliny distinguished between Britain and the land of the Hyperboreans, as did Pomponius Mela.

Since there is no source of amber near Stonehenge, it does not lie at the mouth of a river, and the longest day there (on latitude 51) lasts not seventeen but sixteen hours, it cannot be the temple described by Hecataeus. However, that it should *resemble* that temple is easy to explain; since Stonehenge in its phases II and III was built by 'colonists from Jutland', they would naturally have used a model from their old homeland.

That there were such models in the Nordic culture area is shown by the many stone circles and 'troy towns' that are found there. Moreover there are many designs worked on ritual stones or bronzes from the Late Neolithic and Early Bronze Ages, which are 'not merely similar, but identical' with the designs of these enclosures (Schwantes 1939, p. 547). An example is a brooch from the Bronze Age hoard found at Vegstorp (south-west Sweden). Upon. it the world- or heaven-pillars are represented in the middle of a 'troy town' composed of five concentric circles.

Sword hilt and brooches from the hoards of Bildschön (Torun region, Poland) and Vegstorp (south-west Sweden)

That very large enclosures of this type existed in the Nordic culture area has been shown by a recent discovery on the island of Zealand, Denmark.

Aerial photographs taken in 1967 near Birkendegård, about 8 km east of Kalundborg, show the traces of three large stone circles. The stones themselves are no longer there, but it can be clearly seen from the photographs that there were once three concentric circles, with a stone tomb (dolmen) at their mid-point. As at Stonehenge, standing stones had been let into holes about 1.4 m deep, and many smaller stones rammed in to provide a firm foundation. On photographs taken after a heavy fall of rain, the dark patches of the holes could be seen clearly, with lighter patches above the stone packing where the earth dried out more quickly.

The outermost of the three rings, where the standing stones had been, had a diameter of 320 m. This is much bigger than Stonehenge (30 m) and close to that of Avebury, the other major British Megalithic monument, which has a diameter of 400 m. Thorkild Ramskou, the director of the National Museum in Copenhagen, who has carried out exploratory investigations at Birkendegård, has said: 'There can be no doubt that it belongs to the same class as Stonehenge and Avebury' (1970, p. 59, p. 66). In the stone packing of one of the holes a flint blade was found, from which Ramskou concluded that 'there are traces of Stone Age settlement' and, 'The notable site of the grave-mound, with wide views in all directions, inspired the Bronze Age sun-worshippers to erect their temple here.'

Whether these stone circles, which at present can only be partially traced, will be found to have had calendrical significance as at Stonehenge, cannot be decided from the exploratory dig alone. 'There is plenty of work to do,' Ramskou ends his report.

If we look at all the researches that have been carried out on the stone circles or 'troy towns' of northern Europe, and the wide area covered by the Megalithic culture, then it becomes obvious that what the Atlantis narrative describes, on the 'holy island', upon which orichalc/amber was found 'in quantities in a number of localities', is a 'troy town', a sun temple like those at Stonehenge or Birkendegård.

The Atlantis narrative states that around the 'hill of no great size', which lay in the middle of the holy island, and on which stood the most sacred shrine with the pillar of Atlas as its mid-point, five concentric circles were drawn, 'as though measured with compasses'. The five circles formed three moats filled with water and separated by two rings of land. Poseidon, the father of Atlas the first king, had laid them out in the beginning, when 'there were still no ships or sailing'. Originally the hill was 'inaccessible to man' (*Criti.* 113d). 'The largest of the rings, to which there was access from the sea, . . . [was] enclosed by a stone wall all around' (*Criti.* 115e).

As early as 1906, W. Pastor wrote: 'What Plato describes as the holiest shrine of the Atlanteans, is a *Walburg*, surrounded by regularly drawn circles', and he pointed out that these *Walburgen* or 'troy towns' were ancient sun temples. He went on to say that the concentric circles of varying width represented the course of the sun; and asserted that such 'troy towns' could only have been designed in the North, because it is only there that during the year the sun follows circles of different size in the sky.

In 1973 a study of these 'troy towns' appeared in the journal for European prehistory, *Vorland.* In it the author concluded that 'This would prove, what Krause saw as the only possible conclusion, that the strange coiled design originated in the North.'

In the 'troy town' of Atlantis, as in so many of the others, a young woman was said to be enclosed. In the Atlantis narrative she is called Cleito; she is probably the same as the Leto of whom Hecataeus spoke (see page 87). The sources agree in saying of Cleito/Leto that she was born on this holy island. 'In terms both of phonology and meaning,' the Germanist H. Gehrts explained in a letter to me (23 January 1967), 'the names are connected with a number of names that appear in the Norse Helgi Lays (which are of very ancient derivation and have other possible links with Heligoland). For instance, *Hlétbjorg* – Kleitoburg [i.e. glory fort]. In the shorter *Voluspá* (in the *Poetic Edda*), a goddess Hlédis is mentioned, who is quite simply the glory-*dis*, i.e. the glory goddess – the goddess Cleito.'

It can hardly be doubted that the 'troy town' described in the Atlantis narrative, that lay on the holy island of Basileia, is identical with that, *sphairoeide to schemati*, in the land of the Hyperboreans, where, too, amber was found. When Hecataeus reported that this shrine was laid out 'after the pattern of the spheres', he was recalling the ancient tradition that Atlas, the first king of the island, had been a great astronomer and mathematician, and the first to introduce the theory of the spheres – *to sphairikon logon*; so it was only natural that on his holy island he would have a shrine 'after the pattern of the spheres'.

The world-pillar or heaven-pillar

In .the midst of the 'troy town' enclosures stood a pillar, which represented the heaven-pillar or world-pillar, the support of the universe. It is probable that the model for this conception of the prop of the world was the centre-post which stood in the middle of a house or tent, supporting the roof. In the earliest times people supposed that the heavens were held up in the same way. In Old Norse this centre pole is called *ás*, plural *aesir*, which became the name for one of the races of the gods. Hauer said of this name: 'strangely, the same word signifies a beam, rafter or post' (1940, p. 175). 'In every work of Germanic mythology one reads of the gods that they were called *Aesir,* i.e. "pillars of the world"' (Hohenöcker 1973).

This design, with outstretched arms and rounded or rolled-up ends, is also known as a 'volute'. Professor Willy Wirth has published a learned article on this subject (1966). He described the volute as 'the god-symbol of a sacred principle of world-organization', and pointed out its great antiquity and its later development which passes into Christian symbolism. He wrote: 'We find the volute symbol in many different culture areas. The consistency of the form, the ever-present religious significance and the extent of its distribution over every continent all show that we have here one of the oldest symbols of an early religious world-view; one of the first great conceptions of a world order.' (p. 427.)

Atlas, the god of the world-pillar, is said to hold up the heavens with his two upraised arms. This explains the two volutes stretching out on either side of the pillar. The wedge-shaped point in between them is the 'resting point of the heavens' which the Assyrians located 'in the amber land of Kaptara on the Upper Sea, where the pole star stands at the zenith' (Eiler 1928, p. 28; Andrée 1951, p. 84). The pole star was known among the Germanic peoples as the 'nail star', because it was believed to be the nail which held the vault of heaven to its point of support. Above the point of the wedge appear light symbols; the pole star for the night sky, the sun for that of the day.

Virgil (*Aeneid* 6.797) described the North as 'where Atlas, the heaven-bearer holds on his shoulders the turning sphere, inset with blazing stars.' Sophocles on the other hand called the point of the heaven-pillar 'the resting-place of the sun', because the sun stays there during the night (Wirth 1966, p. 438).

The Romans called such pillars '*metae*'. This was also the word for the turning post in the circus, round which the chariots had to swing. Since the distance covered in the race was reckoned by 'metae', they served also as measuring posts, hence their name, from the Latin *metri* (Greek *metrein*), to measure. The *metae* were, then, both turning posts and measuring posts. The use of the same term for the heaven-pillars shows that they were similarly held to measure the revolutions of the heavens. Likewise in the *Völuspá* (7.2), the heaven-pillar or world-tree is called *mjöt-vithr,* i.e. 'measuring-tree'. Hauer said on this subject: 'With the idea of the supporting beam was connected that of proportion, hence of order and measure . . . thus the symbol of the world-pillar expressed the belief in the firm foundation of the universe, in which measure and strict order ruled, and which was firmly upheld by an eternal support' (1940, p. 345).

The world- or heaven-pillars would stand in the middle of the sanctuary, often on a three-tier pyramid, or on the altar stone.

To prevent the heavens from falling and the world from collapsing should the pillar break or fall, it had to be anointed with sacrificial blood. This custom has been reported from many countries in which the cult of the heaven-pillar was practised. The ancients believed that this rubbing or pouring on of blood, preferably that of a bull, would be effective in holding up the world. This is why on representations of the world- or heaven-pillar a zigzag pattern is so often found, a design which also occurs on ritual vessels as far back as the Megalithic age. 'On these vessels it can be interpreted as a symbol of flowing water, or for the blood of sacrifice. In the world-pillar cult the design may be a reference to the 'reddening of the post' – the custom of rubbing the blood of sacrifice into the sacred post, or letting it flow over it.' (Wirth 1966, p. 442.)

A memory of this custom is preserved in the *Eddas*. In the *Hyndluliód* (st. 10) it says:

For me a shrine	of stones he made
And now to glass	the rock has grown,
Oft with the blood	of beasts was it red,
In the goddesses ever	did Ottar trust.

('glass' = *gleri*, i.e. glass or amber).

Hauer was the first to recognize in the cult described in the Atlantis narrative 'the primitive Indo-Germanic cult of the world- or heaven-pillar'.

Their rule and their community [of the ten kings] were governed by the injunctions of Poseidon, enshrined in the law and engraved by the first kings on an orichalc pillar in the temple of Poseidon in the middle of the island . . . And before any prospective judgement they exchanged mutual pledges in the following ceremony. There were in the temple of Poseidon bulls roaming at large. The ten kings, after praying to the god that they might secure a sacrifice that would please him, entered alone and started a hunt for a bull, using clubs and nooses but no metal weapon; and when they caught him they cut his throat over the top of the pillar (*kata koryphen autes*) so that the flood flowed over the inscription. And on the pillar there was engraved, in addition to the laws, an oath invoking awful curses on those who disobeyed it. When they had finished the ritual of sacrifice and were consecrating the limbs of the bull, they mixed a bowl of wine and dropped in a clot of blood for each of them, before cleansing the pillar and burning the rest of the blood. After this they drew wine from the bowl in golden cups, poured a libation over the fire, and swore an oath to give judgement according to the laws written on the pillar, to punish any past offences, never knowingly in future to transgress what was written, and finally neither to give nor obey orders unless they were in accordance with the laws of their father. (*Criti.* 119c–120b.)

This description shows that we are dealing with a most ancient cult. The ten kings were not permitted to hunt the sacrificial bull with the usual weapons of the Bronze Age, but only with clubs and nooses, the oldest weapons of mankind. They had to do this alone, just the ten of them. This suggests that the cult dates from an age when the chiefs of the tribe, originally also its priests, captured the wild aurochs for sacrifice. It is generally held that this was the original purpose of the capture of animals. Men wanted to capture a living beast for the proper fulfilment of a ritual; this was done long before they began to capture animals for domestication (Wahle 1924–32). The capture of the sacred bull is a practice from the hunting stage of human evolution. It stands out in the later, agricultural society described in the Atlantis narrative like a megalith in a landscape of our own day. O. Höfler's phrase, 'the extraordinary tenacity with which cultic forms survive the millennia' fits this case precisely.

On two gold drinking cups, found in 1888 at Vaphio near Sparta, the capture of the sacrificial bull with nets and clubs is strikingly represented. It looks as though the Spartans, who were the direct descendants of the North Sea Peoples who entered the Peloponnese about 1200 BC, had kept up this bull sacrifice for some time. Schachermeyr has pointed out the importance which the sacrifice of bulls had in the cult of Poseidon (1950, p. 33). This god was worshipped as 'bull-formed' (*taureos*) and in that shape he inhabited rivers and seas. One is reminded of the legend of the *Elbstier*, the bull who dwells in the mouth of the river Elbe, and in his rage arouses the floods (K. Stuhl 1937, p. 65); or of the story that the ancestor of the Merovingian kings was a sea-monster in the shape of a bull; and perhaps also of how the holy island of Fositesland was also known as 'Farria', which may mean 'bull island'. It was there that Willibrord slaughtered 690 sacred beasts, and thereby brought on himself the anger of the king of the place (*Vita Willibrordi*, ch. 10).

The dedicated bull was slaughtered 'over the top of the pillar'; the Greek text has *kata koryphen autes, koryphe* = the upper part of the pillar, i.e. the volute, known as *às* in ancient Germanic languages, in Hebrew as *kaphthor*. All these words mean the two outspread arms of the upper part of the pillar. From the Germanic *às* comes the name Asgard for the holy island in the *Eddas*. The Hebrew *i Kaphthor*, from which the Philistines were said to have come (Jer. 47:4; Amos 9:7), is an exact translation of the Germanic *holmr Asgard*.

If there was room on the top of the pillar for the kings and also the sacrificial animal, then the arms of the volute must have been spread out wide.

Heaven-pillar on a bowl of the North Sea Peoples, from Cyprus, end of the thirteenth century BC

The sun-chariot of Trundholm (from Reinerth, vol. 1)

A Philistine bowl, which can be dated since it was found in association with a scarab with the seal of Ramses IV (died 1160 BC), shows the wide outspread arms of the volute. Very similar is the '*Irminsul*' on the Extern-stones. There are more primitive representations on Philistine cups or vessels from the period around 1200 BC (Hrouda 1964, p. 128), or on a bowl which dates 'from the end of the thirteenth century' (Karageorghis 1968, p. 266) which was found in Cyprus, a place visited by the North Sea Peoples. The wide outspread arms of the volute are found in all these designs.

The Philistines, who were the leading tribe of the North Sea/Atlantean Peoples – were also known as the 'pillar people' on account of this pillar cult; in Hebrew 'Kaphthorites', literally 'people of the capital of the heaven-pillar' (Gen. 10:14; Deut. 2:23; 1 Chron. 1:12). Repeatedly the children of Israel are given the command, 'Ye shall overthrow their altars, and break their pillars, and burn their groves with fire; and ye shall hew down the graven images of their gods' (Deut. 12:3; see also Num. 33:52; Deut. 7:5).

Rudolf of Fulda recounted in his *Frankish Annals* for the year 727: 'Charlemagne captured the Eresberg, reached the Irminsul, and destroyed the shrine.' In the *Translation of Saint Alexander* it says: 'To dense woods and springs [the Saxons] gave divine honours. They had erected a wooden block of great size, and worshipped it under the open sky. They called it in their tongue *Irminsul*, the All-Pillar, that holds up the universe.' The word *irmin* in fact means 'powerful', and was at the same time the name of the highest god, Irmin, who was originally called Er, with Ear, Eor or Ermen as alternative forms (Krause 1891, p. 247). This recalls the place-name 'Eresberg', where the *Irminsul* stood, or the Bavarian word *Erchtag* for judgement-day or the Styrian word *Ertag* for Tuesday. The Greeks also called Atlas, the Heaven Bearer, *Er* (Richardson 1926, p. 118ff.).

Schuchhardt saw the menhirs or standing stones erected near many Megalithic enclosures as Irminsul pillars or their forerunners (1934, p. 313).

W. Wirth explained: 'For thousands of years this symbol [the volute] retained its original meaning. The leaders of the later Western nations still carried it, as a sceptre or sacred emblem. So the lily of France is prefigured in Hittite, Assyrian and Scythian examples. The formal shape is identical.' F. Seitz (1953, p. 24) has shown clearly that the royal lily evolved out of the old *Irminsul*. In this context it is worth noticing that on old compasses the sign for north is shaped like the royal lily; an indication that people knew almost up to the present day that *Irminsul* was a symbol for the north.

We may also recall here the representation of the Heaven Bearer on the Bronze Age brooch from Vegstorp, where the world-pillar is shown

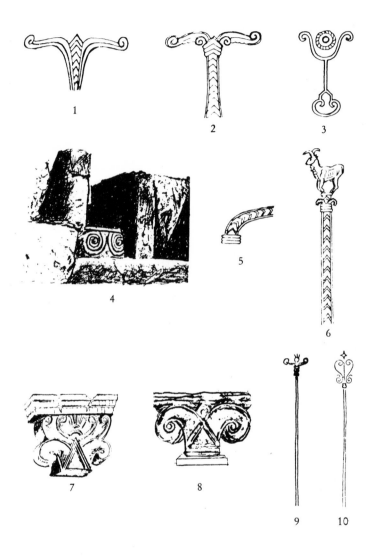

The Volute: (1) on a Philistine bowl, 1160 BC. (2) Old Saxon Irminsul (3) Bronze Age brooch from Vegstorp (4) Hal Tarxian, Malta (5) shaft of the Assyrian royal war-chariot with zigzag design (6) Assyrian cultic pillar with zigzag design (7) stone capital from Cyprus (heaven-pillar with sun, half-moon and stars) (8) stone capital from Cyprus (9) sceptre of Arcesilaus (born c. 315 BC.) (10) sceptre of Darius I (born 521 BC.). From Wirth 1966, p. 436

in the midst of a 'troy town' pattern. (See above page 89.)

These pillars became known in the South in quite early times – perhaps through the amber trade. So, for instance, many Egyptian texts speak of 'the pillars of heaven that stand in the North', or of the fame of Pharaoh which extends 'from the southern lands of the Negroes to the marshes on the borders of darkness, where stand the four pillars of the heavens.' A text of the time of Ramses III speaks of 'up-holding gods, who stand in the darkness (the far North)'. Ramses III said that the North Sea Peoples came 'from the pillars of heaven'. Homer sang of 'The malevolent Atlas, who knows the sea in all its depths and with his own shoulders supports the great columns that hold earth and sky apart' (*Od.* 1.52ff.).

In Euripides's tragedy *Hippolytus* (428 BC), the Chorus sings:

O to escape, and lurk high under steep crags,
At the touch of a god to rise,
A wing'd bird among flying flocks!
To soar over the swell of the Adrian coast,
Above the waters of Eridanus
Where, in lament for Phaethon,
His sisters drop their piteous tears
Which glow like amber in the dark stream;

And then to reach that shore planted with apple-trees
Where the daughters of evening sing,
Where the sea-lord of the dark shallows
Permits to sailors no further passage,
Establishing the solemn frontier of heaven
Which Atlas guards;
Where divine fountains flow beside Zeus's marriage-bed;
Where holy earth offers her choice fruits
To enrich the blissful gods.

Hippolytus 734ff.

Euripides cannot have derived these verses from the Atlantis narrative because they mention ancient traditions from the land of amber which the narrative does not contain. For instance, the river Eridanus, which can be identified as the Eider (see above page 48), the Heliades who weep for Phaethon; and the Hesperides ('daughters of evening') who guard the golden apples.

It is remarkable that Euripides described the river and sea waters as 'purple', for this is the literal meaning of *porphyreos*, translated above as 'dark'. Before the protective sea-wall was built, the sea around Heligoland was coloured red by the crumbling of the soft red sandstone; it was known locally as 'Heligoland crab-soup' (von Bülow 1935, p. 244).

In Oldenswort, on the north-west bank of the Eider, the geologist H.L. Heck has found, 10m below the present marshland, a layer of red sandstone; near the adjacent village of Süderhoft, large lumps of it were found on the sand-flats, or the ground surface. Heck said of this find: 'This old sandstone mountain ridge is the underlying framework which explains the formation of the peninsula, extending so far to the west.' The sandstone is, according to Heck, 'indistinguishable from that of Heligoland' (1935; Wolff 1936).

It is possible, therefore that this sandstone, lying so close below the surface, was washed away by the water of the Eridanus/Eider, staining it purple-red.

Note that Euripides, too, said that Atlas stands in the land of amber, and there 'guards [or 'holds' – *echei*] the solemn frontier of heaven'. Euripides knew also that there was the marriage-bed of Zeus, king of the gods. In the Atlantis narrative it is told how Poseidon, also a king-god, on the island of Basileia (also called the metropolis = mother city) lay with Cleito, and begot the ten royal twins.

He knew also that here 'the sea-lord of the dark [purple] shallows / Permits to sailors no further passage.' This too is told in the Atlantis narrative, where it speaks of the 'impenetrable mud which prevents the free passage of those who sail to the sea beyond [the Baltic]'.

These verses of Euripides contain a most ancient tradition, whose various components are mentioned in texts long before his time. In the context of this enquiry the important point is that Atlas 'guards the frontier of heaven' in the land of amber, near the amber river Eridanus.

Scymnus wrote: 'At the furthest limit of their [the Celts'] country stands the Northern Pillar (*stele boreios*); it rears its head above the sea. Around this pillar dwell the Celts, whose boundary it marks; beyond are the Eneti and the Istri.' Up to the second century BC the Celts inhabited the North Sea coast as far as Wörpe, north-east of Bremen. So Scymnus was talking about a pillar in the North Frisian area.

Hecataeus too (see above p. 87) said that the holy place of the Hyperboreans, which was built 'after the pattern of the spheres' lay 'in the regions beyond the land of the Celts' on 'an island in the ocean'. It must be remembered that the ancient authors could not distinguish between Celts and Germans. Orosius (5th century AD) described the Germans as one of the Celtic tribes: Livy (59 BC–AD 17) also described the Cimbri, Teutons and Ambrones as Celts.

These 'Northern Pillars' also got the name of 'Pillars of Heracles (or Hercules)' because of the very ancient story that Atlas gave the hero Heracles the heavens to hold. After the fifth and sixth centuries BC, as the north of Europe became culturally more and more isolated from the Mediterranean peoples, the term 'pillars of Heracles' was applied to pillars north of the Straits of Gibraltar. But Apollodorus of Athens still

maintained explicitly that it was *not* these pillars in the West, but those in
the North, that Atlas gave Heracles to hold.

This makes understandable the following passage in Tacitus's *Germania:*

> Both sections [the greater and the lesser Frisians] have the Rhine as a frontier
> right down to the Ocean, and their settlements also extend round vast
> lagoons, which have been sailed by Roman fleets. We have even ventured
> upon the Northern Ocean itself, and rumour has it that there are Pillars of
> Hercules in the far north. It may be that Hercules did go there; or perhaps it
> is only that we by common consent ascribe any remarkable achievement in
> any place to his famous name. Drusus Germanicus did not lack the courage
> of the explorer, but Ocean forbade further research into its own secrets or
> those of Hercules. Since then no one has attempted it. It has been judged
> more pious and reverent to believe in the alleged exploits of gods than to
> establish the true facts. (Ch. 34.)

It is often supposed that the 'Pillars of Hercules' mentioned here are
the red and white cliffs of Heligoland. This is a fallacy. Natural rock
formations were not what was originally meant by 'Pillars of Heracles
(Hercules)'. Those at the Straits of Gibraltar were not, as one so often
reads, the rocks to the north and south of the Straits, but two man-made
pillars which stood before the temple of Heracles at Gades (present-day
Cádiz), about 100 km north of the Straits.

The Greek historian Posidonius (*c.* 130–*c.* 50 BC), who in about the
year 90 BC, spent a month studying the tides at Gades, stated as much
explicitly. Other ancient authors, such as Artemidorus and Pliny, spoke
of the 'sacred pillars of Heracles at Gades' – not, therefore, the rocks on
either side of the Straits, which are called by their ancient names Abila
and Kalpe. Pillars are mentioned in connection with other shrines of
Heracles. For example, Alexander the Great, at the easternmost point of
his conquests, erected an altar with 'pillars of Heracles' (Strabo
Geography 3.5.5). In Sogdiana between the Jaxartes and the Oxus
(present-day Uzbekistan), there was said to be an altar with 'Pillars of
Heracles' (Pliny *Natural History* 6.49).

So 'Pillars of Heracles' did not originally mean natural rocks or
mountains, but man-made sacred pillars. Consequently by the 'Pillars
of Hercules' which Drusus Germanicus wanted to discover we must
understand not the cliffs of Heligoland, but artificial pillars on the
'sacred island'.

The reason why Drusus, as Tacitus has told us, was not able to
discover them, emerges from a fragment of a poem by the Roman officer
Albinovanus Pedo. He had served under Drusus in Germany, and his
verses probably refer either to the expedition mentioned by Tacitus, or
to some other similar attempt to penetrate the mystery of the 'Pillars of

Hercules' in the North Sea. On this voyage the Roman ships ran into severe storms, and when these subsided the ships ran onto sandbanks, on which they remained stuck. They had come '*ad rerum metas extremaque littora mundi*', i.e. 'to the measuring or turning-posts of things, the remotest shores of the world. . . . But the gods cry "Back!" It is not permitted for mortal eyes to see the limits of the earth. Why do our rudders trouble the strange seas, the peaceful seat of the gods?' The poem is preserved in the *Suasoriae* of the Elder Seneca (died *c.* AD 40) (1.15).

Here then, the *metae rerum* are described as the 'peaceful seat of the gods', and as lying in a sea of mud, in the 'sacred waters' (*sacras aquas*) a description unique in ancient texts. These pillars must still have existed in the year AD 689, for Wulfram, who in that year met Willibrord on Fositesland, saw 'wonderfully decorated pillars' there.

F.R. Schröder has shown that these pillars, the *metae rerum*, were also held to be 'seats of the gods'; he has described the cult pillars that stood before or in the temple as the 'high-seat-pillars of the gods' (1929, p. 27, p. 66). In the *Eddas* the Heaven-Pillar is also called the World-Tree or the World-Ash, presumably because of its widespread arms or branches; and in the *Eddas*, too, the Aesir have their seats and give their judgements at the foot of the tree.

E. Jung, R. Haupt, O. Strabismus, and others have ventured the opinion that the 'Roland pillars' which are found in so many market places in northern Germany, derive from the World Pillar, *Irminsul*. In the Middle Ages the seat of the magistrates was beside the Roland pillar; at its foot trials were held and oaths were sworn, just as they were beside the sacred pillar on the royal island in the Atlantis narrative.

The sacred cauldron and the golden drinking cups

At the feast of the bull sacrifice, when the limbs of the victim had been consecrated to Poseidon, the ten kings filled a bowl with wine, each one dropped into it a clot of blood, and they then drew wine from the bowl in golden cups, poured it on the fire, and swore to obey faithfully the laws of Poseidon.

Large mixing vessels and sacrificial bowls are often found in the territory of the Nordic culture area.

On the island of Fyn, Denmark, a large bronze cauldron has been found, and inside it eleven gold drinking cups. On the cauldron is a picture of the sun, sailing in a ship with a swan-headed prow. This design perhaps represents the night journey of the sun, which is carried by swans across the nether ocean to its rising-place. The same design

appears on a large bronze cauldron from Siem, 14 km north of Hadsund
in north Jutland, and two almost identical ones from Granzin in
Mecklenburg. The ritual character of these vessels is clear from the fact
that similar ones have been found mounted on wheels: for example one
in Peckatel, Mecklenburg, and the remains of another at Warin in the
same area. Very similar is the wheeled cauldron from the 'Trushöj' in
southern Zealand, Denmark.

Golden drinking cups, apart from the eleven just mentioned from
Fyn, are often found; for example two hemispherical gold bowls from
Avernakø, decorated with sun symbols and dating from the early
Bronze Age; two golden bowls from different spots on the remarkable
terraced hill of Borgbjerg near Boeslunde in the Skelsör area; two bowls
and two cups, all of gold, from a bog near Midskov; and two gold bowls
from a single find in the same area (Bröndsted 1962, vol. 2, p. 114, p. 168,
p. 298). Bröndsted in his work on the Danish Bronze Age has described
many other finds of the same kind.

Equally famous are the eight gold bowls from the great hoard at
Eberswalde, 45 km north-east of Berlin, which have the same sun
symbols and other designs as many of the Danish ones; and two from
south Dithmarschen, in the south-west of Schleswig-Holstein (Hoffmann 1938, Taf. 6; Schwantes 1939, Taf. 55). 'A great number' of gold
bowls have been found in Schleswig-Holstein (Schwantes 1939, p. 408);
they all come from treasure hoards, and Schwantes (1939, p. 521) has
conjectured that they were used for ritual purposes.

The high feast on the royal island, which the Atlantis narrative
describes, is perhaps portrayed, in the style of the rock scribings, on the
decorated panels of a tomb at Kivik, in south Sweden about 40 km east
of Lund. This is a tomb of the Middle Bronze Age, i.e. of about
1400 BC. On one of the panels a chariot is shown with a figure standing
in it, drawn by two horses. In front and to the left of the chariot a large
fish is shown, perhaps a dolphin. Possibly it represents the sun god in his
chariot, drawn by his horses across the heavens. The great fish or
dolphin was in ancient times thought of as the guide of the sun across the
ocean below the earth; later a swan appeared instead of the fish.
Underneath the chariot two unattached horses are shown. These are
perhaps the horses of the sun, which run free during his night journey.
On the lower rim, eight figures in long robes are shown, led by a man
wearing a sword. Perhaps these are nine of the ten kings who went to the
feast in 'the most splendid dark blue ceremonial robes'.

In the middle of another panel is a large cauldron, with four figures
approaching it from the left and five from the right – presumably to
draw out the sacrificial drink. Above them stand figures blowing on
horns, accompanying the feast with their music. In the upper left-hand
corner of this panel are two men holding a drilling apparatus, loaded

with heavy weights. This is 'perhaps a ritual drilling' (Schwantes), i.e. the drilling of the new fire. In folk custom, still practised up to early modern times, this had to be done by a pair of twins (Huth 1939, p. 128; Johannes Reiskius 1696; Plischke 1957). The custom of quenching the old fire and kindling the new, which was widespread among the Germanic tribes, is suggested by the words of the Atlantis narrative: 'Then when darkness fell and the sacrificial fire had died down they all put on the most splendid dark blue ceremonial robes and sat on the ground by the embers of the sacrificial fire, in the dark, all glimmer of fire in the sanctuary being extinguished. And thus they gave and submitted to judgement.' When the sacrificial fire went out, and all other fires were extinguished, then naturally a new fire, called among the Germanic peoples 'hnotfiur', had to be kindled. This custom, too, seems to be an inheritance from the Megalithic era, since it is reported from among the Canarians, Indians, Greeks and Latins. In the *Rigveda* it is told that the sacred task of drilling the new fire had to be accomplished by the holy twin-pair, the Acvins, closely related to the primitive-Germanic word *Alcis* (Almgren 1934, p. 186; Huth 1939, p. 128). The Spartans too, direct successors of those North Sea Peoples who entered the Peloponnese, practised this custom and carried the new fire with them in a tent when they went to war (Lüdemann 1939, p. 30).

On each of the other panels of the tomb at Kivik are two horses (a twin symbol?), one pair following one another, the other pair facing each other. Sun discs, zigzag lines, and sacred axes, which from their shape can be dated to the Early Bronze Age, are also shown. On one tablet above the sun wheels two volutes can be recognized; the usual wedge-shaped point between the two arms is not visible because of the poor state of preservation of the stone. Between the two axes is a pointed pillar. The position of the sun, and hence the time, could be measured by the shadow thrown by the pillar. The relation of the shadow to the height of the pillar showed the latitude of a particular place. These pointed pillars correspond to the *metae rerum*, the 'measuring posts'.

From the similarity between the designs on the panels of the Kivik tomb, and the description of the high festival on the royal island of Atlantis, we may guess that it is the tomb of one of the kings of Atlantis who had played his part in the great feast.

The statue of Poseidon

Of the statue of Poseidon we read that the temple: 'Contained gold statues of the god standing in a chariot drawn by six winged horses, so tall that his head touched the roof, and round him, riding on dolphins, a hundred Nereids (that being the accepted number of them at the time)' (*Criti.* 116d–e).

The details of this account may be exaggerated. Perhaps the Egyptian priests who gave the narrative to Solon embellished the account, with features suggested by the temples of their own country, where there were giant gilded statues of gods.

However, in the Eddaic Saga of Ragnar Lodbrok it is said that on the island of Samsø there stood a statue of a god made of wood which was 40 ells high. On the Scandinavian rock scribings of the Bronze Age the figures of gods are two or three times as tall as the people in the processions. So it is clear that very large statues did exist.

The god 'standing in a chariot drawn by six winged horses' is also shown on one of the panels of the tomb at Kivik, together with a dolphin. The statement that the horses were winged probably means that they were the sun horses that drew the sun across the heavens. Though the scenes depicted on the panels of Kivik are not on the lavish scale described by the Egyptian priest, they do show that in northern Europe as early as the Middle Bronze Age, and perhaps much earlier, there was a cult of a god standing in a chariot, drawn by horses and led or accompanied by a dolphin. Altogether, six horses are shown at Kivik; are these the six of which the Atlantis narrative speaks?

The god Poseidon, according to the researches of the Swedish archaeologist and religious historian Martin P. Nilsson, came from 'an original homeland in the North'. It seems that in very early times he was connected with chariots, sacred horses, and dolphins. F. Schachermeyr (1950) gave many connections between this god and chariot driving, horses and dolphins from Greek religious cults. Admittedly by the time of the Homeric poems, Poseidon 'plays the part of a retreating storm'. The historian of religion W.F. Otto has said: 'He must once have been much more powerful than he appears in the *Iliad*. In numerous ways, and not least by acute characterization, the Homeric poems indicate that his true greatness belongs to the past. Occasionally they confront him with the younger deities, and upon each occasion he appears to be somewhat awkward and old fashioned before the bright and buoyant spirit of an Apollo.' (1947, p. 30.)

In the *Iliad* 21.445f.) Poseidon built 'a wall for the Trojans round their town, a strong and splendid one to make the place impregnable'. So in quite early times he was thought of as the builder of Troy, and the 'troy towns'; this is confirmed by what we are told of the 'troy town' on Atlantis (*Criti*. 113d). There, the walls or defences had been erected by Poseidon in the dawn of time, 'when there were neither ships nor sailing'.

Among the Achaeans, 'who were descended from Indo-Germanic peoples who formerly lived in south Scandinavia and north Germany as far as the Weichsel' (Bühler 1947, p. 8f.), Poseidon had already sunk into the background behind newer deities. A renewal of his cult occurred

Nordic rock scribings: two slabs from the tomb at Kivik (from Schwantes 1939)

only with the arrival of the North Sea Peoples in their great migration
(Schachermeyr 1950, p. 46) and it is not surprising that it was in Sparta
that Poseidon and his cult began once more to play a dominant part.
There, the Dorian nobility venerated Poseidon as their tribal ancestor,
as did the kings of Atlantis.

The Philistines too, who were related to the Dorians by blood and
tribal affiliation, honoured Poseidon; for H. Hitzig has shown that the
'Dagon' of the Old Testament is no other than Poseidon. In Gaza and
Ashdod they erected great temples, where the god was shown riding in a
chariot and accompanied by a great fish, as on the tomb at Kivik.•

There are therefore indications that the statements of the Atlantis
narrative about the statue of Poseidon in the temple on the royal island,
though perhaps exaggerated, may well be basically correct.

The temple of Poseidon on Basileia – an amber temple?

In the midst of the great 'troy town' on the royal island of Atlantis stood
a temple to Poseidon. The account tells us:

> The diameter of the island on which the palace was situated was five stades
> [about 920 m]. . . . The construction of the palace within the acropolis was as
> follows. In the centre was a shrine sacred to Poseidon and Cleito, surrounded
> by a golden barrier, through which entry was forbidden, as it was the place
> where the family of the ten kings was conceived and begotten; and there
> year by year seasonal offerings were made from the ten provinces to each
> one of them. There was a temple of Poseidon himself,˙a stade [183 m] in
> length, three plethra [92.5 m] wide, and proportionate in height, though
> somewhat outlandish in appearance. The outside of it was covered all over
> with silver, except for the figures on the pediment which were picked out
> with gold. Inside, the roof was ivory picked out with gold, silver and amber
> (orichalc), and all the walls, pillars and floors were covered with amber
> (orichalc). (*Criti.* 116.)

All this sounds so improbable that one might be tempted to assign it
to the realm of fantasy. However, S. Pfeilstücker and O. Huth have
demonstrated that the extremely rich decoration of Germanic temples
in pre-Christian times is not a figment of poets' imagination, but
'corresponds with Germanic custom'. Pfeilstücker has cited accounts of
'almost incredible wealth of decoration in gold, silver and amber, found
in Germanic temples'.

The student of Nordic antiquities Hermann Müller wrote about the
account of the temple and palace: 'This description agrees remarkably
well with those of the castles of the gods in Germanic mythology; we are
told of these that they gleamed with gold and silver, had many rooms,
were covered with copper, and surrounded by walls and moats. Even in

the bridge which connected the palace with the rest of the country, one seems to recognize the bridge Bilfröst of the Nordic legend.' (1844, p. 478.)

Of the temple of Forseti, who is certainly identical with the Frisian Fosite, it was said:

> There is a hall called Glitnir;   its pillars are gold
> And its roof with silver is set.
> There most of his days   does Forseti dwell
> And sets all strife at end.
>
> *Grímnismál* 15.

And again in the *Gylfaginning* (17): 'There, too is the (hall) called Glitnir, whose walls, and all its posts and pillars, are of red gold, but its roof of silver.'

Wulfram, who in the year 689 preached on Fositesland, told of 'a temple of extraordinary splendour' (*Vita Wulframni*, ch. 10). Liudger, who in 780–785 baptised its inhabitants and destroyed all the heathen shrines, carried away with the help of his followers 'a great treasure which they had found in the temples' (*Vita Liudgeri*, ch. 7).

Folklore, which so often preserves true memories of ancient events, tells of a 'golden city' which lies sunken on the Steingrund near Heligoland. Its inhabitants were so rich that 'in the old times they had canals and drains made of copper' (Siebs and Wohlenberg 1953, p. 234). A story from Butjadingen (the area between the Weser and Jade Bay) tells how the inhabitants of the country that later sank into the North Sea were so rich that 'They shod their horses with golden shoes, and ploughed the land with silver ploughs. They could afford to harness four white horses to a dung-cart. The drains that drained the land were built not of wood or stone, but of copper.' (Lübbing 1928, p. 7f.)

One might dismiss these as mere fairy-stories. Serious prehistorians do not do so. Research has frequently shown that local tradition has preserved truths about long past times. The contents of unopened Bronze Age tombs has several times been correctly reported in local legend (see Chapter 6). H. Jankuhn said of one such legend: 'We must certainly reckon with the existence of an oral tradition reaching back more than thirty-five generations. For we know of historical traditions that go even further back.' (1937, p. 330.) E. Jung (1939, p. 42–62) gave many examples of accurate traditions going back thousands of years. So instead of simply rejecting the story of the vanished 'golden city' on the Steingrund, with its copper land-drains and immeasurably wealthy inhabitants, it should be regarded as having a kernel of truth.

The same assumption may be made about other legends that are told along the coasts of the North Sea about a '*Glasberg*' or a '*Glastempel*' which sank beneath the waves (see above page 54). In all these words, the first part – '*glas*' – may be interpreted as meaning 'amber'. The same attitude can be taken to the old Heligoland story that on the Steingrund, 'A hall of fabulous splendour lies below the waves. The walls and floor were made of glass, clear as water, adorned with a rich inlay of gold and pearls. Precious jewels shone and glittered from the roof.' (Krogmann 1952, p. 142; Jensen 1865, p. 86.)

The story of the 'princess on the glass mountain', or the 'ascent of the glass mountain' is, according to O. Huth (1955, p. 18, p. 25) 'very widespread; over thirty variants are found in western, northern, and eastern Europe. . . In the Danish medieval ballad, Brunhild (Bryniel) sits on the glass mountain on which her father has placed her, and Siegfried (Sigward) rides up it on his horse. . . The island in the North Sea is the glass island, and the glass mountain is the amber mountain.'

Many of the stories of the glass mountain say that it was surrounded by a triple ring of water and could not be climbed by ordinary mortals. The same was true of the 'hill of no great size' on Atlantis, which Poseidon surrounded with a triple ring of water, 'making the place inaccessible to man (for there were still no ships or sailing in those days)' (*Criti.* 113e).

Heine-Gelder's opinion was that these legends or fairy-stories are 'myths of the sacred mysteries of the Megalithic age'; and Huth (1950, p. 17 f.) agrees.

It is not easy for modern people to fathom the meaning of these ancient myths. Very likely the union of Poseidon with the maiden Cleito signifies the '*hieros gamos*', the 'sacred marriage', the magical source of fertility and plenty. We may recall the verses of Euripides, who knew that there, in the amber country, was the 'marriage-bed of Zeus'.

This is a widespread myth; it is recalled, for example, in the marriage of Siegfried and Brunhild; or in these verses from the Danish ballad of 'Sivard, the King's son of Denmark':

> Sivard had a colt, which he had tamed himself. He won proud Bryniel on the glass mountain; all in the bright day. They rode to win her, the knights and squires and all the bravest men; none could climb the mountain, to win the fair maiden. The mountain was both high and slippery; her father had set her upon it; there was no man on earth he wished to have her hand.

Finally, Sivard announces his determination to try, and sets out: 'The way was long; the path led far; Sivard looked boldly at the glass mountain; the maiden smiled at him so sweetly.' Then he reaches Bryniel and marries her. The Bryniel of this story is the Brunhild of German legend.

That the hill on the amber island, not to be climbed by ordinary mortals, was 'smooth' or 'slippery' is attested by the Atlantis narrative, where we read that Poseidon had smoothed off the hill (*Criti.* 113d).

Stories of glass mountains and sacred marriages are known throughout the world. As O. Huth has said: 'They reappear almost word for word in Indonesia and Polynesia, where they certainly date from before European contact... The spread of this story must be related to the spread of the Megalithic culture' (1950, p. 16). That it comes from the North, or is set there, is shown by the fact that in many versions the glass mountain must be sought under the pole star. Even in the Indian legend of the mountain of Meru, in which the same story is told, the mountain lies under the pole star. 'The name "*Meru*" like "*Glasberg*" means "the shining mountain". Directly over it stands the pole star, and "the stars wheel about it in nearer and farther circles." It has three circular storeys or tiers . . . on the summit of mount Meru live the gods, and the souls of the ancestors.' (Huth 1955, p. 29.)

All this points to the conclusion that on the amber island near Heligoland, as early as the Megalithic era, there was an important shrine which either served as model for all these widespread legends or was itself modelled upon them. Here, we may suppose, the *hieros gamos* or sacred marriage shown on many Scandinavian rock scribings was celebrated.

The Atlantis narrative states that the temple of Poseidon was 'somewhat outlandish (or barbarous) in appearance'. 'This statement applies to all the monuments of the Megalithic culture, as we know them, but not at all to those of Crete or Santorin, where some have supposed Atlantis to lie' (Hohenöcker 1974, p. 17). So we may imagine the temple of Poseidon on the holy island as a great Megalithic enclosure, whose innermost shrine was a hall richly ornamented with amber, sacred to Cleito and Poseidon, where the profane public were forbidden to enter.

The axe cult

In the Neolithic period and the Bronze Age, the cult of the sacred axe spread throughout the Megalithic culture area. Axes are often found in graves, under standing stones, in dwelling sites and hearths; in quantities and in positions which show clearly that they must be interpreted as ritual offerings. Often an axe is set in the earth upright, with the cutting edge in the air, and held in place by small stones.

Among such finds are: two unpolished, narrow-backed flint axes at the edge of a great stone near Lottorf in Schleswig; four identical ones under another great stone near Sorring Skov in the neighbourhood of Århus; a polished, pointed axe found under the hearth at a dwelling site in Troldebjerg, Langeland, and three flint axes set in a triangle near Bedsted on the Thy peninsula, Denmark. Near the last lay some amber

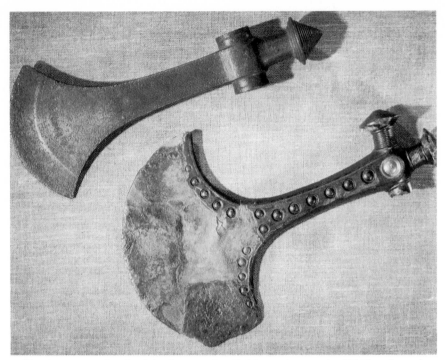

Two bronze axe heads of the fourteenth and thirteenth centuries BC. Top: from the 'Krogsbolle', Denmark. Bottom: from Brondsted, Gaverslund, Denmark. Danish National Museum, Copenhagen (photo from the Museum)

beads, which had clearly been placed on purpose near the votive axe.

In Brittany, the French researcher G. de Mortillet discovered axes in six of the seven Megalithic tombs which he investigated; they had been stuck in the earth, cutting-edge upwards. Five smaller stone axes, four of diorite and one of fibrolite, were found in the same position at the foot of a menhir at Mané-er-Hroek (south-east of Locmariaquer). Inside burial chamber no. 1 at St Michel near Carnac, thirty-nine stone axes, ten made of jadeite, were found, all buried edge-upwards. The list could be continued with similar finds in England and Ireland.

Prehistorians speak of an 'axe god', or a god to whom the axe was sacred. Undoubtedly this was the god to whom were offered the many axes which were carefully placed in tombs, or in fields or bogs. Many of them are new and unused; others are broken, with the fragments carefully laid together. Often they are made of rare or valuable materials. For example, in a deposit near Hørdum on the Thy peninsula, five large shaft-hole axes made of amber were found (Bröndsted 1960, vol. 1, p. 330). In other places axes made of copper – a valuable material at the time – have been found with spirals or decorative plaques of the same metal. Under one of the menhirs of the semicircular enclosure or cromlech of Kerlescan, Brittany, a copper axe was found which had been buried edge-upwards before the stone was set in place.

Undoubtedly too the many miniature axes in copper or earthenware, which were worn as pendants round the neck, were symbols of the axe god. In the passage-grave period such axe-shaped amber pendants were 'the height of fashion' (Sprockhoff 1938, p. 141).

The axe god, or perhaps one of his worshippers, carrying a large axe, is shown on a rock surface at Simrishamn, south Sweden. At Schülldorf near Rendsburg, a shafted axe is incised on a stone tablet decorated with numerous small hollows or cup shapes, which resemble similar ones at Mané-er-Hroek and Mané-Kerinoed in Brittany and Stonehenge in England.

Certainly the god of the axe was especially honoured during the Megalithic era; however, the cult itself may stem from much earlier times. Schwantes supposed that it came originally from the North, since in that area was found 'the oldest axe in the world, with which mankind begins a new civilization' (1938, p. 216). Since these most ancient axes were chipped out of a flint core, they are known as 'core-axes'. They are first found in mounds of discarded mussel shells or 'kitchen middens' of the Middle Stone Age (Mesolithic). One example even has a shaft. The forerunners of these flint axes were made of deer or reindeer antler, with cutting edges either of bone or of flint-chips let into the antler. The first polished axes, too, come from the north of Europe (Schwantes 1938, p. 165), and the first double-edged axes are found in this area. Schwantes said of the latter: 'This is clearly a genuinely Nordic weapon, since here we can follow its gradual evolution from early types with edges, to the most completely developed form. These battle-axes spread to western Europe, to England and Brittany. However, they cannot have their origin there, but must be derived from a stimulus in *our* territory.' (1938, p. 208.)

Schwantes dated this oldest axe in the world to the seventh millennium BC, a dating which now after the work of Colin Renfrew must be put back by at least a thousand years. The oldest known axes from Brittany and England come from the fourth or third millennium BC, so one must surely agree with Schwantes that the home of the Megalithic culture whose principal weapon was the axe, and of the cult of the axe god, lay in Denmark and Schleswig-Holstein.

But who was this axe god? Perhaps the rock scribings will help to answer the question. On one of the carved panels at Kivik two upright axes are shown, with their edges turned towards a pointed pillar. Evidently there was a close connection between the pillar and the axe.

The same connection is shown by the many axe offerings that are found under or at the foot of pillar stones and by the engravings of axes on standing stones. Thus on one of the uprights at Stonehenge, the shapes of four axe-heads with the edge uppermost, together with a dagger, were found. In front of the passage grave at Mané-er-Hroek there formerly stood a menhir, which has now been set up inside the tomb. On its upper part are engraved four shafted axes. Inside the tomb were found 102 stone axes and a quantity of beads, undoubtedly left there as offerings. These objects and engravings suggest that the god to whom the axe was sacred was also the god of the pillar.

The Atlantis narrative states that the amber pillar on which the laws of Poseidon were written was erected at the mid-point of the temple. Clearly Poseidon here appears in the role of pillar god and god of the axe. This agrees with the fact that in Greece in the earliest times, Poseidon was worshipped at pillars and that he carried the axe or the double-axe (Schweitzer 1922; p. 93f.). Among the later Greeks, Atlas, son of Poseidon, became the god of the heaven-pillar, the heaven-bearer, and Apollo the god of judgements and oaths. In place of the axe, Poseidon then received the trident as his symbol. It is a commonplace of the history of religions, that sons or 'hypostases' of older gods take over their functions.

It is worth noticing in this context that in the old legend about the origin of the Frisian laws the Frisian god Fosite – who corresponds to Poseidon not only in function but in name, which has the same derivation – steered the twelve Frisian *Asegen* (law-givers) over the stormy sea to the sacred land. There the god threw his axe onto the shore 'and there gushed forth a spring, whence the place is called "Axenshowe" (*howe* = temple). And at Eswai they landed and sat around the spring' where the god taught them the laws. 'Therefore they must deliver their judgements at "Axenshowe" and at "Eswai"' (K. von Richthofen 1882, vol. 2, p. 419, p. 435, p. 447, p. 459f.).

So Fosite too was an axe god, teacher of the law, highest judge, saviour from danger at sea, waker of springs, just like Poseidon. This, surely, was also the god to whom the pillar and the axe were sacred, and the pillar is universally the symbol of the heaven-pillar, on which the sky rests.

O.S. Reuter has shown that the idea of heaven resting on a pillar, identified with the pole star,

> could only have originated in the North, where the pole star, even though inclined towards the north, remains broadly speaking overhead – but not in the South, where it sinks progressively towards the northern horizon. If traces of this conception remain among southern peoples (e.g. the Sumerians or the Egyptians), it must have been carried there during the migration of peoples . . . The astronomical facts do not admit of the borrowing being the other way (1922, vol. 1, p. 83, p. 86 ff.; also vol. 2, p. 29 f.; 1934, p. 234.)

Cleito, the 'Magna Mater'

The name 'Poseidon', according to philologists, is related to the Greek word *posis* = spouse, and is explained as meaning the 'spouse' of the Magna Mater (Kretschmer, *Glotta,* vol. 1 (1909), p. 27 ff.; vol. 14 (1926), p. 201; vol. 15 (1927), p. 187; in agreement are: W. Schulze, U. von Wilamowitz-Möllendorf, O. Kern, F. Schachermeyr and others).

In agreement with this, the atlantis narrative names Poseidon as the spouse of Cleito, who was born on the amber island. The passage goes:

> At the centre of the island, near the sea, was a plain, said to be the most beautiful and fertile of all plains, and near the middle of this plain about fifty stades inland a hill of no great size. Here there lived one of the original earth-born inhabitants called Evenor, with his wife Leucippe. They had an only child, a daughter called Cleito. She was just of marriageable age when her father and mother died, and Poseidon was attracted by her and had intercourse with her, and fortified the hill, where she lived, smoothing it over, and enclosing it with concentric rings of sea and land. There were two rings of land and three of sea, which looked as if they had been measured with compasses, with the island at their centre and equidistant from each other, making the place inaccessible to man (for there were still no ships or sailing in those days) . . . He begot five pairs of male twins, [and] brought them up. (*Criti.* 113d–e.)

I have already quoted the description of the shrine of Cleito and Poseidon, in which at the beginning the ten kings had been born; a forbidden place surrounded by a golden *peribolos*. The costly decoration and the barrier of gold surrounding this most sacred spot show that here was the central shrine of the far-flung Atlantean community. Here, the successors of the ten children, from all their ten kingdoms, brought their offerings.

The word '*peribolos*' comes from the verb *periballo* = to throw around, to encircle. It signifies here a golden chain, which was hung around the sacred place. This sounds unlikely at first, but we know that in later times (tenth century AD) a golden chain was hung around the greatest of the Swedish shrines, at Uppsala; 'The shrine is surrounded by a golden chain which hangs from the gables of the building, and glitters from afar at all those who approach it' (Scholiast on Adam of Bremen's 'Hamburg Church History', 4.26; *c.* 1050).

Because the 'mother' Cleito had been born there, and had brought her ten sons into the world there, the city on the island of Basileia was also called the 'Metropolis', i.e. mother-city (*Criti.* 115c). The question arises, whether we have any evidence for the worship of the 'great mother' in northern Europe, or indeed anywhere in the wide area through which the Megalithic culture spread. There is no doubt that we have.

In Beldorf, in the Rendsburg district of Schleswig-Holstein, a stone pillar as high as a man has been found, dating from the Megalithic era. It is decorated in the front with many longitudinal and lateral grooves and on the back with cup markings. The head is shown by a grooved circle and two cup markings stand for the eyes.

Before this pillar lay a stone tablet also engraved with cup markings. All prehistorians who have commented on it have connected it with other similar stone pillars or rock scribings of the Magna Mater found throughout the area in which the Megalithic culture was diffused. The correspondences are so close that the Beldorf pillar may be referred to as a representation of the Magna Mater.

From the passage-grave era we have vessels from northern Europe which show the 'owl face' or the great rayed eyes of the goddess. One of them corresponds almost exactly with a vessel from a passage grave at Los Millares, near Almería, Spain, showing the same rayed eyes. Even the number and arrangement of the twenty-seven rays which go out from each eye are exactly the same. I shall return to these rays and their significance.

The owl face, the great rayed eyes, and also the serpent, which often appears in the Scandinavian rock scribings, seem to be the sacred symbols of the Magna Mater.

From the Bronze Age of northern Europe, from Fandal, Fangel-Torp, Viskö, Farö, Ferreslev, and from Pomerania, we have several small female statuettes, which represent 'copies of larger statues of the female deity' (Bröndsted 1962, vol. 2, p. 226).

The statuettes from Viksö (North Zealand) and Farö (Fyn) are shown with the hands raised to the breasts. (In the case of the second, the arms are missing, and one can only recognize the two hands below the breasts.) This attitude corresponds to that of the Magna Mater on menhirs in France (Benezet, St Sernin) and Spain (Almería, Los Millares).

Particularly numerous in north Europe are votive deposits of women's ornaments, often very costly. 'It can only have been a feminine deity to whom these offerings were dedicated' (Bröndsted 1962, vol. 2, p. 207).

There is therefore plenty of evidence that as early as the Neolithic period, as later in the Bronze Age, the Magna Mater was worshipped in northern Europe.

The home of the Megalithic culture and the problem of dating

Many scholars have supposed that the cult of the Magna Mater in the Megalithic age came to northern Europe from the Orient, along the sea route via the Mediterranean islands and the coasts of the Iberian peninsula, France and England. This is unlikely.

It is much more probable that the Atlantis narrative is correct when it states that in the beginning when 'there were still no ships or sailing', the Great Mother Cleito was born on the amber island, the daughter of 'one of the original earth-born inhabitants'. The cult of the Magna Mater, so widespread in the Megalithic era, must have begun in the area of the Great Mother's home, 'the obvious starting point' (Schwantes 1939, p. 221) of the Megalithic culture itself.

Until recently few prehistorians placed the home of the Megalithic culture in northern Europe. The reason for this was the inadequacy of the dating methods which were available until comparatively recently. Earlier prehistorians, taking as their device *'ex oriente lux'*, dated all archaeological finds in northern and western Europe several centuries *later* than finds of the same type in Egypt or Mesopotamia, where the dates are known from written records.

In 1952 the American scientist Willard F. Libby in his book *Radiocarbon Dating* showed a new method of calculating the age of prehistoric finds, which made it possible to assign broadly reliable dates to any object which contained deposits of carbon (e.g. wood, bone, or peat).

Since then, however, it has been demonstrated that this method is not accurate and often gives dates which are in fact much too recent. Radiocarbon datings can be corrected, however, with the help of dendrochronology, or tree-ring dating. This method is based on the fact that a living tree adds a new growth-ring to its trunk every year. Therefore by simply counting backwards from the time the tree was felled or died, it is possible to tell in what year each ring grew. Since the rings formed in good years are broader than those formed in years of drought, one can see the variations in climate through the years. Charles W. Fergusson, of the University of Arizona, has been able to use very old bristle-cone pines to build up 'a continuous absolute chronology reaching back almost 8200 years' (Swan 1971, p. 48).

Comparisons between datings of pieces of wood given by the two different methods – radiocarbon and tree-ring – showed considerable differences. 'The divergence . . . is not serious after 1500 BC. Before that time the difference becomes progressively larger and amounts to as much as 700 years by 2500 BC. The carbon-14 dates are all too young.' (Renfrew 1971, p. 68.)

The British Professor of Archaeology, Colin Renfrew, has explained
the consequences of this corrected perspective for European prehistory
in a dramatic article 'Carbon 14 and the prehistory of Europe' (1971).

> The revision of carbon-14 dates for prehistoric Europe has a disastrous effect
> on the traditional diffusionist chronology. The significant point is not so
> much that the European dates in the third millennium are all several
> centuries earlier than was supposed, but that the dates for Egypt do not
> change . . . now it is clear that the megalithic tombs were being built in
> Brittany earlier than 4000 BC, a millennium before monumental funerary
> architecture first appears in the Eastern Mediterranean, and 1500 years
> before the raising of the pyramids. The origins of these European burial
> customs and monuments have to be sought not in the Near East but in
> Europe itself.

The Megalithic town of Los Millares in Southern Spain, which was
formerly dated by the carbon-14 method to about 2350 BC, was in fact
built about 2900 BC. 'The central moral is inescapable. In the past we
have completely undervalued that originality and creativity of the
inhabitants of prehistoric Europe. . . . The old diffusionist view of links
connecting Europe and the Near East is no longer tenable. . . . It
transforms our picture of what happened in prehistoric Europe and of
how Europe developed.'

In the present context what this means is that the widespread
assumption that the worship of the Magna Mater derived from the Near
East must now be rejected because the stone pillars of the goddess in
Brittany – and with them the others in northern Europe – are *older* than
4000 BC, and therefore older than those in the Near East.

The statement of the Atlantis narrative that mother Cleito was born
on the sacred amber island – not brought there from far off – thus gains
additional support. From a separate tradition come the statements of
Hecataeus cited on page 87 about the Hyperboreans. The legend
recounted there is that 'Leto was born on this island'. The Cleito of the
Atlantis narrative is identical with the Leto of the Hyperborean
tradition. That Cleito became Leto, with the passing of the Hyperborean story into the Greek language, is 'perfectly understandable . . . In the Germanic dialects Cleito became *Hlet-is* and *Hled-is*,
names which occur in lists of ancestors in the *Hyndluliód*. In the Helgi
Lays, with their antique style and Heligoland connections, we find
Hlethbjorg, i.e. *Hleth*-castle. . . . These correspondences apply to both the
meaning and the sounds of the names.' (Gehrts 1967). According to
Gehrts the names Cleito, Leto and Hledis all mean 'glorious one', and
Hlethbjorg = 'glory-castle' (Greek *kleitos*; Latin *inclutus*; Old High
German *hlut* = famous, glorious). Perhaps the Heligoland story that the
footsteps of St Ursula could once be seen on the island; and the special

honour given there to this saint (Siebs and Wohlenberg 1953, p. 234), are a memory of this goddess, transformed in Christian times.

A 'city' in the Megalithic Age?

It has been denied that a 'city' like the metropolis depicted in the Atlantis narrative could have existed anywhere in the northern Europe of the Bronze Age. But Hecataeus spoke of a 'city' on the holy island of the Hyperboreans, and Diodorus of a walled city of the Atlanteans, founded by their first king. The discovery of a great walled settlement belonging to the Megalithic age near Büdelsdorf in the Rendsburg district of Schleswig-Holstein gives colour to these reports of a walled city in the north of Europe at that time.

In a dried-up former bend of the river Eider, which had surrounded on three sides a plateau about 18 m high, a large fortified settlement of the Megalithic culture, covering ten hectares, was discovered in 1969. Protected on three sides by the river and the sheer fall of the ground, it had been secured on the fourth by a triple ditch 300 m long and 2.5 m deep, and a stockade of stout tree trunks.

Besides a quantity of potsherds, flint implements and arrow heads, the foundations of houses were found there. One was 22 m long; others measured 6 by 10 m. Among the objects found were a baking oven, earthenware plates and dishes, and much more.

These excavations have shown that people's former assumptions about the life of the Megalithic people of the new Stone Age were false. Such a large stttlement, which could well be described by the Greek word '*polis*' could only have been built by a well organized community under unified direction, and with command of considerable technical expertise. The fortified settlement at Büdelsdorf is twice as large as that at Los Millares, which is five hectares in size and hitherto had been the largest known inhabited Megalithic site. According to carbon-14 dating, the Büdelsdorf settlement belongs to 2400 BC. But, as I have mentioned, the dates given by this method are far too recent; rather, like Los Millares, it must be put at 2900 BC.

The many Megalithic stone circles and other monuments, often of vast size, found all over the area occupied by this culture, should have warned prehistorians against describing their builders as 'settled pastoralists and peasants, with little social organization, living in extended family groups in small hamlets'.

So the as yet incomplete excavations at Büdelsdorf strengthen the supposition of the existence of a walled city of the Megalithic people in northern Europe.

Any settlement in the shelter of the Heligoland cliffs would be likely to grow into an important port, for here at the common estuary of the Elbe, Eider and Weser rivers prospects for the growth of a town were particularly bright. The information that the Atlantean metropolis had three harbours suggests that trade by sea had great importance here. As a port on the Elbe, the Weser and the North Sea, it would have had the significance that later attached to Hamburg or Bremen. It was equally important as a port from which one could sail 'to the sea beyond [the Baltic]', for the route via the Eider and the Schlei would spare the seafarers of the Megalithic age, like those of the Viking age after them, the long and dangerous voyage round Cape Skagen. The metropolis lay in the area where in Neolithic times the precious Heligoland copper ore was worked, and where the 'gold of the North', amber/orichalc, was found in the earth 'in a number of localities'.

In addition to the extraordinarily propitious site of the metropolis, there was the uncommon fruitfulness of the Stone Age and Bronze Age marshland, which, because of its high lime content, was even more fertile than it is in the present day.

Here again folklore contains memories of the fruitfulness of the sunken land. According to a Frisian legend: 'The farmers were free lords and held their own court of law under the blue sky. Their land bore grass and fruit in plenty, and was so rich that men's shoes grew yellow from the clover when they walked through it. If a man put down his spear in the grass, in the night it was overgrown and the next morning no longer to be seen.' (Lübbing 1929, p. 4.)

In this extremely promising site, protected from the North Sea storms by the rock massif of Heligoland – then much larger – it was natural that a settlement should grow into a rich and powerful trading port, where 'Their wealth was greater than that possessed by any previous dynasty'.

Prehistorians have long recognized that 'the sea traffic of the Neolithic and Bronze Ages went mainly towards the West, across the North Sea', and they attribute 'the great prosperity which we find in the settlements of the North Sea coasts and islands' to this trade, and 'above all to the trade in amber, whose main sources in the Stone Age and early Bronze Age lay on the North Sea coast of Jutland' (Schwantes 1939, p. 572). By this overseas trade with England, Ireland, France and Spain is to be explained the 'extraordinary quantity of gold which these Northern farmers had at their disposal' (*ibid.*). Ahrens agrees that the island of Heligoland played an important part in the early Bronze Age amber trade. Since the rocks of Heligoland could not geologically be a source of amber, Ahrens has placed the amber island between Heligoland and the mainland (1966, p. 245).

So prehistoric research has confirmed the statement of the Atlantis narrative: 'Because of the extent of their power they received many imports, but for most of their needs the island itself provided.' (*Criti.* 114d.)

The narrative also says of the three harbours on Basileia that they 'were crowded with vast numbers of merchant ships from all quarters, from which rose a constant din of shouting and noise day and night' (*Criti.* 117e). Perhaps this too may prove to have been true.

Elephants on Atlantis

In previous sections I have shown that the statements in the Atlantis narrative on the site of the royal island, the copper and amber that it produced, the organization of the kingdom, the recruitment of the army, the importance of sea trade, the religious life, and much more, must be accepted as historically correct. The same applies, as will be seen from later chapters, to the statements in the narrative on the terrible natural catastrophes which ended the 'Golden Age' of northern

Jürgen Spanuth with an elephant tusk

Europe, and about the great military expedition of the Atlanteans through Europe and Asia Minor to the frontiers of Egypt.

There is, however, one statement in it which *cannot* be correct: that among the animals on Atlantis were 'numerous elephants' (*criti.* 114e).

There are various ways of explaining how elephants got into the text of the *Critias.*

One possibility is of mistranslation. Other mistranslations in the text are, as I have already pointed out, 'orichalc' for amber, and 'year' for the Egyptian lunar month.

We learn from *Criti.* 113a that the Atlantis narrative was translated twice: 'Solon intended to use the story in his own poem. And when, on inquiring about the significance of the names, he learned that the Egyptians had translated the originals into their own language, he went through the reverse process, and as he learned the meaning of a name wrote it down in Greek.' So these foreign names were translated first into Egyptian, then into Greek.

In the course of this double translation, mistakes could easily occur. As Paul Kretschmer has shown, the word 'elephant' stems from a common Indo-Germanic word belonging to an earlier stage of Indo-Germanic.* Its original form was *elebhant,* from which the Gothic *ulbandas* was derived. This name was initially applied to the aurochs or wild cattle. The Hebrew for the first letter of the alphabet, *aleph* or *eleph,* and the Greek for the same letter, *alpha,* are a reminder of it, for this letter represents a bull's head: ၓ . 'The names of these great animals were often confused, since the animals themselves were scarcely or not at all known' (Kretschmer 1952, p. 309). Kretschmer's view is supported by Burchardt (1912).

So perhaps a 'barbarian' word, i.e. a primitive Indo-Germanic word sounding something like 'elebhant' was mistranslated, either by the original, Egyptian, translators, or by Solon himself.

Or we may conjecture that, as the text and pictures from Medinet Habu show, North Sea captives and Libyan captives were interrogated together. At that time, as rock carvings show (Frobenius 1925) and much later too, as Herodotus (4.191) tells us, there were large numbers of elephants in Libya. It could well be that the accounts of Northern and Libyan prisoners were mixed up.

* Indo-Germanic: the language family including nearly all the languages of Europe and many north-Indian languages; more usually known as Indo-European. The supposed original parent language, Proto-Indo-European, can only be reconstructed from its derivatives. The same term is sometimes applied to the people(s) speaking those languages.

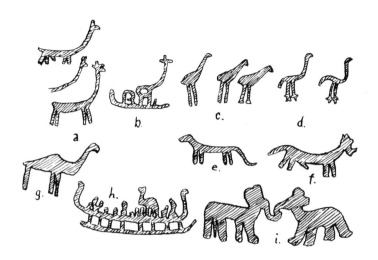

African (?) animals from the Bronze Age rock scribings of south-west Sweden; (a) giraffes (?) (b) giraffe on a ship (?) (c,d) ostriches (?) (e) Panther (?) (f) (?) (g) camel (?) (h) camel on ship (?) (i) elephants (?)

The theory that there were really still elephants in the north of Europe in the Bronze Age is, on the other hand, quite unconvincing. This theory relies on the fact that elephants are shown in Swedish rock scribings at Bohuslän. L. Baltzer reproduced pictures of elephants found in these carvings and said of them: 'The animal can only be an elephant. This interpretation will naturally arouse storms of indignation, in which I readily join. I am myself indignant at this fact, but I do not know whether this is more because such animals are depicted there, or that people have refused to see them because they are awkward. . . The great ears and the curved trunk show that this is the African elephant.' (1919, p. 46.)

It should be mentioned here that during a diving expedition an elephant tusk was found. Heligoland fishermen also assert that in 1914 lobster-fishers on the Steingrund found a well preserved elephant skull with both tusks, which could still be seen on the island up to the heavy bombardment during the Second World War but has not been heard of since.

The rock scribings of elephants at Bohuslän, however, should not be taken as evidence that there were such animals in northern Europe in the Bronze Age, but rather that Northerners on their voyages to Africa had seen elephants there and on coming home had engraved their likeness on the rocks.

Certainly, the question of how the elephants got into the *Critias* is
hard to answer. To mention it does not outweigh, however, the many
other proofs that the Atlantis narrative is the *Germania* of the Bronze Age.
Those who would place Atlantis in some other spot – near the Azores (I.
Donnelly), the Canaries (D. Wölfel), on Crete (J.V. Luce), or Thera
(A. Galanopoulos) – cannot use it as evidence against locating it in
northern Europe. For there were no elephants in any of these other
places either.

Brandenstein said in his very thorough study of the question:
'Wherever one may place Atlantis, there can have been no elephants
there . . . consequently we must accept them as an embellishment of
Plato's – or rather of Solon's, who might have brought the knowledge of
this animal back with him from Egypt' (1951, p. 80).

The ten realms of the kings of Atlantis

Of the kings of Atlantis and their descendants we read: 'On this island of
Atlantis had arisen a powerful and remarkable dynasty of kings, who
ruled the whole island, and many other islands as well and parts of the
continent; in addition it controlled, within the strait, Libya up to the
borders of Egypt, and Europe as far as Tyrrhenia. This dynasty,
gathering its whole power together, attempted to enslave, at a single
stroke, your country and ours and all the territory within the strait.'
(*Ti.* 25b). Elsewhere we find that Atlas, the eldest brother, received the
original kingdom or heartland, which was called Atlantis after him, and
his twin brother Gadirus 'the furthest part of the island towards the
Pillars of Heracles and facing the district now called Gadira'
(*Criti.* 114b). After the names of the five pairs of twins have been given,
we read: 'They and their descendants for many generations governed
their own territories and many other islands in the ocean and, as has
already been said, also controlled the populations this side of the straits
as far as Egypt and Tyrrhenia' (*Criti.* 114c).

In *Criti.* 119c it is stated that the rule and community (*arche kai
koinonia*) among the ten twins and their descendants were governed by
the injunctions of Poseidon.

For many scholars these statements are enough to make them dismiss
the Atlantis narrative as an 'unhistorical fairy-tale' or 'a Utopia without
historical foundation'. A. Schulten said of this passage, 'The account
here loses touch with reality and becomes pure fantasy' (1948, p. 12).
They simply cannot believe that in prehistoric times there can have been
such a widespread political confederation.

But solid archaeological facts, and written texts from the time of
Ramses III, once again contradict the opinion of the sceptics. There was

indeed in all these areas, in the Neolithic Age, perhaps even in the Mesolithic, an association 'which shows close ties between the peoples who inhabited them' (Schwantes 1939, p. 221).

The 'close ties' or 'community' between the peoples who lived on the coasts and islands of north, west, and south-west Europe, and North Africa, are particularly clear from the similarity of the Megalithic monuments and tombs found in all these areas.

In North Africa are found the same Megalithic tombs, stone circles, menhirs and burial rites as in all the other areas of this culture (Schwantes 1939, p. 221). The rock pictures of North Africa 'are amazingly similar, indeed often identical with those of the North' (Frobenius 1925). In both areas, figures with rayed crowns, figures blowing horns, swastikas, sun symbols, 'troy towns', spirals, rune-like signs, footsteps, and cup markings are scratched or engraved on the rocks. The folk-tales of the Berbers are the same as those of the peoples in the Megalithic culture area. The skulls and skeletal remains that have been found in the Megalithic tombs there belong overwhelmingly to the Cro-Magnon race, as they do in the other areas. The Tamahu, the builders of the Megalithic monuments in North Africa, are shown in the Egyptian wall-paintings as fair and blue-eyed, and accompanied by the 'ship sign' ⌣ just as it appears so often on the Scandinavian rock scribings. The war chariots of the Libyans in the North African rock pictures are the same as those, for instance, on the tomb at Kivik: the charioteer does not stand on the axle, but on the shaft, and clearly drives the two horses. Wölfel says of it: 'This is quite different from the type of chariot usual in Egypt' (1942, p. 108).

These and other common features led D. Wölfel to speak of an 'intimate connection' between the peoples of White Africa – as he calls those areas inhabited by the Tamahu and the Libyans – and the Megalithic peoples in south-west, western and northern Europe. This 'intimate connection' is also attested by the texts of Ramses III, where he speaks of a 'confederation' between the Tamahu and the Libyans, and other peoples, with the North Sea Peoples, and says the North Sea Peoples were the leaders (Medinet Habu, tablet 46).

The first archaeologists to demonstrate the close connection between the North African Megalithic monuments and those of Europe, were the French researchers Férand and Latourneux. They investigated the North African Megalithic tombs, stone circles, menhirs and tomb offerings, and concluded that there had been 'a stay of several centuries in the wanderings of the Northerners' in this area (quoted by E. Krause 1891, p. 69). They also wrote:

> In Bu Merzug within a radius of two miles the whole country, which is surrounded by springs, the mountains and the plain, is covered with Megalithic monuments: dolmens, half-dolmens, cromlechs (i.e. stone

circles), menhirs, stone avenues and grave-mounds. . . The builders of these
were the dolmen people, who came from the shores of the Baltic, wandered
through England, France and the Iberian peninsula, until finally as the
blond and blue-eyed Libyans, and the Northern people of the Tamahu, they
troubled the borders of Egypt. (Krause 1891, p. 69.)

The Tamahu appear in ancient Egyptian texts 'at the latest about
2400 BC; they belong to a population-wave of Nordic, European, type'
(G. Möller 1920/21, p. 428). The Libyans appear first, under that name
at least, in the year 1227 BC. Some scholars consider that the Libyans
were the direct descendants of the Tamahu; others that they were
related by blood and tribal affiliation but represent a new wave of
immigration. The Tamahu must not be confused with the Tehennu, as
the Egyptians called the dark-skinned and black-haired people who
were probably the original inhabitants of North Africa. The Tehennu
are named in Egyptian texts long before the Tamahu. W. Hölscher
pointed to the 'close connection' between the Tehennu and the Egyptians themselves (1937, p. 16), and showed that the Tamahu, Libyans
and Meshwesh 'are distinct from the Tehennu in every respect' (1937,
p. 12).

The 'close connection' or the 'community' between the Tamahu and
Libyans and the North Sea Peoples is also shown by the fact that these
white peoples of 'Nordic, European type', venerated Atlas, after whom
they named their highest mountain range, and also, as Herodotus
related (2.50, 4.188), Poseidon. So the same Megalithic monuments, the
same burial rites, the same racial characteristics, the same religious cult,
the same types of ship and chariot, and much more besides, all show the
'intimate connection', or as the Atlantis narrative puts it, the 'community' between the inhabitants of White Africa and the peoples of the
Megalithic culture as far as northern Europe.

There were also close connections between these peoples and an
early wave of immigration in the Canary Islands. 'All the archaeological
finds made of recent years in the Canaries go to prove that these islands
were the outposts of an early high culture, with all the marks of such a
culture, however provincial and "barbarized". Large city-like
settlements have been discovered, imposing grave layouts, and finds of
inscriptions keep accumulating.' (Wölfel 1955, p. 181.) Wölfel mentioned engravings of ships on a rock wall on Gran Canaria 'which
indisputably belong with the representations of ships in the Scandinavian rock pictures', and went on, 'Those daring seafarers of the
Megalithic age, who had set up close cultural connections between
southern Spain, Brittany, the British Isles and Scandinavia, had clearly
also reached the Canaries' (ibid. p. 185). The people of the Canaries
worshipped a god of the world-pillar, whom they called 'The God Who

Holds the Heaven' (Rössler, 1941/2, p. 360). The name 'ataman' for 'heaven' on the Canaries led Wölfel to the theory that this god should be seen as 'a sort of giant Atlas, a god of the world-pillar' (*ibid.* p. 361).

> This sacred rock whose very name means 'the upholder', was for the Canarians not simply a stone, which must be prevented from falling and injuring people; rather it was the foundation of the very being of the world, the prop that held heaven and earth fast; in a word, the world-pillar, which, as in the beliefs of many peoples, was thought to be always in danger, so that the menace of its fall must be prevented by sacrifice. The strength of this world-pillar had to be maintained by constant offerings of liver – for the liver is according to widespread belief the seat and bearer of life ... The Canarians show unmistakable connections (racial, cultural, religious) with the more northern European peoples, in fact, with the Indo-Germans. (*Ibid.* p. 362-3.)

Here too the skulls and skeletal remains show that the population belonged to the Cro-Magnon race (Wölfel 1942, p. 100) and the first Spanish discoverers described the inhabitants of the seven Canary Islands as white-skinned, fair, and blue-eyed. The Spanish scholar Joseph de Viera y Clavija stated that he himself saw mummies of Guanche women ('Guanche' was the name of this people) 'with well-preserved, golden hair' (Rössler 1941/2, p. 357).

The Canarians had the institution of double kingship; their temple was decorated with red, white and black stones; they knew the axe offering. Rock pictures of horses and chariots show that they had the domesticated horse (Biedermann 1974, p. 14).

These and many other features of the Canarian culture led Huth to the conclusion: 'We certainly have here the remains of the west-European-Nordic Megalithic culture' (1939, p. 133). The Canarians had a tradition of a terrible catastrophe, which thousands of years before had devastated the earth with earthquakes and floods. Their own homeland had been engulfed, but their ancestors had saved themselves by climbing onto the peaks of the highest mountains, which stuck up out of the waves (Braghine 1939, p. 129).

In about 1200 BC Gran Canaria must indeed have been devastated by a disastrous volcanic eruption. After a long period of dormancy, the volcano on the island broke out and covered it with a thick layer of lava and ash. As on Thera/Santorin, a wooden post and pine trunk were found underneath this volcanic layer. A carbon-14 dating by Professor H.U. Schminke of Bochum gave an age of 3075 years plus or minus 100. So the eruption must have occurred sometime between 1000 and 1200 BC.

So the Canaries, like the lands of 'White Africa' may be reckoned to belong to that 'community' of which the Atlantis narrative tells.

Another part of this community lay 'in Europe as far as Tyrrhenia'. By this we must understand the coastlands and islands of the western Mediterranean. And indeed a Megalithic culture is found there with passage graves, cromlechs and menhirs, identical with those in the other areas.

Among the many monuments one of the most important is the Megalithic 'city' of Los Millares about 14 km north of Almería and near the rich copper mines of the Sierra de Gador. The settlement was built, like the one at Büdelsdorf (see page 117), on a piece of high ground, rising out of the fertile valley of the Anderax. Here too were found the remains of a bank and stockade, of an aqueduct which brought water from a nearby spring to the town, of houses made of dry-stone masonry. Nearby is a cemetery with seventy-five Megalithic tombs, some among them having a 'spirit hole' i.e. a (generally round) hole in the entrance slab. Often the mounds, which were piled over the Megalithic structure of the grave-chamber, were surrounded with several circles of stones, as they are in the other parts of this culture area. Many idols of the Magna Mater have been found at Los Millares showing her with the 'owl face' and the great rayed eyes, and with her hands raised to her breasts. One bowl shows two large eyes from each of which radiate twenty-seven rays, or 'eyelashes', which corresponds exactly to a carving on a Danish passage grave (see page 114). Often in these tombs, axes had been left as offerings, or necklaces with miniature axe-pendants (one of them of amber) just like those from the graves in Denmark or Schleswig-Holstein. Naturally, as well as these typically Megalithic grave-goods some from other culture areas have been found. This is just what one would expect given the overseas trade in which the inhabitants of Los Millares engaged.

The eye motif, on a vessel from a Danish passage grave, about 2000 BC. The two sets of twenty-seven eyelashes and the two pupils of the eyes give a total number of 56.
Right: bowl from Los Millares, with eye motif

The gold hoard from the mound of Borgbjerg on the island or Zeeland (from Schilling 1940)

This settlement was built about 2900 BC and is therefore considerably younger than those of Brittany, which were built before 4000 BC, but *older* than any monumental tomb architecture in the eastern Mediterranean. It is *not*, therefore, 'a degenerate copy of eastern Mediterranean and Near-Eastern monumental architecture' (Childe 1950; Cles Reden 1960) but an older, more primitive stage of the later tomb architecture of the Near East and Egypt. That the Megalithic tombs are older than, and forerunners of, the Egyptian mastabas from which in turn the pyramids derived, was first convincingly demonstrated by Elise Baumgärtel in 1926.

A second Megalithic centre in the south of Spain lies north of Málaga at the foot of the Sierra de Torcales, on the rim of a fertile plateau near Antequera. There, gigantic Megalithic tombs have been found, which speak of the power of great chiefly families. Very probably the Megalith builders of Antequera, like those of Los Millares, exploited the rich ores of silver, copper and lead in the neighbourhood. Particularly notable is the passage grave of the Cueva del Romeral, with an entrance passage of 23 m leading into a chamber 4 m high. The corbelled roof of the chamber is closed at its summit with a slab 6 m long and 80 mm thick. Behind this chamber is a smaller one, the burial chamber, walled with thick slabs. The whole building covers 44 square metres. The resemblance between the Cueva del Romeral and the famous 'Treasury of Atreus' is astonishing. But this Megalithic grave is no 'barbarized form' of the Atridean tomb, but an earlier stage of its development.

A second magnificent passage grave is the Cueva del Menga, also in the neighbourhood of Antequera. This is excavated from the side of a limestone hill. A passage 25 m long leads to a burial chamber whose roof is made of a single gigantic block. Mighty upright stone pillars about 3 m high hold it up; it weighs about 170 tonnes. Like the other slabs and uprights, it was dragged there from a quarry about a kilometre away. Sybille von Cles Reden wrote: 'Looking at the huge masses of stone which were moved in order to build the Cueva de Menga, one is amazed at the way in which the Megalith builders overcame the technical problems; for engineering was then still in its cradle' (1960, p. 204). But we shall see that in Brittany even larger masses of stone were transported over even greater distances, and that the engineering technique of that time was by no means 'in its cradle'.

Other passage graves at Antequera, such as the Cueva de Viera, are smaller; all the same, the latter has a passage 21 m long; the passage and the chamber are neatly walled with slabs.

On the south coast of France, too, especially in Languedoc but also in Provence, there are several Megalithic tombs like those in Spain. In them have been found copper flange-hilted daggers, rings, spirals of copper, beads of amber and gold, and many bell-beakers which were clearly imported from southern Spain. These finds show that the tombs belong to the Copper Age, and are therefore younger than the dolmens and the older passage graves of Brittany and northern Europe, where copper first appeared only in the later passage-grave period. Here, too, many axes were found, clearly placed as offerings. Numerous female Menhir statues – about fifty in Languedoc alone – often with 'rayed eyes' or holding the hands to the breasts, or both, show that the cult of the Magna Mater flourished in this area.

The name of the population of these coasts is not known. It is possible that some of the names in the Medinet Habu list of the great confederation which attacked Egypt about 1200 BC belong to the peoples of this area. Among these names – which otherwise cannot be assigned to any locality – are the Seped, the Meshwesh, the Pebekh, the Isi and the Menesen (Medinet Habu, tablets 22, 44).

The French expert on prehistoric metallurgy, Jean R. Maréchal, has shown by means of numerous finds that one of the three great hordes that marched through Europe from the North at the end of the thirteenth century BC, travelled along the great rivers of France – the Seine, Rhône, Loire and Garonne – to the French coast. Maréchal placed 'the epicentre [of the great migration] in southern Scandinavia and the Danish islands and the nearby sea', and spoke of 'a far-flung Atlantic community, which spread from Scandinavia to the Iberian peninsula and even to the Mediterranean' (1959, p. 232 ff.).

J. Wiesner, too, has shown (1943) that the great migration reached to the coasts and islands of the western Mediterranean.

On the islands in the west Mediterranean, there is also a Megalithic culture which is similar to, or identical with, those already described. On these islands it lasted longer and attained richer and more complex forms than, for example, in northern Europe.

'The very large number of Megalithic monuments on the Mediterranean islands is due not only to the better chances of preservation there than on the mainland, but also to the fact that the bearers of the Megalithic culture clearly stayed longer on the islands than on the mainland. There, protected from other migrants and conquerors, they could build their monuments undisturbed.' (Hülle 1966/7, p. 14.) It was owing to this protected situation that Megalithic tombs were still being built on the islands right up to Mycenaean times; this is shown by the Mycenaean artefacts that have been found in them. The inhabitants had guarded themselves against foreign conquest by great fortified enclosures. These are known on Majorca and Menorca as *talayot*, and on Sardinia as *nuraghi*. On Sardinia alone there are about 7000 of them, the largest being at Barumini. These great fortresses can be dated by the radiocarbon method to somewhere between 1400 and 1200 BC (*Logbuch*, Karawaneverlag, 1002a).

To this period belong the famous Sardinian bronzes. About 3000 have been found in the various *nuraghi* but most came from one great hoard dating from the thirteenth century BC. Most of them are figures of warriors, but there are also some female figures, and some models of ships.

Some of the warrior figures are particularly interesting as they are armed with horned helmets, round shields and swords, just like those in the Swedish rock scribings or the murals of Medinet Habu. J.R. Maréchal has said of them: 'The little votive figures which represent warriors in horned helmets and round shields, show signs of Scandinavian influence' (1959, p. 259f.). W. Hülle has stated: 'Many items are the same in the area of the west Mediterranean Megalithic culture, and in its outposts in the Atlantic area' (1966/7, p. 20).

So there existed between the Megalithic culture of these Mediterranean islands, and that of the other areas, a *koinonia,* a community 'which shows the existence of close ties between the populations living in them' (Schwantes 1939, p. 221).

Towards the end of the thirteenth century BC this old *koinonia* was renewed. On the Balearics, on Corsica, Sardinia and Sicily, there are signs of the influx from northern Europe. Among these indications are the flange-hilted swords and daggers, brooches, axes, spearheads and shield-bosses that are known from the Nordic realm and the areas through which the 'great migration' passed (Wiesner 1942, p. 225ff.). The custom of cremation was introduced; until then it was unknown in the Mediterranean area, though common in the North. The first iron implements appeared in Sicily and Sardinia. Finds of bronze bits and two-wheeled chariots show that towards the end of the thirteenth century horses were brought to the islands. 'These finds are all the more remarkable in that the horse is not native to the islands' (Wiesner 1942, p. 229). The texts of Ramses III show that the coasts and islands of the western Mediterranean still belonged to the community of the North Sea Peoples at the end of the thirteenth century. These texts state that on the side of the 'ten kings' of the North Sea Peoples there fought the Sherden (Sardinians), Shekelesh (Siculi from Sicily and southern Italy), Teresh (Tyrrhenians), the 'Wasasa of the sea' (according to Biollay these were perhaps the inhabitants of Corsica) and the Lebu (Libyans). The American translators say about the word which Ramses III used of these peoples: 'The word occurs only in this passage . . . the meaning is "community", or "league"' (Edgerton 1936, p. 53; tablet 46, note 17g).

Another of the realms of the ten sons of Poseidon was that of the second brother, Gadirus, twin of Atlas, the eldest; it lay 'towards the pillars of Heracles and facing the district now called Gadira', i.e. on the west coast of Spain and Portugal (*Criti.* 114b).

The similarity of the Megalithic monuments of this area to those of

Brittany, England and northern Europe has often been noticed. This fact and the frequent finds of amber objects in this area show that there was constant traffic between the people there and those of the Megalithic culture area of northern Europe (La Baume 1924).

Amber must have been exchanged for the daggers and bell-beakers which seem to have been the characteristic products of the Iberian megalith builders, both at the end of the Neolithic and even more during the first period of the Bronze Age.

The rich veins of copper, tin and silver ores in this area led to a blossoming of the Megalithic culture. The finds show that they had trade connections not only with northern Europe and England, but with Egypt and the Near East (Ritchie Calder 1961, p. 134f.).

It may be assumed that part of the population of Gadira took part in the great military expedition against Egypt. Maréchal noted a collection of flange-hilted swords which was fished out of the harbour of Huelva at the mouth of the Guadiana north-west of Gades/Cádiz and 'which might just as well have come from Denmark or Schleswig-Holstein' (1959, p. 259).

Of the ten territories which formed part of the *koinonia*, the Atlantean community, four have been accounted for, as they are named in the Atlantis narrative itself: the heartland in Northern Europe, 'Libya as far as Egypt', 'Tyrrhenia', and 'the district of Gadira' on the coast of the Iberian peninsula. The other six are not named in the narrative, but it may be assumed justifiably that they include all the areas to which the Megalithic culture spread, in its several thousand years of existence. That is to say, Brittany, Normandy, Ireland, England and Scotland. Maréchal, on the evidence of numerous prehistoric finds, reckoned these as part of the 'far-flung Atlantic community', and wrote: 'A large number of characteristic weapons have been found along the east coast of Scotland, in the Firth of Forth, and in the Thames. The seafaring warriors sailed along the north coast of Scotland and landed in Ireland. Their settlements were to be found in Wessex, Brittany and in southern Spain, by the sixteenth century BC or even earlier.' (1959, p. 261f.)

R. Ströbel (1940) has described in his detailed study of the period how England, Scotland and Ireland were settled 'soon after 2000 BC' by 'battleaxe people from Jutland'. So here too the Atlantis narrative appears to give the facts correctly, when it tells us that the ten kingdoms of the Atlantean Community included, besides the four named, many other coastlands and islands.

The Atlantis narrative offers the solution to the 'great mystery' of the Megalithic culture, of which Schwantes wrote: 'It cannot be doubted that the European/North African/ Mediterranean Megalithic culture area shows that there must have been close ties between the peoples dwelling in it. But what the nature of those ties may have been – that is

Megalithic stone alignments and tombs at Carnac, Brittany

the great mystery which we cannot unravel' (1939, p. 221).

The conclusions I have reached so far are supported by the opinion of the French philologist A. Meillet, who convincingly showed that 'the origins of the closely related Indo-European languages are to be explained in exactly the same way as the birth of the Romance languages from Latin: the official language of an – in this case prehistoric and preliterate – empire overlay the various native languages of its provinces and thus split up into different local dialects' (1908, p. 431f.).

Meillet identified this 'empire' with the Megalithic culture, and considered that the megalith builders must have spread their 'official language' to all the territories over which they ruled, and that this accounts for the origin of the Indo-European (or Indo-Germanic) language family.

Many have agreed with Meillet's conclusions and many have disputed them; the latter mainly among those scholars who consider that the megalith builders were not Indo-Germanic speakers. But this hypothesis is rejected by many philologists. Foremost among them is Wolfgang Krause of Göttingen, an expert on the Nordic, Celtic and Tocharian cultures, who has demonstrated both that the megalith builders were Indo-Germans and – since he places the home of the Megalithic culture in northern Europe – that 'there is no more doubt that the original home of the Indo-Germans was in the North Sea/Baltic area' (B. von Richthofen 1970, p. 67). The most recent researches in the fields of astronomy and geometry support Meillet's conclusion.

Throughout the whole area of the Megalithic culture, from the Hebrides to Spain, from Ireland to East Germany, in which measurements and astronomical orientations have been taken, the same astronomical and geometrical knowledge is found and the same unit of measurement, the 'megalithic yard', was used. 'The existence of this unit and its consistency over so great an area show an expertise in geometry almost like that of a high civilization, and which is in no way inferior to the astronomical expertise which we have also found'(Schlosser 1976, p.192).

But the diffusion of all this astronomical and geometrical knowledge could not have been possible without a common language. The megalith builders also needed a written record for their astronomical data and evidence of this has been found in the signs and ideograms that are on many megalithic structures (Földes-Papp 1975, p. 62–67; G. and V. Leisner, *Röm.–Germanische Forschungen*, Bd. 17, Taf. 72; Reyna 1950 and 1970).

The Atlantis narrative says that the ten kings of the far-flung Atlantean empire met together every fifth and sixth year alternately on the island of Basileia. They could only have understood one another by using the 'official language' posited by Meillet.

Technical and organizational capacities of the megalith builders

Uncommon technical and organizational abilities were needed to build megalithic structures. These temples, grave-mounds, stone pillars and avenues of standing stones are gigantic and their builders 'altered whole landscapes by removing entire mountain tops and cliffs' (R. Müller 1970, p. 100; also Hülle 1967).

I have already discussed the impressive monument of Stonehenge. There, the transport of the sandstone blocks, weighing up to 25 tonnes each, from the Marlborough Downs about 3 km away (the nearest source of this type of stone) was a considerable technical achievement. An even greater one was the transport of the sixty bluestones, which can only have come from one particular place, 240 km away from Stonehenge, in the Prescelly Hills in Dyfed. Probably they were carried mainly by sea (Atkinson 1959, p. 56ff.).

Even larger in its area than Stonehenge is the temple at Avebury. Much of this has been destroyed in the course of the centuries, but many of the stones which composed its four circles still remain, either in place or fallen, and the holes in which the stones originally stood can still be located. The outermost circle was surrounded by a bank and ditch, and included an area of about 11.5 hectares. Once it consisted of 100 sandstone monoliths, each one weighing about 60 tonnes. Thirty of them still remain, the rest are only shown by the holes in which they stood.

The layout of the two inner circles is the same. A double row of standing stones, known as the avenue, leads up to the enclosure; it is 2.5 km long. According to Ramskou the newly discovered circle at Birkendegård is surpassed in size only by Avebury.

Megalithic tombs, too, are often of astounding size. Passage graves, 12-13 m long, 2-3 m wide and 2-2.5 m high, surrounded by huge stone slabs and covered by gigantic capstones, are found in Denmark and North Germany. Near Werlte in the Hümmling region of Lower Saxony, a burial chamber has been preserved with an interior 27 m long. Sprockhoff mentioned chambers 'almost 30 m long' (1938, p. 18). Passage graves or gallery graves in England, Ireland, Brittany, Spain and Portugal are often as large or larger. For their construction great weights had to be dragged to the building site.

Near Locmariaquer in Brittany stands the partly ruined gallery grave known as the Table des Marchands. Seventeen uprights and three covering stones remain of it. The uprights are rather more than 3 m high, and one of the now-broken covering stones measures 5.72 m by

Megalithic tomb on Sylt (photo Spanuth)

Megalithic tomb on Minorca (photo Spanuth)

3.95 and is 0.85m thick at its middle point. Its weight has been calculated at about 50 tonnes (Hülle 1967, p. 100).

Above these chambers, enormous mounds were often heaped. So, for example, Silbury Hill in the south of England near Avebury is the largest man-made prehistoric mound in Europe. It is 168m wide at its base, and its 354,000 cubic metres of limestone, chalk and turf form a cone 40m high, whose flat top measures 30m across (Wernick 1974, p. 17).

The mound over the 'chief's tomb', a gallery grave near St Michel in the neighbourhood of Carnac, is 125m long at its base, 60m wide, and 10m high. Its interior has a capacity of 50,000 cubic metres (Hülle 1967, p. 107).

Often the temples or stone circles are approached by long alleys or avenues of standing stones. To the north and west of Carnac lies an area which is dotted with huge grave-mounds and great stone avenues. Nearly 3000 menhirs (from the Breton words *men* = stone, and *hir* = long) extend in rough alignments across the heathland: ten, eleven, even thirteen rows side by side, generally ending in a stone circle or oval. In most cases the stones on the eastern end are smaller. The line gradually increases in height, until those at the western end are twice as tall as a man. Not long ago, Alexander Thom, Professor of Engineering Science at Oxford until his retirement in 1961, proposed the theory that these alignments preserve the astronomical knowledge of prehistoric observers of the heavens, knowledge that was only rediscovered in the sixteenth century AD. He has supported his opinion with comprehensive measurements and calculations.

These menhirs are often of astonishing size. Several of them are hewn out of single blocks 9, 10 or 12 metres high. The largest is now lying broken in four parts beside the Table des Marchands. It was thrown down and broken up only in post-Roman times, for Roman remains were found underneath the broken pieces. When upright it stood 20.3m high; its weight has been calculated at 350 tonnes. Its name is Er-Grah. *Er* = *hir* = great, *grah* = fairies, so 'great stone of the fairies'. The type of granite from which it is made is not found near its present position; the nearest source is on the west coast of the Quiberon Peninsula, known as the Côte Sauvage, about 10km away. The huge stone pillar is thought to have been hewn from the cliffs, loaded onto a raft and floated round the peninsula into the Gulf of Morbihan, there landed and dragged, presumably on rollers, to its present site. It is calculated that this would have needed at least 3000 men.

Taken all together, these often gigantic Megalithic monuments show that the people of this culture were no 'primitive nomads', but men with considerable expertise in the handling of heavy loads. The task of transporting stone pillars weighing several hundred tonnes, the building of huge burial chambers, tall mounds, and stone avenues kilometres in length, all require a central political authority.

The strong connections between the Megalithic cultures of the west Mediterranean and those in western and northern Europe have often been commented upon. So it may be that Diodorus Siculus, whose *Library of History*, written in the first century BC, made use of many ancient works now lost to us, preserved a genuine tradition when he wrote (3.56):

> Now the Atlanteans, dwelling as they do in the regions on the edge of the ocean and inhabiting a fertile territory, are reputed far to excel their neighbours in reverence towards the gods and the humanity they showed in their dealings with strangers, and the gods, they say, were born among them. And their account, they maintain, is in agreement with that of the most renowned of the Greek poets [Homer] when he represents Hera as saying:
> > For I go to see the ends of the bountiful earth,
> > Oceanus source of the gods and Tethys divine their mother.

This is the account given in their myth: their first king was Uranus, and he gathered the human beings, who dwelt in scattered habitations, within the shelter of a walled city and caused his subjects to cease from their lawless ways and their bestial manner of living, discovering for them the uses of cultivated fruits, how to store them up, and not a few other things which are of benefit to man; and he also subdued the larger part of the inhabited earth, in particular the regions to the west and the north. And since he was a careful observer of the stars he foretold many things which would take place throughout the world; and for the common people he introduced the year on the basis of the movement of the sun and the months on that of the moon, and instructed them in the seasons which recur year after year. Consequently the mass of the people, being ignorant of the eternal arrangement of the stars and marvelling at the events which were taking place as he had predicted, conceived that the man who taught such things partook of the nature of the gods, and after he had passed from among men they accorded him immortal honours, both because of his benefactions and because of his knowledge of the stars, and then they transferred his name to the firmament of heaven, both because they thought that he had been so intimately acquainted with the risings and the settings of the stars and with whatever else took place in the firmament, and because they would surpass his benefactions by the magnitude of the honours which they would show him, in that for all subsequent time they proclaimed him to be the king of the universe.

Uranus, as the ancestor of the Atlanteans is here called, was in Greek mythology the father of Poseidon (by Gaia) (Hesiod *Theogony* 137f.). According to *Criti.* 144, Poseidon was the father of Atlas. It is often the case in the history of religion that whole families of gods consist of 'hypostases', having the same functions and in the final analysis being simply different names for the same god. Fundamentally these are all examples of the same myth: that the ancestor of the Atlanteans, whether he be called Uranus, Poseidon or Atlas, founded a walled city for his people, that he was a famous astronomer, and that the Atlanteans had ruled countries which were (from the Sicilian-Mediterranean point of view) 'to the west and north'.

The megalith builders' knowledge of astronomy and geometry

The 'community' of the megalith builders, the ancestors of the Atlanteans, in all their ten provinces or colonies, is shown not only by the similarity of their monuments and religion, by their technical and organizational abilities and their command of deep-sea navigation, but by their astonishing knowledge of astronomy and geometry.

This fact has become clear only in recent times, with the investigation and measurement of numerous Megalithic sites from an astronomical point of view. Professor Rolf Müller has collected the results of these researches in his important work *Der Himmel über den Menschen der Steinzeit* ('The sky above Stone Age man') (1970), in which he has drawn on the investigations of Professor A. Thom and others.

Professor Thom has examined the astronomical significance of 450 stone circles, alignments and tombs from the north of Scotland to Wales and his remarkable conclusions were published in a number of articles, which have been collected in his book, *Megalithic Sites in Britain* (1967). Müller has investigated numerous sites in Germany (on Sylt, on the Ahlhorner Heide, near Boitin, in Mecklenburg, near Odry in West Prussia, the *Externsteine* near Horn, in the southern Teutoburg Forest and others) and his conclusions agree with those of Thom.

In his introduction Müller first discusses the relationship between astronomy, economic life, cult and religion, and says that the megalith builders demonstrated in their great works of construction not only their religious ideas but also a tradition of knowledge of mathematics, land measurement and above all astronomy. 'Researches by English and American astronomers have in the last few years opened up sources which must command all our attention, for their work reveals a new picture of the astronomical observations of Stone Age man, which surpasses anything we had previously supposed' (Müller 1970, p. 2).

These researches have shown that the megalith builders were outstanding astronomers, who not only observed, by means of sight-lines, the courses of the sun and moon and several of the fixed stars, but were able to predict solar and lunar eclipses.

It also becomes apparent that they used a single consistent unit of measurement, the 'megalithic yard', of 829 mm. This is very nearly the same as the Spanish *vara* of 838 mm, which the Spaniards were still using in the time of Columbus, and carried to Mexico, Peru and Texas. Moreover the Megalithic constructions show that their builders understood the 'Pythagorean' theorem, the value of the ratio of the circumference of a circle to its diameter (π) and the fifty-six-year astronomical cycle.

Knowledge of the 'Pythagorean' theorem enabled the megalith builders to set out right-angled triangles with sides of, for example, 3, 4 and 5 units (say, 'megalithic yards') ($3^2 + 4^2 = 5^2$).

It has been found repeatedly that this type of triangle was used in the building of stone circles. 'He [the megalith builder] was almost obsessed with the desire to construct his monument on the basis of as many right-angled triangles as possible. And it was clearly felt to be important that all three sides of the triangle should be multiples of the basic measurement – the megalithic yard.' (Müller 1970, p. 45.)

The value of π was also 'undoubtedly known to the geometricians of the Stone Age' (*ibid.* p. 111). Presumably they did not know the mathematical theory behind it, but found the number by trial and error.

Hecataeus stated that the Hyperboreans knew the nineteen-year cycle; he wrote: 'The god visits the island every nineteen years, the period in which the return of the stars to the same place in the heavens is accomplished; and for this reason the nineteen-year period is called by the Greeks "the year of Meton"' (Diodorus Siculus 2.47).

Meton was a Greek astronomer of about 432 BC and he calculated this cycle. The Hyperboreans, who are undoubtedly identical with the megalith builders, knew it more than a thousand years earlier.

However, the interval at which the phases of the moon correspond with the course of the sun is not precisely 19 years, but 18.61 years. So after every two nineteen-year cycles one of eighteen years must be substituted, to correct the error. $19 + 19 + 18 = 56$ years. The knowledge of this fifty-six-year cycle and its component cycles of nineteen and eighteen years, can be shown to be built into the construction of Stonehenge. According to the researches of the American astronomer G.S. Hawkins, 'The fifty-six Aubrey holes were the counters in a calculating apparatus, which made it possible for the priests to predict the course of the moon year by year, and so warn the people of coming eclipses, so that they would not be alarmed by the sudden darkness' (Müller 1970, p. 67).

Hawkins has shown how the builders of Stonehenge could, by moving the posts or stones that used to stand in the fifty-six 'Aubrey holes', predict 'with great accuracy every important event that would affect the moon for three hundred years' (*ibid.* p. 67). He has also shown

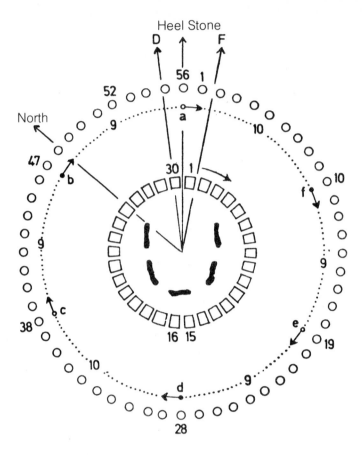

The Stonehenge 'computer', in which the 56 'Aubrey holes' give the figures. The Aubrey circle is 88 m in diameter. (After G.S. Hawkins)

that the fifty-six crooked lines on one of the supporting stones of the Table des Marchands, 'on account of the order of the lines, and the other symbols found with them, should probably be seen as a moon calendar' (*ibid.* p. 70). So here again the moon cycle of fifty-six years is represented on a Megalithic site.

Müller has come to the same conclusion about the 'rayed eyes' of the Magna Mater shown on a bowl from a Danish passage grave. 'Each eye is surrounded by twenty-seven "lashes", which together with the eyes themselves add up to fifty-six' (*ibid.*). Remember that on the bowl from the passage grave at Los Millares the rayed eyes are shown with exactly the same number of 'lashes'.

Professors Thom and Müller have also pointed out 'how highly in the

Megalithic era the techniques of geodesy and land-surveying were developed' (*ibid.* p. 72), and that the numerous stone circles show 'an art of construction which, while simple, yet shows an astounding knowledge of geometry, and of which there are dozens of examples' (*ibid.* p. 43). Again, Müller speaks of 'the highly developed geometrical knowledge of the builders of the stone circles' (*ibid.* p. 43, p. 84, p. 110).

Professor Thom has suggested that some remarkable stone circles in northern Scotland were 'practice sites,', 'where those wise men, who transmitted their knowledge to future generations, put their craft of land-surveying to use in the service of astronomical observation' (*ibid.* p. 95).

Thom has guessed that somewhere there must have been a centre from which all this knowledge, and the standard measurement of the 'megalithic yard', were disseminated; 'but his investigations gave him no clue whether this was on an island or the mainland' (*ibid.* p. 36).

Perhaps the old Greek traditions will give a clue in looking for this centre. I have already cited the tradition that the eldest son of Cleito and Poseidon, born on Basileia, was the first king there; he, so the traditions say, 'invented the lore of the spheres', and on the holy island of the Hyperboreans built a temple 'after the pattern of the spheres'. Atlas is described as a great mathematician and astronomer (Pliny *Natural History* 7.57; Lycophron, quoted in Tzetze, 873). Diodorus (4.27) said: 'Atlas had worked out the science of astrology to a degree surpassing others and had ingeniously discovered the spherical arrangement of the stars.'

Perhaps this shows that Thom's 'centre' must be looked for where Atlas was born and reigned as first king, on the island of Basileia, in the metropolis of the far-flung *Koinonia* of the Atlantean megalith builders.

The area around Heligoland was inhabited in the Middle Stone Age. This is shown by three core-axes which have been found there (Ahrens 1967, p. 298ff.) of which Ahrens has written:

> These axes are the oldest traces so far found of human habitation on Heligoland. In the time they were deposited, one must imagine the present island – or rather group of islands – as a small mountain peak, perhaps a landscape of broken slopes, at the end of a promontory sticking out into the North Sea from where Eiderstedt is now. It is quite likely that the settlement of Heligoland goes back to even earlier times. In any case the chances of finding Palaeolithic or early Mesolithic artefacts on the small area that still remains of the old Heligoland must be judged very slim, since the very parts of the land which offered the best conditions for human habitation (nearness to the coast, fresh water) have long fallen victim to the sea. (1967, p. 299f.)

W. Matthes, Professor of Prehistory and Ancient History at the University of Hamburg, has published finds from Heligoland and the nearby Steingrund, which he considers to be carvings of men and animals (bears, mammoths) from the old and middle Palaeolithic (Matthes 1969).

As for the Neolithic and Bronze ages, the numerous finds, and the thirteen grave-mounds that have been found on the quite small surface of the present-day Oberland (plateau) of Heligoland indicate 'a dense settlement' there up to the thirteenth century BC (Zylmann 1952, p. 39).

The Megalithic culture came from the North

So far I have produced a succession of pieces of evidence that the Megalithic culture did not, as was previously thought, travel from Egypt and the Near East to northern and western Europe, but on the contrary originated in Europe and spread to the Mediterranean. The master engineers of the Megalithic sites in northern and western Europe were erecting their monuments while the Egyptians were still building in wood and plaster. The megalith builders can no longer be dismissed as mere copyists of the work of higher cultures. They had made their own culture long before the 'high cultures' of Egypt and Mesopotamia arose.

The gallery graves of Brittany are now dated to about 4800 BC, and even earlier than those are their forerunners, the simple dolmens, with only one stone on each side and one cover stone. Schwantes has written of the dolmens:

> If we may take the form of the tomb as the criterion for its age – then the oldest forms of Megalithic tombs belong to the North. This is the only area in which one can see the Megalithic tomb, as it were, unfurl out of older forms of burial; the simple grave chamber whose supports were perhaps of wood, hidden under a round or long mound of earth, is replaced first with a stone construction. The small and narrow chamber at first served to hold only one corpse, but now, since the stone tomb would survive its initial use instead of collapsing, it could be used to receive other members of the same family. All this appears as the result of an unbroken line of development from the burial customs of the Middle Stone Age. (1939, p. 218.)

Sprockhoff came to the same conclusion:

> Undoubtedly the countryside richest in dolmens is that of Holstein. In this area are found all the forms, from the most basic to the many-chambered tomb, the earliest simple cists with surrounding wall-stones of equal height, the longer, narrower dolmens with low entrance-stones, the extended dolmens, and those with complex ground-plans. Nowhere else do we find the whole evolutionary series present in a single small area. It follows that Holstein is part of the primitive homeland of the dolmen culture. (1938, p. 24.)

Elsewhere he writes: 'The oldest forms – the original dolmens – are found mainly in Schleswig-Holstein. This area belongs to the primitive territory, the heartland, of the Nordic Megalithic, which otherwise includes only southern Sweden. From Holstein the dolmens spread, in their extended or polygonal forms, eastwards and southwards.' (1936, p. 260.) As the oldest form of Megalithic tomb, the simple dolmen, is not found in England, France or the Iberian peninsula, it may be assumed that the Megalithic culture spread from northern Europe, its 'heartland', to western and south-western Europe along the coasts.

There are other indications that the home of the Megalithic culture must be sought in northern Europe. I have already mentioned that the oldest axes in the world, and also the oldest double-edged 'Amazonian axe', have been found in northern Europe. Remains of pottery have also been found in the area in the Mesolithic 'kitchen middens' culture. As Schwantes has said: 'Here the axe was discovered, and perhaps also the art of pottery making' (1939, p. 575). Also the belief that heaven rests upon a pillar can, according to O.S. Reuter, have arisen only in the North (see page 112). The high value placed on amber by the megalith builders can only have originated in the area from which the amber itself derived, which in the Neolithic and Bronze ages was the west coast of the Cimbrian peninsula, and in particular the area between Heligoland and Eiderstedt. Here too the oldest copper implements were smelted from the Heligoland copper ore. According to the researches of J.R. Forssander (1936) and K. Kersten (undated, p. 72f.), the trade in copper goods, originally very valuable, was in the hands of the Megalith people and in the dolmen and gallery-grave periods they spread the use of flat axes, dagger blades, spirals and necklets along the sea-routes. That Atlas was connected with amber, called in Greek *electron*, is shown by the old legend that one of the seven daughters he had by the Oceanid Pleione was called Electra – the amber maiden.

Even Sybille von Cles Reden, who sought the home of the Megalithic culture in the eastern Mediterranean on the basis of datings that have since been superseded, noted that in the Megalithic era 'unusual creative powers were concentrated' in Jutland, Schleswig-Holstein and the surrounding islands 'achievements of unique beauty and the highest technical skill' in the working of pottery, stone and metal are found there (1970, p. 289).

So it does not seem too unlikely a theory, that the 'centre' postulated by Professor Thom, from which the knowledge and achievements of the megalith builders were spread, is to be sought where the Atlantis narrative placed the metropolis, the capital of the far-flung *koinonia* of the Atlanteans and the birthplace of the great astronomer and mathematician Atlas, after whom the whole island and surrounding ocean were named (*Criti.* 114a); that is, on the amber island of Basileia, near Heligoland.

The Vanir and the Aesir

It is not known what gods the megalith builders worshipped, apart from the Heaven Bearer and his spouse the Great Mother. F. Behn was certainly mistaken, however, when he attributed to them and their descendants a 'monotheistic concept' (1948, p. 224).

Much more probable is the idea held by many prehistorians, who see the Vanir, so often mentioned in the *Eddas*, as the gods of the megalith builders, and the Vanir's opponents the Aesir as the gods of the megalith builders' human antagonists, the Corded-ware People. The theory has often been proposed that the war between the Aesir and the Vanir, described by Snorri in the *Prose Edda* and more fully in his history of the kings of Norway, the *Heimskringla,* is a memory of the immigration of the so-called 'Corded-ware' or 'Battleaxe People' into the homelands of the Megalith People on the Cimbrian peninsula and the Danish islands. The *Heimskringla* relates: 'Odin (the King of the Aesir) attacked the Vanir with his army, but they were well prepared and defended their land, and so each side in its turn had the victory; each harried the land of the other and did them harm. But when both were weary of fighting, they held a parley and made peace, and exchanged hostages.' (1.4.)

The Megalithic People had inhabited the North Sea and Baltic area at least since the Middle Stone Age. Some time after the middle of the third millennium BC, there was a northward movement of the Corded-ware People, who had been settled in central Germany and further east.

The condition of some Megalithic tombs suggests that there were occasional armed clashes. However, in the subsequent. period the Megalithic and Corded-ware peoples became entirely assimilated, and from this mixture arose, about the turn of the second and third millennia, the Germanic peoples. The *name* 'German' is admittedly much more recent. It appears for the first time in the Roman records of 'triumphs' in the Capitol for the year 222 BC. But it is conventional to refer to the ancestors of the Germanic peoples by this name (Schwantes 1952; H. Hingst 1952; Sprockhoff 1954; E. Meyer 1968; Pokorny 1968; Bosch-Gimpera 1968; B. von Richthofen 1970; and many others).

It has long been a matter of dispute which of these peoples should be considered to be Indo-Germans. Often the Corded-ware People are thought to have been so, while the megalith builders are seen as non-Indo-Germanic. But Wolfgang Krause published in 1941 an exhaustive philological study in which he stated: 'There is *no* evidence that the bearers of the Megalithic culture were non-Indo-Germanic' and that 'one may be inclined rather to see an original relationship between the Nordic Megalithic culture and the Battleaxe People, than to suppose that the Nordic Megalith People came from the West.' Bolko von Richthofen agrees with this opinion (1970).

After the assimilation of these two originally related peoples, the connections between the megalith builders and their old associates in the British Isles, in France and on the Iberian peninsula were maintained. This is shown by the many battleaxes that have been found in these old colonies of the megalith builders.

The gods of the two peoples, the Vanir of the megalith builders and the Aesir of the Corded-ware People, also amalgamated with one another. So arose the bewildering pluralism of the Germanic gods, with parallel forms like Fricco/Freyr or Freya/Frija/Frigga, which can scarcely be distinguished from one another. From the Megalithic religion there remained the worship of the Magna Mater; and the sacred marriage, 'a concept known everywhere among the Germanic peoples' (Laur 1949); and no doubt much more. In Christian times the Irminsul became the Roland pillar, the Magna Mater the Virgin Mary, and the sacred marriage the folk drama of the May King and May Queen.

CHAPTER 4

THE NATURAL CATASTROPHES
OF THE THIRTEENTH
CENTURY BC

The fall of Phaethon

According to the ancient traditions, the 'Golden Age' ended in a rush of terrible natural disasters. Climatologists call these 'the great divide' (Bülow 1933, p. 55), 'climatic catastrophes of world-wide impact' (Paret 1948, p. 124) or, because of the effect of their final phase, the 'climatic revolution' (Behn 1948, p. 123; Ahrens 1966, p. 45; Pokorny 1968, p. 200) or the 'climatic drop' (Gutenbrunner 1939, p. 26). K. von Bülow called this 'great divide', 'the most important of all climatic alterations since it brought to an end the Golden Age' (1933, p. 55).

Greek and Roman authors preserved traditions of these catastrophes, above all in the story of the fall of Phaethon, 'the shining one'.

In its broad outline the story is as follows: Phaethon, son of the sun god Helios, begs his father to be allowed for one day to drive the chariot of the sun. In spite of his father's grave doubts and warnings, he persists in his desire, and Helios has to grant it since he has sworn by the Styx to grant his son one wish, as an acknowledgement of his paternity. When the horses of the sun feel an inexperienced hand on their reins, they break out of their normal track and plunge towards the earth. Terrible fires destroy forests and cities; rivers and springs, the Nile among them, dry up in the heat; once-fruitful lands, including Libya, become deserts; fearful earthquakes shake the world; everywhere the ground explodes; mountains, including Etna, burst into flame; ash and smoke cover the world with darkness; three times the sea shrinks back, only to return with overwhelming floods.

Finally Zeus takes pity on the tormented earth, and with a thunderbolt throws Phaethon from the chariot. He falls in the estuary of the river Eridanus, on whose banks his sisters, the daughters of Helios (Heliades) mourn with tears of blood, which become transformed into amber.

146

Of the many ancient authors who treated this legend, the most important is Ovid, who in his *Metamorphoses* gave the Phaethon story in its fullest form. Ovid preserved material from older mythological works and histories which are otherwise lost (Vosseler 1959, p. 5).

The cataclysms of which this legend tells can be dated by the fact that they include two unique events: 'Libya became a desert' and 'the Nile dried up'.

These two events are recorded· in the ancient Egyptian inscriptions on only one occasion. In the Karnak inscription it says that in the fifth year of the reign of Merneptah(1232–1222 BC) 'Libya has become a barren desert; the Libyans come to Egypt to seek sustenance for their bodies' (Hölscher 1937, p. 61f.). In the Medinet Habu texts, Ramses III reported: 'Libya became a desert; a terrible torch hurled flame from heaven to destroy their souls and lay waste their land . . . their bones burn and roast within their limbs.'

The Medinet Habu texts also report the drying up of the Nile. There we find, among other references, 'The Nile was dried up and the land fell victim to drought' (tablet 105). The other texts from the same period report the same catastrophes.

So the fall of Phaethon must be placed in the second half of the thirteenth century BC.

This story was also mentioned by the Egyptian priest who translated the ancient texts into Greek for Solon. He said: 'Your own story of how Phaethon, child of the sun, harnessed his father's chariot, but was unable to guide it along his father's course and so burnt up things on the earth and was himself destroyed by a thunderbolt, is a mythical version of the truth that there is at long intervals a variation in the course of the heavenly bodies and a consequent widespread destruction by fire of things on the earth' (*Ti.* 22b–c).

O. Paret, who wrote an exhaustive study of the thirteenth-century cataclysms, also cited the Phaethon legend (1948, p. 150, p. 167, p. 174) and said that Plato, in the *Timaeus* and the *Laws,* 'correctly understood these events' (1948, p. 174).

Other ancient writings also tell of the fiery comet, which the Greeks called Phaethon. To the Egyptians it was known as Sekhmet. In the texts of Sethos II (about 1215–1210 BC) we read: 'Sekhmet was a circling star, which spread out his fire in flames, a fire-flame in his storm' (Breasted 1906, vol. 3, p. 117).

In an inscription from Ugarit (Ras Shamra) which dates from shortly before the fall of that city in the last quarter of the thirteenth century, we read: 'The star Anat has fallen from heaven; he slew the people of the Syrian land, and confused the two twilights and the seats of the constellations ' (Bellamy 1938, p. 69). In the Avesta, the holy book of the Zoroastrians, which preserves vivid memories of that era, the fiery

star which unleashed first terrible fires and then a flood is called Tistrya.
There are endless traditions from different peoples who under different
names recall the appearance of a fiery star in a time of widespread
burning and flooding.

Many ancient authors, such as Lydus, Servius, Hephaestion, Junc-
tinus and Pliny, mention this star. Pliny said: 'A terrible comet was seen
by the people of Ethiopia and Egypt, to which Typhon, the king of that
period, gave his name; it had a fiery appearance and was twisted like a
coil, and it was very grim to behold: it was not really a star so much as
what might be called a ball of fire' (*Natural History* 2.23). The Egyptian
king Typhon, whom Pliny mentioned, is the same who on the shrine of
El Arish is called Tawi-Thom, who reigned for only a short time after
the death of Merneptah, and in following 'the rebels' (by which is meant
the Children of Israel) was drowned in Lake Serbonis, now Sebchat-
Berdawil, east of the Port Said (text from Al-Arish translated by Goyon
1936).

So it may well be true that as many ancient traditions assert, the 'ball
of fire', which in the second half of the thirteenth century BC circled the
earth on a course like that of the sun, was the cause of the world-wide
droughts, burning, earthquakes and floods. These cataclysms are
described in detail in the Atlantis narrative, and a wealth of scientific
and archaeological evidence confirms that they are described correctly.

Drought, drying up of rivers and springs, destruction of forests, famines

Before the time of these catastrophes, so the Atlantis narrative tells us,
Greece was rich and fertile; the plains covered with fruitful soil, the
mountains crowned with thick forests, streams and rivers flowing
everywhere. The numerous population enjoyed 'an excellent soil, an
abundant water supply, and a well balanced climate'. I have already
shown that this is an accurate description of conditions in Mycenaean
times.

But then the rivers and springs dried up, the forests were destroyed,
and the fertility vanished.

> You are left (as with little islands) with something rather like the skeleton of a
> body wasted by disease; the rich, soft soil has all run away leaving the land
> nothing but skin and bone... for some mountains which will now only
> support bees produced not so long ago trees which when cut provided roof
> beams for huge buildings... and the shrines which still survive at [the]
> former springs are proof of the truth of our present account (*Criti.* 111e.)

It is a fact that in the second half of the thirteenth century BC, there
began an abnormally hot and dry period, which led, not only in Greece

but in all the areas whose climatic development has been studied (Europe, the Near East, North Africa), to a catastrophic drought, to the disappearance of forests, and to famines.

O. Paret (1948) also dated this period of heat and drought to the time soon after 1250 BC, and produced large quantities of evidence for this dating.

For example: it is to this period that the so-called 'pile dwellings' which are found in various European countries, belong. Paret suggests that the posts which are found planted in the beds of many lakes and rivers (for example the Rhine and the Danube), often as deep as 7 metres, were not as is generally assumed piles to support buildings on a platform above, but part of the walls of huts built at ground level on the shores of lakes or rivers shrunken in the great drought. This would show that in the thirteenth century BC the water table in Europe had sunk by 7 metres. Paret said that this 'unparalleled recession of the water table' was a 'world-wide phenomenon', which can only have been caused by 'an extraordinary drying up of the climate' (p. 228 f.). '[This catastrophic drought] set the peoples of all southern and central Europe in motion, toppled the old world and laid the foundations for a new one. It unleashed "the storm that altered the destiny of the world".' (Quotation from Bachhofer in Paret 1948, p. 188.)

Another piece of evidence for this period of drought is contained in the 'boundary horizons' and 'burning horizons' which are found in many European bogs. 'Boundary horizons' occur when the growth of the bog is interrupted during a period of drought. The interrupted or dead growth then forms a recognizable layer, the 'boundary horizon'. Since the bogs first began to grow after the Ice Age, there have been several periods of drought, so there are generally several such 'horizons' in any bog. 'Of all the boundary horizons', said Bröndsted, 'the most noticeable is the one that falls at the beginning of the Iron Age' (1960, vol. 1, p. 17). Elsewhere he spoke of the 'well known boundary horizon of the transition from the Bronze to the Iron Age' (1962, vol. 2, p. 261). This horizon, which is so clear and is found in all the bogs, 'must be considered as contemporary in all cases' (Lehmann 1954, p. 508). Hitherto it has been dated, with the imprecise technique of pollen analysis, to 'about 1000 BC' or '3000 years ago' or 'about 1200 BC' (Schwarzbach 1961, p. 179). But with the help of the contemporary texts from Medinet Habu, the catastrophic heat and drought which caused the horizon can now be dated more precisely.

'In central Europe, too, the period of drought must have begun soon after 1250' (Paret 1948, p. 144). It was then that the 'great migration' of the Burial-mound and Urnfield people began. The sinking of the lakes made their dried-out shores habitable. Segments of the population from near and far, driven by thirst and hunger, gathered by what remained of the lakes and built the huts that were formerly taken to be 'pile dwellings'.

Out of the many pieces of evidence for the extraordinary heat of the time, I shall mention only the following. In 1947/48 the Swedish oceanographer Hans Pettersson led a research expedition to the Mediterranean. They obtained a number of drill-cores from the sea bed, which made it possible to test for changes in climate over several millennia. In these cores they examined the remains of foraminifers, small shellfish whose various species can only survive within quite specific temperature ranges. It is therefore possible to tell, by the presence of particular species of foraminifers, the temperature of the sea at the time a particular stratum of the sea bed was deposited. Now it became apparent from the sequence of the various strata, that the temperature of the Mediterranean had slowly risen after about 5000 BC, until it reached a peak about 3200–2400 years ago, when it was roughly the same as the temperature of the Caribbean today. Then the deposits of 'warm foraminifers' were overlaid with layers of ash left by volcanic eruptions. The cores also showed that the volcanoes had previously been dormant, or had had only minor eruptions which left no layers of ash on the sea bed. The thickness of this volcanic layer showed that this series of eruptions was much the most violent of the last 10,000 years, and that the volcanoes of the eastern and western Mediterranean had been active at much the same time. *Above* these layers of ash were found strata with foraminifers that can only live in cold water, showing that *after* the eruptions a period of cold set in which lasted for several centuries; and the temperature of the Mediterranean fell more steeply than at any other time in the last 7000 years. The period of this 'climatic drop' is estimated at '3000 years ago', with an uncertainty factor of plus or minus 5 per cent.

The texts from the time of Ramses III report in great detail the terrible earthquakes, the floods and fall of ash, which followed these eruptions. 'Egypt lay devastated' when Ramses came to the throne. However, in the texts of Merneptah, who died about 1222 BC, these catastrophes are not mentioned. They must therefore have occurred *after* the death of Merneptah, and *before* the accession of Ramses, i.e. between 1222 and 1200 BC. Various indications suggest that the catastrophes reached their peak a few years after the death of Merneptah, in about 1220 BC.

Fire from heaven

The Egyptian priest who told the Atlantis narrative to Solon said of the story of Phaethon that it was 'a mythical version of the truth that there is at long intervals a variation in the course of the heavenly bodies and a consequent widespread destruction by fire of things on the earth' (*Ti.* 22b). The priest, then, accepted the 'truth' of the Phaethon legend, which tells of a great burning that destroyed forests and cities.

That in fact there was a 'destruction by fire of things on earth' in the second half of the thirteenth century BC is proved both by contemporary texts and by numerous archaeological and geological discoveries.

Some of the texts I have already quoted. These reports of fire which fell from the heavens in Libya, Egypt, Syria and India may be supplemented by the statements in the Medinet Habu texts about the home of the North Sea Peoples the Atlanteans: 'Their forests and fields are burnt with fire.' 'The heat of him [i.e. Sekhmet] has burnt their countries.' 'The fire of Sekhmet has burnt the lands of the nine bows.' 'As mighty fire was prepared for them.' 'They had before them a sea of flame.' (Tablets 17, 46.)

Of the archaeological discoveries I will describe only a few.

B. Hrouda has described in a comprehensive study the mounds of ruins found in Palestine (1964, p. 126ff.). In all of them he found 'thick strata of burnt material' and he noted that, 'These burnt strata are evidence of a major catastrophe which, shortly *before* the arrival of the Philistines in Palestine, destroyed the settlements of towns such as Megiddo, Jericho, Lachish and others.' He came to the conclusion that, 'These catastrophes must have occurred before the colonization of the area by the Philistines' (1964, p. 133). Since he placed the beginning of this colonization process at or shortly before 1200 BC these fires must have raged 'about 1220 BC' (1964, p. 134).

In the traditions of Israel in the 'pre-Prophetic' period there are numerous stories of how, before the arrival of the 'Northerners' (*ha Saponi*) whose leading tribe was the Philistines, fire fell from heaven and burnt up the entire country.

In Ugarit, then the capital of Syria, excavations have shown that there was destruction by violent earth tremors and outbreaks of fire at the end of the thirteenth century. The cataclysm can be dated because *underneath* the layer of ruins it left behind, a long sword was found bearing the seal of the Pharaoh Merneptah (died about 1222 BC), while *above* it was found Philistine pottery (Schaeffer 1955, vol. 3, p. 169ff.; 1948, p. 71; Schachermeyr 1957, p. 122; Kimmig 1964, p. 234f.). So the 'final destruction' must have occurred here between 1222 and 1200 BC.

In a kiln in Ugarit was found a clay tablet which should have been baked; but the city was wrecked before that could be done. The tablet is of interest because on it is written a message from the last king of Ugarit, 'Ammurapi, to the King of Alasija (Cyprus) in which he speaks of the landing of seven enemy ships. 'Does my father not know', the letter continues, 'that all my troops are in the land of the Hatti (Hittites) and all my ships in the land of Lukka?' He asks that news should be sent to him immediately should any more enemy ships be sighted (Otten 1963, p. 9). But before the message could be sent, destruction fell upon Ugarit; so this occurred shortly *before* the colonization by the Philistines and the other peoples associated with them.

In this context the inscription from Ugarit quoted above may be recalled: 'The star Anat has fallen from heaven; he slew the people of the Syrian land.' The 'catastrophe stratum' of the earthquakes and fires has been found in all the other towns and settlements in Syria that have been excavated (Schaeffer 1948). That these destructive fires were *not* caused by the Northern peoples is shown by excavations in Assur (Assyria), which those peoples never reached. This city too was laid waste by fire at the end of the thirteenth century. 'Nobody can explain the origin of this intense heat which melted together hundreds of fragments of brick, and reddened and vitrified the entire core of the building' (Zehren 1961, p. 87).

In Asia Minor, too, all the towns and villages were burnt. B. Hrouda mentioned 'the devastation by burning' of many towns there. Of particular interest are the conditions found in the capital of the Hittite kingdom, Hattusa:

> The city was destroyed in a great catastrophe. Wherever we set our spades, on Buyukkale or in the first temple in the residential quarters or in Yazilikaya, we found unmistakable signs of a devastating fire that had consumed everything that would burn, reduced brickwork to reddened masses of slag, and made limestone blocks explode in fragments. Sometimes one got the impression that the materials that happened to be in the buildings could never have been enough to raise such a blaze, such a heat; rather, fuel must have been brought in from elsewhere to build up the fire. A few accidental local fires cannot have caused such devastation. Here, unquestionably, was human madness at work, nothing, not a house, not a temple, not a hut escaped it, and where the fire did not find the way of itself, anything was carried in to accomplish the work of destruction. (Bittel and Naumann 1952, p. 27.)

Many writers have attributed the burning of the cities of that time to human agency. They did not know the contemporary Egyptian and Syrian reports which tell how the comet Sekhmet, or Anat, fell from heaven. Conquerors would surely not have kindled a fire which destroyed every house and every hut, so that, 'according to the evidence of the excavations, the walls of the citadel houses and temple burned for days, perhaps weeks' (Ceram 1955, p. 170), nor destroyed for ever the olive groves and woods which, according to the remaining Hittite texts, had surrounded the capital (Hicks 1974, p. 92, p. 217). This was not 'human madness at work' but the comet Sekhmet, Anat, Phaethon, or whatever else that ball of fire may be called. Even from far-away China comes a report of 'a great star, whose flames devoured the sun'. It is dated between 1300 and 1200 BC (report in *Frankfurter Allgemeiner Zeitung*, 9 December 1970).

The traces of this burning have been found in Europe also, in fortresses and settlements, in forests and bogs. All the palaces and settlements on Crete and the Greek mainland were destroyed by fire – it is to this we owe the preservation of the Linear B tablets since they were baked hard and thus could survive the millennia. To quote all the excavation reports that give the evidence of these catastrophes would take several pages.

In Macedonia, in what is today Hungary, and in central Germany, villages and fortified camps were destroyed by great fires at the end of the thirteenth century. Again and again great masses of cinders have been found, and often walls and fortifications vitrified by the heat. C. Schuchhardt said of these: 'They occur everywhere where the wall of a fortress or a palace was built both of timber and stone such as basalt, and then burnt' (1941, p. 237 f.).

The forests of Europe also burned. For instance, in the sphagnum bogs of the eastern Alps, which lie 2600 m above sea level, the remains of burnt trees have been found. And regularly in these high mountain bogs a 'burning horizon' is found, which by pollen analysis can be dated to 'about 1000 BC' (Wilthum 1953, p. 83).

The situation is the same in the sphagnum bogs of the Black Forest, where Karl Müller, Professor at the University of Freiburg, examined burnt strata which he found to lie between the pollen maxima of fir and beech, and which he placed at 'about 1000 BC.' In the burnt strata in both these areas are the remains of mountain pines.

Pollen analysis shows that in the Black Forest, after a long period of warmth and favourable climate, in which the mountains were covered with beech woods, a time of drier weather followed, in which the beech woods were replaced by mountain pines characteristic of such a period. It was these mountain-pine forests that burnt up. They were followed, in about 1000 BC, by coniferous forest, which is indicative of a colder and damper climate. K. Müller wrote: 'Since it is unknown, so far as I am aware, for mountain-pine forests to catch fire by lightning, these burnings must have been deliberately caused. However, as far as we know the upper slopes of the northern Black Forest were not inhabited at that time, and so it is hard to understand the purpose of such a burning. The problem of how the burnt stratum occurred is therefore still unsolved.' (1953.)

This burning horizon with its evidence of terrible fires that raged 3000 years ago is found in all the bogs of Holland, North Germany and Scandinavia. It regularly occurs just above the 'boundary horizon' which, as mentioned above, marks the long period of drought in the thirteenth century. Clearly, the dried-out bogs burned for a long time.

In Scandinavia the same sequence is found. Here the Bronze Age was the time of 'climatic optimum' and the country was thickly forested as far as the Arctic Circle. Warmth-loving deciduous trees were present in many places up to the northern coasts. Towards the end of the Bronze Age, these deciduous woods burnt up, as the burning horizon, which is found everywhere, attests.

J.G. Andersson said: 'It must have been by fire that the people of this time began the destruction of nature. But it is hard to know how far the prehistoric forest fires, whose traces we find constantly, are to be attributed to human agency, and how far to lightning.' (1914, p. 16.)

So Andersson attributed the destruction of the forests and bogs of that time to human agency and only brought in the possibility of lightning as an afterthought.

But why should the people of that time have set fire to the woods on the mountains of Asia Minor, Greece, the Alps, the Black Forest and Scandinavia – none of which was then inhabited? Why should they have wanted to fire the – often vast – bogs, all of which show the 'burning horizon' at that time?

As though to refute the assertion that these fires were caused by men, the contemporary Egyptian text declares: 'The fire of Sekhmet has burnt the lands of the nine bows.' (For the other texts, see above page 151.) Moreover, the fires burned in places where neither the North Sea Peoples nor any other enemies had come. I have mentioned that this was so at Assur. It was the same in Egypt, which the North Sea Peoples had not then reached; and yet the eye-witness account of Ipuwer says: 'Nay, but the gates, columns and walls are consumed with fire . . . Behold, the fire will mount up on high.' (Ermann 1923, p. 95, p. 100.) And in another text of the time it says: 'The fire was to the end of heaven, and to the end of the earth' (Wainwright 1932).

No! Neither in the towns and fortresses nor in the forests and bogs was 'human madness at work' causing these terrible fires. Both the contemporary texts and the traditions of many peoples tell of a shining appearance in the heavens, to which they give different names, which kindled the world-destroying fire.

Ovid has given us the tradition of this heavenly phenomenon, which he, like the other Greek and Roman writers, called Phaethon:

> The earth caught fire, starting with the highest parts. With all its moisture dried up, it split and cracked in gaping fissures. The meadows turned ashy grey; trees, leaves and all, were consumed in a general blaze, and the withered crops provided fuel for their own destruction. But these are trifles to complain of, compared with the rest. Great cities perished, their walls burned to the ground, and whole nations with all their different communities were reduced to ashes. The woods on the mountains were blazing, Athos was on fire, Cilician Taurus and Timolus, Oeta and Ida, a mountain once famous for its springs, but now quite dry. Helicon, the Muses' haunt, was burning, and Haemus, later to be linked with Orpheus's name. Etna's flames were redoubled, and shot up to immense heights, the twin peaks of Parnassus and Eryx and Cynthus were alight, Othrys and Rhodope, destined at last to lose its snows, Mimas and Dindymus and Mycale and Cithaeron, the natural abode of sacred rites. Scythia did not escape, in spite of its chilly clime, Caucasus was in flames and Ossa too, and Pindus; Olympus, a greater mountain than either of these, was ablaze, as were the airy Alps and cloud-capped Apennines.
>
> Then, indeed, Phaethon saw every part of the world in fire, and found the scorching heat more than he could endure. He breathed in blasts of burning air, like those from some deep furnace, and felt his chariot glowing white hot. No longer could he bear the cinders and sparks which were flying through the air; enveloped in hot smoke and pitchy darkness, he did not know where he was, or whither he was going, but was swept along, according to the whim of his swift-footed team.

(*Metamorphoses* 2.210f.)

It has recently been suggested that the comet Phaethon is identical with Halley's comet (Zanot 1976, p. 26). This got its name from Edmund Halley, colleague and friend of Newton and astronomer at the Greenwich Observatory. Halley observed that three heavenly bodies, which had appeared in 1531, 1607 and 1682, had apparently covered identical courses. After making the necessary calculations he reached the conclusion that he was dealing with three appearances of the same object, which reappeared at intervals of seventy-six years. This comet is still held by astronomers to be one of the greatest in our solar system. 'Its head is immense, and its tail about 30 million kilometres long' (Zanot 1967, p. 14). In its course it circles the sun, and then moves away from it as far as the planet Neptune. Seen from the earth, it appears to come *out of the sun;* hence the myth among the ancients which made Phaethon the son of the sun god. Halley calculated that in the middle of April 1759 the comet would reach its perihelion, i.e. the nearest point in its course to the sun. And indeed it did reappear and passed its perihelion shortly before the expected moment, on 12 March 1759. It appeared again, at almost precisely the expected times, in the autumn of 1835, and on 20 May 1910. Its next appearance is expected in 1986.

Before Halley's comet's appearance in 1910, the Heidelberg astronomer Max Wolf had calculated that the earth on its course would cross the tail of the comet near the head, passing through its core. The consequences would be catalysmic. 'About 4.25 a.m. our planet will be enveloped in a deadly cloud of poisonous gases and cosmic dust that makes up the tail of the comet. Hydrogen, carbon, nitrogen, hydrogen cyanide and potassium cyanide will turn the globe into a monstrous gas-chamber. No one will escape, or at most a fortunate few in the areas around the poles, who may not be directly struck by this terrible fate which is approaching us out of space' (quoted in Zanot 1976, p. 13). The Berlin astronomer Wilhelm Meyer was equally pessimistic, explaining: 'There will be a catastrophe. The sun will become dark, glaring lightning will illuminate the pitch-black sky, monstrous fiery masses will plunge from heaven. The eruption of the chained volcanic fires will alter the face of the earth.' (Zanot 1976, p. 19.) Other prophecies were: 'The axis of the earth will be displaced. The bodies of water in the oceans will leave their beds and break over the continents. A hundred thousand human beings will meet a terrible end in this new deluge, and all traces of our civilization will be obliterated in a single night.' (Zanot 1976.)

There is no way of knowing whether these scientists had been inspired by Ovid's account of the catastrophes which followed the appearance of the comet Phaethon, or if they calculated the results of the approach of Halley's comet purely theoretically. What is certain is that humanity was gripped by a wave of panic, well described by Zanot.

Fortunately, the astronomers' calculations were mistaken. Max Wolf later explained, 'It [the comet] was drawn from its regular course by the gravitational pull of Jupiter and Saturn.'

In fact our planet encountered the tail of the comet, not near the head, but far away from it. An eye witness described the scene afterwards:

Minutes become eternities. Two a.m.; three o'clock; four o'clock. In silence, the world awaits its end. Suddenly, the sky begins to grow phosphorescent, the stars grow pale, a greenish aura surrounds the moon. Now only the huge, terrible comet lights up the vault of heaven. It is 4 18, 19, 20; many people fall on their knees, cover their eyes with their hands, and pray. 425 – the end! For a moment, the earth trembles, the aureole of the moon becomes a brilliant blue, the strange light becomes more intense and thousands of meteors fall in a fearful firework display; for a moment a terrible wave of heat passes over the earth. Then, at last, dawn. Men once again look up at the heavens. The sun rises. The comet, moving at a rate of 54km per second, is already far away. All over the world, people draw breath in relief. (Zanot 1976, p. 21f.).

The German astronomer Archeschold explained at the time why the predicted cataclysm did not occur. 'The part of the tail which we encountered was a long way from the core. Consequently the gases were extremely diluted, and the earth's atmosphere acted as a shield against them. Naturally none of us can say what would have happened if the gases had penetrated our atmosphere. Who knows what will happen when Halley's comet returns once more in 1986?' (Zanot 1976, p. 22.)

Since Halley's comet shows irregularities in its course, and therefore also in the point in time at which it will reach its perihelion, one cannot precisely calculate at what point the earth's course will cross the comet's tail. If it crosses it near the head, the most disastrous cataclysms will follow; if near the tail, the consequences will be negligible.

By counting backwards into the past it can be seen that Halley's comet also appeared in, among others, the years AD 451, the year of the birth of Christ, and 1226 BC.

In July AD 451, Halley's comet appeared just at the time of the battle against the Huns at the Catalaunian Fields (the Mauriac plain near Troyes). Isidore of Seville (AD 560–636) recounts in his *History of the Goths, Vandals and Suevi:*

> At the same time [as the battle] terrible signs were to be seen in the heavens and on the earth, whose monstrous nature fittingly accompanied the horror of the war. After several severe earthquakes, the moon in heaven was darkened; in the west a comet appeared, and shone for some time, being of enormous size. But in the north, the sky became red, looking like fire and blood, against which fiery red, lighter rays like ruddy spears were interspersed.

His source for this account was the work of the historian Damascius, who was born in AD 470, only twenty years after the battle, so that he certainly must have got his account from contemporary witnesses of the events (Hennig 1950, p. 145, p. 150). From the same source comes the information that those who fell in the battle fought once again in the sky, and 'filled the heavens with the noise of war'. The idea that a battle is taking place in the sky – generally between gods or fallen heroes – is commonly associated with the aurora borealis, which often accompanies the appearances of comets (examples in Hennig 1950, p. 45 ff.) Damascius claimed that, on seeing these phenomena, the Huns were overwhelmed with terror and gave up the battle. So the appearance of Halley's comet on that occasion may have had fortunate consequences for Western civilization.

It has also been calculated that Halley's comet appeared in the year of Christ's birth, and in fact can be identified with the Star of Bethlehem (Zanot 1976, p. 18). 'At that time it was moving across the constellation of Gemini, rather to the north of Castor and Pollux, in fact on latitude

31.42 north. Two thousand years ago these two stars were to be found at about latitude 32, and passed through the zenith daily over Bethlehem. Consequently Halley, too, must in the year zero have been found directly over Jesus' birthplace.'

Another year in which it appeared was 1226 BC. I have already noted that the fall of Phaethon should be dated to the second half of the thirteenth century BC, and have suggested that the worst of the catastrophes that were unleashed by the comet occurred shortly after the death of Pharaoh Merneptah in 1222 BC.

The difference between the astronomers' dating of the comet in 1226, and mine in about 1220, is explained by the fact that the 'absolute chronology' of the pharaohs of that time is still disputed. By 'absolute chronology' is meant the dating of an event as a precise number of years either BC or AD. 'Relative chronology', on the other hand, means the knowledge that some one event is earlier or later than some other, without knowing by how many years, decades, or centuries. A typical example of a relative chronology is provided by the occupational layers in an inhabited site. It is obvious that the upper layers are the later ones, and the lower ones the earlier, but it is not possible to say how much earlier or later, or in what precise year any of them were laid down.

The ordering of the lives or reigns of the pharaohs into a relative chronology is easy, since we know from the inscriptions and lists of the various pharaohs in what dynasty each lived and reigned. But to fit them into an absolute chronology presents serious problems. Among Egyptologists there are partisans of a 'long chronology' and a 'short chronology', while the supporters of a 'middle chronology' seek for a compromise between the two! None of the three chronologies is definitive.

So, for example, the death of Ramses II is set by F. Bilabel in the year 1246, by A. Scharff in 1234, by Breasted in 1232, by J.V. Beckerath in 1224 and by S. Lehmann in 1223. Since it is also uncertain for how long Ramses' successor, Merneptah, reigned – 'perhaps ten years' (Breasted) – there is an area of uncertainty of twenty-six years in the absolute chronology of the period.

I have followed the American Egyptologist J.H. Breasted and assumed that Merneptah died ten years after his father Ramses, i.e. in 1222. However, this assumption is far from certain. Bilabel, for instance (1927, p. 164), suggested that Merneptah reigned only seven years and died in 1239. It is certain only that Merneptah was on the throne for at least five years. So the date of his death could have been any time between 1239 and 1213. Since the texts of his reign do not mention the terrible natural catastrophes which are described so vividly in those of his successor Ramses III, I have assumed that the catastrophes began shortly after Merneptah's death, i.e. at any time between 1239 and

1213. This fits in perfectly well with the calculations of the astronomers that Halley's comet appeared in 1226 BC.

It can therefore be assumed, with the modern astronomers, that the comet Phaethon is identical with Halley's comet. The cataclysms which accompanied its appearance are explained by the supposition that the earth passed through the tail of the comet near its core. In that case all the disasters shown by contemporary accounts and archaeological evidence were only to be expected.

It was Max Wolf's opinion that the tail of Halley's comet consisted of hydrogen, carbon, nitrogen, hydrogen cyanide and potassium cyanide. This was confirmed by research into comet Kohoutek in 1973.

This comet was discovered on 9 March 1973 by the Czech astronomer L. Kohoutek, at that time working in the observatory at Hamburg, and was named after him. The tail of this comet was analysed with the most modern techniques by American space-research laboratories, which established 'with absolute certainty' that 'the tail of the comet consisted of hydrogen cyanide, methyl cyanide and hydrogen' (Zanot 1976, p. 64). When the reports of the thirteenth century BC say that 'men shudder at the taste of the water' (Ipuwer papyrus) or 'the river stank . . . and all the Egyptians digged round about the river for water to drink; for they could not drink of the water of the river' (Exod. 7:21, 24) then this could be due to the hydrogen cyanide and potassium cyanide in the tail of the comet, which had contaminated the earth.

Earthquakes

In the Atlantis narrative we find:

> At a later time there were earthquakes and floods of extraordinary violence, and in a single dreadful day and night all your [Athenian] fighting men were swallowed up by the earth, and the island of Atlantis was similarly swallowed up by the sea and vanished; this is why the sea in that area is to this day (*kai nyn*) impassable to navigation, which is hindered by the very thick (*karta bracheos*) mud, the remains of the sunken island. (*Ti.* 25d.)

It was by this same earthquake .that the spring on the Athenian Acropolis 'on the northern side' was choked (*Criti.* 112d). I have already described how archaeological research has discovered this spring, which was destroyed in the thirteenth century BC.

The ancient Egyptian texts of the time tell of those 'years of terror', when 'the foundations of the earth trembled'.

In the Ipuwer papyrus we find: 'Nay, but the land turneth around as doth a potter's wheel . . . gates, columns and walls are consumed with fire . . . the southern ship [Upper Egypt] is adrift. The towns are destroyed . . . great and small say, "I wish I were dead!" . . . Behold, a thing hath been done, that happened not aforetime . . . the Residence is overturned in an hour.' In the third and fourth poems, a large number of lines begin 'Destroyed is. . .'; what follows is illegible, but presumably it was the names of places and buildings that had been destroyed. At the end it says: 'Mankind is destroyed . . . all these years are confusion . . . thou hast kept alive [a few] people among them, but they cover their faces for fear of the morrow' (Ermann 1927, p. 95–108).

In papyrus 1116b Eremitage it says:

> Mine heart, lament the land whence thou art sprung. . . That which was made is as though it were never made, and Re might begin to found [the world] anew. The whole land hath perished, there is nought left, and the dirt of the finger nail surviveth not of what should be there. This land is ruined. . . This land is taken away and added to, and none knoweth what the issue will be. . . I show thee the land in lamentation and distress: that which never happened before hath happened. . . The land is destroyed . . . that which was made is as though it had not been made. . . I show thee the land in lamentation and distress. (Ermann 1927, p. 112–115.)

In the Medinet Habu inscriptions the catastrophes are described in similar terms. There too it is reported that the Nile dried up, the land was parched, the people starved: 'The house of the thirty [chief nobles] is destroyed . . . the earth shakes; all the water is useless . . . Egypt was without shepherds.' The refrain, 'That which never happened before hath happened' is repeated. It seems these words are meant to emphasize the uniqueness of the catastrophe. This is underlined in the Atlantis narrative also, when it speaks of 'the greatest of all destructions' (*Ti.* 23c), 'earthquakes and floods of extraordinary violence' (*Ti.* 25c) and 'one appalling night of flood' (*Criti.* 112a).

The archaeological evidence confirms these statements. The eastern Mediterranean is one of the regions of this planet most often visited by earthquakes. It is evident that many palaces had to be restored and rebuilt after earthquake and flood. This has been established on Crete, on Cyprus and even on Thera. But there was no rebuilding after the worst destruction, which happened at the end of the thirteenth century. The 'catastrophe horizon' of this period is found everywhere: in Greece, in Crete, Thera, Cyprus and all over the Near East.

'Here let us notice only the appalling extent of the catastrophe, which laid waste all the cities from Troy to Jericho, from Bogazköy (Hattushash) to Megiddo and Byblos' (Kehnscherper 1963, p. 49).

'From Troy VII to Palestine a chain of devastation can be traced' (Wiesner 1943, p. 122).

'A catastrophe which was one of the worst in world history' (Schachermeyr 1944, p. 78).

'The results of these [catastrophes] make them some of the most frightful in the history of the world' (Lesky 1947, p. 2).

In these cataclysms, the Mycenaean culture of the Greek mainland, the Minoan culture on Crete and Thera, the Hittite in Asia Minor, Syria with its great capital city of Ugarit, Palestine, with its strongly fortified city of Jericho, were all destroyed, and everywhere 'only a few survivors remained' as the Atlantis narrative says of Greece. Archaeological evidence proves it. Of 320 settlements in Greece in the thirteenth century, only forty were still inhabited in the twelfth. The population had shrunk to a hundredth of what it had been only a century before (Luce 1975, p. 39).

Comparative statistics have been gathered for the towns of the Peloponnese in the twelfth and thirteenth centuries, and these figures give a glimpse of the magnitude of the disaster (Desborough 1964, passim; 1972, ch. 1).

Area	Number of known settlements in the thirteenth century	Number of known settlements in the twelfth century
Messene and Triphylia	150	14
Laconia	30	7
Argolis and Corinth north of the Isthmus	44	14
Boeotia	27	3
Phocis	19	3
Attica	24	12

In Mycenaean times these places were thickly populated; after the catastrophes only a sparse and miserable resettlement is found.

The Atlantis narrative does not explicitly state that it was an *earthquake* that destroyed the island of Atlantis. It says merely: 'the island of Atlantis was similarly swallowed up by the sea and vanished'. However it is not unlikely that earthquakes played a part in its submersion, although the North Sea is not an earthquake zone. (The nearby mainland, over which the kings of Atlantis also ruled, is *not* in question.)

There are a number of eye-witness accounts of devastations on the west coast of Schleswig-Holstein produced by earthquakes. At the time of the terrible Lisbon earthquake of 1 November 1755, 'the whole mainland [of Schleswig-Holstein] was shaken'. 'Shocks were felt' and 'during divine service at Rendsburg the congregation noticed that the three crowns of the great chandelier hanging from the ceiling were in motion; but the canopy over the font moved even more, and swung to and fro uncontrollably.' (Leithauser quoted these eye-witness accounts in the *Husumer Nachrichten* of 27 June 1964.)

In his *North Frisian Chronicle*, Antonius Heimreich described the catastrophic flood of 11 October 1634, in which the island called the 'Strand' went under. This 'monstrous storm was mixed with a shaking of the earth', which was felt as far as the east coast. Fissures opened in the earth, and in several places the ground 'split wide apart'. The walls of houses cracked and, 'Trustworthy persons have given it for truth, that the beds in which they lay, and others, the chairs in which they sat at table, were moved and shaken to and fro' (1666, p. 479). Peter Sax, who experienced the same catastrophe on the mainland at Koldenbüttel, also spoke of earthquakes which were felt on that day and said that 'the foundations of the earth moved, and one could not but think that heaven and earth would fall apart, and the last day was at hand' (1631).

The greatest expert on the geology of Heligoland, Professor O. Pratje, noted that the 'girdle' of the island (as the remains of the once-far-greater rock massif are called) shows, about 300 m from the present west coast, a steep fault 10 m high, which can only have been caused by a sudden sinking of the whole of the former massif. Pratje considered that this must be connected with the abrupt end of human settlement on Heligoland in the thirteenth century BC, and that this was when the island became separated from the mainland. Until then, according to Pratje, and others, the cliffs were connected with it by the so-called 'Südstrand ridge' (1923, p. 57; 1952, p. 25). Since the rate at which the sandstone is washed away by the sea is 10 m every hundred years, this sudden sinking must have taken place 3000 years ago. The sudden sinking of such a large mass must have been accompanied by major earth tremors. The sinking itself can be explained by the existence not far below the sandstone massif of a large salt-plug; more than 3000 m deep. Under high pressure this can become as soft as wax or molten glass. This often leads to a rising or sinking of the ground; so that 'a sinking of the North Sea bed around Heligoland would have been possible' (Professor Voigt, Hamburg 1953).

Volcanic eruptions

The earthquakes were a result of 'an enormous increase in volcanic activity which took place 3200 years ago' (Suball 1958, p. 107). At this time, 'the last great wave of earthquakes and the last peak of volcanic activity devastated our earth' (Suball 1958, p. 106). Of the many volcanoes which erupted at that time, I will mention only those in the area relevant to the Atlantis narrative. The Icelandic geologist S. Thorarinsson has pointed out that '3000 years ago in Iceland there was extraordinarily high volcanic activity' (1944, p. 1 f.). Great lava masses, which with the help of modern methods can be dated then covered the whole of the island. The same observation could be made on the Canary Islands. They too were covered by masses of lava and layers of ash. On Gran Canaria, wooden beams and tree trunks have been found embedded in the lava, and these have been dated by the Carbon-14 method by Dr H.O. Schminke of the Mineralogical institute in Bochum. He concluded that the trees had died 3075 years ago, plus or minus a hundred years (letter to the author 13 January 1972). It is worth noting here that the core profiles from the Mediterranean sea bed give no indications that the volcanoes erupted *before* this time, although the drillings covered a period of about two million years.

The most terrible eruption of that time was that of the volcano on Thera, which with the help of the Medinet Habu texts can be dated to about 1220 BC, and which according to contemporary writings and archaeological evidence took place on a spring day. Geologists, vulcanologists and archaeologists use only superlatives when they write of this event. H. Reck called it 'an eruption of unimaginable power'; the French geologist Fouqué said: 'the eruption of such a vast mass of lava can only be explained by a massive volcanic explosion lasting a long time'; P. Herrman called it 'probably the most terrible catastrophe that humanity had experienced since the Ice Age'; Professor G. Kehnscherper 'the greatest disaster since the Ice Age'; the geologist H. Steinert, 'the most dramatic volcanic eruption in history and the most far-reaching in its consequences' and 'the worst volcanic eruption that has been experienced by man on this planet'.

One could quote more opinions of the same kind. The main cone of the circular island, about 1600 m high, was thrown up into the air to an immense height, and in its place remained a hollow crater 400 m deep. It has been estimated that about 150 cubic km of solid stone was thrown into the air; at the eruption of Krakatoa in 1883 it was only 15–20 cubic km. In both cases this is without counting the huge masses of lava which welled up from the depths and were also thrown into the air.

The masses of ash thrown into the air at the eruption of Krakatoa drifted around the globe for several years and coloured the night sky red because of the reflection of the sun's rays. Sunset and sunrise were for years unusually colourful, the sun and moon appeared redder than usual, indeed the moon was described as 'coppery'. These ash clouds diluted the sunlight by 20 per cent, which led between 1883 and 1886 to unusually cold winters and cool and rainy summers, which resulted in bad harvests.

About 1220 BC volcanoes also broke out on the Sinai peninsula. It is probably quite true that 'When Israel went out of Egypt . . . Jordan was driven back. The mountains skipped like rams, and the little hills like lambs' (Ps. 114). The Children of Israel were shown their way by 'a pillar of a cloud' by day and 'a pillar of fire' by night (Exod. 13:21).

The Exodus of Israel can be dated precisely. In Exod. 1:11 it is reported that the Children of Israel 'built for Pharaoh treasure cities, Pithom and Ramses'. Both these cities were built under Ramses II, the Great. Then, in Exod. 2:23, it says 'it came to pass in process of time, that the king of Egypt died'; Ramses II died after a seventy-year reign in 1232 BC. Only *after* his death did the 'ten plagues of Egypt' begin, as Exod. 7–10 tells, making possible the Israelites' escape. In other words, the terrible earthquake, the fire, the rain of stones from heaven, the thick darkness over Egypt, and the 'rain of blood' – all phenomena which would follow a major volcanic eruption – occurred just a few years after Ramses' death, in about 1220 BC.

Certainly there were other volcanoes that must have erupted at that time, but those mentioned so far would by themselves have been enough to have caused catastrophic consequences for the peoples of Europe, the Near East and North Africa.

Darkness

One of the many consequences, or secondary phenomena, of these volcanic eruptions was the darkness which (like the 'rain of blood') was caused by the great clouds of ash that were blown about the globe.

For these phenomena too we have contemporary reports. Ramses III at Medinet Habu described the 'great darkness' which prevailed before the beginning of his reign. In the Ipuwer papyrus we read: 'Nay but men look like gem-birds [blackbirds]. Squalor is throughout the land. There is none whose clothes are white in these times . . . all are laid low by terror'. (Ermann 1923, p. 95.) In papyrus Hermitage 1116b it says:

> How fareth this land? The sun is veiled and will not shine that men may see. None will live when the storm veileth it; all men are dulled through the want of it. . . The sun separateth himself from men; he ariseth when it is the hour. None will know that it is midday, and his shadow will not be distinguished

[on the sundial]. No face will be bright that beholdeth thee, and the eyes will not be moistened with water [through looking at the sun]. He is in the sky like the moon.' (Ermann 1923, p. 113–14.)

In the papyrus 'Wise sayings of a potter', we are told: 'In the days of Typhon the Nile was empty of water and the sun darkened' (text in von Gall 1926, p. 69ff.).

On the shrine of Al-Arish is written: 'The land was in great distress. Misfortune fell upon the whole earth . . . there was a terrible uproar in the capital . . . for nine days no one could leave the palace. During these nine days of storm there was such a tempest that neither men nor gods [i.e. the members of the royal family] could distinguish the faces around them.' (Griffith 1905, p. 38).

This is very reminiscent of the description of the same catastrophe in the Book of Exodus: 'and there was a thick darkness in all the land of Egypt three days; they saw not one another, neither rose any from his place for three days' (Exod. 10:22–3). This 'thick darkness' is always mentioned whenever the 'ten plagues of Egypt', or the Exodus of Israel that they made possible, are spoken of.

In the *Midrashim* ('Studies'), which preserves valuable ancient traditions from the time of the Exodus, i.e. the thirteenth century BC, we find the following account:

On the fourth, fifth and sixth days the darkness was so thick that they could not move from their places. . . The darkness was of such a nature that it could not be dispelled by artificial means. The light of the fire kindled for household uses was either extinguished with the violence of the storm, or swallowed up in the density of the darkness . . . nothing could be discerned. . . None was able to speak or to hear, nor could anyone venture to take food, but they lay themselves down . . . their minds were in utter confusion, and so they remained, overcome by the visitation. (Ginzberg 1946, vol. 2, p. 360ff.)

Caius Julius Solinus (third century AD), the editor of a 'Collection of marvels' which contains many quotations from lost earlier works, says that in the days of the fall of Phaethon, 'deep night spread over the whole earth' (ch. 11). From every continent there are stories of a long period of utter darkness, or of some great dragon or wolf or other monster who swallowed the sun. Such stories cannot always be dated. But when they tell that at the same time the earth was burnt up and there were terrible earthquakes, it is not unlikely that these too are memories of that time about 1200 BC when, because of the eruption of the great volcanoes, huge masses of ash were thrown into the air and drifted about the world.

The rain of blood

Another product of volcanic eruptions, in particular that of Thera, is a very fine blood-red ash, which in the deposits around Thera forms a layer several metres thick. It was thrown up by the explosion to a great height and presumably drifted in the atmosphere for even longer than the heavier masses of ash and soot. As these often microscopically small, blood-red particles sank to lower altitudes, a water drop gathered round each one, and these then fell to earth as a 'rain of blood'. This has been noticed repeatedly after later eruptions of Thera. Large areas of countryside on which the rain has fallen look as though they had been sprinkled with blood; rivers flow blood-red; even the sea around the island may take on a blood-red tinge for some distance around (Galanopoulos 1963, p. 4; 1964, p. 137; Velikovsky 1951, p. 64). This red colour is caused by a high iron content.

The same thing has been reported after other eruptions. Pliny reported that during the consulate of Manlius Acilius Gaius Porcius 'blood rained from heaven' and coloured large tracts of Italy. Plutarch recounted that in the reign of Romulus the same thing happened. After the major eruptions of Thera, Etna and the Icelandic volcano Hekla in 1755 (which were probably connected with the Lisbon earthquake), 'There fell in western France and Switzerland a rain of blood, a portent of evil. In Locarno suddenly hot steam arose, which turned into a blood-red mist. This fell to the earth as rain, and stained the snow blood-red.' (Hermann 1936, p. 110).

There are many other reports of a rain or snow of blood falling from the sky. D.F. Arago collected numerous accounts of this phenomenon in his *Astronomie Populaire* (1854–7, vol. 4, p. 209ff.).

A number of texts of the thirteenth century BC describe this 'rain of blood', the colouring of the countryside, rivers and sea. Ramses III at Medinet Habu declared: 'The two lands [Upper and Lower Egypt] were as red as blood' (inscription 27). The Ipuwer papyrus says: 'Blood is everywhere . . . Nay, but the river is blood. Doth a man drink thereof, he rejecteth it as human, for one thirsteth for water . . . Nay but the Red Land is spread abroad throughout the country.' (Ermann 1927, p. 95–6.) In papyrus Hermitage 1116b, Egypt is called 'the Red Land'. In the Book of Exodus we are told that the Nile turned into blood and the fish died. The river stank, so that the Egyptians were sickened when they drank its water, and all the water in streams, irrigation channels, ponds and storage vessels turned into 'blood'; 'and all the Egyptians digged round about the river for water to drink; for they could not drink of the water of the river. And seven days were fulfilled, after that the Lord had smitten the river.' (Exod. 7:17–25.)

Many of those traditions from all parts of the world that tell of the great burning, the darkening of the sun, the great flood, also tell of the 'blood' that fell from heaven and reddened the earth.

On top of the 'sacred way' which was built by Ramses II from his palace in Luxor to the temple of No Amun in Karnak, and along which his magnificent funeral procession had moved in 1232 BC, there fell a layer of black volcanic ash 3–4 m thick and above that blood-red volcanic ash about 1.30 m deep. These are striking confirmations of the contemporary accounts of the darkness and the 'blood' which fell on Egypt – and not only on Egypt – shortly after 1232 BC. According to the Hamburg mineralogist Professor H. Rose, volcanic ash has been found in many places in northern Germany, in the area of the boundary horizon of the bogs.

Floods and tidal waves

The Atlantis narrative tells of a time when 'there were earthquakes and floods of extraordinary violence' (*Ti.* 25c). This is certainly correct. At the time when 'the last great wave of earthquakes and the last peak of volcanic activity devastated our earth' (Suball 1958, p. 106), there must also have been 'floods of extraordinary violence' because volcanic eruptions are alway accompanied by floods as well as earthquakes. These floods are known as seismic waves, or else by a Japanese term, 'tsunamis'.

'[An] ominous withdrawal of the sea from its normal stand,' said Rachel Carson of this phenomenon, 'is often the first warning of the approach of seismic sea waves' (1956, p. 129). This retreat is followed, often after several hours, by enormous waves accompanied by a loud rushing and roaring noise. Over a calm sea the water may pile up into one enormous precipitous wave, like a wall of glass, which advances on the shore with an overwhelming roar.

The speed with which tsunamis can move over the sea depends on the depth of the water, and can vary between 700 and 800 km per hour. After the eruption of Thera in 365 AD, which was not remotely as severe as that of 1200 BC, a tsunami was released in the eastern Mediterranean which threw a ship on the Peloponnesian coast 3 km inland, and carried the ships in the harbour at Alexandria over the houses into the countryside (Mavor 1973, p. 67). Ramses III declared on the walls of Medinet Habu that 'the whole delta of the Nile is flooded by the sea'. A report of the Lisbon earthquake of 1755 tells how 'the appalled inhabitants saw the sea first withdraw a long distance, then return like a wall 15 km high, and overwhelm and destroy everything. . . The waves that devastated Lisbon also flooded the coasts of Spain and the Azores. In Cádiz the wave washed 500 men away; on the West African coast it swept whole caravans into the sea.' (A. Herrmann 1936, p. 124.)

A description of the great Krakatoa eruption in August 1883 says: 'Waves up to 30 m high arose, which broke with devastating force over all the neighbouring coasts, rushed on as far as South America, and cost the lives of 50,000 people' (Hennig 1950, p. 61). On 1 April 1946, a quake on the sea bed occurred near the Aleutian island of Unimak. The tsunami swept away a lighthouse which stood 30 m above water level on the coast of Alaska, and after five hours reached Hawaii, 3600 km away, having therefore travelled at an average speed of 770 km per hour (Freuchen 1958, p. 111 f.).

After the volcanic eruptions and earthquakes that in May 1960 attacked southern Chile, a tsunami flooded the coasts of Japan, Hawaii, Australia, New Zealand, California and Alaska. In Japan it was 10 m high and inundated 38,000 houses, of which 5000 were carried away (Deutsche Press–Agentur report, 24 May 1960).

The wave which followed the monster eruption of Thera in 1220 BC must have been higher than any of these. On the island of Anaphe, Professor G. Marinos, geologist at the University of Salonica, found a layer of lava washed up by this wave. It was 5 m thick, and lay at a height of 250 m (!) above sea-level (1959-61, p. 210 f.).

These are the highest traces of a tsunami that have ever been found. Admittedly, Anaphe lies only 25 km from Thera; nevertheless James W. Mavor, member of the Woods Hole Oceanographic Institute, reckoned that there were 'three great waves each having a height at sea of 200 feet just before crashing on the Cretan shore' (1973, p. 98).

W. Brandenstein stated on the basis of archaeological evidence that the eruption of Thera 'produced such an enormous wave that the flood reached the capital (Knossos, on Crete) 8 km inland and 40 m above sea-level and destroyed it' (1951, p. 18). He rightly pointed out ·that a catastrophe which could destroy Crete with all its towns and cities 'must also have done great damage at Athens,' since 'the earthquake started from a point roughly halfway between the two places'. Legends, which according to Brandenstein date back to Mycenaean times, tell how Poseidon in his rage overwhelmed with a flood the fertile plains of Eleusis and all Attica (Brandenstein 1951, p. 65). Athens too was flooded and 'only those who fled to the mountains escaped with their lives'. Pausanias stated that in his time (c. AD 150) there still existed a broad cleft in the rock, north of the Ilissus valley, near the temple of Olympian Zeus, through which the flood waves were said to have rushed in (quoted in Knötel 1893, p. 414). This would mean that at Athens the tsunami was 70 m high. Apollodorus said of this flood: 'Poseidon in his rage let monstrous masses of water overwhelm the land; the Thriassio plain (around Eleusis) was drowned and Attica sank beneath the waves of the sea' (3.14.1).

These traditions agree with the statements of the Atlantis narrative about 'earthquakes and floods of extraordinary violence' and the assertion that only 'the herdsmen and shepherds in the mountains escape' (*Ti.* 22d).

Now it is important to realize that severe earthquakes or seaquakes release tsunamis not only in the seas in which their epicentres lie, but also in distant seas, the Baltic for instance, and even in inland waters. After the Lisbon earthquake of 1755, 'on the Pomeranian coast, when there was not a cloud in the sky or any wind, suddenly near the Treptower Deep waves as big as houses reared up, and flooded over the coast, throwing a heavy barge that was lying in the mouth of the old Rega right up onto the land'. The contemporary chronicle which records this wave says: 'The sea-folk who live along the coast are familiar with this phenomenon, which they call the "sea bear"' (*Peiner Nachrichten,* 3 April 1964). Such 'sea bears' or tsunamis occurred near Leba, Poland, in calm weather in 1778. A great flood, according to the reports, reached as far as this small town which lies well inland. The reports emphasize that at the same time in Kolberg (Kolobrzeg), about 150 km to the west, the sea, during calm weather and without any warning, retreated so that one could walk out 100 m dryfoot on the sea bed. A government report from Henkenhagen of a wave which occurred there in 1795 says: 'the sea was as calm as a pond; suddenly it rose up and a fearful storm raged all around'.

Such waves have also been observed in inland bodies of water, and not only large ones like Lake Constance or Lake Vänern in Sweden, but in small ones too. For instance there is the well known description by Theodor Fontane of the little lake of Stechlin, which threw up waves or whirlpools whenever 'in Iceland or elsewhere volcanoes erupt'.

It is worth noticing a description of the tidal waves which followed the 1755 earthquake:

It is just after 11 a.m. on Lake Retzow [near Neustrelitz in Mecklenburg]; there are only a few fishermen pulling in their nets in the calm weather, when with utter suddenness the water of the lake begins to seethe and heave, then without warning mounts into a wave which rushes at the fishermen who are standing on the shore. Although the slope of the beach is gentle, the water rushes up it, and washes round their feet and legs up to the knees. Startled to death, and fearing to be swept apart by this inexplicable flood, they shout to one another to stand firm. For a few minutes they stand in the water, anxiously waiting to see if anything more is going to happen; then it draws itself back again with such strength that the men are dragged a pace forward towards the lake. Far out into the centre of the lake the water retreats, and there for a few moments it stands like a steep wall the height of a man. Then it breaks once again over the shore; and repeats this forward and backward movement six times altogether. It was 1 November 1755. (Leithäuser 1964.)

Similar events occurred in the lakes of the Brandenburg March, Mahlgast, Roddelin and Libbe. The Eider flooded near Rendsburg, as did the Elbe near Cuxhaven, the Trave at Travemünde (near Lübeck), the rivers and lakes in Sweden, the canals in Amsterdam and the harbours of England (Leithäuser 1964). A contemporary wrote: 'All Europe has been shaken. From Africa, America and Asia more news comes in. The newspapers carry reports every day of how Portugal, Spain, Italy, France, England, Germany and other lands are still receiving shocks.' (A. Herrmann 1936, p. 124.)

I have quoted these reports of flood waves in inland lakes, because it is possible that the 'sudden and simultaneous end' of the so-called 'pile dwellings' (Paret 1948, p. 22) may be attributable to the same kind of tsunami in the lakes at that time.

It has hitherto been generally assumed that the sudden end of these settlements is to be accounted for by a gradual rising of the level of the lakes. Paret says: 'As the climate became wetter, the lakes rose, like the water-table in the bogs. The settlements had to be abandoned, and new ones built on higher or more solid ground' (1948, p. 38) or 'the lakes rose once again and gradually flooded over the remains of the abandoned villages' (1948, p. 212). If in reality through the change in the climate (which will be discussed below) the abandoned villages had 'gradually' been flooded, then the inhabitants would have had time to save their often valuable belongings. However, this clearly *cannot* be the case. For in many of over 400 pile dwellings that are known in Europe, bronze weapons, which were often precious, and jewellery have been found, as well as well preserved cooking pots and other objects of daily use, *in situ* on the beds of the lakes. The inhabitants of the houses had no time to take these things with them. The catastrophe must have fallen on them suddenly. The cause of this sudden and simultaneous ruin of all the pile dwellings must be sudden and simultaneous flood waves in the lakes, of the kind that only occur after the most violent earthquakes.

Modern geological research has repeatedly confirmed and explained the occurrence of seismic waves in inland lakes. The severe earthquake in Alaska on 27 March 1964 provided an opportunity for experts in various fields to investigate this occurrence thoroughly. The results were collected in eight volumes, published by the National Academy of Sciences in 1968. In more than 700 lakes and rivers and even streams, not only in America but in Africa, Asia, Europe and Australia, there were sudden and significant movements of the water level. Tsunami waves of greater or lesser height occurred on the coasts of every continent.

These phenomena, which were unexpected even by the experts, are explained by 'plate tectonics' theory, according to which the outer shell of the earth, the 100 km thick 'lithosphere', is composed of seven major and a number of lesser 'plates', moving like crusts of ice on a substratum of lower viscosity. When these plates move horizontally, they either collide, slide over one another, or move apart. When they collide, the result is earthquakes or volcanic eruptions ('destructive movements'). If the collision is of long duration it leads to the throwing up of mountain ranges, as in the Himalayas, which resulted from the collision of the Indian subcontinent with the Eurasian plate, or the Alps from that of the European with the African.

It has been repeatedly observed that after earth or sea quakes even in distant areas, the coasts of the North Sea and the Baltic, though not themselves in a highly volcanic area, can be visited by tidal waves. The seismic waves in the Baltic have been described above (page 169). Tidal waves on the North Sea coasts are of particular interest because Basileia and the fertile marshland which once lay off the coast of the Cimbrian peninsula were flooded and drowned by just such a wave.

According to an eye-witness account by the writer C.P. Hansen, 'On 5 June 1858, a light south-easterly breeze was blowing, the sea was calm. Suddenly, about 5 p.m., a huge mountainous wave reared itself on the horizon and advanced roaring on the coast. It lashed the beach and flowed into the hollows between the sand dunes' (on Sylt, where Hansen was staying at the time). After the water had retreated the sea was calm again until after a time a second wave 'came out of the south-west with a fearful noise', swirled over the beach, overturned boats, and nearly engulfed one fisherman. These two waves were 'as high as houses'. That night at 9.30 a third came in with the same loud roaring. Another eye witness, W.H. Decker, reported of the same event that it announced itself with an unusually loud rushing noise, that the waves 'threw fishing boats and wreckage up into the dunes, and that 'everything showed that some extraordinary event must have occurred during this otherwise beautiful weather'.

Two other fishermen recalled: 'We saw in the far distance an extremely high wave coming towards us; it broke first on the outer reef and then advanced on the beach at about the height of a house. We had to leave our boat and take shelter among the dunes, until the water subsided. We saw how this giant, this monster, broke over the beach with raging force and drove our boat hard into the dunes.'(*Husumer Nachrichten*, 18 December 1970.) 'These gigantic waves terrified not only the people of Sylt, but those of Dover, Wangerooge, [East Frisian Islands], Heligoland and the western coast of Denmark' (*ibid.*).

On 27 August 1883, the day of the eruption of Krakatoa, a wave about 3 m high overflowed, during otherwise calm and sunny weather, the west coast of Schleswig-Holstein; the Halligen islands went under, and numbers of animals were swept away, according to eye-witness reports.

On 14 June 1964, 'Bathers on Sylt were astonished by a tidal wave several metres high; one visitor was knocked down and injured, and the retreating wave took articles of clothing with it. . . . A sulphur-yellow tidal wave several metres high, coming from the south, struck the beach of Sylt early on Sunday morning, during calm weather and with the sea as flat as a mirror. Hundreds of basket chairs were washed up to the sea-wall. (*Husumer Nachrichten*, 15 June 1964.)

Many similar episodes from earlier times are preserved by the Frisian Chronicles. The waves that followed the Lisbon earthquake in 1755 have already been described. On the same day, about 11.30, 'in still weather', in the harbour at Glückstadt 'several ships and rafts' were torn from their moorings and thrown against the tideway'. In the harbour at Husum 'between eleven and twelve, when the tide was far out, the water was thrown upwards rushing and roaring, as though the fiercest storm were raging' (as a contemporary account put it) (*Husumer Nachrichten*, 20 October 1969).

One can easily imagine that during the monster eruption of Thera and the many other volcanoes in 'the last great wave of earthquakes and the last peak of volcanic activity' on our planet, seismic waves would have broken over the North Sea coasts, which overwhelmed the coastlands and islands, and drowned the old marshland.

These tidal waves have left many traces behind them on the west coast of Germany. In 1935 the geologist E. Becksmann published the results of his researches there. He found that to the west of the Schleswig-Holstein sandy country there was the old Stone and Bronze Age marshland, and the sand itself had spurs sticking out to the west. 'At about the turn of the Bronze/Iron Age', the west coast was flooded by an enormous wave; the spurs of the sand were swept away and the west coast evened off. So, for example, a sandy ridge about 8 m wide near Heide, which once extended far to the west, was washed away, and so was an even larger one running from St Michaelisdonn to Süderdonn and Averlak. The cliffs which the raging North Sea then broke off are to this day known locally as Kliff or Klev. At those places where the old sandy coast had deep inlets, the sea filled them up with great banks of silt, the largest are those between 'Steller Senke', north of Heide, and Nordstrand. This is about 25 km long and up to 10 m high. It is these drifts that make it possible to date the catastrophe. Underneath them soil has been found belonging to the Stone and Bronze Age marshland; on top there are no Bronze Age finds, but numerous Iron Age ones. This shows that during the Stone and Bronze ages it did not exist; but by the Iron Age it was inhabited. These and other observations forced Becksmann to the conclusion that the catastrophe which 'levelled off' the coast in this way occurred between the Bronze and Iron ages. The 'klevs' which were then broken off, and the banks of silt which were thrown up, are striking evidence of the height which those waves reached.

W. Haarnagel has investigated the banks thrown up by the sea in the district of Wursten, and he discovered that like those of Schleswig-Holstein they lie on top of the Stone and Bronze Age marsh. Like the former, they run from north-west to south-east and these too, so he concluded, were thrown up between the Bronze and Iron ages (1951, p. 78).

The geologist W. Wildvang came to the same conclusion during his researches on the south coast of the North Sea between the Ley and the Dollart. In 1911 he published a comprehensive work on the subject, calling it *Eine prähistorische Katastrophe an der deutschen Nordseeküste* ('A prehistoric catastrophe on the North Sea coast of Germany'). He wrote of a 'catastrophe of annihilating force' evidence of which has been noted again and again 'in the course of innumerable drillings and peat-diggings and during the construction of canals and sluices'. Here I will quote only briefly from this very detailed work:

> With all its violent power, the North Sea first rushed over our fluvial-alluvial landscape [i.e. the Stone and Bronze Age marshland] up to the rim of the sandy area, and destroyed all vegetation with its high salt content, for this inundation lasted a long time. It seems that trees were laid flat by the first· rush of the water . . . the remains of the trees thrown down in this catastrophe can be distinguished from the upright stumps of trees mentioned earlier, since they lie at full length; a fact which is explained by the circumstances of their destruction. The tops of these uprooted trees always point to the east, which supports the assumption that the catastrophe was caused by a storm from the west. (1911, p. 36.)

Wildvang also pointed out that 'at various places' skeletons of human beings have been found who had fallen victim to this catastrophe. For instance, near Pilsum was found a skeleton of unusual size. On the breast lay a round shield and near the head a horn. The corpse had been covered with sea mud, and lay quite 2m deep. The thick layer of mud which covered it lay on top of the boundary horizon and burning horizon of a bog. So here too is an indication that after the extraordinary drought which began about the middle of the thirteenth century, 'a catastrophe of annihilating force' broke over the coast, flooding the old marsh up to the rim of the sandy area.

Similar observations have been made in many other places on the North Sea coast. Dr Winberg, for instance, found 'old remains of dry land at a depth of 2.53 below low water level near the island of Memmert; he regarded this as part of the land which had lain there in the Stone and Bronze ages. A similar find was reported by Dr Leege, who discovered a bog meadow laid bare by the sea under the beach at Juist. There were remains of many fresh-water plants, 'the hoof marks of

cattle and horses were also visible, and wagon tracks clearly marked in
the soil' (quoted by Wildvang 1938, p. 14). Similar remains of the
ancient land surface have been found in a more complete state near
Borkum. Wildvang argued that all these discoveries point to 'a sudden
alteration which must have had a catastrophic impact on those who
experienced it' (1938, p. 175).

The same observations have been made on the west coast of
Schleswig-Holstein. From the many researches of modern times I will
quote only those detailed observations made by the Kiel geologist
Forchhammer during the early nineteenth century, which are of
particular value since it would not be possible to repeat them today.
Partly through natural causes (erosion, building up of sand dunes) and
partly through human intervention (farming, spread of towns and
villages, airport construction), a large part of what Forchhammer
observed is no longer available. He found, in many places from North
Jutland to Dithmarschen, the traces of a great flood which had
overwhelmed the islands and coastlands. Remains such as stones and
mussel shells were found as much as 18.84m above sea-level.
Forchhammer wrote: 'If we compare the results of these observations,
we have to conclude that a flood coming from the west once broke over
these coasts, far surpassing in height and extent any other known to
history' (1837, p. 65).

The debris left by this deluge covered the tops of Bronze Age grave-
mounds, which it had also flattened and partially destroyed. It also
covered fields, which could be dated to the Bronze Age by the finds
made in them. Forchhammer therefore came to the conclusion that this
mighty flood had taken place at the end of the Bronze Age and had
washed right up to the edge of the main sandy area.

The Kiel geologist Professor von Maack investigated and confirmed
Forchhammer's conclusions. The latest excavations have also shown
that Bronze Age grave-mounds near Archsum on Sylt are covered by
marine deposits (Kossack 1974).

The datings given by these investigators for this great inundation
can only be vague ('the end of the Bronze Age', '3000 years ago', 'the
change from the Bronze to the Iron Age') because only imprecise methods
of dating were available to them.

Now, however, we are in a position, with the help of contemporary
Egyptian texts, to date it more precisely. The period of drought, as Paret
observed as long ago as 1948, must have begun soon after 1250 BC (Paret
1948, p. 144). The immense volcanic eruptions, the terrible earthquakes
and the tsunamis must have shaken the continent around 1220 BC.

Waves 18 m high cannot be caused simply by storms – though floods
so caused certainly did occur. Such floods never reach a height of more
than 6m; a wave which reaches 18m can only be seismic in origin.

We learn from the Medinet Habu texts that those North Sea warriors who were taken prisoner declared: 'Our islands are uprooted and carried away . . . the might of Nun [the ocean] broke forth and fell in a great wave on our towns and villages'. Medinet Habu also says: 'The head of their cities has gone under the sea; their land is no more' (inscriptions 37, 46, 80, 102, 109). Since the 'head of their cities' is also called *neterto*, i.e. 'sacred land', or *netera*, 'sacred island', we have here a contemporary report of the submersion of the 'sacred island' of the North Sea Peoples, i.e. Atlantis.

Hesiod (about 750 BC) sang of the battle between Zeus and Typhon (another name of the monstrous apparition of the heavens):

> and the heat and blaze from both of them
> was on the dark-faced sea,
> from the thunder and lighting of Zeus
> and from the flame of the monster,
> from his blazing bolts and from the scorch
> and breath of his stormwinds,
> and all the ground and the sky
> and the sea boiled, and towering
> waves were tossing and beating all up
> and down the promontories
> in the wind of these immortals,
> and a great shaking of the earth
> came on . . .
>
> *Theogony* 844–49

The 'climatic drop' or the 'great divide'

In the Atlantis narrative we find that after the period of heat and drought, the burnings, earthquakes and floods, a time began in which a deluge descended (*Ti.* 23a) and the soil of the Athenian Acropolis was 'all washed away in one appalling night of flood' (*Criti.* 112a). These floods of rain carried away the fertile earth from the high ground (*Criti.* 111b) and indeed 'those living in the cities in your part of the world [i.e. Athens] are swept into the sea by the rivers' (*Ti.* 22d). With these floods of rain ended the period in which the Greeks enjoyed 'an excellent soil . . . and a well balanced climate' (*Criti.* 111e).

These statements agree with the conclusions of geologists and students of climate, who have recorded about 1200 BC a 'climatic decline' or 'climatic drop' which K. von Bülow calls 'the great divide'. At that time the average temperature sank by 3–4 degrees, the snow line of the Norwegian mountains, which in the middle of the thirteenth century BC lay at 1900 m above sea-level sank to 1500 m (Schwarzbach 1961, Abb. 115, p. 178). In the eastern Alps there were no glaciers during the Bronze Age but glaciers developed around 1200 BC and reached far down into the valleys (Wilthum 1953). The Swedish climatologist Sernander called this 'a true *fimbul* winter' (see below, Chapter 6). The Austrian F. A. Gessmann spoke of a 'second Ice Age', a 'sudden period of sharp decline' (1935, p. 82 f.). The Americans George Denton and Stephen Porter, relying on investigations into the movement of glaciers in North America, British Columbia, Baffinland, Alaska, Patagonia, southern Chile and Norway, describe the time between 3000 and 2500 years ago as a 'neoglaciation' of the earth (*Scientific American,* 1970).

During this period there must have been, as has often been noted, heavy precipitation of snow in the North and on the mountains and of rain in more southerly lands. In the bogs of northern Europe, above the boundary and burning horizons, is found 'Sphagnum Cuspidatum turf', which can only form *under* water. This shows 'a period of renewed flooding between 1200 and 1000 BC' (Jonas 1944, p. 255). Routes used up to 1200 BC 'became unusable because long stretches of them had become marsh, and were given up' (Jonas 1944, p. 158). Schwantes has also described this climatic decline, and noted: 'The periods of prehistory which follow the Bronze Age fall in an era which is known as the sub-atlantic on account of its cooler climate and increased rainfall' (1939, p. 229). This 'climatic drop' was a world-wide phenomenon; it was 'uniform over the whole northern hemisphere, and has recently been observed in the southern hemisphere also, in New Zealand and Tierra del Fuego' (Schott, 1950, p. 29; Schwartzbach 1961, p. 182 ff.).

Numerous climatologists, archaeologists and historians have produced evidence for this 'climatic drop'. The philologist J. Pokorny has even made the following suggestion:

> I myself have hypothesized that the Germanic sound-shift can be explained in purely physiological terms by assuming that following the catastrophic change in climate in the Baltic area, people, in order to protect themselves from the cold and damp air, closed their mouths more tightly when drawing the breath in; this naturally resulted in a stronger outbreath, and a narrowing of the frictional surface of the air stream . . . if one remembers that the Germanic sound-shift coincides more or less with the beginnings of the Nordic Iron Age, and the climatic drop, then the conclusion is almost forced upon one, that there must have been some connection between these events. (1968, p. 200.)

So the statements of the Atlantis narrative that after the natural catastrophes already described, finally 'floods from heaven' washed the fertile earth off the mountains, and even swept city-dwellers into the sea, are 'correctly observed' (Paret 1948, p. 174).

This also applies to the statement that all the soil of the Acropolis was washed away 'in one appalling night of flood' (*Criti.* 112a). In 1970 Professor S. Marinatos told an archaeological conference at Athens that soil ought to be put back on the Acropolis and once again planted. He explained that 'in antiquity the rock of the Acropolis was not bare, but covered with earth and growing things (Deutsch Presse-Agentur report, 28 November 1970).

The causes of the climatic drop and the heavy rainfall after 1200 BC are known. It has often been noticed that after severe volcanic eruptions, the rays of the sun are blocked by the great clouds of ash which have been released into the atmosphere, and consequently the climate becomes colder.

Thus after the eruption of Krakatoa in 1883, the average annual temperature of the whole earth sank by half a degree Celsius; this led to bad harvests and to the exceptionally rainy summer and snowy winter of 1885–6.

On 11 June 1783 there was a particularly severe eruption of the Icelandic volcano Skaptar. The great clouds of ash which it threw up into the atmosphere were such that in the northern hemisphere in the years 1783–4, the sun was only visible as if through a veil, temperatures sank, and the result was bad harvests, cool summers and abnormally cold, snowy winters. 'Abbott and Fowle observed that, after the 1912 Katmai eruption, the sun's rays, as observed by them from Mount Wilson in California and Bassour in Algeria, were weakened by 20 per cent. According to Brooks, all the really cold years since 1700 have followed after major volcanic eruptions.' (Schwarzbach 1961, p. 207.)

It has recently become known that increased rain and snowfall and sinking temperatures can be caused, not only by volcanic ash in the atmosphere, but by fine meteoric dust. This discovery was made by the Australian astrophysicist Bowen, after many years of observations. He noticed, after the appearance of meteors, broad, vaporous layers in the ionosphere. Regularly, about thirty days after the appearance of this meteoric shower, there were heavy falls of rain on broad, world-wide fronts. The gap of thirty days is explained by the fact that the meteoric dust had to sink from the upper levels of the atmosphere to those in which rain-clouds form. When the American Air Force gave Bowen the use of a high-flying aircraft of the U2 type, he was able, 23000 m above the ocean and the South Pole, to catch in a filter a quantity of fine dust particles, made up of iron, chromium, and rock dust: undoubtedly the remains of meteors. By these and other observations Bowen was able to show that heavy rain or snow falls primarily occur as a result of cosmic dust sinking into the earth's atmosphere.

Taking this into account, it is easy to imagine what catastrophic consequences would follow for the earth's climate if large amounts of meteoric dust *and* ash clouds were present in the atmosphere simultaneously. This was exactly what happened at the end of the thirteenth century BC. The comet, called by the Greeks Phaethon, by other peoples Sekhmet, Typhon, Anat, Tistrya etc., came near to the earth and enormous quantities of meteoric dust mixed with the ash that had been thrown up by the eruption of numerous volcanoes. The result was a severe dilution of the sunlight, a 'climatic degeneration' with very heavy rain and snow falls, which led to a 'true *fimbul* winter', a 'neo-glaciation', a small 'second Ice Age'.

This climatic decline, which occurred in every continent, had particularly catastrophic effects in northern Europe. 'This long period of good weather was ended by a sudden change in climate, which, though it did not reach the low temperatures of the Ice Age, had catastrophic consequences for economic life. Large areas, especially in the North, became unfit for agriculture, since the ripening period was no longer sufficient for the crops . . . the '*fimbul* winter' of the *Edda* preserves a memory of this decisive event in the history of the Northern peoples.' (Behn 1948, p. 123.)

Wheat and vines were grown north of Stockholm in the Bronze Age but their cultivation in those regions has been impossible ever since (Florin 1943, p. 891). Millet, which had been cultivated far to the north, now would only thrive in the extreme south of Sweden. The warmth-loving deciduous woods, which had covered Scandinavia as far as the northern coasts, had vanished, and in their place, from 1000 BC on, grew the coniferous forests which are still typical of the area. 'Humanity had entered a new, harsher time, the "age of iron"' (K. von Bülow 1933, p. 65).

The story of Phaethon tells that in the end, Zeus answered the entreaties of the other gods by quenching the fires that were ravaging the earth with great floods of rain. Here too then we have, as the Egyptian priest put it, 'a mythical version of the truth'.

CHAPTER 5

THE LONG MARCH OF THE ATLANTEANS THROUGH EUROPE AND ASIA MINOR TO EGYPT

Legend or History?

In the Atlantis narrative we are told how the Atlanteans launched an attack through Europe and Asia (i.e. Asia Minor), and also through Libya, up to the frontiers of Egypt. They occupied all the Greek states; only the Athenians, giving the world a proof of their courage and strength, had overcome the invaders and preserved their freedom (*Ti.* 24e, 25b,c; *Criti.* 108e, 120d).

This heroic victory of the Athenians over the Atlanteans was in fact the reason that the priest told the whole story to Solon, 'to do honour both to you and your country' (*Ti.* 23d), and the reason why Solon was so interested in it that he wrote it down and brought it back to Athens, in order to compose an epic about it (*Criti.* 113a).

For all those who have accepted the wrong location for the home of the Atlanteans, or the wrong dating for the whole story, this account of the Atlanteans' great campaign is the main reason for dismissing the whole thing as an 'unhistorical fairy-tale', or 'a utopian romance without historical foundation' (R. Noll). A. Schulten, for example, who located Atlantis near Tartessus and had it destroyed by hostile Carthaginians, explained that with the story of the campaign the account 'takes off into pure fantasy' (1948, p. 12). J.V. Luce, who identified Atlantis with Crete or Thera, which according to him were destroyed by earthquake and eruption about 1470 BC, tried to show that the attack on Athens by the Atlanteans 'is nothing but exaggeration and distortion' (1969, p. 25).

And yet it is precisely this account of the war, and the routes along which the attackers came, which proves that the story which the Egyptian priests told Solon was 'not a fiction, but true history' (*Ti.* 26e). In fact, all the statements in the narrative correspond exactly with the historical events of around 1200 BC.

It will not be possible to describe here in all its details this 'long march' of the Atlanteans, which is known today as the 'great migration', but I have done this in my book, *Atlantis* (1965).

Here I will consider only those statements about the expedition which are found in the Atlantis narrative itself, from the point of view of their historical reliability.

The starting point of the 'great migration'

'Our records tell how your city checked a great power which arrogantly advanced from its base in the Atlantic sea to attack the cities of Europe and Asia' (*Ti.* 24e).

I have shown that the 'Atlantic sea' of the ancients is *not* identical with our Atlantic Ocean, but with the North Sea – or rather, with the North and Baltic seas together. Atlas, after whom this sea was named, was imagined as standing in the North, under the Pole Star, on the amber river Eridanus, 'Where, in lament for Phaethon, / His sisters drop their piteous tears' (Euripides), 'in the land of the Hyperboreans'.

Archaeological research has shown that the north of Europe was thickly populated in the Bronze Age but lost most of its population during the thirteenth century BC. The Swedish archaeologist Count Oxenstierna noted an 'almost total lack of finds on the Danish islands and the Scandinavian mainland, which lasts for 350 years', and has associated this 'widespread and long-lasting gap' in the archaeological materials in a formerly thickly populated area, with the natural catastrophes of that time (1957, p. 17, p. 19).

The German archaeologist H. Hoffmann has also suggested that a major emigration from the Nordic area followed these disasters. He has pointed to the 'extraordinary number of hoards', which are a sign of population movement, since 'goods were buried in this way for the safekeeping of heavy belongings, or as offerings to the gods.' O. Paret agreed, citing the large quantity of hoards of this period, from the North Sea to the Mediterranean: 'Often during this time of climatic catastrophe and flight from famine, the cry must have been "*Sauve qui peut!*" and many would at first have taken their metal goods, but later have left them by the way so as to move faster. The spread of these hoards, then, shows not so much trade routes as escape routes.' (1948, p. 145.)

According to Hoffmann, the 'finds of hoards' in the Nordic area show that:

1 The immigration or flight started from the North.
2 At the end of period III and during period IV the entire Nordic realm was taken over by the great migration movement.

3 The migration was from north to south. The areas of Schleswig-Holstein where graves have been found (i.e. settled areas) and the areas in which hoards have been found (migration routes) never overlap since the migration routes avoided inhabited country so as to escape unnecessary conflict.
4 The migration was caused by the natural catastrophes because the land in the Nordic area could no longer support the population (1938, p. 51).

Hoffmann's conclusions were reached purely on the basis of the archaeological material, without knowledge of the contemporary texts from Medinet Habu. It is striking how precisely the texts support the archaeological evidence since they too speak of natural catastrophes in the homeland of the North Sea Peoples, and say of them: 'Their soul was in utter despair' and 'the need of mouths [hunger] drove them'.

Along the old amber routes through Europe

The statement that this great power 'advanced . . . to attack the cities of Europe and Asia [Minor]' (*Ti.* 24e) also corresponds with the facts. A rich supply of archaeological evidence makes it possible to trace the routes of the Atlanteans on their way south. They used the old amber routes, along which for centuries amber had been carried to the Mediterranean countries. Now, along these routes are found not only rich deposits or hoards, but also urnfields and grave mounds, in which the North Sea People 'who were Urnfield People' (Kehnscherper 1963, p. 5) laid their dead. The typical weapon of the North Sea Peoples, the 'Germanic flange-hilted sword', is found everywhere along these migration routes. The numerous finds of such swords show not only from what area their wearers came, but what routes they took before arriving at their goal, Egypt (see map).

Three different routes can be plainly distinguished. The first went up the Elbe, and thence up the Oder, through Bohemia to the Danube. The Illyrians on the middle and upper course of the Oder were driven out of their territory. 'There are many indications that at that time strangers invaded Illyria from the north, and it may be that then the whole Illyrian people gave way before the overwhelming pressure' (Kutzleb 1940, p. 122). Some of them may have been carried along with the North Sea People; however, they cannot be traced archaeologically in south-east Europe at this time (Berve 1942, p. 31 f.; Milojcic 1948, p. 35 ff.). The majority of the Illyrians moved into the eastern Alps, and from there to the Veneto and Apulia (Schachermeyr 1936, p. 248). Consequently the assertion, frequently made, that the leading tribe of the

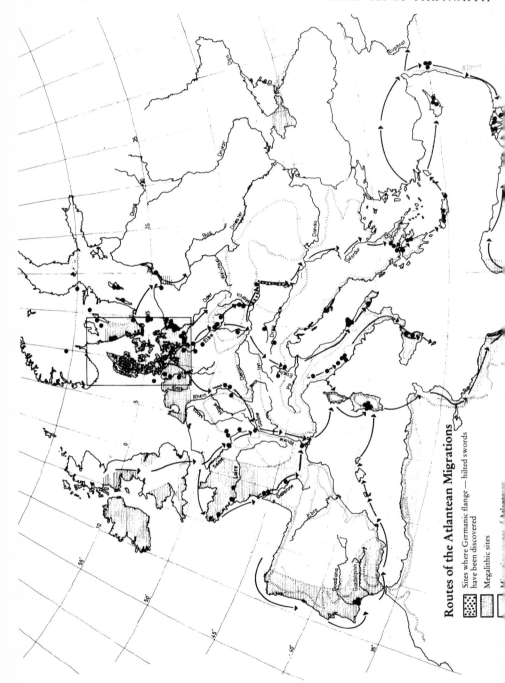

Routes of the Atlantean Migrations

Routes of the Atlantean Migrations

North Sea Peoples – the Prst or Peleset of the Egyptian texts, the Philistines – were Illyrians, is without foundation. The Philistines had nothing to do with the Illyrians, who only entered Greece two or three hundred years *after* the North Sea Peoples (Milojcic 1948, p. 35).

According to the careful researches of the Hungarian archaeologist A. Mozsolics (1957, p. 148 ff.), the Phrygians were then settled 'in the Moldau valley, below České Budějovice, particularly in southern Bohemia'. They fell back on the northern Dalmatian coast, and then followed in the train of the North Sea Peoples, in the second or third wave of the great migration, and took over the country in Asia Minor which they ruled for centuries and which is still called after them.

In the second half of the thirteenth century BC, the North Sea Peoples reached the Hungarian plain. Here the native inhabitants had fortified many of their settlements, presumably in anticipation of the invasion. But they were driven out and retreated to the rim of the Carpathians. What is remarkable is that the 'newcomers from the North never took over the settlements they had presumably conquered, but built themselves new ones on previously unoccupied ground' (Kehnscherper 1963, p. 11). The reason for this is not clear; perhaps it was simply easier to build afresh on empty land than in the ruins of the burnt-out older settlements. What is certain is that the 'invaders from the North', the 'newcomers', brought a new culture to Hungary, the 'Urnfield culture'. There was a 'complete dying out or moving out of the earlier population, and fundamental ethnic changes' (Kyrle in Mozsolics 1957, p. 143). As they had in their own country, the 'conquerors from the North – the North Sea Peoples – built grave-mounds, presumably for their chief men, and urnfields, presumably for the commoners or the poorer people, or for a larger number of dead. The 'burial-mound and urnfield culture' is *not* native to Hungary, but was brought there only by the North Sea Peoples.

The North Sea Peoples settled in Hungary for some time, and evidently left quite a large section of their population behind them. Numerous finds of weapons and other objects, of burial mounds and urnfields, just like those of northern Europe, are there to prove it.

Then, a decade or so before 1200 BC, they broke out once again and, with powerful bands of warriors, and with wives and children, some pressed on up the Danube, across the Bosporus, and into Asia Minor; while others moved along the Morava and Vardar valleys into Greece.

There are indications that the North Sea Peoples entered Macedonia and Greece only *after* the last, most terrible eruption of the volcano on Thera; for the remains of their settlements are always found *above* the burning and ash horizons which that event left behind. So, with the population of Greece greatly reduced, they only met resistance where the remaining groups of Achaeans had gathered and put up fortifications for their defence.

The kings in the palaces and castles of Greece and Crete had already received warning, long before the eruption of the volcano, of the danger that was coming upon them from the north. They had time to prepare for the impending attack. Everything in Greece at that time 'suggests forebodings of the coming storm' (Schachermeyr 1936, p. 244), indeed 'terror' (Palmer 1963, p. 154) fell upon the inhabitants of Mycenaean Greece. Fortified enclosures were hastily built, among them that first wall on the Acropolis mentioned in the Atlantis narrative and the tunnel leading to the spring on the north side. At Mycenae and Tiryns, in the same way, walls were thrown up in the rough 'Cyclopean' style, i.e. built out of unhewn rocks piled upon one another; and inside them, hidden approaches to the wells which would provide water in case of siege. Across the isthmus of Corinth a strong Cyclopean wall was built. Broneer called it 'the last attempt to keep out the invaders from the north' (1948, p. 111f.).

The primitive 'Cyclopean' construction of these walls is a sign, not of 'technological decline' as Palmer asserted, but of the great haste in which these defences had to be thrown up.

Other Achaean chieftains hoped to repel the enemy by sea, and so avoid the labour of building great fortifications. We know about their plans from the many Linear B tablets which have been found in the ruins of their palaces.

The king of Pylos gave one unit of his navy the task of going to Pleuron on the north coast of the Gulf of Corinth, about 30 km west of Naupactus. Probably the object was to prevent the seafaring Northerners, who had already reached the north coast of the gulf, from crossing it. Other ships of Pylos were made ready on the coast nearby and manned with oarsmen. The two tablets in question, which are partly broken, list probably more than 400 rowers. Other tablets read: 'Thus the watchers are guarding the coastal areas'. On others, each section has the heading: 'Command of X in Y' followed by a list of personal names. Chadwick wrote of these tablets: 'It seems clear that the purpose of the operation order is to establish a coastal observation corps, and we may infer from this that an enemy landing from the sea was feared' (1967, p. 105). Yet other tablets show that a communication service of swift e-qe-ta – charioteers – was set up between the watchers on the coast and the palace at Pylos. The king of Pylos, in Chadwick's opinion, was clearly not in a position to defend the whole coast, or to prevent a landing at every point, but 'provided he has speedy news of the attack, he may be able to muster his army to meet the invaders' (1967, p. 106).

But the fleet and the coastal defence corps of the king of Pylos could not prevent the North Sea Peoples from landing on the coast of the Peloponnese. The oracle at Delphi had advised them not to take the land route over the Isthmus of Corinth – a strong defensive wall had been put up there – but to build a fleet at Naupactus on the north coast of the Gulf of Corinth and cross the sea at that point, where it was narrowest. Near Tegea (present-day Tripolis) the king, Echemus, or Echemenus, opposed them. The leader of the North Sea warriors, Hyllus (according to Apollonius of Rhodes, the son of Heracles and Melite, born on the holy island of Electris (*Argonautica* 4.538 ff.)) made the proposal

> that there was no need for the two armies to risk their lives in a general engagement; it would suffice, he suggested, if a champion chosen from the Peloponnesian army met him in single combat upon agreed conditions. The Peloponnesians accepted the proposal and engaged upon oath that, if Hyllus were victorious, the Heracleidae [i.e. the North Sea Peoples] should be allowed to resume the ancient rights of their family, and that if he were vanquished, they should withdraw their army and make no further attempt upon the Peloponnese for a hundred years. (Herodotus 9.26.)

In this duel Echemus slew Hyllus. The Heracleidae abided by the result and passed on, to return only after a hundred years and occupy the Peloponnese. The land was then divided between three great-grandsons of Hyllus: Temenus, the eldest, received Argus; Cresphontes took Messene; and Aristodemus Laconia, with its principal city, Sparta. This Aristodemus was, according to Herodotus (7.204), the ancestor of the Spartan king Leonidas, who in 48 BC fell at the head of his 300 warriors resisting the overwhelmingly superior forces of the Persian king Xerxes.

There is plenty of evidence for the reliability of this tradition. Archaeological research in the Peloponnese has shown that the North Sea Peoples or Heracleidae entered the peninsula shortly before 1200 BC, but then 'The danger passed by' (Matz 1958). It has also become evident that the palaces and settlements of the Peloponnese, like those of all the eastern Mediterranean, were destroyed not by human actions but by earthquake and fire. The remnant of the population collected round the ruined palaces and rebuilt them in part. For about a hundred years there shone from these patched-up edifices the last rays of Mycenaean culture, the stage known to archaeologists as 'Mycenaean III c 1'. 'Then they could no longer resist the renewed assault. This second and last catastrophe, which destroyed Mycenae and Tiryns also, fell between 1150 and 1100 BC. It meant the end of Mycenaean culture.' (Matz 1958.)

The story of the successful duel of King Echemus against the leader of the Atlanteans is also supported by Greek tradition. Before the battle

of Plataea (479 BC) against the Persians, the Tegean contingent asserted
that 'We have always by universal consent been given the privilege of
holding this position [one of the wings of the army – the place of honour]
in every campaign undertaken jointly by the Peloponnesians, both in
recent and in former times. Let us remind you how . . . we won the
privilege. . .' and the story of the duel follows (Herodotus 9.25). So the
allied states of the Peloponnese gave the Tegeans the place of honour
'both in recent and former times', because their king Echemus had
conquered Hyllus. Such traditions do not grow out of mere fantasy, but
from historical memories.

The king of Knossos, like his counterpart in Pylos, had laid plans. He
too erected no walls or defences for his palace, but relied on his strong
fleet to conquer the enemy at sea, or at any rate to prevent them from
landing. However, in case they did nevertheless get ashore, 400 war
chariots were prepared, armour and weapons of all sorts were made
ready, and more than 20,000 sheep and 700 pigs commandeered,
evidently as provisions for the troops. A road network was laid out in
order to bring troops to any part of the coast in case of emergency
(Chadwick 1958). But before the Northerners reached Crete, one spring
day came the terrible eruption of Thera. The weapons and other
remains of the North Sea Peoples are found on top of the layers of
volcanic ash and lava, not under them as would have been the case if
they had arrived before the catastrophe.

So the North Sea Peoples only encountered resistance where some
part of the population who had survived banded themselves together in
a defensible position.

This was the case principally at Athens. So it is historically correct
when the Atlantis narrative tells us: 'Our records tell how your city
checked a great power which arrogantly advanced from its base in the
Atlantic sea' (*Ti.* 24e). 'It was then, Solon, that the power and strength
and courage of your city became clear for all men to see. Her bravery
and military skill were outstanding; she led an alliance of the Greeks,
and then when they deserted her and she was forced to fight alone, after
running into direct peril, she overcame the invaders and celebrated a
victory.' (*Ti.* 25b.)

Archaeologists, independently of the Atlantis narrative, have concluded:

> The mighty Cyclopean walls [on the Acropolis] were built in the thirteenth
> century BC. They were to protect the inhabitants, who, as the latest
> excavations show, abandoned the slopes of the hill about this time. We see
> the onset of the troubles of the age of the great migrations, which were to end
> only with the close of the twelfth century. Archaeological evidence,
> language and tradition all show that Athens and Attica were spared the
> direct impact of these troubles; however, there was fighting, and we must

assume a constant immigration throughout the twelfth century of a pre-Doric Greek population who had been driven out of the Peloponnese. (Kübler 1942, p. 190.)

'Athens was not overwhelmed during the Dorian migrations, thanks to the wall around the Acropolis' (Schefold 1949, p. 61).

Many other archaeologists have similarly concluded that Athens was attacked at the end of the thirteenth century by invaders in the great migration, hitherto known as the Dorian migration, that the population took refuge on the Acropolis and that there they successfully defended themselves behind the newly built Cyclopean wall, won their freedom, and put the enemy to flight.

This victory too is enshrined in tradition. It was told that the leader of the North Sea Peoples/Dorians/Heracleidae, by name Xanthus, 'the fair-haired one', challenged the king of Athens, Thymoitas, the descendant of Theseus, to a duel for possession of the city and the land of Attica. Thymoitas, however, refused the challenge. Then Melanthus, a descendant of King Nestor, who had come as a refugee from Pylos, took it up. He slew Xanthus and so the besiegers, according to the terms agreed, left empty handed. The Athenians deposed the cowardly king Thymoitas and rewarded Melanthus with the kingship.

The tradition is highly plausible. We are told repeatedly that the North Sea Peoples settled the possession of a country by a duel; for instance, with the Tegeans for Arcadia, or with the Hebrews for their land. This is a custom we know of among the Germanic tribes, and no other people. The representation of the rightful king of Athens, descendant of the great Theseus, not as a hero but as a coward and the statement that Melanthus from Pylos took on the duel, speak for an accurate memory. Archaeological evidence shows that refugees from Pylos came to power in Athens and there introduced constitutional changes which took away the divine character of the kingship (Webster 1960, p. 192).

Moreover the language, the culture, the manners and customs which were preserved at Athens from Mycenaean times show that it cannot have been conquered by the North Sea Peoples. The Mycenaean style of pottery was long continued there and the population remained on the whole undisturbed (Berve 1942, p. 34). The Athenians were proud of their Mycenaean inheritance. They called themselves 'autochthones', 'native born', while they referred to the North Sea Peoples, or Dorians, who had invaded the Greek states, as 'newcomers' (Herodotus 1.56).

The centuries-long wars between Athens and Sparta, where they were particularly proud of their Dorian descent, have their roots in this period around 1200 BC, when the rest of Greece, especially the Peloponnese, was occupied by the North Sea Peoples/Hera-

cleidae/Dorians; and Athens alone preserved her freedom and the
Mycenaean tradition. So here too the Atlantis narrative has correctly
described the historical events.

The journey through Asia

The Atlantis narrative is also correct when it states that the Atlanteans
passed through 'Asia' on their way to Egypt.

By this the ancients meant simply Asia Minor. On this point the
Atlantis narrative is confirmed by the Medinet Habu text, which says:
'As for the foreign countries, they made a conspiracy in their isles.
Removed and scattered in the fray were the lands at one time. No land
could stand before their arms, from Hatti, Kode, Carshemish, Yereth
and Yeres on, but they were cut off at one time. A camp was set up in one
place in Amor. They desolated its people and its land was like that which
has never come into being.'

The names mentioned here mean: Hatti = Hittites, Kode = the
south-east part of Asia Minor and southern Syria, Carshemish =
present-day Jerablus on the Euphrates, Yereth is probably Crete, Yeres
= Cyprus, Amor = land of the Amorites = Palestine.

The text continues: 'They were coming, while the flame was
prepared before them, towards Egypt. Their confederation was the
Peleset, Theker, Shekelesh, Denye(n), and Weshesh, lands united. They
laid their hands upon the lands to the very circuit of the earth, their
hearts confident and trusting: "Our plans will succeed!"' (inscription
46).

The names of the various tribes mentioned here cannot all be
identified. Scholars agree, however, that the Peleset are the Philistines
and that the Sakar are the tribe of that name mentioned in the Wen-
Amun papyrus (about 1095 BC) as having settled on the coasts of the
Lebanon after their attempt to conquer Egypt had failed. The Denyen
meanwhile fell back on Cyprus, where at Enkomi they founded a
flourishing settlement on the ruins of the old city which had been
destroyed by the earthquake. The Weshesh are hard to identify.
Professor E. Biollay has suggested that they were inhabitants of Corsica.
The Shekelesh can be identified as the Siculi, who then inhabited
southern Italy and Sicily.

This text thus supports the statement of the Atlantis narrative, that
the confederation of the North Sea Peoples attacked Egypt by way of
Asia Minor and the Near East.

The march through Italy

As well as the Atlantean route that I have described already, a second migration route can be traced by means of the archaeological finds. This leads up the Elbe and the Saale, through the valley of the Regnitz, to the Danube, and from there through the valley of the Inn and over the Brenner, down through Italy to Sicily, and from there to North Africa.

This route is marked by numerous finds, of weapons and belongings, of grave-mounds and urnfields. The archaeologists speak of a 'new cultural stratum', which can help us to grasp 'the effects of the great migration on the Apennine peninsula in its various phases' (Wiesner 1942, p. 202).

As weapons and other objects of this new cultural stratum are found in the so-called 'pile dwellings' (in reality, as I have shown, huts on the shores of the sunken lakes), it is clear that the migration had already reached Italy by the time of the great drought, i.e. soon after 1250 BC. Finds of the new type are particularly rich at Peschiera on Lake Garda, and other Italian 'pile villages' have produced similar finds. Recently, the remains of a thirteenth-century village have been found about 5 m below the present water level of Lake Bolsena. Its abundant contents belong to the 'new culture stratum'. The pottery and weapons (axes, daggers, flange-hilted swords) show that their owners originated in the north of Europe. According to the account published by the Italian Department of Antiquities, this settlement was destroyed as follows: 'A severe earthquake shook the area, and caused a violent tidal wave to wash over the village, leaving only the piles [i.e. the walls of the huts].' This observation supports the thesis that those settlements all over Europe which have been found below the present water level of lakes and rivers were similarly destroyed by earthquake and flood, not by a gradual rising of the water level at the end of the drought.

An earlier generation of scholars interpreted the finds of this new type as belonging to a highly developed culture native to this part of the peninsula, J. Wiesner, the greatest expert on the migration period, contradicted this mistaken assumption as long ago as 1943:

> There is no possibility that these forms developed on the Apennine peninsula; there is nothing there in the previous period from which they could have evolved. About all, Pescheria is *not* to be seen as the place of origin of the new culture. These 'pile dwellings" belong to a culture which at the time these new forms appeared in Italy lacked the technical ability to produce them, particularly in the field of metallurgy. There are no signs of such ability in the Aegean area either. Rather, we have here the arrival of a regular 'type front', whose origins, whether for Italy or the Aegean, must be sought in a common, Northern, original. (1943, vol. 2, p. 75.)

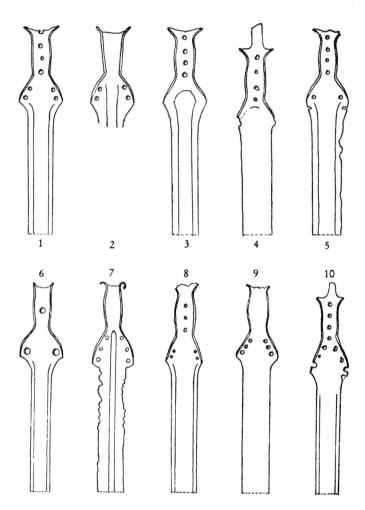

Nordic flange-hilted swords from:

1) Hoilandsvandet, Denmark	6) Annenheim
2) Rügen	7) Near Leoben, Styria
3) Mycenae	8) Near Fucino, Italy
4) Egypt	9) Near Fucino, Italy
5) Beneditto in Perillis, Italy	10) Beneditto in Perillis, Italy

The new culture stratum shows a uniform character from the north of Italy to the south, and is attested by numerous finds in Sicily, Malta Sardinia, and the Balearic Islands (Wiesner 1942, p. 234, p. 225 f., p. 228; 1943, p. 71, p. 112f., p. 115f., p. 117f.). Among the weapon types, flange-hilted swords and daggers appear again and again as do razors, bow-shaped fibulae, shaft-hole axes, and sickles which are all new to Italy and the islands. War chariots and mounted warriors appear, both unknown in Italy till then. Also new is the custom of cremating the dead and laying out great urnfields as cemeteries. However, the newcomers also built large grave-mounds, as they did in the other areas through which they migrated. These immigrants were skilful seafarers, like those who had conquered the Peloponnese, Crete and Cyprus.

As the spread of the new culture stratum through Apulia, Sicily, Malta and the Balearics shows, these coasts and islands were occupied by the sea routes. Bronze snaffles and two-wheeled chariots, which have been found as relics of the great migration, show that horses and vehicles too were transported by sea. A people who cross the sea with their horses and chariots must be most expert sailors.

Thick layers of burnt material and ash *above* the older cultural strata and *below* the new culture stratum show that here as elsewhere 'the flame was prepared before them', as it says at Medinet Habu.

To see where the peoples came from who brought the first wave of the great migration to Italy, we may take the tribe of the Umbrians as an example. These people were not native to Italy but, as their traditions recounted, had been driven by a terrible flood from their home in the Ocean (Wiesner 1942, p. 232, p. 222n.). Excavations in Umbrian settlements have shown that they came with the first wave of the great migration, towards the end of the thirteenth century. Their territory at first included not only the present Umbria but also the area south of Lake Trasimene. Tuscany too was settled by them, as Herodotus (1.94) rightly said and Pliny (*Natural History* 14.112) confirmed. There were also Umbrians on the Ligurian coast and in Upper Italy, north of Rimini, for example, and north and south of Ravenna (Wiesner 1942, p. 231; Kretschmer in *Glotta*, vol. 21 (1933), p. 122).

P. Kretschmer has pointed out that the name of the Umbrians is related to that of the Ambrones. Segments of the same tribe had gone to the making of both the Italic and the Germanic peoples. The close relationship of their language to the Germanic ones also indicates their Northern origin.

A neighbouring tribe to the Umbrians called themselves the Teutones or Teutanes, and yet another, which settled at Ephorus on Lake Avernus, were known as Cimmerians. In these cases too, according to Kretschmer, we must recognize a connection with those Germanic tribes of the same names, who inhabited the Cimbrian peninsula (Pomponius Mela 2.32; Pliny *Natural History* 4.99, 37.35).

1200 years later, in about 130 BC, Cimbri, Teutons and Ambrones were once again driven from their homes by flood and famine, and tried to break into Italy, only to be defeated at Aquae Sextiae (present-day Aix-en-Provence) in 102 BC. Plutarch in ch. 9 of his 'Life' of Marius, the general who commanded the Roman army on that occasion, recounted that on the morning of the battle the following episode occurred:

> The Ambrones . . . did not rush on in a disorderly or frantic course, or raise an inarticulate battle cry, but rhythmically clashing their arms and leaping to the sound, they would frequently shout out all together their tribal name, 'Ambrones', either to encourage one another or to terrify their enemies in advance by the declaration. The first of the Italians to go down against them were the Ligurians, and when they heard and understood what the barbarians were shouting, they themselves shouted back the word, claiming it as their own ancestral appellation, for the Ligurians call themselves Ambrones by descent.

Kretschmer took this story as an indication that on the day before the battle of Aquae Sextiae, the Ambrones, who had long been settled in Italy, encountered their northern Germanic kinsmen, who were once again attempting to invade Italy. F. Altheim and E. Trautmann held the same opinion (1939, p. 66ff.).

S. Gutenbrunner (1939, p. 10ff.) and other researchers have suggested that the name of the island of Amrum in the North Frisian Islands is a memory of the home of the Ambrones and that Himmer (Himmerland = northern Jutland and Ålborg) recalls the homeland of the Cimmerians or Cimbri. The name Thytesysel (Danish *sysel*, Old Norse *sysla* = district) is the homeland of the Teutons (see also Karsten 1932). All these tribes entered Italy with the first wave of migration.

The French expert on prehistoric metallurgy, Jean Maréchal, has shown that the great migration also passed along the French rivers Rhône, Seine, Loire and Garonne, going south. He has also shown that this southward movement in all probability followed not only the land route but a sea route down the west coast; he has called these two movements the 'Continental' and the 'Atlantic' advance. 'We see that their advance by sea is parallel with that on Italy and Greece. The meeting point of these two movements, the Atlantic and the Continental, seems to have lain in Sicily and southern Italy, where objects characteristic of both have been found.' (1959b, p. 252.)

The flange-hilted sword found in the harbour at Huelva (see page 131) is one of the many archaeological discoveries that support the Atlantis narrative's statement that the Atlanteans also entered the Mediterranean 'from without' (*exothen*) and 'attempted to enslave, at a single stroke, both your country [Greece] and ours [Egypt] and all the territory within the strait [of Gibraltar]' (*Ti.* 25b).

This is also confirmed by the text of Ramses III, which says of the North Sea Peoples, 'They laid their hands upon the lands to the very circuit of the earth.'

So, in the second half of the thirteenth century BC, 'all the territory within the strait' except for Athens and Egypt lay in the hands of the

Detail from the mural at Medinet Habu showing the sea battle between the Egyptians and the North Sea Peoples (from *Earlier Historical Records of Ramses III*, University of Chicago Press)

North Sea Peoples – the Atlanteans. The encirclement of Egypt, the goal of their great migration, was accomplished.

The attack on Egypt

We are well informed about the assault on Egypt by the reports of the Pharaohs Merneptah and Ramses III. The first attack by the Libyans, and the North Sea Peoples who were their allies, came in the fifth year of the reign of Merneptah (1227 BC). The reason for this invasion by the Libyans is given: 'Libya has become a desert and without fruit. The Libyans come to Egypt to seek sustenance for their bodies.' (Karnak inscription Z.22, Hölscher 1937, p. 61 ff.)

The drying-up of their country, until then a land of pasture and

meadow watered by great rivers, had brought famine to the Libyans.
Now they hoped to find food in the Nile valley. This hope was not
unfounded, for just at that time, during the reign of Merneptah, there
was a 'great Nile', i.e. abundant flooding. The reason was this: the Nile
has its sources in the high mountainous areas of the Virunga Mountains
(4324m), Kilimanjaro (5895m) and the highlands of Ethiopia whose
highest peak is 4629m. All these mountains had, until the period of
catastrophic heat, 'wide-spreading glaciers' (Flint 1959, p. 70; Schwarzbach 1961, p. 31, p. 165; Suball 1958, p. 44 and elsewhere). During the
heat, these melted, apart from a small residue on the summit of
Kilimanjaro. While this process was going on, the Nile was abnormally
full. Since the fertility of Egypt is produced by the twice-yearly flooding
of the river, with its load of life-giving mud, Egypt became particularly
fruitful just in the years when the rest of the world was hit by the heat
and drought. For example, Merneptah was able, at the plea of the
Hittite king Suppiluliuma II (c. 1225–1201 BC) to send fourteen ships
loaded with corn to Asia Minor to relieve a famine there. The letter of
Suppiluliuma to Merneptah has been preserved, in which he begs for
corn, describing his message as 'a matter of life or death' (Otten 1963).

The drought affected Egypt itself only after the reign of Merneptah
but before that of Sethos II (1215–1210 BC), who once again reported a
'great Nile' which had renewed the fertility of his country. This later
'great Nile' must have been the result of the enormous flood of rain
which followed the volcanic eruptions (see page 175). The failure of the
Nile and the consequent drought in Egypt can only have been of short
duration. As it truly says in the Atlantis narrative: '. . . the Nile, our own
regular saviour, is freed to preserve us in this emergency . . . here water
never falls on the land from above either then or at any other time, but
rises up naturally from below' (Ti. 22e). So the Libyans could
reasonably hope to find 'sustenance for their bodies' in Egypt.

In 1227 BC, under the leadership of their chieftain Merije, son of
Did, the Libyans poured into the western Delta of the Nile, and besieged
Memphis and Heliopolis. The name 'Libyans' appears for the first time
in the texts of this period (Hölscher 1937, p. 61). Before this time, the
white-skinned peoples living to the west of Egypt were known as
'Tamahu' or 'Temehu', or 'Tiamah'. It is not clear whether the Libyans
were in fact a new people, recently arrived in North Africa, or whether
this is simply a new name for the Tamahu, who had been there for
millennia. Both peoples were reckoned by the Egyptians among the
'northern peoples', and both are portrayed as white-skinned, fair-haired
and blue-eyed (Möller 1920/21, p. 427).

On the side of the Libyans there fought the 'northern people from
the islands': Teresh, Sherden, Shekelesh, Luka and Ekwesh. It is
thought that the Teresh are identical with the Tyrsenoi (or

Tyrrhenians), i.e. the Etruscans; the Sherden with the Sardinians; the Shekelesh with the Siculi of Sicily; the Luka with the Lycians (Stadelmann 1968, p. 157; also W.M. Müller, Schachermeyr and others). Many scholars suppose that the Ekwesh are the Achaeans of Greece. If this is correct, it shows that about 1227 BC, the 'northern people of the islands' were still in alliance with the Achaeans.

The advance of this coalition put Egypt in great peril. Then Pharaoh Merneptah had a dream of good omen; the god Ptah appeared at his side in gigantic stature and gave him a sword with the command to abandon all fear (Breasted 1906-7, vol. 3, p. 582; 1927, p. 468).

After a month of preparation, Merneptah's troops were ready to march, and on the morning of 15 April, in the fifth year of his reign (1227 BC), a battle was fought near the royal castle of Perire on the western Delta. The fighting went on for six hours, and by the end of it the Egyptian archers had routed the foreigners, with huge losses (*ibid.*). Among about 9000 enemy dead, there were 6359 Libyans, including six sons of the Libyan king, 222 Shekelesh, 422 Teresh, an unknown number of Ekwesh (there were 2362 severed hands), and an uncertain number of North Sea warriors. The booty included 9111 swords, teams of horses, 1307 head of cattle, and much more.

Sethos II also had to guard against attacks by the North Sea Peoples. But since their main body had not yet reached Egypt, he had to deal only with small bands of warriors, the advance troops of the 'great migration'. It must be as a result of one of these defensive skirmishes that the Germanic flange-hilted sword bearing the cartouche of Sethos II was found in the Nile delta in 1912 (see page 36).

About 1200 BC the North Sea Peoples, the Atlanteans, and the peoples in alliance with them had completed their preparations. In Amurru (Amor), Palestine, under the leadership of the Peleset, the Sakar, Shekelesh, Denye and Meshwesh had pitched their camp. In Crete and Cyprus a strong invasion fleet lay ready for the North Sea warriors. To the west of Egypt came the Libyans and the Teresh (or Tyrrhenians) marching under the leadership of the North Sea Peoples. This time, the Ekwesh and the Luka are missing from the confederation. If the former are really to be identified with the Achaeans, then their absence in the war against Ramses III is perhaps accounted for by the fact that by this time the annihilating eruption of Thera and its accompanying disasters had reduced the population of Mycenaean Greece 'to almost a hundredth' (Luce 1975, p. 39) so that, as the Atlantis narrative says, only a 'few survivors . . . remained' (*Ti.* 23c).

Pharaoh had seen the approaching danger. He had fortified his frontier with a defensive wall, the 'wall of the princes'; he had 'battleships, *mns* ships, and *br* ships' i.e. warships of all kinds, 'manned from the bow to the stern with valiant warriors bearing their arms'. He had armed 'all the recruits that are on the roll of his majesty', and hired African mercenaries as auxiliaries. Proudly the inscription says of this army: 'The soldiers were the choicest of Egypt, like lions roaring on the mountain tops. The charioteers were warriors, and all good officers, ready of hand. Their horses were quivering in every limb, ready to crush the [enemy] countries under their feet.' (Medinet Habu tablet 46; Breasted 1906-7, p. 38.)

In the fifth year of the reign of Ramses III, there followed the general assault upon Egypt. From the west the North Sea Peoples, the Libyans and the Teresh attacked; from the east, the North Sea Peoples and the other tribes I have listed; from the sea, a powerful fleet of the North Sea Peoples sailed up the mouths of the Nile. A battle of major importance for the history of the world was joined. By throwing in his entire strength, and by the gift of especial good fortune, Ramses was able to withstand the three-fold attack. 'Hundreds of thousands' of the North Sea People were slain or taken prisoner. As for the ships that had come up the Nile mouths, 'A wall of metal upon the shore surrounded them, they were dragged, overturned, and laid low upon the beach; slain and made heaps . . . while all their things were cast upon the water.' Many ships were capsized, and the warriors swimming in the water were killed by the archers and spear-men. 'The Nile was red with the blood of the slain' (Medinet Habu).

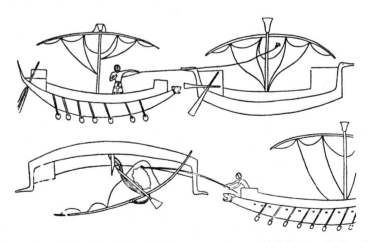

How the ships of the North Sea Peoples were overturned (Medinet Habu, from Edgerton and Wilson, 1936)

The trekkers in ox-wagons, who approached Egypt by land from Amurru, were surrounded and the men killed. The women and children who sat on the heavy carts were killed or taken prisoner. On the Libyan front too, the Egyptians were victorious. Here, as the count of severed hands and phalli shows, more than 25,000 of the enemy fell. Thousands more were made prisoner and taken away in chains. A large, well preserved, mural relief shows the fate of the prisoners. They were chained together in pairs, and taken to a prison camp. There they had to sit in rows on the ground to await interrogation. One by one they were led away by Egyptian officers, who can be recognized by their long kilts, and branded with 'the great name of his majesty' (Medinet Habu tablets 28, 42). Then they were interrogated; numerous scribes wrote down the prisoners' answers; this is why the text says repeatedly 'They say . . . they say. . .' The ten kings of the enemy alliance were taken prisoner and led before Pharaoh; they were interrogated by Egyptian officers and finally killed by Ramses III in person.

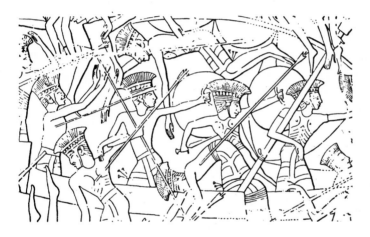

North Sea warriors during the naval battle. One man has fallen overboard wounded and is being held up by his comrades. (Medinet Habu, from Edgerton and Wilson 1936)

The victory of Ramses seemed complete; but it was a 'Pyrrhic victory' as W. Hölscher (1937, p. 66) put it. Several times the Pharaoh had to take the field to protect his country from the North Sea Peoples. In the last years of the reign of Ramses II, 'the great', Egypt had been at the height of her power. Afterwards, she was so weakened by the natural catastrophes and the defensive wars against the North Sea Peoples, that she fell into a 'period of decline', indeed of stagnation (Breasted), and never regained her old greatness.

The Northerners settled in the former Egyptian province of Amurru (Syria and Palestine). The tribe of the *Prst* or Peleset occupied the plain and the coast; these are the Philistines of the Old Testament. The Sakar took over the coasts at the foot of the mountains of Lebanon; the Denye

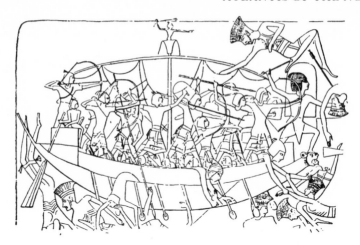

Egyptian warship grapples one of the ships of the North Sea Peoples (Medinet Habu,
from Edgerton and Wilson 1936)

Captive Northerners are branded with the name of Pharaoh

settled in Cyprus; the tribe of the Dori or Duri fell back on the Aegean
islands and the Peloponnese, where they set up the Dorian states. On the
Palestinian coasts the towns of Gaza, Ashqelon, Ashdod, Jamnia, and
Dor, all of which had been burnt up and destroyed in the natural
catastrophes, flourished once more. They joined themselves into a
league of independent cities, which has been compared by the American
archaeologist Elihu Grant (1936, p. 175) to the Hanseatic League of the
German Middle Ages. On the coasts of Palestine, Lebanon and Cyprus,
secure harbours and strong fleets were constructed. So the North Sea
Peoples quickly gained control of the seas in the Eastern Mediterranean,
which became known, after their leading tribe, as 'the sea of the
Philistines' (Exod. 23:31).

Left: captive Northerners are interrogated. *Right:* Ramses III slaying a king of the North Sea Peoples (Medinet Habu, first courtyard, pillar on the south side)

So it is true, just as the Atlantis narrative says, that in the days when the first wall was built on the Acropolis at Athens, i.e. towards the end of the thirteenth century BC, at the time of the great natural catastrophes which left Greece with only a 'few survivors', a powerful people, rulers over many islands and coastlands on the Northern Ocean, together with their allies, 'gathering its whole power together, attempted to enslave, at a single stroke . . . all the territory within the strait' (*Ti.* 25b).

The march of the Atlanteans did indeed take them through Europe and Asia Minor, up to the frontiers of Egypt, and the latter was hard pressed. It is a fact that these peoples commanded a powerful fleet, and attacked Egypt both by sea and by land, in alliance with Libyans and Tyrrhenians. The great army was commanded by ten kings, who, according to the Egyptian texts, were taken prisoner after their unsuccessful campaign. Strong bands of war chariots, and the world's first mounted warriors, were used by the North Sea Peoples, the Atlanteans. In the event, Egypt was rescued from the danger and kept its independence. The Atlanteans had indeed, 'laid their hands upon the lands as far as the circle of the earth', as Ramses III, in agreement with the Atlantis narrative, tells us.

The assertion that only Athens, by its heroic defence, preserved its freedom, is also historically correct; in Attica Mycenaean art and culture survived for another hundred years.

So the statements of the Atlantis narrative are no 'unhistorical fairy-tale', or 'pure fantasy', but, as I have repeatedly stressed, a true record drawn from ancient Egyptian temple inscriptions and papyrus texts, which Solon brought home with him from Egypt.

CHAPTER 6

A GERMANIC ATLANTIS TRADITION

In the foregoing pages I have repeatedly pointed out that oral tradition often transmits memories of long-past times, which are later confirmed by research, at least in their essentials.

S. Kleemann in his book on 'Excavations in Germany' (*Ausgrabungen in Deutschland*) wrote as follows:

> Local legends and fairy-tales are quite astonishingly reliable. What we find indeed borders on the fabulous. . . . Near Schuby, south of Schleswig, the story was told that in a grave-mound in the area lay a headless warrior. The mound did indeed turn out to contain a tomb, in which there lay on a stone slab the skeleton of a man, with the skull laid near the feet. This is quite abnormal in mound-burials. On the Osterberg, near Hamburg, there is a grave-mound inside which, according to the local story, a king sat, like Barbarossa, upright at his table. Excavations revealed an unusual find for the Late Bronze Age: the burnt remains of the corpse had been emptied onto the top of a stone table. In Seddin (Brandenburg) there is a huge mound 11 m high and 90 m in diameter; the old people of the village used to say that in it lay a king in a three-fold coffin. This Iron Age mound was excavated in 1900; inside it was a stone grave-chamber, in the centre of which stood a large earthenware vessel with a lid. Inside this was a bronze urn, holding the cremated remains, and with them a small bronze jug. The bones showed the deceased to have been a robust man of about thirty, among his bones lay those of an ermine. Perhaps he was indeed a king, who wore an ermine pelt (in this case not fully dressed) as a sign of rank. (1962, p. 253.)

Many other examples cited by Kleemann show that the reliability of these legends does indeed 'border on the fabulous'.

The Kiel prehistorian K. Kersten cited similar examples and showed that legends from Schleswig-Holstein preserve remarkable memories of the Bronze Age (c. 1935, p. 8 ff.)

Now it would be odd if folk-memory preserved the truth about comparatively trivial matters, such as the contents of graves or the sites of lost villages, while knowing nothing of the sacred island in the amber country of the ancients, of the terrible natural cataclysms in which it vanished; of the great war expedition of the North Sea Peoples; and of the re-emergence of the holy island.

There are in fact very ancient Germanic legends and traditions telling of all these events, and they are in entire agreement with the facts that I have so far established. These are the traditions concerning Asgard, the 'home of the Aesir', or 'place of the world-pillar'; of the 'holy island', how it sank beneath the sea and later re-emerged; of the terrible natural catastrophes which accompanied 'Ragnarök', the 'downfall of the gods'; of the 'first war in the world' and how 'there was great slaughter all over the earth'. These accounts are preserved in the *Eddas*; the whole body of legend is known to scholars as the myth of Ragnarök, literally 'the downfall of the powers'. The literature on the theme is unusually rich and full of contradictions. The true meaning of these traditions, the age to which they should be dated and the place to which they refer, remains a riddle not yet answered by all the learned treatises on the subject.

It is astonishing in what an inadmissible manner the really quite clear and unambiguous statements in the *Eddas* about Ragnarök have been misinterpreted, misdated and falsely localized.

B. Kummer, for instance, supposed that he saw in them memories of the 'change of faith', the introduction of Christianity (1950, p. 12, p. 24; 1961, p. 35) although no such reference can be detected at any point.

Axel Olrik rightly said of the *Völuspá*, the chief source in the *Eddas* for the Ragnarök tradition, 'Its unusually rich descriptions of nature are *purely physical;* the sun is darkened, storms rage, the earth burns up and then sinks into the sea' (1922, p. 128).

Moreover, there are the statements that after the disasters of Ragnarök,

> · Now do I see   the earth anew
> Rise all green   from the waves again;
>
> . . . .
> The gods in Ida Plain   meet together
>
> *Völuspá* 59–60

'and they will dwell in Odin's hall' (*Völuspá* 62). In the *Gylfaginning* it says of the new age after Ragnarök:

> In that time the earth shall emerge out of the sea, and shall then be green and fair; then shall the fruits of it be brought forth unsown. Vidar and Vali shall be living, inasmuch as neither sea nor the fire of Surtr shall have harmed them; and they shall dwell at Ida-Plain, where Asgard was before. And then the sons of Thor, Modi and Magni, shall come there, and they shall have Mjollnir there. After that Baldr shall come thither, and Hodr, from Hel; and all shall sit down together and hold speech with one another, and call to mind their secret wisdom, and speak of those happenings which have been before: of the Midgard-Serpent and of the Fenris-Wolf. (Ch. 53.)

No sign here of the 'new teachings' or 'change of faith', that

Kummer reads into the *Eddas*. Consequently his dating of Ragnarök to between AD 963 and 1051 falls to the ground (1961, p. 126).

The *Elder Edda*, of which the *Völuspá* forms part, is a collection of ancient poems about gods and heroes, which were written down in Iceland. The events in Iceland since its settlement in the tenth century AD are well known to us from the many realistic narratives which we have in the 'Sagas of Icelanders'. From no other European country of the time do we have so many vivid insights into the lives, thoughts and beliefs of the population as from Iceland. There is no trace in these stories of all the things Kummer imagined were the result of the introduction of Christianity (which he equated with Ragnarök): 'The old peasant culture was destroyed; the light of the old values of heathen life was quenched; the gods went under, fighting to the last; and men felt themselves without home or direction, as the forces of chaos seemed to overwhelm the old order' (1950, p. 9). But the truth is just the contrary; the Icelanders, in the year AD 1000, adopted Christianity by the unanimous decision of their general assembly; for some time heathen and Christian ideas existed side by side; there was no collapse of the old order, no god went under fighting. Kummer himself had to admit this. He wrote of the many Icelandic sagas: 'The reader is understandably surprised when he tried in vain to find . . . the knowledge and experience of the vanishing heathen age' (1950, p. 11). From all this it follows that Kummer's interpretation and dating of Ragnarök are false.

We are left then, with the question posed by the Danish Eddaic scholar Berger Nerman (1958): 'How old is the *Völuspá*?'

The *Völa*, the pagan prophetess or sibyl who speaks in this poem, calls it 'ancient lore of men, the oldest that I know' (*Völuspá* 1).

The *Eddas* do provide some evidence of the time at which most 'ancient lore' originated. They speak of the 'earliest time, in which the gods built Asgard', or say of the gods that on Ida Plain 'forges they set, and they smithied ore' (*Völuspa* 7). There is no mention of iron, only of ore – i.e. copper ore. We are taken back, therefore, to an age when copper was worked, but not iron – i.e. to the Bronze Age. This dating agrees with the name given to this time, 'the Age of Gold' (*Gylfaginning* 14), and the frequent references to gold, golden jewellery and gold-covered temples. All this fits the Bronze Age, when – probably through the amber trade – 'truly immense quantities of gold flooded into the North' (Schilling 1940, p. 313).

'Striking evidence of the prosperity of the Bronze Age Germanic peoples is the great wealth of gold found at this period; not only are unusual quantities of jewellery made out of it, but vessels and dishes of gold, in greater quantity than even in the gold-producing countries, are common finds in the bogs' (Behn 1950, vol. 2, p. 130).

The 'Age of Gold' that ended with Ragnarök is the Bronze Age. In later times, up to the writing of Snorri's (prose) *Edda*, there was never again such wealth or such fruitfulness in northern Europe.

This dating is supported by the description of the catastrophes that brought Ragnarök about. These agree precisely with the events of the thirteenth century BC which I have already described. No such series of events has happened since.

These cataclysms began with a period of extraordinary heat and drought, which dried up the waters, killed vegetation in the bogs and caused them to burn up, and brought severe famines upon the inhabitants of our planet. The *Eddas* and other Germanic traditions state: 'the air dries up' (*Völuspá in scamma* 15), or 'The waters dry up, the bog dies . . . the people wither in terrible need, immeasurable thirst overcomes the sons of the heroes' (*Heliand* 4310). The 'ancient Germanic heathen word' (Braune and Ebinghaus 1962, p. 170) for the drying-up of bogs and streams was *mutspelli* or *muspilli* literally 'destroyer of moisture'.

This time of drought and famine was caused, accompanied, or brought to an end by 'fires falling from heaven' and world-wide burning. In the *Eddas* it says: 'Then . . . shall Surtr cast fire over the earth and burn all the world' (*Gylfaginning* 51).

Surtr fares from the south   with the scourge of branches [fire]
. . . .
The dead throng Hel-way   and heaven is cloven

Völuspá 52

Smoke-reek rages   and reddening fire
The high heat licks   against heaven itself

Völuspá 57

Severe earthquakes follow. 'Ill days among men . . . ere the world totters' (*Völuspá* 45), 'the crags are sundered' (*Völuspá* 52),

Yggdrasil shakes   and shiver on high
The ancient limbs

Völuspá 47

'Then shall come to pass these tidings also, all the earth shall tremble so, and the crags, that trees shall be torn up from the earth, and the crags fall to ruin; and all fetter and bonds shall be broken and rent' (*Gylfaginning* 51). 'Then he [Loki] writhes . . . with such force that all the earth trembles; ye call that "earthquakes"' (*Gylfaginning* 50). 'Then the ash of Yggdrasil shall tremble, and nothing shall be without fear in heaven or in earth' (*Gylfaginning* 51).

The tradition that 'trees shall be torn up from the earth, and the crags fall to ruin', can only be derived from someone who lived through such an event. Human imagination would be hard put to it to invent such a detail.

But precisely this has been observed to happen during severe earthquakes. During the terrible earthquake which visited Chile in May 1960 it was reported that 'whole mountains disintegrated into avalanches of earth . . . trees with all their roots were torn out of the ground and flew through the air' (Dr H. Berger, Puerto Montt, Report on the Earthquake: 21 May 1960). Father Charlevoix, a priest who lived through the devastating earthquake which occurred in Canada in 1662, reported: 'Whole mountains were uprooted and transplanted to another spot. Trees flew up into the air as though a mine had exploded under their roots, and others turned upside down on their heads' (quoted in Hermann 1936, p. 150).

The catastrophes at the end of the Bronze Age were world-wide in their impact. This is shown not only by the texts of Medinet Habu, the legend of Phaethon, and the archaeological evidence, but by the *Eddas*. There we read:

> Then sought the gods their assembly-seats,
> The holy ones,   and council held,
> To find who with venom   the air had filled

'Then [Loki] writhes . . . with such force that all the earth trembles' (*Gylfaginning* 50). 'Surtr . . . shall go forth and harry . . . and burn all the world with fire' (*Gylfaginning* 4).

These earthquakes were followed by great floods. In the *Eddas* we find:

> The monstrous Beast   twists in mighty wrath;
> The Snake beats the waves   the eagle is screaming;
>
> *Völuspá* 50

> The sea, storm-driven,   seeks heaven itself,
> O'er the earth it flows   the air grows sterile   *Hyndluliód* 44

'Then the sea shall gush forth upon the land, because the Midgard Serpent [i.e. the Ocean], stirs in giant wrath and advances up onto the land. Then that too shall happen, that Naglfar [the ship of the dead] shall be loosened . . . Yet in this sea-flood Naglfar shall float. . . The Midgard Serpent shall blow venom so that he shall sprinkle all the air and water; and he is very terrible, and shall be on one side of the Wol.' (*Gylfaginning* 50.)

In these monstrous floods Asgard is submerged:

> The sea, storm-driven,   seeks heaven itself,
> O'er the earth if flows   . . . .
> For the gods are doomed   and the end is death
>
> *Hyndluliód* 44

The skald Arnor Jarkaskald (about AD 1030) recalled the old tradition in his verse:

> The bright sun becomes black
> Earth sinks into the sea
> (Quoted by Kummer 1962, p. 116)

The darkening of the sun and the sinking of the earth into the sea must have happened simultaneously because both were results of the volcanic eruptions of the time. The great clouds of ash thrown up by the volcanoes floated for a long time in the atmosphere and darkened the sun; the earthquakes which followed caused the seismic waves which flooded all flat coastlands.

There is mention elsewhere in the *Eddas* of the darkening of the sun at the time when Asgard sank; for instance:

> Among these one   in monster's guise
> Was soon to steal   the sun from the sky.

> There feeds he full   on the flesh of the dead,
> And the home of the gods   he reddens with gore;
> Dark grows the sun   and in summer soon
> Come mighty storms
>
> *Völuspá* 40, 41

> Whence comes the sun   to the smooth sky back
> When Fenrir has snatched it forth?
>
> *Vafthrudnismál* 47

Fenrir, the monster of the heavens, is called 'the killer of daylight'. There can be no doubt that the words 'Dark grows the sun ... in summer' refer to the same darkening that is described in the Egyptian texts of about 1200 BC. Similarly 'the home of the gods he reddens with gore' corresponds with the reports which describe the 'rain of blood' and the reddening of the earth.

The legends and traditions of many peoples tell of this 'rain of blood' or 'reddening of the world'. When in these legends we are told that the 'rain of blood' coincided with the burning of the world and the flood, then we may assume that they refer to the events of 1200 BC.

In the Finnish national epic, the *Kalevala,* which according to D. Welding (1948) contains '3000-years-old traditions', it says that in the time of the terrible cataclysms which let loose burning and flood, 'the earth was sprinkled with red milk' (rune 9). It was then that the props of heaven gave way, sun and moon were darkened, and later a fiery appearance in the heavens kindled a new sun and moon.

The Tartars of the Altai mountains tell of a world-catastrophe in which 'blood rained from heaven', followed by a burning of the world (Holmberg 1927, p. 370).

The clouds of ash together with the meteroric dust in the atmosphere led to a sharp worsening of the climate, with heavy falls of snow in the North (see page 175). This climatic drop is mentioned in many passages in the Eddas. For example:

> Then follow the snows   and the furious winds
> For the gods are doomed,   and the end is death.
>
> *Hyndluliód* 44 (*Völuspá in scamma* 13)

'There shall come that winter which is called the *Fimbul* [mighty] winter: in that time snow shall drive from all quarters; frosts shall be great then, and winds sharp; there shall be no virtue in the sun. Those winters shall proceed three in succession, and no summer between; but first shall come three other winters, such that over all the world there shall be mighty battles.' (*Gylfaginning* 51). And in the *Vafthrudnismál* we find the anxious question:

> What shall live of mankind   when at last there comes
> The mighty winter to men?
>
> *Vafthrudnismál* 44

I have mentioned that the Swedish geologist Sernander called the climatic drop 'a true *fimbul* winter'; and F. Behn wrote: 'The *fimbul* winter of the *Eddas* perhaps preserves a memory of this event, so decisive for the history of the north European peoples' (1948, p. 123).

The *Eddas* also preserve striking accounts of the comet that the Egyptians called Sekhmet and the Greeks and Romans Phaethon or Typhon. In the *Eddas* it is called 'Surtr from Muspellheim' – *muspell*, like *mutspelli* and *muspilli* means 'destroyer of moisture'. The *Gylfaginning* (51) says of it: 'In this din shall the heaven be cloven, and the sons of Muspell ride thence: Surtr shall ride first, and both before and after him burning fire; his sword is exceeding good; from it radiance shines brighter than from the sun. . . The sons of Muspell shall go forth to that field which is called Vigridr. . . Then straightway shall Surtr cast fire over the earth and burn all the world.'

'We have here an impressive and uncommonly vivid description of a comet: Surtr from Muspellheim with his shining sword as the leader, the glowing head of a whole train of fire-giants, a troop which at first stays together in the heaven, and then at last, like Phaethon of the Greeks, sets heaven and earth ablaze.' (Hohenöcker DGG 1974, No. 2, 8.)

In the *Völuspá* we find:

> Surtr fares from the south   with the scourge of branches
> The sun of the battle-gods   shines from his sword;
> The crags are sundered   the giant-women sink
> The dead throng Hell-way   and heaven is cloven.

Völuspá 52

In the contemporary Egyptian texts and their derivative, the Atlantis narrative, it is described in detail how through these catastrophes the North Sea Peoples, the Atlanteans, were driven to launch a great military expedition, which eventually brought them to the frontiers of Egypt (*Ti.* 25b, *Criti.* 120d).

The *Eddas* too know of the setting out of this force but not what became of it.

In the *Völuspá* we find:

> The war I remember   the first in the world

Völuspá 21

> Forth from their homes   must all men flee

Völuspá 56

> Axe-time, sword-time,   shields are sundered
> Wind-time, wolf-time,   ere the world falls;
> Nor ever shall men   each other spare.

Völuspá 45

'First shall come three other winters, such that over all the world there shall be mighty battles' (*Gylfaginning* 51).

The resurgence from the sea of the 'holy island' is also in the *Eddas*.

> Now do I see   the earth anew
> Rise all green   from the waves again;
>
> . . . .
>
> The gods in Ida Plain   meet together,
> of the terrible girdler   of earth they talk.
>
> In wondrous beauty   once again
> Shall the golden tablets   stand mid the grass
> Which the gods had owned   in the days of old

Völuspá 59–61

The *Gylfaginning*, in the passage already quoted, tells us: 'In that time the earth shall emerge out of the sea, and shall then be green and fair; then shall the fruits of it be brought forth unsown.' The passage ends: 'Then all [the Aesir] shall sit down together and hold speech with one another, and call to mind their secret wisdom, and speak of those happenings which have been before: of the Midgard Serpent and of the Fenris-Wolf. Then shall they find in the grass those golden chess-pieces ["tablets"] which the Aesir had had.' (*Gylfaginning* 53.) That the land 'where Asgard was before' re-emerged from the sea, is an accurate memory. So are the golden 'tablets' which the Aesir formerly used and now find again. On Basileia, the kings 'wrote the terms of the judgement on gold plates which they dedicated . . . as a record' (*Criti.* 120c). Is it also an accurate tradition, when the Aesir are said to remember *runes* ('secret wisdom')?

This brief overview shows that the *Eddas* preserve an astonishingly accurate tradition of the catastrophes which began in the thirteenth century BC. In other words their content is not, as Kummer would have us believe, 'memories of the introduction of Christianity', which at the time when these ancient poems were written down was a matter of very recent history. Rather it is 'ancient lore of men, the oldest that I know', as the wise Sibyl says at the beginning of her song. Comparison between the *Eddas* and the other sources also shows how right Kleemann was when he wrote: 'Local legends and fairy-tales are quite astonishingly reliable.'

This comparison, finally, also shows that Ragnarök and the Fall of Asgard do not belong 'in the spiritual realm of terrible religious struggles', but in the earthly realm of terrible natural disasters.

Where was Asgard?

Asgard was a very earthly city; it was flooded over by the sea; subsequently the island upon which it stood re-emerged from the waters, and Vidar and Vali 'shall dwell at Ida Plain, where Asgard was before' (*Gylfaginning* 53). Of Asgard it is said: 'That house is the best made of any on earth, and the greatest' (*Gylfaginning* 14). All this indicates that some earthly construction served as model for Asgard.

But where was Asgard?

The *Eddas* gave many clues. For instance, we find:

> How call they the isle where all the gods
> And Surtr shall sword-sweat mingle?
>
> *Fáfnismál* 14

So Asgard lay on an island.

To the east of this island lay a 'holy land', for we read:

> The land is holy   that lies hard by
> The gods and the elves together
>
> *Grímnismál* 4

From the east there pours   through poisoned vales (*eitrdala*)
     With swords and daggers   the river Slidr

Völuspá 36

In the *Grimnismál* the river Slidr is named in conjunction with another
river, Hrid (28). These are the old names of the Schlei and the Rheider,
along which ran the important shipping link between the inlet of the
North Sea which is today the Eider valley, and the Baltic (see page 64,
and *Olaf Tryggvason's Saga*). The Danish historian P. Grove was the first
to identify the river Slidr with the Schlei, and the Hrid with the Rheider.
He recognized the Eider valley in the '*eitrdala*'. Further on we find:

Eastward dwells the Old One   in Ironwood

Völuspá 40

In the inventory of King Valdemar II (died 1241), '*Jarnvith*' is the
name of the 'wood on the Jarne', as the river Treene was formerly called
(Gutenbrunner 1949, p. 65).

The place now called Janneby on the Treene (Jarne) was formerly
called Jarneby, and lay in the 'Jarnvith'. The Jarne (Treene) rises south
of Flensburg, and flows southwards, entering the Eider near
Friedrichstadt. So Asgard must have lain west of the 'Jarnvith'.

Other events also take place east of Asgard. Njord is sent east as a
hostage (*Lokasenna* 34); when Thor goes to war against the 'Jöten' he
invariably travels eastwards (*Völuspá* 50, 51). P. Grove identified the
'Jötnar' (generally translated 'giants') with the Jutes. Since the Jötnar
are repeatedly identified with the Danes, he may well be right. The
Jutes inhabited the middle of Schleswig, i.e. to the east of North
Frisia.

Further evidence is provided by the statement that Fenrir fell near
Asgard 'by the mouth of the river' (*Lokasenna* 41). Elsewhere we hear of
the 'turbid (muddy) streams' (*thunga strauma*) in the region stalked by the
Fenris-Wolf (*Völuspá* 39).

Of great help in localizing Asgard are the statements that 'In Asgard
before the doors of Valhalla there is a wood that is named Glasir'
(Neckel 1914, fragment 7, p. 314), for glasir means amber. In the
Helgakvida this wood is called 'Glasislund', amber wood. The fields
around Asgard are likewise known as 'Glasisvellir', amber fields. So
Asgard must have lain in the region of the amber islands, which the
Romans called 'Glaesariae', after the word *glas* = amber.

This serves to pinpoint the location of Asgard – or of that shrine
which served as a model for it. It was in the region of the amber islands,
at the mouth of the amber river, west of Jarnvith, and of the rivers Slidr
and Hríd, in the 'turbid streams' i.e. among the sand or mud banks. This
'holy island' was overwhelmed in the disasters of the thirteenth century
BC, when the sea 'storm-driven seeks heaven itself' (*Hyndluliód* 39), but

rose again from the waves and was later once more known as a 'holy island', a 'holy land' or '*terra sancta*'.

So the *Eddas* are a kind of Germanic Atlantis document; that is to say, an account of the site of the 'holy island' in the amber region in the Bronze Age; of its 'Golden Age', of its destruction in a world-wide conflagration and flood, and of its re-emergence at a later time.

Besides these, there are yet further correspondences between the two 'Atlantis documents'. For example, 'They made for themselves in the middle of the world a city which is called Asgard; men call it Trója' (*Gylfaginning* 9); see Reuter 1921, p. 20). The temple on Atlantis was laid out in the form of a troy-town or *Walburg* (see page 83). In the midst of Asgard stood the *mjöt-vithr*, the 'measuring-tree' also known as the 'ash Yggdrasil' (*Völuspá* 2, 46, 47; Kummer 1961, p. 44). This is a symbol of the centre-pole or pillar of heaven. According to the *Eddas:*

> Now to glass (*gler* – amber)   the rock was grown
> Oft with the blood   of beasts was it red
>
> *Hyndluliód* 10

which is also reported of the pillars in the centre of the temple on Basileia. Beside this 'measuring tree' or heaven-pillar, the Aesir assembled; there they had their judgement seats, as we are told also of the kings of Atlantis.

That the 'holmr Asgard', the island of Asgard, was a centre of the cult of the heaven-pillar is shown by the name itself, which, like the name 'Aesir', derives from the word *ás* meaning centre-post or king-post. So 'holmr Asgard' means the island of the centre-post, or the island of the heaven-pillar. According to the *Eddas,* two springs flow there, called 'Mimis brunnr' and 'Urd brunnr' (*Völuspá* 5, 11, 33; *Gylfaginning* 15). The temples of Asgard are decorated with gold, silver and amber (*glass*). Of Asgard it is said: 'That house is the best made of any on earth and the greatest; without and within it is all like one piece of gold' (*Gylfaginning* 14).

Asgard is surrounded by a palisade (*bordveggr*), like the temple and palace on Basileia. Just as in the Phaethon story Phaethon fell into the mouth of the river Eridanus, so the terrible heavenly phenomenon Fenrir fell into the mouth of the river near Asgard, 'By the mouth of the river / the wolf remains / till the gods to destruction go' (*Lokasenna* 41). As in the territory of Atlas the Hesperides guard the golden apples (*Argonautica* 4. 1397), so Idun 'guards in her chest of ash those apples which the gods must taste whensoever they grow old; and then they all become young' (*Gylfaginning* 26). As the ten kings at their great *thing* wear long blue mantles, so Odin in Asgard wears the blue heaven-mantle. On both Basileia of Atlantis and on Asgard the highest *thing* and court of law were held; on both islands there were·golden 'tablets' with inscriptions; on both there was a great wealth of gold. On both copper ore was worked and amber found. Both sank into the sea and re-emerged.

That the submersion of Asgard, like that of Basileia, occurred about 1200 BC is shown by another piece of evidence as well as those already cited. The Hebrew word *kapthor* means precisely the same as the Germanic *ás* – supporting beam, king-post, the out-spread arms of the upper part of a pillar. The name *i kaphthor* is a literal translation of *holmr Asgard*; both mean 'island of the heaven-pillar', or literally, 'island of the top of the pillar', 'island of the heaven-bearing beam'.

The Philistines were known as Kaphthorites, i.e. 'pillar people' and this is also the meaning of 'Atlanteans', since the heaven-pillar stands in their country.

So the Bible's description of the Philistines, the leading tribe of the North Sea Peoples, the Atlanteans, as 'the remnant of the country of Caphtor' (Jer. 47:4) may be translated 'the survivors from the island of Asgard'. Because the time at which the Philistines entered Palestine is fixed beyond doubt between 1220 and 1200 BC, the *i kaphthor*, the *holmr Asgard*, must have sunk shortly before that time.

With the knowledge of the events which took place in the thirteenth century BC, we have the key to unlock an old problem.

It has repeatedly been noted by historians of religion, that the Egyptians, Israelites, Persians, Indians, Chinese, Greeks, Romans, Germanic peoples and many other nations in the most diverse parts of the earth, all possess an 'eschatological schema', i.e. a tradition about the end of the world and of mankind, which is astonishingly consistent. All these eschatologies mention a monstrous fiery apparition in the heavens, which is referred to as a 'fiery star', a 'fiery comet' or a 'ball of fire'. This phenomenon unleashes catastrophes on earth; the ground shakes, the sea overflows the land, fire falls from heaven, sun and moon are darkened, darkness covers the earth, blood rains from heaven, in southern lands there are enormous floods of rain; in northern areas or on high ground, equally great falls of snow. In the Parsee tradition, the 'great winter' lasts four years, in that of the *Eddas,* three. During this time the sun is darkened and there is no summer. Finally both gods and men die.

The similarities between the eschatologies of these different peoples have led to various hypotheses about which of them could have borrowed from which other. The Israelites are said to have had it from the Egyptians, or the Persians, the Persians from the Indians, the Indians from the Chinese, the Greeks from the Persians or the Hebrews, the Romans from the Greeks, and the Germanic peoples from the Old Testament prophets. There are as many theories as there are scholars.

But we can now see that no such borrowing took place; the

similarities have quite a different explanation. People all over the world experienced the disasters of the thirteenth century BC in the same way, as a kind of 'end of the world'. Those who survived were convinced that when the actual end of the world did arrive, it must repeat those events. So the eschatological schema consists of memories of that time projected into the future. These memories were frequently refreshed. Every time a comet appeared – and this happened repeatedly; Halley's comet returns every 76 years – then people feared that the whole series of events was about to repeat itself and bring the world to an end. So the tradition was constantly renewed, and thus, often in fixed formulae, preserved over the centuries. The similarity in the traditions is not due to borrowing, but to the fact that all these peoples had experienced the same events in the same way.

The myth of Ragnarök is therefore not, as Pipping, Neckel, Kummer and others conjecture, taken from the Old Testament prophets. It is a native, ancient, independent tradition of the catastrophes surrounding the destruction of the island of Asgard, and of its subsequent reappearance.

Various students of the *Eddas* have shown that the traditions concerning Asgard refer to the west coast of Schleswig-Holstein. Axel Olrik was the first scholar to point out that stories of flourishing lands that sink into the sea and later reappear are very common on the Schleswig-Holstein coast, but are not found elsewhere in the Germanic world. Later, Hugo Pipping examined the names which occur in the *Völuspá* and showed that 'within the Nordic realm, they occur only in southern Denmark' (quoted in Gutenbrunner 1949, p. 66f. – Pipping includes Schleswig-Holstein in 'southern Denmark'). Gutenbrunner came to the same conclusion: 'Part of the Schleswig-Holsteiners' traditions of the end of the world is preserved in verses 40–42 of the *Völuspá*' (1949, p. 67).

So the location of Asgard on the west coast of Schleswig-Holstein is in agreement with the opinions of German and Danish scholars. The riddle I began with is solved: 'What is the true meaning of these traditions, the age to which they should be dated, and the place to which they refer?' The tradition of Asgard contains memories of a holy island which sank into the sea about 1200 BC and later in part reappeared; and of the most sacred shrine of the Germanic peoples during the Bronze Age. This island lies in the amber region of antiquity, between Heligoland and the mainland, and is identical with 'Basileia', the 'sacred island' of the Atlantis narrative.

CHAPTER 7

HOMER AND ATLANTIS

The historical reliability of the Homeric epics

In antiquity many readers were tempted to try to discover the actual scenes of the various events recounted in the epics of Homer. The poet was seen as a god-like, omniscient being (Schadewald 1942, p. 51) and it was generally believed that in his poems he had described real events and places. Many islands and cities competed, not only for the reputation of being Homer's birthplace, but for that of being the island of Circe or Calypso, or the land of the Cicones or the Cyclops, or the Royal Island of the Phaeacians.

Later Greek scholars, however, gave up all attempts at localization. Eratosthenes (about 210 BC) coined the epigram: 'Whoever would find the places Odysseus visited, must first find the cobbler who made the leather bag where Aeolus kept the wind' (quoted by Strabo 1.24). For Eratosthenes, Homer had simply drawn all his stories from his imagination, and from many centuries, scholars shared this opinion.

Indeed, a century and a half ago, they began to see not merely the Homeric poems but Homer himself as a product of the imagination. The poems were analysed into numerous fragments, which were attributed to different hands and dates at the whim of the writer. So the poet was dissolved into a crowd of anonymous rhapsodists, and Homer dismissed, together with his subject-matter, into the realm of fable.

But a change was on the way. A passionate admirer of Homer, Heinrich Schliemann, appeared, armed with the conviction that the origin of the Homeric epics was not fantasy but history. Schliemann received the same sort of treatment as I did when I first made the same claim for the Atlantis document. Insults and wild accusations were heaped upon him, and he was openly called a madman and a fraud.

Among the antagonists of Homer, certain occupants of professorial chairs were especially prominent. Professor Stark, then 'a German authority' (Ludwig 1932, p. 187), described Schliemann's publication on Troy as 'a staggering piece of humbug'. When Schliemann exhibited his finds a museum director wrote, 'This man is a fraud!' The influential director of the Athens University Library wrote: 'After all, this German-American, who now promises us a house in which he wishes to display his finds, got his treasure-trove by smuggling. Perhaps he found these objects not in the earth but in a junk-shop? And what has he found? Pots! Who is to say his pots are not forgeries?'

A scholarly Mafia attempted to discredit Schliemann publicly, calling him a 'dilettante'. Among these gentlemen were some who totally refused to read Schliemann's work or to look at his finds!

But Schliemann, convinced of the validity of his researches, dared to defy the learned world of his time, to despise the insults of his opponents and to pursue his course undeterred. He had such confidence in the Homeric texts that he paced out, watch in hand, the distance from the foothills where, according to the poet, the Greek camp by the ships had been, to make sure where the walls of Troy would be found. From this he concluded that, contrary to tradition and learned opinion, Troy could not lie at Bunarbashi, but must be under the mound of Hissarlik. Here, although the learned world called him a fool and a fantasy-monger and condemned him for daring to take Homer's statements seriously, he began his excavations. And he found more than even he himself had hoped: he found the ruins of city walls and palaces; he found innumerable pots and shards; he found a treasure of gold, which he called 'the treasure of Priam'. Even though this turned out to be older than Schliemann had thought – the technique of archaeological dating was then in its infancy – it showed that Homer's Troy 'rich in gold' had indeed been found.

Of course the learned world tried to deny even this proof of the correctness of Schliemann's theories. There were suggestions that he had 'planted' the treasure; he was called forger, fraud, charlatan, 'fit for the madhouse'.

The archaeologist A. Furtwängler, father of the famous conductor, described Schliemann as 'a disagreeable fellow, muddle-headed and unstable' (Furtwängler 1965, p. 75).

Today Schliemann's researches are acknowledged everywhere. The scandalous behaviour of his learned opponents seems disgraceful; he is celebrated as the pioneer of Greek archaeology, and his battle with his scholarly enemies is played down. The great scientist Max Planck was right when he wrote: 'A new scientific truth does not become established because its opponents are won over and accept it, but rather because they gradually die out, and the rising generation is familiar with the truth from the start' (1948, p. 22).

The triumph of Schliemann was the triumph of Homer. He appeared now as *the* poet; in E. Drerup's phrase, 'the true, great and immortal Homer'. The climate of opinion on the historical status of the Homeric epics changed so radically that Professor W. Dörpfeld, Schliemann's collaborator, adviser and friend, could write: 'If in my book *The Return of Odysseus*, like Walter Leaf in his *Homer and History*, I have taken the Homeric epics as a priceless factual source for early history, I do so not with uncritical naïvety, but after long and serious study.' The Viennese archaeologist Professor Schachermeyr claimed: 'The Homeric epics must be utilized as a historical source, since, along with some material which is altered or inserted, they also preserve much accurate information on Mycenaean times' (1929, p. 56). If, then, in what follows I put more trust in Homer's geographical knowledge and descriptions than, in spite of everything, is generally done today, then I am only following in the footsteps of Schliemann and Dörpfeld, whose trust in the poet's factual accuracy was so uniquely vindicated.

In more recent times the conviction of the historical worth of the epics has received new confirmation from the decipherment of the Linear B script by Michael Ventris and John Chadwick. It is hardly necessary to say that both researchers, who were 'outsiders and dilettantes' were attacked and slandered by some scholars. For example, Professor B. Hrozný, a Czech scholar, who in his youth had earned a great reputation by his discovery, in 1914, that the Hittite language recorded in cuneiform script was Indo-European, wrote: 'This is nothing but madness and fantasy.'

The decipherment of Linear B gave a new impetus to Homeric studies. For it proved what had until then been held impossible, that the Mycenean Achaeans already spoke Greek, and that they had a script in widespread use. Until then it had been assumed they were illiterate; and yet the many thousand verses of the Homeric epics could only have arisen in an era when there was a writing system in Greece. The Greek alphabet was held to be the earliest such system, and that was supposed to have been introduced in the ninth or eighth century by the Phoenicians. Consequently it was thought that Homer had written at that time. As recently as 1952, Albin Lesky could write: 'Today we no longer attempt to date Homer at the end of the Mycenaean age' (1952, p. 54).

But now everything is changed. The decipherment, together with a quantity of new archaeological discoveries, transformed the situation. In 1967 the philosopher Dr Kahl-Furthmann published a book with the title *Wann lebte Homer?* ('When did Homer live?') in which she demonstrated, with a wealth of evidence, that Homer belongs to the Mycenaean age, and is many centuries older than the experts had until then maintained. Once again it fell to an outsider to solve one of the greatest riddles of antiquity. But once again it was professional academics and occupants of professorial chairs who described her work as 'insanity' and tried by every means to hinder its publication.

Finally, one professional scholar had the courage to declare his open support for the results of her researches. Professor Franz Vonessen of Freiburg wrote in 1969:

> This book proves that Homer is Mycenaean and about 500 years older than the consensus of Homeric research has hitherto allowed. Note: this book does not merely assert this, it *proves* it. It also proves that the *Iliad* and *Odyssey* each form a single whole, which, apart from a few interpolations, is of one piece throughout. This too is not only brilliantly argued; it is plainly demonstrated. . . . The proofs are striking, the supporting instances innumerable. No one can doubt it, but Homeric studies will need time to become open to the new discoveries, so that the whole truth can be assimilated. But let us take this as a touchstone, a test-case, to see how far an academic discipline of the present day is governed by the love of truth and how far it is under the rule of disputatiousness and vainglory.

Of the experts in Homeric studies who rejected Kahl-Furthmann's work and tried to prevent its publication, Vonessen wrote:

> But it must be remembered that blindness is notoriously no monopoly of the naturally blind; more often it is, in allegorical terms, the child of 'self-love enthroned', of received opinion, *doxa*: a small sprig of that tree of vice that springs either from *luxuria* (lust for power – thus in Livy) or sometimes from *superbia* (pride, arrogance), but is always closely entwined with *scurrilitas* (loutish mockery) and *rancor* (malicious intrigue). (Vonessen, 1969, p. 636.)

Kahl-Furthmann's researches have demonstrated that Homer belonged to the high period of Mycenaean culture, and thus that he could not have known anything of the destruction of the Mycenaean and Minoan civilizations in the cataclysms that occurred after about 1250 BC. He could have known nothing of the ruin of the great fortresses and palaces of Mycene, Tiryns, Knossos etc., or of the migration period and the many changes it brought. He lived, therefore, at a time when Basileia, the royal island of the Atlanteans, had not yet sunk beneath the waves but, as the Atlantis document tells us, was carrying on a flourishing trade, in amber (orichalc) and other goods. Amber merchants carried their precious wares to the southern lands, and great hoards of it are found in many Mycenaean tombs.

Naturally these merchants would have talked about the royal island in the North, where the amber, 'splendid gift of the gods', was dug out of the earth, and would have described it as a rich and fertile land. The descriptions of this island in Homer are so vivid and close to life, but also so foreign and un-Mycenaean, that Professor Kitto said: 'It is obviously a picture of something that he (Homer) has seen' (1957, p. 39). Now, I do not agree with Kitto that Homer had himself seen or walked upon this fortunate island. But in his description of it, he made use, as he did in other passages, of the topographical descriptions and sailing instructions which were available in Mycenaean times. Many scholars have pointed out that Homer used real models for his descriptions of places (Hennig 1934, p. 50) and was concerned so far as possible to incorporate into his work all the strange stories of far countries and seas that were current in his time, and to bring them into relation with the adventures of his heroes (Hennig 1934, p. 3). This applies particularly to his description of the royal island of Phaeacia.

The royal island of the Atlanteans and the royal island of the Phaeacians

In the *Argonautica* of Apollonius of Rhodes, the 'holy island of Electris' (the 'isle of amber'), which lies in the Cronian Sea (i.e. the North Sea) near the river Eridanus, is identified with the royal island of the Phaeacians. On this island reign the Phaeacian king and his wife Arete, and from here Hyllus had migrated with a party of native Phaeacians to the shores of the Cronian Sea, only to be later killed in the land of the Mentors. On the shores of the island, the Eridanus throws up great masses of amber; the inhabitants of the place are called alternately Phaeacians and Hyperboreans.

It is irrelevant for our purpose whether Apollonius took this identification of the Phaeacians with the Hyperboreans and the inhabitants of the amber island from the work of Pytheas, as D.S. Stichtenoth maintains, or from some older work, a pre-Homeric Argonaut epic. The important thing is simply that from a quite early date in Greece, the equation was made: royal island of the Phaeacians = holy island of Electris = holy island Helixoia of the Hyperboreans. In all probability the identification, like the description of the Phaeacian land, stems from the period when the amber trade flourished between Greece and the 'amber country of the ancients', i.e. in the golden age of Mycenaean culture, the fourteenth and thirteenth centuries BC.

Since, as I have shown, Atlantis is the amber country, it follows that Phaeacia and Atlantis are one and the same. The identity of these two 'royal islands' has already been noted by many scholars.

In the seventeenth century the Swedish scholar Olaf von Rudbeck (1630–1702) noticed the remarkable parallels between the descriptions of the two islands. Later writers, for example the American I. Donelly, the Germans P. Borchardt and R. Hennig, A. Schulten and F. Kluge, have also noticed how almost completely similar the two descriptions are. 'Between Homer's description of the land of the Phaeacians and Plato's story of Atlantis there are so many and such remarkable parallels that they cannot possibly be coincidental. There are solid grounds for deriving both accounts from some common source.' (Hennig 1934, p. 64.)

Hennig originally agreed with Schulten and placed Atlantis at Tartessus. However, since he became acquainted with my own work, he has changed his mind and agrees 'wholeheartedly' with my view that the Basileia of the Atlantis document is the same as the Basileia of the Phaeacians and the Basileia of Pytheas, which lay at the mouth of the Eider, between Heligoland and the mainland.

To demonstrate that the descriptions of Homer and Plato refer to one and the same island, Hennig drew up a list of parallels, which I have used and added to in the following table:

Of the royal island of the Phaeacians we are told that:	**Of the royal island of the Atlanteans we are told that:**
1 It lay in the Ocean (*Od.* 4.568, 5.275 ff., 12.1).	1 It lay in the 'real ocean' (*Ti.* 25a) 'opposite . . . the Pillars of Heracles' (*Ti.* 24d), 'in the Ocean' (Diodorus Siculus 3.56).
2 Phaeacia was in the North (see below – 'The Course to Phaeacia'.)	2 Atlantis was in the North, in the 'Atlantic sea' of the ancients.
3 The Phaeacians dwelled 'at the end of the world': they were the 'remotest' (*eschatoi*) human beings (*Od.* 6.23, 6.205, 6.280 etc.).	3 The Atlanteans dwelled 'at the end of the earth' and were the 'remotest' (*eschatoi*) of mankind (Diodorus Siculus 3.56).
4 Immediately in front of the island of the Phaeacians stood a steep cliff falling sheer into the sea (*Od.* 5.400f.).	4 Immediately in front of the royal island of the Atlanteans lay cliffs, which 'rose precipitously' from the sea (*Criti.* 118a).
5 The Phaeacian Basileia lay at the mouth of a great river (*Od.* 5.440f.).	5 The Atlantean Basileia lay at the mouth of a great river (*Criti.* 118a).
6 On the coast of the Phaeacians' royal island, near the water, there were hills and dunes (*Od.* 5.470, 5.475).	6 On the coast of Basileia, behind the cliff, lay hills and dunes, 'which came right down to the sea' (*Criti.* 118a).
7 Behind the hills along the water lay a fertile plain, 'the rich land of Phaeacia' (*Od.* 6.258, 13.322).	7 Behind these hills lay a flat, very fertile plain (*Criti.* 118).
8 The palace and the temple of Poseidon were not directly on the coast, but some way inland (*Od.* 6.317f.).	8 The palace and the temple of Poseidon were not directly on the coast, but 50 stades (9.2km) inland. (*Criti.* 115, 117).

9 The royal city was surrounded by high embankments and broad harbours (*Od.* 6.262, 6.8, 7.44f.).

9 The royal city was surrounded by high embankments and broad canals (*Criti.* 115).

10 The embankments were built of earth and high enough for a ship to sail through (*Od.* 6.264, 7.44f.).

10 The embankments were made of earth, and high enough for a ship to sail through (*Criti.* 115f.).

11 Before and behind the embankments lay a fine harbour, and the way through is narrow (*Od.* 6.264).

11 Before and behind the embankments was a harbour; the way through was so narrow that only one ship could sail through (*Criti.* 115).

12 A canal led across the plain and through the embankment and so made it possible to sail right up to the palace (*Od.* 6.264, 8.5).

12 A canal led across the plain and through the embankments, so making it possible to sail right up to the palace (*Criti.* 115).

13 The gods gave the Phaeacians *aglaá dora* = beautiful or shining gifts. The word *aglaá* comes from the root *glas* = amber.

13 On the royal island amber/orichalc was mined in a number of localities' (*Criti.* 114).

14 In the middle of the royal island stood a beautiful temple to Poseidon, and the palace of Alcinous (*Od.* 6.266, 7.85f., 7.135f.).

14 At the mid-point of the island stood a magnificent temple to Poseidon, and the palace of the high king (*Criti.* 115, 116).

15 The palace was magnificently adorned with gold, silver and copper, 'a radiance like that of the sun or the moon lit up the high-roofed halls of the great king' (*Od.* 7.85, 7.135).

15 The palace was magnificently decorated with gold, silver, copper and amber, and its 'size and beauty were astonishing to see' (*Criti.* 115).

16 The temple of Poseidon and the palace were surrounded by a wall (*Od.* 6.303, 7.113).

16 The temple of Poseidon and the palace were surrounded by a wall (*Criti.* 116).

17 In front of the temple of Poseidon stood golden statues (*Od.* 7.91).

17 In front of the temple of Poseidon stood golden statues (*Criti.* 116).

18 Perhaps the description of the statue of Poseidon in the *Iliad* 13.21 ff. is a memory of this statue. There Poseidon is described as: covered in gold, driving winged

18 Among them was a statue of Poseidon in gold and surrounded by Nereids and dolphins (*Criti.* 116).

horses and accompanied by sea monsters.

19 Bulls were sacrificed to Poseidon by the Phaeacian kings; the high king led the sacrifice (*Od.* 13.24, 13.182 ff.).

19 Bulls were sacrificed to Poseidon by the Atlantean kings; the high king led the sacrifice (*Criti.* 119).

20 The Phaeacian kings were not absolute monarchs like the Mycenaean kings; they had to take the opinion of their 'captains and counsellors' and hold assemblies (*Od.* 6.54 f., 7.189 ff., 8.11 f.).

20 The kings of the Atlanteans were not absolute monarchs like the Mycenaean kings; they had to take the opinion of their colleagues and hold judicial assemblies (see page 72).

21 The kings of Phaeacia drank from golden cups (*Od.* 8.430).

21 The kings of Atlantis drank from golden cups (*Criti.* 120).

22 Beside the temple of Poseidon was a beautiful grove and a garden with fruit trees (*Od.* 6.295, 6.321, 7.112 ff.).

22 Beside the temple of Poseidon was a beautiful grove and a garden with fruit trees (*Criti.* 117).

23 And with two springs (*Od.* 7.129).

23 And with two springs, a warm and a cold one (*Criti.* 117).

24 The Phaeacians loved a hot bath (*Od.* 8.249).

24 The Atlanteans loved hot baths (*Criti.* 117).

25 Surrounding the temple of Poseidon and the palace were meeting places and sports grounds (*Od.* 6.266, 8.5, 8.110). There were no sports arenas in Mycenaean Greece.

25 Surrounding the temple of Poseidon and the palace were meeting places and sports grounds (*Criti.* 117).

26 The Phaeacians exercised themselves in these sports grounds at 'boxing, wrestling, jumping and running' (*Od.* 8.100 f.).

26 In these sports grounds the Atlanteans exercised themselves in gymnastics of all kinds (*Criti.* 117).

27 Poseidon was the ancestor of the Phaeacian royal house (*Od.* 8.56 f.).

27 Poseidon was the ancestor of the Atlantean royal house.

28 One of their ancestors belonging to this line of Poseidon once led

28 One of the ancestors of this house once led the Atlanteans to their

the Phaeacians to their country, built them a city and surrounded it with embankments, built them their houses and temple, and shared out the farmland among them (*Od.* 6.7ff.).

country, surrounded their city with embankments, weaned the inhabitants from their lawless and animal life, and taught them farming (Diodorus Siculus 3.56).

29 King Alcinous was at the head of twelve lords (*Od.* 8.41, 8.390f.).

29 The high king of Atlantis was the leader of ten kings (*Criti.* 114).

30 The Phaeacians were all descended from Poseidon (*Od.* 7.205f., 13,130f.).

30 The Atlanteans were all descended from Poseidon (*Criti.* 114, 120).

31 The Phaeacians were the best sailors and had the fastest ships: 'They pin their faith on the clippers that carry them across the far-flung seas, for Poseidon has made them a sailor folk' (*Od.* 7.34, 7.320).

31 The Atlanteans were outstanding sailors; they had a fleet of 1200 warships (*Criti.* 117, 119).

32 The Phaeacians were of 'godlike nature', and are called the 'godlike Phaeacians' (*Od.* 6.41, 13.130).

32 The Atlanteans loved the divine 'to which they were akin' (*Criti.* 120).

33 'We ... come in contact with no other people' (*Od.* 6.205).

33 They were 'once unmixed with other, mortal stock' (*Criti.* 121).

34 The climate of Phaeacia was uncommonly favourable. 'There is never a time when the West Wind's breath is not assisting, here the bud, and here the ripening fruit' (*Od.* 7.119f.).

34 The climate of Atlantis was once extremely good; a gentle breeze blew constantly; they could harvest twice in the year (*Criti.* 115, 118; Diodorus Siculus 5.19).

This parallel treatment shows clearly that the royal islands of Atlantis and of the Phaeacians were identical. Certainly, mythological and fairy-tale elements have found their way into both narratives. That is all part of the traditional style of antiquity. The *Iliad* and *Odyssey* also contain many such traits, but nobody today would deny that they also preserve correct historical and geographical data. This has been repeatedly demonstrated by the excavations and researches of the last hundred years.

The same is true of Homer's description of Phaeacia. As Hennig said: 'A kernel of firm topographical fact underlies it' (1934, p. 60).

The correspondences between the two descriptions are so numerous
that one might suppose that Solon or Plato had used Homer's Phaeacia
as a model and copied from it. However, this idea can easily be shown to
be mistaken.

In the Atlantis document there are many statements that are not
found in Homer's account, and therefore cannot be taken from it. For
example, in the Atlantis document the colours of the 'cliffs that stood
before the island are correctly given as black, white and red; the distance
between the coast and the 'hill of no great size' on which the city stood is
given as 50 stades; it is reported that orichalc (amber) is 'mined in a
number of localities'; the world-pillar in the midst of the temple is
described. Finally, we are told of the destruction of the island by
earthquake and flood, and of the 'sea of mud' that replaced it. The great
military expedition of the Atlanteans through Europe, the successful
defence of Athens, the march of the Atlanteans through Asia Minor,
their alliance with the Libyans and Tyrrhenians and the assault on
Egypt, and so on, are all described. Besides, Solon stated that 'he and all
his countrymen were almost entirely ignorant about antiquity'
(*Ti.* 22a). All of which shows that Solon did not use any Greek source,
not even Homer's Phaeacia; rather, as we have repeatedly pointed out,
he drew his account from ancient Egyptian temple inscriptions and
papyrus texts. The two accounts are alike because both describe the
same place, not because one was copied from the other.

The same is evidently true of the tradition concerning the Hyperboreans. This was copied neither from Homer's Phaeacia nor from the
Atlantis document. Rather it is, as E. Jung stated in 1939, 'a very
ancient tribal legend' of the Dorians, 'which preserves accurately the
memory of the north European origins and southward migration of the
ruling classes in Greece and Rome' (1939, p. 33f.).

It is no argument to assert against the location of Phaeacia in northern Europe that Homer could not have had any knowledge of so distant
a region. We know that information about northern countries came to
Greece with the amber trade, which was at its height in Mycenaean
times. Homer evidently wove this information into his *Odyssey*. He sang
also of other northern lands besides Phaeacia; for example there are the
verses on the land of the Cimmerians (*Od.* 11.31 ff.) or those on his
journey to the Laestrygones:

> For six days we forged ahead, never lying up even at night, and on the
> seventh we came to Telepylus, Lamus' stronghold in the Laestrygonian
> land, where shepherds bringing in their flocks at night hail and are
> answered by their fellows driving out at dawn. For in this land nightfall and
> morning tread so closely on each other's heels that a man who could do
> without sleep might earn a double set of wages, one as a neatherd and the
> other for shepherding white flocks of sheep. (*Od.* 10.80 ff.).

Krates of Mallos (about 170 BC) pointed out that this refers to the short summer nights of the extreme northern latitudes. Hesiod had asserted that day and night are neighbours in the far north, where Atlas stands:

> Atlas, son of Iapetus, stands
> staunchly upholding
> the wide heaven upon his head
> and with arms unwearying
> sustains it, there where Night and Day
> come close to each other
> and speak a word of greeting
> and cross on the great threshold
>
> Hesiod *Theogony* 747-9

'Here we have described the short summer night so characteristic of the northern latitudes, which must have made a deep impression on travellers from the south... It is only natural to find in this passage a reference to the "white nights" of the north, as do Müllenhoff, Much, and most other commentators.' (Gutenbrunner 1939, p. 34.)

Odysseus describes the land of the Cimmerians as being by 'the deep-flowing River of Ocean and the frontiers of the world', i.e. in the North Sea. As Posidonius (*c.* 135–*c.* 50 BC) explained, 'The Greeks formerly called the Cimbri "Cimmerians"' (in Strabo 7.2). Plutarch too made it clear that the Cimbri and the Cimmerians were the same; this people, he says: 'Live on the farthest sea, in a dark and tree-covered land, where the rays of the sun hardly penetrate, in the neighbourhood of the north pole' ('Life of Marius' 11). Diodorus said of the Cimbri, who a few decades before his birth had attacked the Roman Empire and only in 102 BC been crushed by Marius at Aquae Sextiae: 'It was they who in ancient times overran all Asia [i.e. Asia Minor] and were called Cimmerians, time having slightly corrupted the word into the name of Cimbrians, as they are now called' (5.22). So the Cimmerians were identical with the Cimbri, whose home was the 'Cimbrian peninsula'.

Eratosthenes, arguing that the *Odyssey* was nothing but fantasy, accused Homer of placing in southern lands places and situations which could only be found in the extreme north. Strabo (first century BC) devoted almost the whole of the first book of his *Geography* to defending Homer against this charge. He argued that since his descriptions show a knowledge remarkable for his time of extreme northern latitudes, and since he even laid some of Odysseus's adventures in the North Sea, he must have owed his information to the Cimmerians themselves, who had at an early period raided Greece (quoted in E. Krause 1891, p. 37 f.).

Tacitus wrote in the *Germania*: 'Ulysses (Odysseus) also, in all those fabled wanderings of his, is supposed by some to have reached the northern sea and visited German lands, and to have founded and named Asciburgium, a town on the Rhine inhabited to this day' (ch. 3). Claudian also (fourth century AD) placed many of Odysseus's adventures in the North Sea (*In Rufinum* 133 f.); and Procopius (AD 500–562) agreed with him (*Histories* 4).

Modern research has reached the same conclusions as these Greek and Roman authors. F.G. Welcker published in 1832 a detailed study of the question, in which he concluded, on the evidence of many ancient authors, that Homer's Phaeacia must be in the North Sea area. He considered that these and other traditions came from the 'Hyperborean regions'. Later the distinguished Germanist E. Krause showed, by comparing Nordic traditions and legends with those that are preserved in the *Iliad* and *Odyssey* 'that we have here the very ancient traditions of a Northern people who migrated to the south' (1891, p. 38).

'What we have here is perhaps an old tradition which reached the Greeks in their original homeland, to the north of that which they occupied in historical times, when they were more closely connected with the Germanic peoples. Indeed we may see here traces of that Bronze Age Greek-German connection, with which we have already explained the appearance in Greek of the originally Germanic word *pyrgos.*' (Gutenbrunner 1939, p. 35.)

So, in agreement with Apollonius and the other writers, Phaeacia may confidently be identified with the 'holy island of Electris' in the amber country, and also with the royal island of Atlantis.

The course to Basileia

In order to show the astonishing knowledge that Homer had of the royal island of the Phaeacians, the easiest way will be to accompany Odysseus on his journey there, and in his experiences on the island.

For this journey, he had precise sailing instructions given him by the goddess Calypso, on whose lonely island of Ogygia he had stayed for seven years. Students of Homer have often noted that in the *Odyssey* there are sailing instructions that read like books of instructions for travellers, which must have existed at that time (Schadewaldt 1942, p. 76).

Clearly, Homer must have had before him such a descriptive account, or *periplus*, that gave exact instructions on the course to set, and the distances between the various islands and coasts.

The course would be given by the constellations or by the prevailing winds. The distances are reckoned by a sailing day (distance covered in twenty-four hours) of 1000 stades, i.e. 100 nautical miles. This can be worked out from the various distances given in the Homeric poems (Köster 1923, p. 179; Hennig 1925, p. 109; Hennig 1934, p. 42; Berve 1942, p. 62; P. Herrmann 1952, p. 172; Pauly and Wissowa 1912, s.v. '*Nachrichtenwesen*'). Other writers in antiquity also reckoned according to this average day's distance (Köster 1923, p. 179), which seems to be if anything too conservative an estimate. In the time of Herodotus they reckoned with a day's sail of 1300 stades; and in the *Periplus* of Scylax (fourth century BC) the distance from Carthage to the pillars of Heracles (8400 stades = 840 nautical miles) is given as seven days, which gives 1200 stades per day.

The information given in the sailing instructions which Odysseus received for his voyage from Ogygia to Phaeacia has been tested by experts. A. Breusing, former director of the School of Navigation in Bremen, stated that 'the nautical information in Homer is very intelligently thought out, and remarkably true to the facts' (1889). Hennig said of these sailing directions: 'The instructions of Calypso are – though admittedly one could not tell this at first sight – remarkably precise, so that even today any sailor by following them could hold a clear and accurate course. It is in fact one of the strongest pieces of evidence that Homer took his descriptions from life, and not from fantasy.' (1934, p. 44.)

Calypso's sailing directions are as follows:

> It was with a happy heart that the good Odysseus spread his sail to catch the wind and used his seamanship to keep his boat straight with the steering-oar. There he sat and never closed his eyes in sleep, but kept them on the Pleiades, or watched Boötes slowly set, or the Great Bear, nicknamed the Wain, which always wheels round in the same place, and looks across at Orion the Hunter with a wary eye. It was this constellation, the only one which never bathes in Ocean's Stream, that the wise goddess Calypso had told him to keep on his left hand as he made across the sea. So for seventeen days he sailed on his course, and on the eighteenth there hove into sight the shadowy mountains of the Phaeacians' country, which jutted out to meet him there. The land looked like a shield laid on the misty sea. (*Od.* 5.269 ff.)

To test this course, it is first necessary to find out what its starting point is. At the beginning of his voyage, Odysseus is on the island of Ogygia, which lies across a 'vast expanse of salt sea water' and is uninhabited by men. This island is also called the 'navel of the sea'. On it there is a great cave, in which the goddess dwells. The ancient Greek scholiast noted that Ogygia must have lain in the Ocean Stream. Strabo too said as much, and pointed out that there is nowhere in the Mediterranean where one could sail for seventeen days, with a following wind, without touching land. Distances of this kind are only found in the Ocean.

Ulrich von Wilamowitz-Möllendorf pointed out that the name itself, *nesos ogygie*, shows that it lay in the outer ocean, since *ogygie* and *okeane* have the same meaning. The French Hellenist Victor Bérard translated *nesos ogygie* as '*l' île de l' Ocean*', 'the Ocean island' – taking *ogygie* not as a proper name but as an adjective.

Now, outside the Straits of Gibraltar, which Homer calls Scylla and Charybdis (Breusing 1889, p. 66f.; Hennig 1934, p. 39f.; Schulten 1950, p. 57; Herrmann 1952, p. 162 etc.), there are the following islands: the Canaries, Madeira and the Azores. All of them have been suggested as being Ogygia (Hennig 1925, p. 41; 1934, p. 43; Schulten 1948, p. 683f.; P. Herrmann 1952, p. 126). But we may reject the Canaries and Madeira for the following reasons: (1) Ogygia is repeatedly stated to be empty of human habitation, but the Canaries and Madeira have been inhabited since the Stone Age. (2) Odysseus is told to steer, during the same night, by Boötes and the Pleiades. According to Villinger, in the summer, when Odysseus made his voyage, these two constellations are never visible on the same night south of latitude 35 (Hennig 1934, p. 44). So Odysseus must have been on an island north of latitude 35 – and this leaves only the Azores, which consequently must have been the starting point of his seventeen-day sail to Phaeacia.

There are other reasons for this identification. Odysseus had passed Scylla and Charybdis, which Hennig on various grounds identified as the Straits of Gibraltar. From there, after a voyage of nine days, he reached Ogygia on the tenth. According to the reckoning used by Homer, in nine and a half days he would have covered 9500 stades, or 950 nautical miles. This corresponds exactly with the distance between Gibraltar and the island of São Miguel in the Azores (952 nautical miles).

. Ogygia is called 'the navel of the sea'. This is in fact the old name of São Miguel. This island, with its 23,000 m high Pico Alto, bore, up to the eighteenth century, the title *umbilicus maris* (Wilamowitz-Möllendorf 1914, p. 1042f.; 1916, p. 497f.; Hennig 1934, p. 41), not merely on account of the shape of its old volcanic cone, but perhaps for another reason. The word *omphalos* was used by the Greeks to mean not only the navel, but any middle point. For example the stone on the race-track around which the runners had to turn – the mid-point of the course.

According to information kindly supplied by the Director of the School of Navigation in Lübeck, Dr Mein Harms, sailing ships when they used to go from Gibraltar to the North Sea ports, entered on an 'obligatory course' which led from Gibraltar to the Azores, round the latter and then north-east by east to the English Channel, and thence to the North Sea. This course was forced upon them by the prevailing winds and currents. For the Azores are the mid-point of air- and sea-currents which turn clockwise around them.

The Gulf Stream, which flows north of the Azores in a north-easterly direction, divides at Ushant: one arm flows through the Channel, the other is diverted southwards along the west coast of France and flows through the Bay of Biscay along the west coast of Spain to Gibraltar. There it turns westward, and circles the Azores, to rejoin the Gulf Stream once more. And since an 'Azores high' is an extremely common, indeed normal, meteorological condition, and since winds in the northern hemisphere move clockwise around an area of high pressure, the winds too on the west coasts of Europe generally blow from north to south. A sailing ship, if it attempted to sail up the west coast of Spain, would therefore be going against both wind and current, which would be time-consuming and also, because of the nearby coast, dangerous. But if it sailed *with* the normal winds and current, round the Azores, the voyage would be both quicker and safer, in spite of the greater distance. The Azores, with the Pico Alto forming a sea-mark visible from far off, form the *omphalos*, the mid-point, of this course, for north of the islands the ship will enter the Gulf Stream, moving north-east at 3 knots. In the Channel, with a west wind, the speed may be greatly increased – speeds of 15 knots have been recorded. The Gulf Stream north of the Azores is about 150 km broad, its dark indigo can be clearly distinguished against the cold bottle green of the northern seas, and 'in winter the temperature change across the current boundary is so abrupt that as a ship crosses into the Gulf Stream her bow may be momentarily in water 20 degrees warmer than that at her stern, as though the 'cold wall' were a solid barrier separating the two water masses' (Carson 1956, p. 142). It is therefore not hard for a ship to keep to the Gulf Stream.

The Mycenaean seafarers must have known this 'obligatory course' from very early times. This is not surprising, for we know that in the Neolithic period the bearers of the Megalithic culture from the North Sea area were sailing to Spain, North Africa and the Canaries, and taking their culture with them. And the seafarers who had brought tin from Britain or amber from near Heligoland to the Mediterranean must have taken this course in their northward voyage. When in the *Odyssey* (1.52) it is said that Atlas, ancestor of the Atlanteans, 'knows the sea in all its depths', this may be a reference to the knowledge of the sea that men owed to Atlas and his descendants. So it is likely that in Odysseus's sailing directions we have a most ancient description of the 'obligatory course' of ships sailing from the Mediterranean to the North Sea.

So the *omphalos thalasses,* the 'navel of the sea', was São Miguel in the Azores, which continued to bear this name as late as the Middle Ages.

When Odysseus began his voyage, there was an 'Azores high', with a 'warm and gentle breeze' (*Od.* 5.268), a 'following wind' (*ouron opisthen*) (*Od.* 5.167) from Ogygia. He had been told to steer by the rising of Boötes and the Pleiades. R. Hennig consulted an expert on prehistoric astronomy and discovered that at that period these two constellations rose 'almost exactly at the same point in the north-east (to be precise, north-east by east)'. Odysseus kept this course, the wind and current with him, right up the Channel and into the North Sea. The voyage lasted seventeen days. On the eighteenth he saw the cliffs of the Phaeacian coast coming into sight (*Od.* 5.279).

It can be objected that he must have passed through the Straits of Dover and yet there is no mention of a coast to either north or south. But this is true of other itineraries which Homer gave for Odysseus or the Greek fleet.

> We must accustom ourselves to the fact that on the voyage from the Syrtes to Sardinia there is no mention of Tunis or Sicily, just as on the way from Ismarus to Malea we are told nothing about the intervening islands. The poet is not writing a travel diary, with description of every routine stopping place, which any seaman knew already. He is concerned with the extraordinary and the unexpected, which even in a seafaring nation was not in everyone's experience. (Zeller 1959, p. 49.)

Homer was not a captain keeping a log, but a poet who made his – possibly fictional – hero experience all the adventures and visit all the coasts and islands of Mycenaean sailors' tales. Certainly there were itineraries, with sailing directions and descriptions of all the coasts with which the Mycenaeans had trading contact. A. Breusing (1889) and Schadewaldt (1942) have pointed this out. Homer has cross-fertilized these two strains; the factual information of the itineraries and the seamen's yarns that were told in the harbour taverns. So his work is a mixture of reliable geographical data, and the true or invented experiences of Mycenaean travellers. As I wrote in 1955:

> Homer has clearly used old travellers' guides from the Mycenaean age, but not stuck to them slavishly. His only object in most cases – indeed as far as we can tell at present, in all cases – was to give the direction, length, and destination of a voyage, but not to describe the coasts which the traveller passes *en route.* On the journey through the Mediterranean to Scylla and Charybdis (Gibraltar) Homer mentions none of the islands or coasts that one would have to pass. On the way from Crete to 'holy Ilion', too, none of the islands that lie between are mentioned. But who would doubt, on that account, that Odysseus went to Troy? (Spanuth 1955, p. 97.)

On the eighteenth day, according to the reckoning that Homer used for distances, Odysseus would have found himself 1750 nautical miles from Ogygia (São Miguel) and therefore about 10 nautical miles from Heligoland (São Miguel to Heligoland = 1760 nautical miles).

A good sailors' guide should include an accurate description of the coast towards which he is steering. In modern sailors' handbooks there are always sketches of the coastlines; the same was true of such handbooks in antiquity (Köster, 1924, p. 188).

The coast of Phaeacia 'looked like a shield laid on the misty sea' – a shield is a flat surface, from which a boss protrudes in the middle. It is easy to see this as a description of the cliffs of Heligoland (the boss) and the low coastline of Basileia behind it.

As Odysseus approached the cliffs, Poseidon – who had a grudge against him – noticed his arrival and struck his ship with a sudden storm. Odysseus was thrown up on to the rocks. Now follows a striking description of this great crag in front of the Phaeacian coast:

But when he had come within call of the shore, he heard the thunder of surf on a rocky coast. With an angry roar the great seas were battering at the ironbound land and all was veiled in spray. There were no coves, no harbours that would hold a ship; nothing but headlands jutting out, sheer rock, and jagged reefs. When he realized this, Odysseus' knees quaked and his courage ebbed. He groaned in misery as he summed up the situation to himself:

When I had given up hope, Zeus let me see the land, and I have taken all the trouble to swim to it across those leagues of water, only to find no way whatever of getting out of this grey surf and making my escape. Offshore, the pointed reefs set in a raging sea; behind, a smooth cliff rising sheer; deep water near in; and never a spot where a man could stand on both his feet and get to safety. If I try to land, I may be lifted by a roller and dashed against the solid rock – in which case I'd have had my trouble for nothing. While, if I swim farther down the coast on the chance of finding a natural harbour where the beaches take the waves aslant, it is only too likely that another squall will pounce on me, and drive me out to join the deep-sea fish, where all my groans would do no good. Or some monster might be inspired to attack me from the depths. Amphitrite has a name for mothering plenty of such creatures in her seas; and I am well aware how the great Earthshaker detests me.'

This inward debate was cut short by a tremendous wave which swept him forward to the rugged shore, where he would have been flayed and all his bones been broken, had not the bright-eyed goddess Athene put it into his head to dash in and lay hold of a rock with both his hands. He clung there groaning while the great wave marched by. But no sooner had he escaped its fury that it struck him once more with the full force of its backward rush and flung him far out to sea. Pieces of skin stripped from his sturdy hands were left sticking to the crag, thick as the pebbles that stick to the suckers of a squid when he is torn from his hole. The great surge passed over Odysseus' head and there the unhappy man would have come to an unpredestined end, if Athene had not inspired him with a wise idea. Getting clear of the coastal breakers as he struggled to the surface, he now swam along outside them, keeping an eye on the land, in the hope of lighting on some natural harbour with shelving beaches. Presently his progress brought him off the mouth of a fast-running stream, and it struck him that this was the best spot he could find, for it was not only clear of rocks but sheltered from the winds. (*Od.* 5.400f.)

Never has the 'rugged shore', with its 'jagged reefs' and 'smooth cliff rising sheer' of Heligoland been more vividly described than in these verses of Homer. Poseidon had sent his storm from the north (*Od.* 5.385) and so Odysseus was carried round the south point of the cliff massif into the mouth of the river that flowed through the plain behind it. Apollonius (see page 252) identified this as the amber river Eridanus, and gave the name of its god as Aegaeus.

Odysseus swam into the mouth of this river, where 'it was not only clear of rocks but sheltered from the winds'.

The poet evidently pictured the river as running from east to west, for only then could one of its banks – the north one – provide shelter from a northerly wind; and Odysseus had been sailing towards the coast from west south-west. The description fits the contemporary facts exactly, since the Eridanus/Eider then flowed into the North Sea immediately south of Heligoland and its course ran from east to west. Even today the old river bed can be seen clearly on every sea chart, engraved deep on the sea bottom. As late as the Middle Ages the god of this river, called Aegis or Ögis, was held in honour, and is said to have had a temple there (Jensen 1900, p. 100).

But before Odysseus could clamber ashore he had another problem. He had seen the flat shore of Phaeacia, without cliffs, and the current had carried him into the mouth of the river. Then, however, the direction of the flow changed and the hero was no longer able to swim against the stream to reach the shelter of the bank.

He prayed to the god of the river and a marvellous thing happened: the god checked the current, and it carried Odysseus in the opposite direction, to the land (*Od.* 5.451f.).

Eratosthenes, who considered that all Homer's stories were pure moonshine, picked out this description of the upward-flowing stream as clear evidence that the poet was a liar, 'since he made a river flow backwards, a thing quite impossible anywhere in the world' (quoted in Welcker 1833, p. 20).

Eratosthenes was wrong. On any coast where there are tides, the rivers flow upstream at their mouths twice a day. Hennig says on this point:

It must have seemed to them [the Greeks] miraculous that a river could flow backwards or, at high tide, stop flowing into the sea. The hero Odysseus owed his safe landing on Phaeacia to such 'miracle'. But in the Mediterranean such a thing is unknown. This seems to me to be the final proof. Nothing else shows so clearly that Homer must have seen an actual river . . . It is absolutely out of the question that a Greek could have described, purely by poetic inspiration, such a phenomenon as the tidal current in a river mouth, which occurred in no river known to him. This alone should be enough to show that in the description of Phaeacia we have no mere product of fantasy, but that the poet had factual descriptions, indeed remarkably precise and correct ones, available to him when we consider that Pytheas, 400 years later than Homer, was the first of the Greeks to study the ebb and flow of the ocean tides, and also the tidal currents and their effect on rivers – then the precise description in the fifth book of the *Odyssey* seems all the more amazing. (Hennig 1925, p. 52f.)

I agree entirely with this opinion and the following passages from this episode in the *Odyssey* will act as further proof: 'He unwound the goddess's veil from his waist and let it drop into the river as it rushed out to sea' – so Homer tells a few verses later on. Then he tells us how the next morning Nausicaa, daughter of King Alcinous of the Phaeacians, brought the laundry down to the river 'in which there was enough clear water always bubbling up and swirling by to clean the dirtiest clothes' (*Od.* 6.87). The phrase *kalon hydor*, which Homer used here, must surely be understood as 'sweet water', since everyone knows that salt water would not 'clean the dirtiest clothes'. So the next morning the river was no longer running with salt water but sweet. This could only happen in a river where during the flood tide salt water is driven into the mouth, while at ebb tide sweet water flows out.

At another place Homer says that there was 'high water' in the harbour, so the Phaeacians chose that time to launch their ship into the 'deep water' (*Od.* 8.50f). This seems to show that there was also 'low water', when they could not have done so.

So the account which Homer had before him clearly described the tides, and the tidal current on the coast of Phaeacia; all this supports the idea that he was using an itinerary of the time.

Recently, Professor K. Bartholamäus of Düsseldorf has checked once more the astronomical and nautical data given in the sixth book of the *Odyssey,* and sent the results of his calculations to me in a twenty-page article. In his covering letter (12 February 1976) he said:

An important supporting argument [for the thesis that Phaeacia is the island beside Heligoland] is the course followed by Odysseus. I have therefore personally checked it, and tests at the planetarium at Bochum support my calculations. There is only one possible course, one possible landing point.

The centre of both constellations (centre of Boötes = Izar, centre of Pleiades = Alcyone), always points to 55 degrees, which leads from the Azores through the English Channel in the direction of Heligoland.

I should like to record here my thanks to Professor Bartholomäus for so thoroughly testing and confirming the older calculations.

The description of the royal island of the Phaeacians

Of the many experiences and adventures which Homer makes his hero Odysseus go through in his ten years of wandering, one of the most delightful is his encounter with the 'white-armed Nausicaa', daughter of the king of Phaeacia. The poet describes the whole episode with particularly loving care, and gives more wealth of detail in his description of the Phaeacians' country than about any of the other coasts or islands that Odysseus visits. It looks as though he had particularly full and accurate information about the place.

Several students of early German literature have been struck by the resemblance between the story of Nausicaa and the German story of Gudrun, told in the medieval poem of the same name. André Moret, Professor of Germanic Studies at the University of Lille, said that 'Gudrun is the Nausicaa of the North' and gave it as his opinion that both legends are native to the peninsula of Jutland. R. Wisniewski also noted the similarity between the two stories, and claimed, on the evidence of the place-names, to locate the action of *Gudrun* on the coast of North Frisia. S. Gutenbrunner said, '*Gudrun* is a prehistoric legend put into verse', and considered that it comes 'from the German-Danish frontier area' perhaps near Haithabu (1949, p. 86). The learned Germanist J.K. Eggers pointed to some of the names occurring in the Gudrun poem, such as Holzanelant = Holstein, Dietmers = Dithmarschen, Abalie = Abalus; 'From this series of names one is led to think of the Insulae Saxones of the Romans and of the island of Abalus which was known to the Greek Pytheas' (Eggers 1968).

So we come back to the same island upon which the story of Nausicaa is laid: Basileia/Abalus, between the mainland and Heligoland.

In both stories, it is told how the daughter of the king of the country goes down to the shore early in the morning to wash the family clothes. Both Nausicaa and Gudrun meet shipwrecked strangers on the shore; in each case the castaway is taken by the princess to her father, to whom he reveals his identity.

We are not concerned here with the legendary or fairy-tale motifs, but with the many accurate details about life on the island of the

Phaeacians, which Homer may have owed either to a pre-Homeric epic about the Argonauts, or to amber merchants of the Mycenaean age.

After he landed on the river bank, Odysseus threw back into the water the veil of the sea goddess Ino, by whose magical power he had been saved.

L. Radermacher pointed out that this is reminiscent of an old Norse fairy-tale in which a shipwrecked hero is rescued by the veil of a mermaid and then throws it back into the sea, as he had promised (Radermacher 1915, p. 178ff., Pauly and Wissowa, 2nd ed. 1894, s.v. '*Phäaken*').

After his rescue the worn-out Odysseus climbed the slope near the river. Low hills near the coast are also mentioned in the Atlantis document (*Criti.* 118). They must be the diluvial hills of sandy geest, which form the Südstrand ridge and stretch from east to west near the former bed of the river Eider. Homer here used the unusual word *klitys*, which is related to the Old Frisian and Danish world *klit*, meaning a hill sloping down to the sea.

Beyond the hills Odysseus saw the 'rich Phaeacian land' lying before him. The city, however, was so far off that he could not see it. He fell into a sleep of utter exhaustion and did not wake till the middle of the following day when he was roused by the cries of Phaeacian maidens, who had come down to the beach with Nausicaa and were amusing themselves by playing ball. Odysseus left the bush in which he had been sleeping, approached the terrified girls and begged for clothing and help. 'Muddied from the sea he made a gruesome sight' (*Od.* 6.137) – there seems to be a reference here to the 'sea of mud'.

Nausicaa took pity on him, gave him clothes and drove with him to the city on her wagon.

The two animals which drew the wagon are referred to as 'mules', *hemionoi*. I pointed out in Chapter 1 that in Egyptian, Hebrew, and Greek texts, the 'Nordic stiff-maned horse' is referred to as a 'mule', because of its typical bushy mane and stocky build.

The journey to the city took till sunset (*Od.* 6.321). The royal city of the Atlanteans was 50 stades (9.2 km) from the coast. The way led through 'honey-sweet meadows' – this could refer to the honey-sweet white clover which grows in the marshlands of the Frisian coast. Odysseus saw along the road 'fields and the works of men' (*agrous kai erga anthropon*); perhaps among the 'works' were the canals and water channels which according to the Atlantis document criss-crossed the fertile plain.

Finally Nausicaa, Odysseus and the maidservants came to the tall embankments (*teichoi*) which surrounded the royal city (*Od.* 6.262).

The construction of these embankments is further described later;

they were 'long and lofty' and 'surmounted by palisades' (*Od.* 7.44).
Within and without them lay an excellent harbour, and the way
through is narrow (*Od.* 6.263). The embankments of Basileia in Atlantis
are described in just the same way, and in the *Argonautica* of Apollonius
we hear of 'towered ramparts' around the Phaeacian capital, which he
also calls the island of Electris (4. 1182). Round Asgard also there was a
bordveggt, i.e. a palisade or stockade (see page 210). The narrow entrance
through the embankment must have had a bridge over it; in North
Frisia today this is known as a 'covered sluice'. This is also described in
the Atlantis document: 'At the bridges they made channels through the
rings of land which separated those of water, large enough to admit the
passage of a single trireme, and roofed over to make an underground
tunnel' (*Criti.* 115). When on the holy island of Electris, where Antinous
ruled, these embankments are described as 'towered', then these
'towers' are surely the built-up bridges over the 'covered sluices'.

   In the following verses of the *Odyssey,* the various features of the city
are described, just as in the Atlantis document: the temple of Poseidon,
surrounded by the market place (6.266), the royal palace nearby
(6.301), the sacred grove (6.291, 7.112f.), the two springs (7.129), the
sports areas (8.5ff., 8.110ff.) and the moorings and boat-houses of the
Phaeacians (6.265ff.). But even in these descriptions it is evident that
Homer was not using the Atlantis document as a model, but that the
correspondences arise from their both describing accurately the same
things.

The seafaring of the Phaeacians

Homer had high praise for the Phaeacians' seamanship. 'They pin their
faith on the clippers that carry them across the far-flung seas, for
Poseidon has made them a sailor folk' (*Od.* 7.35) and they have
'extraordinary skill in handling ships at sea' (*Od.* 7.108). The details
which he gave of their ships suggest that he had reliable information to
go on. He said they had boat-houses for them, which is stated of no other
people in the story. The Atlantis document too speaks of the '*neosokoi*' of
the Atlanteans into which even large triremes could be dragged.

   The ships of the Phaeacians are described as 'double-tailed'. This
description can be understood by looking at the pictures of the ships of
the North Sea Peoples – who are identical with the Phaeacians – on the
walls of Medinet Habu, or the Bronze Age rock scribings. There the
ships of the Northerners are shown with high 'tailed' stems at bow and
stern, so that they are indeed 'double-tailed'. According to Homer the
ships had masts which could be unstepped; and in the murals of Medinet
Habu, some of the Northerners' ships have had their masts taken down,
something that was never done on Egyptian ships. These pictures also

show that the Northerners had their own method of setting .the sail. It was carried on a single yard; the lower yard (the 'boom') was omitted. This yard was not lowered to the deck when the sail was no longer needed, as on Egyptian ships. Instead the sail was hoisted up to the yard by a special rope, the 'clew' or 'bunt-line', which could be done from the deck; and it then hung from the yard in swathes. This method of stowing away the sail is first found among this people. Köster, studying these ships as they are depicted in the Egyptian reliefs, concluded with almost the same words as those which Homer used about the Phaeacians: 'The Northern Peoples of the time of Ramses II were the most expert sailors of their day' (1923, p. 42, p. 52). This technique of furling the sail was used later by the Vikings, and continues to the present day: the sails of small fishing vessels are still managed in the same way.

Homer also said that the Phaeacians anchored their ships with the help of a pierced stone (*Od.* 13.77). Such stone anchors (*stjori* in Old Norse) were used during the Viking age and only much later replaced by metal anchors. When the Steingrund was investigated by divers in 1953, two large stones with holes bored through them were found; were these such stone anchors?

In the passage describing how the Phaeacians made a ship ready to sail, King Alcinous says: 'when they have all made their oars fast at the benches' (*Od.* 8.37) and a few lines later we find that they 'fixed the oars in their leather loops'. So the Phaeacians fastened their oars to the tholes with a leather thong, a method which is still in use in the North Sea area today.

These Phaeacians very clearly showed the 'wild joy in seafaring of the North Germanic peoples' (Schadewaldt 1942, p. 77), which was unknown to the ancient Mediterranean. For the peoples of classical antiquity seagoing was a necessary evil. Homer made even a god say: 'Who would choose to scud across that vast expanse of salt sea water? It seemed unending.' (*Od.* 5.100.) But he said of the Phaeacians that they 'joyfully sail to the farthest shores' and that they 'have no use for the bow and quiver, but spend their energy on masts and oars and on the graceful craft they love to sail across the foam-flecked seas' (*Od.* 6.270 ff.). In these words we catch the same delight in seafaring that shows, for instance, in the Old English poem 'The Seafarer' from the Exeter Book (about AD 870):

> Now come thoughts
> Knocking my heart, of the high waves,
> clashing salt-crests, I am to cross again.
> Mind-lust maddens, moves as I breathe
> soul to set out, seek the way
> to a far folk-land flood-beyond
>
> (Alexander 1966, p. 75)

These are almost the same words that Homer puts in the mouths of the
Phaeacians. The names too which he gives to the Phaeacian characters
are, as Schadewaldt (1942, p. 76) pointed out, peculiar, and show this
people's passion for the sea. They can be translated as: Topship,
Quicksea, Paddler, Seaman, Poopman, Deepsea, Lookout, Go-ahead,
Up-aboard, and Seagirt son of Manyclipper Shipwrightson. Such
names were not used elsewhere in classical antiquity, but in Old Norse
literature similar formations are common. We find there names like
Swift-sailor, Wave-breaker, Far-farer, England-farer, Jerusalem-farer,
Wave-nose, Cod-biter, Whale-belly and many others.

Sand-dune formation in Phaeacia

The sea brought the Phaeacians troubles as well as joy. Poseidon, we
learn, was angry with them for 'giving safe-conduct to all and sundry'
(*Od.* 13.174) and threatened 'that one day he would wreck one of our
fine ships on the high seas as she was returning from such a mission, and
would overshadow our city with a ring of high mountains' (*Od.*
13.175f.). At the time of Odysseus's visit the first part of this threat had
already been fulfilled – Poseidon had transformed one of their ships into
a rock near the shore – and the Phaeacians were terrified that he would
carry out the second part and surround the city with mountains.

The anxiety of the Phaeacians about these 'mountains' only makes
sense if they constitute a threat to their fertile land and their shipping.
Clearly the reference is to the danger from wandering sand-dunes,
which could cover the 'rich land of Phaeacia' and block the harbour.
Jessen put forward this interpretation: 'Does this not mean the danger,
always present on flat, sandy coasts, of great drifting sand-dunes? And is
not "mountains of Poseidon" a poetic metaphor for dunes?' Hennig
commented: 'I find this interpretation particularly happy' (1925, p. 61).

So the fields and the harbours of Phaeacia were threatened by dunes.
How terrible a danger this can be in the area where Basileia lay is shown
by the fate of the island of Trischen, which lay between Heligoland and
the coast of Schleswig-Holstein. Its fertile marshland was within a few
years covered completely by the shifting dunes. Meanwhile, since the
dunes which up to then had protected the coast had moved away, the sea
flowed over the land and destroyed it, so that only a small section of the
island now remains. The same danger seems to have threatened
Phaeacia; in the verses of Homer we hear plainly the people's fear of
these 'mountains of Poseidon'.

'In earlier times these dunes, known as the "white death", were a
terror to the inhabitants of North Frisia. In the course of the centuries
they have buried whole villages, broad meadows, tall churches and

solidly built houses, as at old List and Rantum.' (*Husumer Nachrichten*, 27 May 1976.)

Sports and games in Phaeacia

Just as the Atlantis document tells of the love of the Atlanteans for sports of all kinds, so Homer tells us how the Phaeacians loved sporting contests, games and gymnastic exercises. Alcinous the king says to his nobles: 'Let us go out of doors now and try our hands at various sports, so that when our guest has reached his home he can tell his friends that at boxing, wrestling, jumping, and running there is no one who could beat us' (*Od.* 8.100 ff.). And Laodamas, the son of Alcinous, says to Odysseus: 'Nothing makes a man so famous for life as what he can do with his hands and feet' (*Od.* 8.147 f.).

These words express the same 'competitive spirit' that we find among the Atlanteans. Contests of all kinds went on at the many sports grounds. Referees kept order and the competitions were watched by gatherings 'many thousands strong' (*Od.* 8.109).

As well as the sports listed above, we find mentioned discus-throwing, with a stone discus, and a particular form of ball game. The sort of large stone discus the Phaeacians used existed in the North in the Bronze Age, as finds have shown (E. Krause 1893, p. 35; Schröder 1914; Broholm 1953, p. 93).

The ball game, in which the Phaeacians showed great skill, filled Odysseus with amazement. He had never seen anything like it. Such ball games were extremely popular in the Germanic North in later times. Huge crowds gathered to watch these games, which were called *knattleikr, soppleikr,* or *sköfuleikr.*

Just as the Phaeacians held their ball game in honour of Odysseus, so in later times in the North it was customary to hold a great ball game in honour of a noble guest. As among the Phaeacians, the game was played between two teams. To this day such games, known as *bosseln,* are much appreciated in Dithmarschen and North Frisia.

The ritual dance among the Phaeacians

In discussing the temple of Basileia and the old legend that Poseidon himself had erected it in order to keep Cleito imprisoned there, I showed that it was probably one of those 'troy-towns' that were constructed in the Neolithic and Bronze Ages. Many of these troy-towns have traditions connected with them of a sacred dance, which was probably meant to represent the course of the sun. One would expect to find such a dance on Basileia; however, none is mentioned in the Atlantis document. But Homer described such a dance, called the 'sacred round'. In honour of Odysseus the Phaeacian king called on selected youths, particularly expert in the dance, 'to beat out the sacred round with their feet' (*Od.* 8.264).

We are told that the ground on which the dance was to be held was carefully measured out and smoothed over, and that the nine stewards watched over the dance as well as the games. Demodocus, the 'godlike singer' of the Phaeacians, stood in the midst of the dancers. That it was a sacred dance is shown by the content of the song which accompanied it (*Od.* 8.266 ff.).

Many centuries later, Tacitus mentioned similar dances by the youths of the Germanic tribes (*Germania* 24). Such dances were held in Germany up to the Middle Ages. A chronicler described the dance of the young men in Büsum in 1647:

> They dance, now in a circle, now crosswise past one another. Now they leap with great skill over swords; now they lay the swords together in a pattern not unlike a rose; now they lift them up, so that each dancer holds a quarter of this rose above his head. At last they entwine them together, with such art, that their king, as they call the leading dancer, may not only tread upon them but raise them on high with one hand. Truly, a most ingenious dance. (Heimreich 1666, p. 119.)

That the Phaeacians had such swords is clear from *Od.* 8.402, where Euryalus, the young Phaeacian who insulted Odysseus during the sports, gives him in atonement a sword, described as *aor panchalkeon* (*Od.* 8.403) – a phrase which is not used of any other sword in the whole epic. *Panchalkeon* means 'all of bronze', a remarkable expression, when we consider that at the time in question (the thirteenth century BC), the 'whole-handled sword' was very common in the Germanic area. This weapon, in which blade, guard and grip were cast in one piece out of bronze, would accurately be described as *'panchalkeon'*. The word *aor* for 'sword', which is not used elsewhere in Homer, is derived from *asfor,* which is related to the German word *Schwert* and the English 'sword'. It is worth noticing that in the Egyptian inscriptions of the thirteenth century BC, the swords of the Northern Peoples are described as 'all of bronze' and three or four spans long. Homer said that the Phaeacian sword was decorated with silver nails. This kind of decoration is found on many 'whole-hilted swords', of the period. On the island of Sylt, one was even found which had a hilt made of gold (Jensen 1900, p. 83; Bröndsted 1962, p. 50; Schwantes 1939, p. 371).

The art of weaving in Phaeacia

Homer described the Phaeacian women as they 'weave at the loom, or sit and twist the yarn, their hands fluttering like the tall poplar's leaves, while the soft oil drips from the close-woven fabrics they have finished. For the Phaeacians' extraordinary skill in handling ships at sea is rivalled by the dexterity of their womenfolk at the loom, so expert has Athene made them in the finer crafts, and so intelligent.' (*Od.* 7.105 ff.)

Among the precious gifts given to Odysseus was a marvellous linen cloth.

The great skill of the Germanic women of the Bronze Age in weaving, knitting and braiding has often been described. 'What tremendous skill there is in the textiles of this period! What was formerly seen as crude cobbling – for instance, men's tunics, apparently pieced together anyhow – turns out to be the product of extremely clever design.' (Schwantes 1939, p. 574.)

Indeed, the 'geometric' style of vase painting, which the Northern Peoples brought with them to Greece about 1200 BC, has been thought to be derived from weaving techniques.

> Semper has correctly argued that both the details and the general character of this style are derived from a particular craft, that of weaving. The threads crossing one another at right angles produce the linear character, the straight lines and angular forms of the designs. The fact that they used on their pottery designs based on the technique of a different craft, shows that we have here a survival from a culture and period in which weaving, braiding and knitting – done, naturally, by women – were the dominant crafts which set the style for all other attempts at figurative arts. (Conze 1870, p. 522.)

Conze thought that the characteristics of the geometric style in Greece grew out of the 'Nordic ornamentation of the Bronze Age' and said: 'So the makers of these ancient Greek vessels stand right on the artistic level of their Northern kinsmen, and we may confidently assume that this similarity is due to their common heritage of artistic skill.' This theory has been often repeated. Von Oppeln-Bronikowski, for example, said that the early geometrical style must be derived 'from very ancient weaving and braiding patterns from the North' (1931, p. 9).

That the Northern Peoples were famous from very early times for their skill in weaving linen, is shown by the Egyptian word *Tuimah*, or *Ta-mahu* for those peoples. *Ta-mah* means 'north-land'. Brugsch showed that the Egyptians called linen *mah*, so *ta-mah* is the 'land of linen' or 'land of flax' (Baranski 1903).

It may also be noted that Ramses III marks the Northern Peoples and their allies with a flax plant as a symbol of their northern origin

(Baranski 1903, p. 148), probably because flax, which is native to the oceanic climate of the North Sea and Baltic area, was principally grown by the people there and was characteristic of them.

That flax was already cultivated and woven in the Nordic culture area in the Neolithic period, is shown by a find from a house-site in Øxenberg on Fyn, where an ox-horn was discovered bound with a linen thread (Brøndsted 1960, p. 221).

The imprints of flax seeds have often been found on clay vessels dating from the Bronze Age. Clearly the seeds must have been added to bread or other food to enrich it with their oil. But the find at Øxenberg is the earliest evidence anywhere of the spinning of flax into thread. It may be assumed that during the following centuries this craft was improved and refined in the Nordic area. Tacitus mentioned that the women of the Germanic tribes wore 'outer garments of linen ornamented with a purple pattern' (*Germania,* ch. 17) and Pliny said that 'The German women know no finer stuff than linen' (*On Natural History* 19.9).

All these observations show that Homer was right in praising the skill of the Northern women in the art of weaving and the preparation of linen and woollen stuffs.

There is a whole series of further details about the Phaeacians in the *Odyssey* which probably derived from actual observation. For instance, among the Phaeacians food and drink were passed around 'sunwise' (i.e. clockwise) (*Od.* 7.183), a custom which is still strictly kept in North Frisia and probably has its origin in the cult of the sun and thus originates from the Bronze Age.

According to Jan de Vries, the Frisian words *warf* and *werf* derive from the root-word *hverbandrehen.* They can signify a whole range of varied meanings, including 'court of law', 'graveyard', 'dike or bank'.

> This suggests that these words originally referred not to a place but to a kind of movement. In the descriptions of the pagan Germanic 'guilds', known as *hvirfingr,'* which had the ritual banquet as the centre of their cult, the word *hvir-drehen* is used to mean the passing around of the consecrated mead-horn in the direction of the sun. It was this direction which ensured the beneficent power of the banquet. Here we can see the relevance of this circular movement to the sun, and thus to the sun-cult. . . . This sunwise circling movement, whether at a banquet, a court of law, or a burial, has a deep significance whose roots appear to lie in the cult of the sun. (De Vries 1934, p. 257 f.)

In the eighth book of the *Odyssey* we are told that the Phaeacians prepared a hot bath for Odysseus and then invited him to a banquet. There, each guest had his own table and his own seat. Exactly the same is reported of the Germanic tribes by Tacitus: 'After washing they eat a meal, each man having a separate seat and table' (*Germania,* ch. 22). (At Greek and Roman banquets the guests reclined round a single table.)

The Phaeacians' feast was held round the open hearth, which was kept burning all day. This too was reported by Tacitus of the Germans. Among Mediterranean peoples it was not usual, on account of the warmer climate. The Phaeacians had 'flaming torches' (*Od.* 7.101) to light the guests at their evening meal. The Northern Peoples had no oil-lamps, which were normal in Mycenaean Greece. So the Northerners did not, as Kahl-Furthmann supposed, forget the use of lamps during their migration to Greece; they never had them. No lamps for burning oil or fat dating from the Bronze Age have been found in northern Europe.

Golden ewers, golden cups and a copper cauldron were used in the palace of the Phaeacian king (*Od.* 7.172, 8.426, 8.430) just as they are also reported in the Atlantis document and as we know them from finds of the period in the Nordic culture area.

The Phaeacians knew the music of lyre and harp (*Od.* 8.98 etc.). The same is reported by Greek writers of the Hyperboreans who, as I have shown, are identical with the Atlanteans. Probably the instruments referred to are the *hrotta*, which is still used in Sweden under the name *Tannenharfe*, and the *win* or *winne*, which is closer to the lute, and was played in the North. Though examples of these instruments have not survived from the Bronze Age, it is nevertheless plain from the many *lurs* or trumpets which we have from that period that the construction of musical instruments, and no doubt the art of performing on them, was highly developed.

The place of honour in the king's hall was 'at the hearth', 'by the great pillar', 'in the midst of the hall' (*Od.* 6.305, 8.66). It was the same in later times among the Germanic peoples, and indeed this arrangement was usual in North Frisia up to modern times; this can be seen from the placing of the high-seat pillar directly by the hearth in the 'Osterfelder House' at Husum. 'The rectangular house with a central hearth is typical of the North' (Spiess 1934, p. 46).

Perhaps the palace of Alcinous was a 'ridge-pole house', i.e. one in which the long roof-pole was held up by one or more pillars. According to the well known expert on prehistoric building techniques, Saeftel, this style was in use in the Nordic realm in the Bronze Age. The house of the king of the Philistines at Gaza, whose roof collapsed when Samson pulled down the two main pillars, must have been the same type of construction. Saeftel pointed out the remarkable correspondences between the old Nordic type of house construction and that of the Philistines.

According to Homer's descriptions, the Phaeacians dressed in 'cloak and tunic' (*Od.* 7.234). Such cloaks and tunics, or kirtles, are known from finds of the Bronze Age, and Tacitus described them as the normal costume of the Germanic peoples of his time (*Germania*, ch. 17).

The Phaeacian king speaks of the three implacable sisters who spin the threads of men's lives. This is clearly a reference to the three Norns, who in later Germanic belief spin the life-threads of men and cut them.

Nowhere else does Odysseus receive such hospitality, and both Nausicaa and the 'grey old man Echeneus' describe it as a holy duty to entertain the stranger. This recalls the words of Tacitus: 'It is accounted a sin to turn any man away from your door. The host welcomes his guest with the best meal that his means allow' (*Germania,* ch. 21). And altogether the night banquet of the Phaeacians recalls the nightly feasts which Tacitus described (*Germania,* ch. 22).

The English classical scholar T.B.L. Webster, who together with John Chadwick published the results of the decipherment of the Linear B tablets after the early death of Michael Ventris, also noted the following points, comparing on the one hand the contents of the tablets and the finds in the Minoan palaces, and on the other the description in Homer of the position of King Alcinous and the decoration of his palace.

The Mycenaean kings had a divine character; they were honoured as gods or demigods (Webster 1960, 35 ff., p. 30 f.). In contrast to this theocratic system is the description of the status of Alcinous, who, while the chief priest of his people, did not himself receive divine honours but was merely *primus inter pares.* The Mycenaean kings had numerous slaves; Alcinous in Homer, and the kings of Atlantis in the Atlantis document, had not. The thrones of the Mycenaean kings were surrounded by figures of lions, sphinxes and gryphons. In the house of the Phaeacian king there is no mention of such symbolic 'royal beasts'. There are only gold and silver dogs, which Hephaestus had made for the home of Alcinous, standing on either side of the door (*Od.* 7.91 f.). This recalls the hound Garmr who stood as watchdog before the gates of Asgard (*Völuspá* 44, 49, 58; *Grímnismál* 44).

So the verses of Homer's Phaeacian episode contain details which, taken separately, would be of little weight, but together convey an inescapable impression that the poet was using remarkably accurate information in describing the island. Not only do the general statements about this northern land and its people stand up to investigation, but also apparently minor details – palisaded embankments, sand-dune formation, boat-houses, 'all-bronze' sword, skill in weaving – are historically correct. Since most of these details are lacking in the Atlantis document, we have added support for the assumption that Homer must have had as his source, not the Atlantis document, but some other highly reliable account. Indeed, according to Tacitus, 'Ulysses . . . in all those fabled wanderings of his, is supposed by some to have reached the northern sea and visited German lands' (*Germania,* ch. 3).

The English author Ernle Bradford published in 1964 a book entitled *Ulysses Found,* in which he identified Phaeacia as Corfu. I have myself sailed around the coasts and islands of the Aegean and Ionian seas and can therefore claim to be in a position to judge Bradford's statements. His adventures *en route* make entertaining reading, but his identifications of the coasts and islands of the Mediterranean with those visited by Odysseus do not stand up at any point. One would have to write an entire book to refute them. To start with, he has completely overlooked the fact that the wanderings of Odysseus, and in particular the voyage to Phaeacia, are set in the outer Ocean, not in the Mediterranean.

Nothing in Homer's account of Phaeacia matches Corfu. There is no stretch of the Mediterranean where one could sail for eighteen days, as Odysseus did on his way from Calypso's island, with following winds and currents on a north-east course. From Cape Colonne one would reach Corfu, steering Odysseus's course of north-east by east, after 120 nautical miles. A ship which took eighteen days to do this would be travelling at 6.5 nautical miles per day. I have sailed in this precise direction to Corfu and, with its many mountain peaks, one over 900 m high, it does not look 'like a shield laid on the misty sea' but like a jagged mountain top. On Corfu there is no river with a tidal current, no broad water-channel leading from the coast to the city, no broad fruitful plain. Archaeologists have shown that there was a small population there in Mycenaean times, but no great royal city, no temple of Poseidon, no race-courses, no embankments 'which were surmounted by palisades and presented a wonderful sight' (*Od.* 7.44) as we are told of the city of the Phaeacians.

Corfu was not, for the Achaeans of the Mycenaean age 'the end of the earth', nor were its people 'the outposts of mankind' (*Od.* 6.203 etc.). Finds of amber in many Mycenaean tombs and Mycenaean finds in the Nordic area show that they traded as far as the North Sea coasts; and finds of their wares in southern France, Sicily, Egypt and Asia Minor show that their horizons reached much further than Corfu – they knew perfectly well that it was not 'the end of the world'. Rather, like later Greek and Roman geographers, they believed that the earth ended on the coasts of the North Sea, the Cronian Sea, the Hyperborean Ocean. So Phaeacia cannot be Corfu (P. Herrmann 1952, p. 126).

The sailing directions to the land of the Phaeacians, the description of the island with its many correspondences with that of Basileia on Atlantis and the fact that Apollonius of Rhodes identified Phaeacia with the 'holy island of Electris' at the mouth of the Eridanus (upon which amber and copper were found) can leave no doubt that what Homer described is the royal island that once lay at the mouth of the Eider in the shelter of the cliffs of Heligoland. Homer described not only 'holy Ilion' but also the 'holy island' of the North Sea Peoples in his immortal verses. It is his verses and not those of Albinovanus Pedo which are the oldest known on the subject of the North Sea (Nissen). They are part of a '*Germania*' of the

Bronze Age, from that golden period of Nordic culture before it was destroyed by the terrible catastrophes of the thirteenth century. If we compare his description with the reality, as it remains today and as it is recorded elsewhere, then we cannot help but exclaim of this great singer of Europe, as he himself said of the bard of the Phaeacians when he sings of 'holy Ilion': 'It is wonderful how well you sing the tale – almost as though you had seen it all yourself!'

CHAPTER 8

MISTAKEN ATTEMPTS AT DATING AND LOCATION

No other story from antiquity has attracted so many attempts at dating and location as the Atlantis document.

> Two millennia have passed since that evening in ancient Athens when Plato's friend Critias told the story which Solon himself had brought home from Egypt, the story of Atlantis, the land that sank beneath the sea. Through twenty centuries wise men and fools, story-tellers and poets, philosophers and scholars, heretics and church fathers, have argued the question: did Atlantis really exist, or was it simply an ornament to Plato's discussion on political and economic organization; a fable invented in order to set the free, democratic Athens up against an authoritarian conquering power, which made the earliest attempt at the *Gleichschaltung* of Europe - to use a modern term - and almost succeeded? (Pettersson 1948, p. 1.)

Pettersson called the Atlantis document 'the most thoroughly argued-over of all stories' and spoke of 'countless attempts at explanation'. The attempts to explain Atlantis, and to date and locate it, are indeed 'countless'. 'Since Plato's day approximately 20,000 volumes have been written on the Atlantis theme, though no one has yet been able to prove the existence of this mythical continent' (*Ceram* 1949, p. 405). Whether there are indeed 20,000 volumes on Atlantis is not important. It is certain that the theme has gripped men of every culture with a peculiar fascination.

Out of all the enormous number of Atlantis hypotheses, only the most recent and important can be discussed here.

Atlantis as Thera or Crete

Recently the hypothesis has been put forward several times that Atlantis, or the royal island of Atlantis, is identical with Thera, or Crete. On 17 November 1975, many newspapers carried a report that the

Greek government was about to finance, with 1.8 million dollars, a large-scale diving expedition by Jacques Cousteau in his special yacht *Calypso*, in order to search for traces of Atlantis in the extinct volcanic crater of Santorin-Thera. 'Since the remains of the drowned civilization have been hard to reach, owing to the depth of the water (300 m) this theory has up to now not been supported by concrete evidence' (*Die Welt*, 17 November 1975).

The Greek archaeologist Spiridiou Marinatos was the first, in 1938, to put forward the theory that what underlay the legend of Atlantis was the fall of the Minoan civilization of Crete at the end of the Bronze Age.

The Greek seismologist Angèlos Galanopoulos took it up and in 1960 published a modified version in which he suggested that the royal island of Atlantis was identical with Thera, and that Basileia with its harbours and canals had once lain where the caldera, the vast water-filled crater, now is. It had been destroyed in the monster eruption of the Thera volcano at the end of the Bronze Age. 'Perhaps traces of the harbours or the canals that Plato described will be found in the depths of the crater of Thera' (quoted in Mavor 1973).

In 1969, the American oceanographer James W. Mavor Jr took up this idea, and published a book, *Voyage to Atlantis*, which appeared in a paperback edition in 1973. Also in 1969 the English scholar J.V. Luce published a book, with the title *The End of Atlantis*. J. Rehork, the German translator of Luce's book, has argued vehemently that it has proved that Atlantis is identical with Thera, and Basileia with Crete.

Whether the identification is with Crete or Thera is immaterial: both hypotheses are quite untenable and can easily be refuted, even though they were greeted in 1969 as 'a breakthrough' in archaeology, and Luce's book was acclaimed with the words: 'history's greatest riddle solved!'

Those who would look for Basileia 'in the depths of the crater of Thera', have fallen victims to a gross logical error. 'It [the island of Thera-Santorin] was once about ten miles in diameter, and was covered by cone-shaped peaks whose sides were scored by steep ravines. In the centre was a summit of perhaps 1600 metres in height.' (Luce 1959, p. 58) 'The Thera caldera was formed as a result of a great eruption, or series of eruptions, which wrecked the island' (Luce 1969, p. 58–9.) Now, the German geologist Hans Reck confirmed in 1936 what had been pointed out by the French geologist Fouqué in 1879: the formation of the crater was due to the last and most terrible of the Bronze Age eruptions. This is shown by the fact that in this final, gigantic explosion, the great layers of lava, 60 m thick, were laid on top of the remains of the old tertiary volcano. In other words, before this last eruption, which left the crater, there stood on the spot the 1600 m high main volcanic cone. The crater itself was formed by this eruption and did not exist before it.

Now, the Basileia of Atlantis, with its three harbours and its canals, which were laid out by Poseidon at the beginning of time, and its rivers, is supposed to have lain in this crater – *before* the great explosion, when the crater did not exist. And yet a port could hardly be built on top of a 1600 m high volcanic cone.

It is amazing that the many writers who have swallowed this hypothesis have not recognized the obvious fallacy on which it is based.

Moreover, none of the other facts that we have about Basileia or the kingdom of Atlantis fit either Thera or Crete.

Neither Thera nor Crete lies in the 'Atlantic sea' but in the sea of Crete, which is clearly referred to in *Criti.* 111a and is obviously not the 'Atlantic sea' of *Ti.* 24. Neither island lies at the mouth of a great river; neither was 'swallowed up by the sea and vanished' (*Ti.* 25d); the Aegean never became 'impassable to navigation' (*ibid.*); Solon and Plato could never have said of the Aegean that passage there was hindered by 'impenetrable mud' (Criti. 108e) for both had sailed through it – their contemporaries would have laughed at them if they had made such an absurd assertion.

Luce has ignored the statement, repeated twice over, that where Basileia sank there was an 'impassable sea of mud', because he knows well that the Aegean had been navigable for as far back as memory reached, and all its coasts and islands were well known to the Greeks. These, and all the other statements – about the mining of amber and copper, about the *koine*, the community, between Atlanteans, Libyans, Tyrrhenians, the inhabitants of Gadira and the many other islands in the Ocean, about the great military expedition through Europe and Asia Minor to Egypt, and the successful resistance of Athens etc., etc. – all these fit neither Crete nor Thera. In fact this 'great breakthrough in archaeology' is a bubble that burst long ago.

Atlantis as Tartessus

Another hypothesis is that of the German archaeologist Adolf Schulten. 'Plato has described the capital of Atlantis and its province near Tartessus, and thus given an imaginative picture of the rich and fortunate city of Tartessus, at the mouth of the Guadalquivir' (1930, p. 342). Schulten's hypothesis, first published in 1922, has found wide acceptance among German scholars. Professor Jessen expressed the view that 'Schulten's identification, Atlantis = Tartessus is the egg of Columbus' (1925, p. 185).

But one can bring many arguments against this hypothesis. Schulten asserted that the destruction of Tartessus around 500 BC by the Carthaginians, on account of 'trade rivalry', was transformed into the sinking of Atlantis into the 'sea of mud'. After its destruction the city 'vanished abruptly from the historical horizon of the Mediterranean peoples'. But Solon, who brought the story from Egypt in 560 BC, would hardly have known that sixty years later Tartessus was due to be destroyed by the Carthaginians. In any case, it is not true that Tartessus suddenly vanished from the knowledge of the Mediterranean peoples. Many writers in the centuries *after* 500 BC mentioned it. Herodotus (died *c.* 420 BC) did so several times (*History* 1.163, 4.152, 4.192); Aristophanes (*c.*450–*c.* 385 BC) praised the taste of 'Tartessian morays' (*Frogs* 475); Rufus Festus Avienus (fourth century AD) spoke of Tartessus and called the Guadalquivir 'Tartessus river'. Pliny (*On Natural History* 4.120) also wrote about it, as did many other Greek and Roman authors.

Schulten himself admitted 'there is no doubt of the identity of the Biblical Tarshish with Tartessus' (1950, p. 21). Now Tarshish/Tartessus is frequently mentioned in the Bible, including books – Esther, Judith, Jonah – which were certainly written after 300 BC.

The Mediterranean peoples continued through the centuries to trade with Tartessus, in spite of Schulten's assertion, since it was a centre of the tin and silver trade (Haussig 1955, p. 645). Avienus, who had accurate information about the area from Britain to the south coast of France, and made use of a lost Greek *periplus* in writing his book *Ora Maritima*, said: 'Here are the pillars of Hercules, and here is the city of Gades, which was formerly known as Tartessus' (265).

So there is no doubt that Tartessus is identical with Gadir, present-day Cádiz, and the Gadira of the Atlantis document, which never disappeared from the knowledge of the Mediterranean world.

Equally false is Schulten's assertion that the Carthaginians had closed the Straits of Gibraltar, and that this is the origin of the passage in the Atlantis document: 'The sea in that area is to this day impassable to navigation, which is hindered by mud just below the surface, the remains of the sunken island' (*Ti.* 25d).

The Straits of Gibraltar were never closed. Herodotus described a voyage of Hanno to the west coast of Africa, shortly after 500 BC and continued: 'Somewhat later than Hanno's journey was that of the Persian Sataspes, who set out through the Pillars of Heracles, in order to circumnavigate Africa' (*History* 4.43). Pytheas of Massilia sailed through the Straits about 350 BC. Posidonius stayed for a month at Gades in 90 BC and said nothing to suggest that the Straits had ever been closed.

There is nowhere any evidence that the Carthaginians ever barred the Straits of Gibraltar, apart from this one misinterpreted passage.

So, when Schulten wrote that apart from this passage 'everything else is sheer fantasy' (1948, p. 12), he showed clearly the flimsiness of the basis for his own hypothesis.

In spite of all his incomprehensible errors and many misquotations,

Schulten asserted, when a reporter questioned him about my own thesis: 'Today, the greatest nonsense gets the most publicity and success. My book is too simple for people.' (*Kristall*, 1953, no. 21.)

Atlantis as near the Azores or the Canaries

The hypothesis that Atlantis lay around the Azores, and that the islands themselves are the mountain peaks of the sunken realm, was first put forward by the Jesuit priest Athanasius Kircher in his work, *Mundus Subterraneus*, in 1665. Later it was taken up and elaborated by many other writers. The American politician Ignatius Donnelly was an enthusiastic proponent of this view: 'Nor is it impossible that the nations of the earth may yet employ their idle navies in bringing to the light of day some of the relics of this buried people. Portions of the island lie but a few hundred fathoms beneath the sea . . . a systematic investigation of the sea bed around the present-day Azores would certainly produce worthwhile results.' (Donnelly 1911, p. 340.)

Donnelly could not know at the time when he wrote, that the Azores are *not* the peaks of a sunken land mass, but on the contrary the tops of a great mass of volcanic rock thrown up from the deep. This has been proved beyond doubt by the researches of the last few decades. The most important of these were carried out by the American research vessel *Glomar Challenger*, which since 1968 has made numerous borings on the ocean bed in that area.

The great plates of the earth's surface which carry the Americas on the one hand, and Africa and Europe on the other, drift apart, and through the cleft between them masses of volcanic rock gush up from a great depth; this forms the Mid-Atlantic Ridge, which stretches from Spitzbergen to the Antarctic Ocean. The islands along this ridge: Spitzbergen, Iceland, the Azores, St Paul's Rocks, Ascension, St Helena, Tristan da Cunha, and also the Canaries and Cape Verde Islands, are *not* the mountain peaks of a sunken continent, but the highest points of the 'upwelling zone', i.e. of these masses of volcanic rock, bursting out of the earth's interior.

The many bore samples that the *Glomar Challenger* brought back from the Azores area show that for the last two hundred million years – for the tests reached this far back in time – there has been no inhabitable land there, and certainly no continent of Atlantis. The only type of sediment they found on the sea bed, down to a very great depth, is that which occurs regularly far from any coast; proving that there was certainly no land anywhere near. But long before this American research, Professor Pettersson had written, on the evidence of geological research on the islands themselves: 'The idea of Plato's Atlantis on the

Azores is, geophysically, a corpse which no geologist, however influential, could recall to life' (1948, p. 63). The same goes for the Canaries. They too lie on the cleft between the African and Eurasian plates, and they too are formed from volcanic rock that welled up from below. There was never any 'continent of Atlantis' there.

Pytheas of Massilia

I have described how the island of Basileia, after it was submerged in the thirteenth century BC, re-emerged in the recession of the sea during the Iron Age. About 350 BC, Pytheas of Massilia (present-day Marseille) visited the island and described its position exactly, using its old name of 'Basileia'. Pytheas was a highly educated man, the first to introduce astronomical observations and mathematical calculations into geography. For this reason his statements are of great value. Unfortunately his major work, *On the Ocean,* has not survived. But his discoveries were so new and important that many ancient geographers disputed them and in the process quoted passages from his works, which have thus been preserved.

Pytheas reported his journey to the amber country and the mouth of the Eridanus particularly fully. Since this area was of special interest to the ancients, an especially large number of quotations about it have come down to us. J.H. Mette, in 1952, and D. Stichtenoth, in 1959, have made collections of these quotations, gathering them together from the most varied sources.

'The surviving fragments of Pytheas's description of this journey grow ever more numerous as we move northwards, because the ancient writers, whether they believed Pytheas or were trying to discredit him had little else to go on when they came to describe the unexplored north (Gutenbrunner 1939, p. 50). From these quotations we learn that Pytheas's other name for the island of Basileia was 'Abalus'; that it lay in the 'sea of mud' a day's sail from the coast; that in front of it stood a crag 'with cliffs of various kinds', upon which Hephaestus, god of the smithy, had furnaces, brazen anvils, bellows etc. (Pliny, *Natural History* 37.35f.; Apollonius Rhodius *Argonautica* 4.580, 4.585f., 4.760f., 4.820). Near the island the river Eridanus flowed into the North Sea. It was into the Eridanus that Phaethon, son of Helios, had once fallen; his sisters, the Heliades, mourned the death of their brother with tears that fell into the river and became the amber which was washed up on the shore of the island of Basileia. For this reason the island was also called 'Electris', the 'Isle of Amber' (Apollonius Rhodius *Argonautica* 4.505, 4.600f.). It lay in the 'sea of mud', 'in the direction of the Ocean' (Diodorus Siculus 5.23), i.e. not actually *in* the ocean. The sea of mud was 'no longer either land properly so-called, or sea, or air, but a kind of substance concreted from all these elements, resembling a sea-lungs – a thing in which the earth, the sea, and all the elements are held in suspension; and this is a sort of bond to hold all together, which you can neither walk nor sail upon' (Strabo *Geography* 2.4.1).

The simile 'resembling a sea-lungs' (a marine creature which is like a jellyfish and which expands and contracts as though breathing) suggests that Pytheas had picked up a local idiom from the inhabitants, for the people there to this day say 'the sea is breathing'. Theodor Storm wrote of 'the seething mud's mysterious breath'. This phenomenon is due to the fact that millions of sandworms, mussels and mud crabs, which lie a few centimetres below the surface at low tide, send out tiny jets of air and water. This causes the 'mysterious breath' and the impression of a 'lung'.

There is another passage which also suggests that Pytheas had borrowed a local idiom from these Northern peoples.

Geminus (about 70 BC) used Pytheas as a source and said: 'In these regions, where the longest day lasts seventeen or eighteen hours, Pytheas himself travelled. He says . . . "The barbarians showed me the sleeping place of the sun", for it is sure that in these regions the night is very short, only two or three hours long, so that the sun after setting rises again after a brief interval' (quoted by Gutenbrunner 1939, p. 58). Similarly Cosmas (early sixth century AD) wrote: 'Pytheas says in his work, *On the Ocean,* that when he was staying in the regions of the extreme north, the barbarians of that country showed him the "bed" of the sun, for it is always at that point during the night' (*Topographia*, 2, 82, 18).

> The expression *hopou ho helios koimatai,* 'where the sun rests' or 'sleeps', is worthy of note, since it does not come from the normal Greek vocabulary and looks rather like a literal translation of a foreign idiom. We find one like it in the Middle High German phrase, *die sunne get ze reste* (*reste* = resting place or bed). Compare also these lines from the epic of '*Dietrichs Flucht*':
>
> > nu wolt die sunne ze reste
> > und ouch ze gemache nider gan.
>
> ('Now the sun goes down to his resting place, and to his bedchamber.') It seems we may confidently see in the Pytheas quotation in Geminus, a literal translation of a Germanic idiom (Gutenbrunner 1939, p. 58).

Pytheas certainly talked with the natives of the countries through which he travelled. In the various surviving fragments of his work we read 'the inhabitants told me. . .'; 'so it is said among the local people. . .', or 'the barbarians say that. . .'. His work consisted of personal observations, astronomical measurements, and the statements of the inhabitants of the coasts and islands that he visited.

We learn from his work that the island of Basileia was the first important distribution point in the trade in amber; from Basileia it was carried to the tribes of the nearby mainland. The amber drifted onto the shore of the island in such quantities that 'the inhabitants of the region use it as fuel instead of wood and sell it to the neighbouring Teutones' (Pliny *On Natural History* 37.35). Upon the island of Basileia there was a palace, or king's house, walls with towers, and a secure harbour behind the cliffs (Apollonius Rhodius *Argonautica* 4.537).

Pytheas called the inhabitants of the holy island of Electris 'Hyperboreans' (*ibid.* 614), and also 'Phaeacians' (*ibid.* 538, 548, 769, 823 etc.).

That he should call them Hyperboreans is understandable, since there was an ancient tradition that placed the Hyperboreans in the amber country, on the river Eridanus (see Preller and Robert 1884–91, s.v. '*Hyperboreer*'). More puzzling is his designation of them as 'Phaeacians'. I have already shown that the identification Electris = Phaeacia = Land of the Hyperboreans is correct; the question is, how did Pytheas arrive at it? Did he, like Homer, know of an ancient Mycenaean tradition about the amber country of Phaeacia? There was a pre-Homeric 'Argonautica' (Scheffer, 1947, XIf.), which told of the Argonauts and their bold voyage which took them as far as the North Sea. Perhaps this 'most ancient epic of the Argonauts' voyage' (Scheffer) was the common source for the description of Phaeacia in both Homer and Pytheas.

It is unlikely that Pytheas, or Apollonius Rhodius whose poem draws on his account, took the identification from Homer himself, for in Apollonius's *Argonautica* there are names and stories from the amber country which are not in Homer's account of Phaeacia, and so cannot be copied from it – for instance, the names Electris and Eridanus, and those of the river god Aegaeus and his daughter Melite. There is also the story of the fall of Phaethon and the tears of his sisters. Also among the traditions found only in the *Argonautica* is an alternative story, according to which the amber was formed, not from the tears of the Heliades but from 'the many tears that Apollo shed for his son Asclepius when he visited the sacred people of the North. He was banished from the bright sky by his father Zeus, whom he blamed for having killed this son of his' (4.546 ff.).

Another story in the *Argonautica* that was not derived from Homer tells how Heracles in the land of the Phaeacians got with child Melite the water nymph, daughter of the river god Aegaeus, and she bore 'the mighty Hyllus'. The story continues: 'But by the time Hyllus had reached man's estate he felt that he had lived long enough in the island of his birth under the stern eye of King Nausithous. So he collected a party of native Phaeacians and, assisted by the king himself, migrated with them to the Cronian Sea. And in those parts he settled, and was killed – by the Mentors, in the course of a cattle raid.' (4.538 ff.) The North Sea is called the Cronian Sea by many ancient authors (Welcker

1832, vol. 1, p. 25 ff.; Ukert 1846, vol. 3, p. 405 ff.).

Nausithous is given in Homer as the ancestor of the Phaeacian royal house (*Od.* 6.7 ff.). I have mentioned Hyllus on page 185 – he was the leader of the North Sea Peoples, who fell in the duel against Echemus of Tegea. Because Hyllus was the son of Heracles by Melite in the amber country, the North Sea Peoples were known as 'Heracleidae' = children of Heracles.

These names and stories cannot have been taken by Pytheas from the Homeric epics, since they do not occur there. On the other hand, the *Argonautica*, which, according to D. Stichtenoth, draws on the work of Pytheas, omits many important elements in Homer's Phaeacia, which Pytheas would surely have included had he been using the *Odyssey* for his description of the country. The central theme of Homer's Phaeacian episode is the stay of Odysseus among the Phaeacians. The *Argonautica* knows nothing of this theme. Both works mention the royal couple, Alcinous and Arete, but in Homer their daughter Nausicaa plays an important role, whereas in Apollonius' *Argonautica* she is not mentioned.

So, between the description of Phaeacia in Homer and that in the *Argonautica*, there are many correspondences, but also many differences. Each of the two poets drew on information which the other did not know. All of which suggests that Homer and Pytheas, or Apollonius, used an older, pre-Homeric work, perhaps a very ancient Argonaut epic, for their descriptions of the country and consequently that the more recent *Argonautica* does not depend directly on the 'Phaeacia' of Homer.

The relevant points are that Pytheas described the land of amber on the west-coast of Schleswig-Holstein as the land of the Hyperboreans and also as the land of the Phaeacians; and that he described precisely the location of the 'holy island of Electris', and even gave its exact latitude. Pliny, who took his information from Pytheas, said that the ninth circle goes 'across the Hyperboreans and Britain, with a seventeen-hour day' (*Natural History* 6.219). This is an exact indication, for the longest day lasts seventeen hours just on latitude 54° 1′ N. (Müllenhoff 1870, p. 342; Stichtenoth 1959, p. 73). Heligoland lies at latitude 54° 7′ N. Pytheas also wrote, as the quotation in Scymnus (5.139) shows, of the 'northern pillar, that rears its peak high above the ocean'. In my view this refers to the heaven-pillar, which according to the Atlantis document stood in the midst of the temple.

Pytheas statements about the island of Basileia/Abalus/Electris have provoked a large literature. The Kiel geologist and oceanographer E. Wasmund located it on the ridge, now lying beneath the sea, which connects Heligoland with Eiderstedt, and was once known as the Süderstrand. This conclusion, which is confirmed by my own researches, is accepted by all the genuine experts on the geology and history of the area (see pages 55–8).

If we may infer from Pytheas's account that in the fourth century BC one or more islands existed between Heligoland and the mainland, and the isobath chart supports the idea, then it follows that even after the island was completely separated from the mainland, the prehistoric population of Heligoland could reach the mainland over various 'stepping stones'. In other words, Heligoland was the last, largest and highest of a chain of islands, which once stretched into the open sea from the Cimbrian peninsula. (Ahrens 1966, p. 238.)

CHAPTER 9

SUMMARY

The Atlantis document of Solon, and the 'Phaeacia' of Homer, bring us living witness of the Nordic culture area as it was in the Bronze Age. Up to now this period has been known only from silent tombs and archaeological finds, which left many questions unanswered, or admitted of various, often contradictory, explanations. Now, however, with the help of these two amazingly reliable documents, many of those questions can be answered and the falsity of many older theories can be proved.

Until now the *reasons* for the great migrations were not known.

Eduard Meyer suggested that overpopulation lay behind this 'great event'. O. Spengler thought it was the invention of chariots, J. Wiesner, that of mounted warriors, which set off this 'world-shaking, indeed world-transforming movement'.

Now, however, we discover from the Atlantis document and its Egyptian sources that in the thirteenth century BC terrible natural catastrophes broke over our planet, and forced many peoples to migrate from homelands that were destroyed by drought, fire, earthquake or flood.

Hitherto there has been great confusion about the *starting point* of these great migrations, which moved through Europe and Asia Minor. The Egyptologist E. Otto selected the Aegean isles, R. Stadelmann and others, the Balkans, W. Kimmig, the 'broad area between the eastern Alps, the Carpathians, and the Balkan mountains' (1964, p. 269), R. Herbig identified it as the homeland of the Illyrians 'in the area of East Germany and Poland' and called them 'the Illyrian migrations' (1940, p. 66f.). Schachermeyr (1929, p. 31) believed that 'the savage wilds of Europe, and in second place, many parts of Asia Minor that had remained barbarous' are possible candidates. G. Spitzlberger (1972, p. 21) is of the opinion that the originators of the great migration were none other than the inhabitants of Switzerland and south-west Germany, who moved out on account of the flooding of their pile-villages.

One cannot help asking oneself where in all these areas can be found the 'Ocean in the North' with the 'islands that were plucked up and

washed away', and where 'the might of Nun [the Ocean] broke out and
struck our towns and villages in a great wave' and 'the head of their [the
North Sea Peoples'] cities was sunk in the sea'?

But now we learn from the Atlantis document and its Egyptian
antecedents, and also from Homer's Phaeacia, that the homeland of
peoples who advanced against Egypt at the end of the thirteenth
century lay in the Ocean of the North, in the amber country of the
Bronze Age.

Up till now the North Sea Peoples have generally been held
responsible for all those terrible fires whose traces are found in the
forests, bogs, settlements and palaces of the time. What is more they are
supposed to have torn down the walls of the burnt-out buildings, so that
quite often (as at Tiryns, Mycenae and Knossos) blocks of stone weighing
a ton or more are found many metres from their original positions. The
North Sea Peoples also – so it was thought – reduced the populations of
the countries they moved through or settled in (Crete, Syria, the Hittite
kingdom), to small remnants or even wiped them out altogether.

Schachermeyr wrote of 'plundering hordes', of 'utter barbarians,
whose cultural distance from the East Mediterranean civilizations was
so great that at first they did not know how to do anything but wreck and
rob' (1929, p. 31). Childe (1950) called the North Sea Peoples 'barbarian hordes', and Kahl-Furthmann has written of 'the invasion of the
barbarian hordes' (1976, p. 15). The leading tribe of the North Sea
Peoples, the Phrs/Philistines, is described as 'the most atrocious'.

But now we learn from the Atlantis document that it was *not* the
Atlanteans, the North Sea Peoples, who had burnt up all these regions
but that 'the comet Phaethon burnt up the surface of the earth'. The
contemporary Egyptian texts support these statements, and precise
stratigraphic researches have shown that the destructive fires raged
before the incursion of the Philistine North Sea Peoples.

Equally false is the assertion, which one often meets, that the North
Sea Peoples decimated or even wiped out the populations of the lands
that they entered.

From the Atlantis document we hear of the terrible earthquakes and
floods in which 'all your fighting men were swallowed up by the earth'
(*Ti.* 25d) and even the spring on the Acropolis was 'choked by the
earthquakes and survives only in a few small trickles' (*Criti.* 112d).

But throughout Egypt, and in Assyria and many other regions to
which the North Sea Peoples never came, the palaces and temples are
also ruined by earthquakes; this, together with the statements of
contemporary Egyptian texts, ought to have warned archaeologists
against making the North Sea Peoples responsible for all this terrible
destruction, and the decimation or annihilation of the peoples in the
affected areas.

From the Atlantis document we find that it was the earthquakes and floods that were the cause of the reduction in the population of Greece, so that only a 'few survivors' remained (*Ti.* 23). Archaeological research has also shown that in Greece, including the areas to which the North Sea Peoples never came, only about a hundredth of the former population survived the catastrophes.

Many archaeologists have noted that the extensive burnt strata are everywhere found to have been laid down *before* the arrival of the North Sea Peoples, and that objects connected with these peoples are never found *in* the destruction layers.

'If Troy VIIA was destroyed "about 1200", but no traces of the destroyers themselves were found, then this is only the same situation that we find all over the eastern Mediterranean: nowhere are there archaeological traces of the "immigrants"' (Kimmig 1964, p. 249). 'So we have the Egyptian reliefs depicting the invaders, and the destruction layers in the towns dated to "about 1200", but the destroyers themselves are invisible. There has been no actual find on the ground which, after critical examination, can be confidently attributed to the migrations.' (*Ibid.* p. 252, p. 262.)

What is more, the Greek tradition knows of no 'plundering hordes'. It does indeed tell of conflict between the surviving native population and the incoming North Sea Peoples, or Heracleidae, but the legends tell only of chivalrous duels and loyally kept bargains. When their champions, Hyllus and Xanthus, had lost their respective duels, the newcomers retired without further violence and came back only about a century later (see pages 185 and 186). And at this 'return of the Heracleidae' there was, according to the tradition, no plundering or murdering either. The terribly reduced population clearly received the returning tribes without resistance, and Greek stories tell only of friendship and alliances with the Hyperboreans, the North Sea Peoples (Diodorus Siculus 2.47). These Northerners from the land of amber had, so the traditions told, founded the principal Greek shrines at Delphi and on Delos. Herodotus (4.33, 4.34) told of the solemn embassies and sacrificial gifts of the Hyperboreans who came to Delos. The gods Apollo and Artemis were said to have come to Greece from the country of the Hyperboreans, and a few Hellenes had themselves visited that country, and in their turn dedicated costly gifts at its shrines. Similarly in ancient times a Hyperborean named Abaris had come to Greece, and renewed the old friendship and alliance with the Delians.

No people tells stories like these about another which has massacred and robbed them. The 'plundering hordes' of the North Sea Peoples are a figment of the imagination of modern archaeologists, who for lack of accurate stratigraphical research have ascribed the layers of burning and destruction to these peoples, who in fact arrived only afterwards.

Until now the period between 1200 and 800 BC, during which the early classical culture of Greece was germinating, was 'veiled in darkness and mystery' and seemed 'an epoch in Greek history which has hitherto resisted all attempts at investigation' (Curtius 1926, p. 2). Of course it was impossible to attribute the first blossoming of Greek culture to 'utter barbarians' who 'did not know how to do anything but wreck and rob'. But now we know from the Atlantis document and from Homer's Phaeacia, that the North Sea Peoples, the Atlanteans, were a people with a high culture and a developed political, judicial and military organization, all of which they carried with them into a Greece ruined and stripped of its inhabitants.

That the rise of early Greek culture is due to them and not to the pathetic remnant of the Mycenaean population that had survived the catastrophes, is recognized by many archaeologists.

'In every case, the new, progressive, developments were set off by the great migrations' (Berve 1948, p. 47).

'What is beginning now [in Greece] has nothing to do with Crete and Mycenae; it is a new creation' (Riemschneider 1952, p. 129).

'Out of this chaos the new Greek world was born' (Webster 1960, p. 379).

'New powers on earth, new gods in heaven, new styles in art and architecture, new types of armour and new acts of war, the alphabet, iron! Crete and Egypt are *passé*; the glorious days of classical Greece lie before us!' (Macalister 1914, p. 27).

And there are many other such judgements concerning the influence of these invaders that one could quote.

Scholars likewise agree that it was only by the great migrations that the orientalization of south-eastern Europe and Asia Minor, which up to then had gone forward without interruption, was finally brought to a halt. Above all, Greece, 'which seemed to be lost to Europe for good' (Wirth 1938, p. 225), was torn from the orient. Now, 'Everywhere there is Europe' (Kimmig 1964, p. 273) and Greece becomes the crucible of European culture.

There are other questions that can now be answered for the first time and which take us back long before the period of the migrations. For instance, the question of the origin of the copper articles that are found in northern Europe in the neolithic period, at the time of the Megalithic culture. Until now, prehistorians were convinced that the peoples of northern Europe at that time had no source of copper ore in their own territory. The copper of that period is said to be 'certainly an import from eastern Europe' (Bröndsted 1960, vol. 1, p. 187). Sprockhoff and Schwantes also gave it as their opinion that all the copper, and, in later times, the bronze, must have been brought from other lands (Schwantes 1939, p. 215; Sprockhoff 1938, p. 70). Sprockhoff considered that these

objects were imported from Spain, Schwantes favoured the Carpathians; while according to Montelius they came from Babylonia.

But now we find from the Atlantis document that the Atlanteans
mined copper from the rock that lay in front of their own royal island.
And indeed the rock massif of Heligoland does contain copper ore, in a
distinct stratum that 'leaps to the eye'. Fragments of charcoal and slag in
a Bronze Age grave-mound on the top of the rock, finds of copper
'blanks' in the sea near Heligoland and spectrum analyses of the oldest
copper objects found in the North all show that the Heligoland copper
was mined, worked and widely distributed as early as the Megalithic
era. Axes made from copper ore with this spectrum, and of the shape
common in northern Europe, appear 'for the first time in large numbers
in the bell-beaker period in Portugal' (Sangmeister 1966, p. 141 f.). The
Nordic copper axes of the Megalithic period are described by
Sangmeister as 'the first true copper forms'. As the distribution map of
the finds of copper objects in the Neolithic period shows, there is a clear
relationship between the distribution of these objects, and the sea coast,
with the Megalithic culture which is found along it. But Schwantes was
not correct when discussing this map to conclude: 'Since the Northern
copper mines were not exploited until a later period, all the copper, and
later the bronze, must have been brought from other lands' (1939, p.
215).

Spectrum analyses have shown that the finds marked on this distribution map are made from Heligoland copper ore. So the megalith
builders of the North did not have to import all their copper from foreign
lands; they had, on the cliffs of Heligoland, a deposit of ore which
sufficed for their needs.

The Atlantis document can also answer another important question,
which always arises in connection with the spread of the Megalithic
culture. 'It cannot be doubted that the European/North
African/Mediterranean Megalithic culture area shows that there must
have been close ties between the peoples dwelling in it. But what the
nature of those ties may have been – that is the great mystery, which we
cannot unravel.' (Schwantes 1939, p. 221.)

From the Atlantis document we learn that all these areas had since
the times of the ancestors acknowledged the 'rule and community' of the
kings of Atlantis; that the ten kings, who ruled these ten countries, were
all held to be descendants of the first king who ruled on the amber island
of Atlantis; and that each fifth and sixth year alternately they had to
meet in the 'metropolis' in order to 'consult on matters of mutual interest
and inquire into and give judgement on any wrong committed by any of
them' and finally that they all swore 'that they should never make war
on each other, but come to each other's help if any of them were
threatened with a dissolution of the power of the royal house in his state;

in that case, they should follow the custom of their predecessors and consult mutually about policy for war and other matters, recognizing the suzerainty of the house of Atlas' (*Criti.* 120).

This shows how close were the ties between the Megalithic peoples who inhabited Europe, North Africa and the Mediterranean area. Through the contents of the Atlantis document this 'great mystery' is unravelled. The similarities of form in the Megalithic tombs and the other monuments; in the pottery, in the jewellery, especially the amber jewellery; the skeletal remains, which nearly all belong to the Cro-Magnon race; the fact that in all the areas of Megalithic culture the same unit of measurement is found, the 'megalithic yard', and the same technical and organizational skills: all this is explained by the information in the Atlantis document.

And so the Atlantis document solves an old riddle, perhaps the greatest known to prehistory. It was not 'missionaries from the East' who spread their cult, along with the knowledge of farming, among the 'savages' of northern and western Europe, but the megalithic people, who carried with them their arts, skills and knowledge.

This was the earliest 'European Community'. As the Atlantis document tells us, it was founded as early as the Neolithic age, by the Megalithic people, with their knowledge of navigation on the high seas, farming, herding, astronomy, geometry and land surveying.

This first 'European Community' continued in existence until the thirteenth century BC, for it was then that the various peoples from the territories of the old Megalithic culture, under the leadership of the House of Atlas (*Criti.* 120d), the king 'from the pillars of heaven' (Medinet Habu), attacked Egypt, from Libya, from the sea, and from Amurru (Palestine).

The political, cultural and religious centre of this community lay 'in the Ocean in the North', i.e. in northern Europe, the original home of the Megalithic culture, on the amber island, Basileia, the 'metropolis', the 'mother-city'. Of the central shrine that stood there, it is said: 'In the centre was a shrine sacred to Poseidon and Cleito, surrounded by a golden wall through which entry was forbidden, as it was the place where the family of the ten kings was conceived and begotten' (*Criti.* 116c). This was Pytheas's 'holy island of Electris', upon which stood Asgard, 'the best made house of any on earth, and the greatest' (*Gylfaginning* 14).

And now we are in a position to solve yet another unsolved riddle of ancient history, namely the question of the whereabouts of the island of Nerthus, of which Tacitus wrote:

> The Reudigni, Aviones, Anglii, Varini, Eudoses, Suarines, and Nuitones, [dwell] . . . safe behind ramparts of rivers and woods. There is nothing note-

worthy about these tribes individually, but they share a common worship of Nerthus, or Mother Earth. They believe that she takes part in human affairs, riding in a chariot among her people. On an island of the sea stands an inviolate grove, in which, veiled with a cloth, is a chariot that none but the priest may touch. The priest can feel the presence of the goddess in this holy of holies, and attends her with deepest reverence as her chariot is drawn along by cows. Then follow days of rejoicing and merrymaking in every place that she condescends to visit and sojourn in. No one goes to war, no one takes up arms; every iron object is locked away. Then, and then only, are peace and quiet known and welcomed, until the goddess, when she has had enough of the society of men, is restored to her sacred precinct by the priest. After that, the chariot, the vestments, and (believe it if you will) the goddess herself, are cleansed in a secluded lake. This service is performed by slaves who are immediately afterwards drowned in the lake. Thus mystery begets terror and a pious reluctance to ask what that sight can be which is seen only by men doomed to die.' (*Germania* ch. 40).

C. Woyte rightly called this 'a description based on direct, living testimony' (1926, p. 65).

'What Tacitus tells us about Nerthus surpasses in its significance, vividness and solemnity all the other evidence for the religion of the time' (Schneider 1938, p. 244).

Because of the enormous importance of this document, many writers have been at pains to identify the island of Nerthus. But all attempts have hitherto failed.

'Which island is meant, remains uncertain' (Woyte 1926, p. 25).

'The North Sea has been searched in vain; it should rather be sought in the Baltic' (Schneider 1926, p. 65).

So the island of Nerthus has been identified as Zealand (Much), Als (Laur), Rügen (Scheel) or even as Bornholm (Clemen).

But all these attempts to place it in the Baltic are excluded by the clear statement of Tacitus: '*Est in insula oceani*'. The Greeks and Romans used 'Ocean' only of the outer, tidal sea, never of an inland sea like the Mediterranean or the Baltic. This applies also to Tacitus, who counted the North Sea as part of the Ocean (*Germania* ch. 34, ch. 37) but called the Baltic 'Mare Suebicum' (ch. 45). Also, it is impossible to drive with a chariot from one of the Baltic islands to the mainland inhabited by the Anglii – i.e. the present-day district of Angeln in north-east Schleswig-Holstein, the Varini (Warnen) in north Schleswig, the Reudigni, who probably lived in Holstein (Gutenbrunner 1949, p. 11) and all the other Nerthus peoples. One can only travel by chariot from an island to the mainland if that island lies in a 'sea' of mud or sand, which becomes dry at low tide.

That the North Sea has been searched in vain for the island of Nerthus is easy to explain: it vanished for good in the floods of the fourteenth century AD. The island of Nerthus is in fact identical with

'Basileia', upon which stood the 'metropolis', the 'mother-city'. On both islands there stood a temple with a 'holy of holies', on both there was a sacred grove, and statues of gods ('*agalmata*', *Criti.* 116d; '*numen*', *Germania* ch. 40). Both temples were central shrines for all the surrounding tribes. At the high feasts 'every iron object is locked away'; and the sacred bull hunt had to take place using 'no metal weapon' (*Criti.* 119e). On the metropolis the bull was consecrated to Poseidon and, as is evident from the Nerthus account, the cow to the Terra Mater. The fact that her chariot was drawn by cows is an extremely ancient tradition from the Megalithic age, when the horse was not known as a draught animal.

'Nerthus was a goddess belonging to the race of the Vanir' (Schneider 1938, p. 16); her spouse and brother was Njord, 'the Nordic Poseidon' (Krause 1891, p. 202), who was of course also one of the Vanir. Now, as I have shown, the Vánir were the gods of the Megalithic people and thus of Indo-Germanic prehistory. H. Schneider said in his discussion of the Nerthus account: 'Here we have at last historical evidence of that deity whose picture we have already met – the lady of the sacred chariot' (1938, p. 244). These pictures are the Megalithic portrayals of the Magna Mater, and the Bronze Age statuettes, which are 'small copies of larger statues of the female deity' (Bröndsted 1962, vol. 2, p. 226). Bröndsted said of the statuette of the goddess of Fardal that she is shown in the attitude of one driving a wagon. Referring to the Nerthus account, he said that in the famous cult wagon of Dejbjerg, which dates from the first century BC, we can recognize the kind of 'chariot' that must have been used for the progress of Nerthus. 'The find at Dejbjerg points not only to Tacitus's goddess Nerthus, but also back to the wagon-riding goddess of the Bronze Age' (1963, vol. 3, p. 116).

Such a solemn cult is unimaginable without prayers and hymns; and so we may take the very ancient Anglo-Saxon charm invoking the earth mother as an inheritance from the time of the cult of Nerthus, brought by the Angles and Saxons from their home in Schleswig-Holstein to England:

> I pray to the earth and high heaven
> Erce, Erce, Erce, Earth Mother,
> May the Almighty Eternal Lord
> grant you fields to increase and flourish
> fields fruitful and healthy,
> shining harvest of shafts of millet,
> broad harvests of barley.
> Hail to thee, Earth, Mother of Men!
> Bring forth now in God's embrace
> filled with good for the use of men.

In these verses the name Erce is enough to show their very early origin.

The name Erce for the Terra Mater is connected with the name of her spouse, the god Er, Erch, or Ir. Er and Erce must have been the names of the divine ancestral couple among the Megalithic peoples; in the *hieros gamos*, the sacred marriage, the 'god's embrace', they begot new life, and at the beginning of the spring magically encouraged the fertility of the fields.

In this context we may once again recall the verses of Euripides, saying that by the waters of Eridanus:

> His sisters drop their piteous tears
> Which glow like amber in the dark stream;
> And then to reach that shore planted with apple-trees
> Where the daughters of evening sing,
> Where the sea-lord of the dark shallows
> Permits to sailors no further passage,
> Establishing the solemn frontier of heaven
> which Atlas guards;
> Where divine fountains flow beside Zeus's marriage-bed;
> Where holy earth offers her choice fruits
> To enrich the blissful gods.
>
> *Hippolytus* 739ff.

This passage, taken from old myths, is important not only because it gives the precise location of 'Zeus's marriage bed', but also because it shows that the sacred marriage was a most ancient custom at that shrine.

All researchers who have studied the Nerthus account agree that at her shrine the sacred marriage played an important part in the cult. If Tacitus did not mention it, this is simply because the act took place in the inmost shrine (*penetrali*) of the temple 'surrounded by a golden wall through which entry was forbidden, as it was the place where the family of the ten kings was conceived and begotten' (*Criti.* 116c). For the general congregation the act was hidden from view, and so this 'description based on direct, living testimony' could not describe it. But the sacred marriage was the heart of the spring festival. It is shown on Bronze Age rock scribings; it is mentioned in the *Edda* (*Lokasenna* 32), and in the collection of old tales from the island of Flatey, Iceland, known as the *Flateyjarbók* (1.337f.).

The ritual progress of Nerthus was the spring procession of the Terra Mater, which brought fertility to the lands of her worshippers. So in this account we have a description of the spring festival, and in that of the Atlantis document one of the midsummer feast, with its bull sacrifice, midsummer fire, and the assembly of the ten kings.

The Nerthus account shows how long the Megalithic cults maintained themselves on her sacred island after it had re-emerged from the sea. Finally, it also shows that it was possible, in the first century AD, to

Marriage, death and resurrection of the fertility god (from Almgren 1934, p. 121)

drive from this island to the mainland. The Südstrand ridge, which is known to have existed later, was thus at that time only partly dry land; but those parts which lay under water could still be crossed at low tide. There is no question of the area between Heligoland and Eiderstedt being, as Gripp claimed, 'under the sea for the last six thousand years'.

So the Atlantis document provides answers to these questions, and many others, which would otherwise be answered doubtfully or not at all.

We must – to recall Professor Schmied-Kowarzik's words – give thanks that Solon, 'the wisest of the seven wise men' brought the Atlantis document from Egypt; and that Plato, the most important thinker of antiquity, esteemed its importance so highly that he reproduced it in his dialogues; and that Homer, the great poet of the Greeks, sang in immortal verse of the royal island of the Phaeacian-Atlanteans, with its inhabitants and its high culture, and much more – independently of the Atlantis document and long before the latter was brought to Europe.

'Scholarship now has a great task before it' (Schmied-Kowarzik). Scholarship will never accomplish this task if the Atlantis document is dismissed unread as 'mere fantasy' or 'a Utopia without historical foundation'.

That it is no such thing, but rather 'a most ancient and yet living narrative from the thirteenth century BC', this book has, I hope, sufficiently proved.

APPENDIX

THE ATLANTIS NARRATIVE

For convenience, a recent English translation, by Sir Desmond Lee, of relevant passages from Plato's *Timaeus* and *Critias* is reproduced in this appendix (by kind permission of Penguin). The quotations in the text have all been taken from this translation, with some minor modifications, noted below, to bring it in line with Mr Spanuth's own German translation.

Plato wrote these pieces in the form of dialogues between his teacher, Socrates (469?–399 BC), and Timaeus, Critias (Plato's great-grandfather) and Hermocrates.

From the **Timaeus**

In the introductory conversation, Socrates discusses the previous day's talk:

I had this in mind yesterday when I agreed so readily to your request for an account of my ideal society [20b]: I knew that there was no one more fitted to provide the sequel to it than you – you are the only living people who could adequately describe my city fighting a war worthy of her. So when I had done what was asked of me, I set you the task I have just described. You agreed to put your heads together, and return my hospitality today; and here I am dressed in my best and looking forward to what I am about to receive [20c].

HERMOCRATES: I assure you, Socrates, that, as Timaeus here said, there is no lack of willingness on our part and we don't want to excuse ourselves from our part of the bargain. Indeed we were considering it as soon as we got back yesterday to Critias's house, where we are staying, and even before that while we were on the way there [20d]. Critias then produced a story he had heard long ago. Tell it again now to Socrates, Critias, so that we can see whether it is suitable for our purpose or not.

CRITIAS: I will, if the other member of the trio, Timaeus, agrees.

TIMAEUS: I agree.

CRITIAS: Listen then, Socrates. The story is a strange one, but Solon, the wisest of the seven wise men, once vouched its truth [20e]. He was a relation and close friend of Dropides, my great-grandfather, as he often says himself in his poems, and told the story to my grandfather Critias, who in turn repeated it to us when he was an old man. It relates the many notable achievements of our city long ago, which have been lost sight of because of the lapse of time and destruction of human life. Of these the greatest is one that we could well recall now to repay our debt to you and to offer the Goddess on her festival day a just and truthful hymn of praise [21a].

266

SOCRATES: Good. And what is this unrecorded yet authentic achievement of our city that Critias heard from Solon and recounted to you?

CRITIAS: I will tell you; though the story was old when I heard it and the man who told it me was no longer young. For Critias was at the time, so he said, nearly ninety, and I was about ten [21b]. It was Children's Day in the festival of Apatouria, and there were the customary ceremonies for the boys, including prizes given by the fathers for reciting. There were recitations of many poems by different authors, but many of the competitors chose Solon's poems, which were in those days quite a novelty. And one of the clansmen, either because he thought so or out of politeness to Critias, said that he thought that Solon was not only the wisest of men but also the most outspoken of poets [21c]. And the old man – I remember it well – was extremely pleased, and said with a smile, 'I wish, Amynander, that he hadn't treated poetry as a spare-time occupation but had taken it seriously like others; if he had finished the story he brought back from Egypt, and hadn't been compelled to neglect it because of the class struggles and other evils he found here on his return, I don't think any poet, even Homer or Hesiod, would have been more famous.' 'And what was the story, Critias?' asked Amynander. 'It was about what may fairly be called the greatest and most noteworthy of all this city's achievements, but because of the lapse of time and the death of those who took part in it the story has not lasted till our day.' 'Tell us from the beginning,' came the reply; 'how and from whom did Solon hear the tale which he told you as true?' [21e]

'There is in Egypt,' said Critias, 'as the head of the delta, where the Nile divides, a district called the Saïtic. The chief city of the district, from which King Amasis came, is called Saïs. The chief goddess of the inhabitants is called in Egyptian Neïth, in Greek (according to them) Athena; and they are very friendly to the Athenians and claim some relationship to them. Solon came there on his travels and was highly honoured by them, and in the course of making inquiries from those priests who were most knowledgeable on the subject found that both he and all his countrymen were almost entirely ignorant about antiquity [22a]. And wishing to lead them on to talk about early times, he embarked on an account of the earliest events known here, telling them about Phoroneus, said to be the first man, and Niobe, and how Deucalion and Pyrrha survived the flood and who were their descendants, and trying by reckoning up the generations to calculate how long ago the events in question had taken place [22b]. And a very old priest said to him, 'Oh Solon, Solon, you Greeks are all children, and there's no such thing as an old Greek.'

'What do you mean by that?' inquired Solon.

'You are all young in mind,' came the reply: 'you have no belief rooted in old tradition and no knowledge hoary with age. And the reason is this. There have been and will be many different calamities to destroy mankind, the greatest of them by fire and water, lesser ones by countless other means [22c]. Your own story of how Phaethon, child of the sun, harnessed his father's chariot, but was unable to guide it along his father's course and so burnt up things on the earth and was himself destroyed by a thunderbolt, is a mythical version of the truth that there is at long intervals a variation in the course of the heavenly bodies and a consequent widespread destruction by fire of things on the earth [22d]. On such occasions those who live in the mountains or in high and dry places suffer more than those living by rivers or by the sea; as for us, the Nile, our own regular saviour, is freed* to preserve us in this emergency. When on the other hand the gods purge the earth with a deluge, the herdsmen and shepherds in the mountains escape, but those living in the cities in your part of the world are swept into the sea by the rivers; here water never falls on the land from above either then or at any other time, but rises up naturally from below [22e]. This is the reason why our traditions here are the oldest

---

* The meaning is uncertain, but there may be a reference to Egyptian irrigation systems.

preserved; though it is true that in all places where excessive cold or heat does not prevent it human beings are always to be found in larger or smaller numbers [23d]. But in our temples we have preserved from earliest times a written record of any great or splendid achievement or notable event which has come to our ears whether it occurred in your part of the world or here or anywhere else; whereas with you and others, writing and the other necessities of civilization have only just been developed when the periodic scourge of the deluge descends, and spares none but the unlettered and uncultured, so that you have to begin again like children, in complete ignorance of what happened in our part of the world or in yours in early times [23b]. So these genealogies of your own people which you were just recounting are little more than children's stories. You remember only one deluge, though there have been many, and you do not know that the finest and best race of men that ever existed lived in your country; you and your fellow citizens are descended from the few survivors that remained, but you know nothing about it because so many succeeding generations left no record in writing [23c]. For before the greatest of all destructions by water, Solon, the city that is now Athens was preeminent in war and conspicuously the best governed in every way, its achievements and constitution being the finest of any in the world of which we have heard tell.' [23d]

Solon was astonished at what he heard and eagerly begged the priests to describe to him in detail the doings of these citizens of the past. 'I will gladly do so, Solon,' replied the priest, 'both for your sake and your city's, but chiefly in gratitude to the Goddess to whom it has fallen to bring up and educate both your country and ours – yours first, when she took over your seed from Earth and Hephaestus, ours a thousand years later [23e]. The age of our institutions is given in our sacred records as eight thousand years, and the citizens whose laws and whose finest achievement I will now briefly describe to you therefore lived nine thousand years ago; we will go through their history in detail later on at leisure, when we can consult the records. [24a]

'Consider their laws compared with ours; for you will find today among us many parallels to your institutions in those days. First, our priestly class is kept distinct from the others, as is also our artisan class; next, each class of craftsmen – shepherds, hunters, farmers – performs its function in isolation from others [24b]. And of course you will have noticed that our soldier class is kept separate from all others, being forbidden by the law to undertake any duties other than military: moreover their armament consists of shield and spear, which we were the first people in Asia to adopt, under the instruction of the Goddess, as you were in your part of the world. And again you see what great attention our law devotes from the beginning to learning, deriving from the divine principles of cosmology everything needed for human life down to divination and medicine for our health, and acquiring all other related branches of knowledge [24c]. The Goddess founded this whole order and system when she framed your society. She chose the place in which you were born with an eye to its temperate climate, which would produce men of high intelligence; for being herself a lover of war and wisdom she picked a place for her first foundation that would produce men most like herself in character [24d]. So you lived there under the laws I have described, and even better ones, and excelled all men in every kind of accomplishment, as one would expect of children and offspring of the gods. And among all the wonderful achievements recorded here of your city, one great act of courage is outstanding [24e]. Our records tell how your city checked a great power which arrogantly advanced from its base in the Atlantic [sea]* to attack the cities of Europe and Asia. For in those days the Atlantic was navigable. There was an island opposite the strait which you call (so you say) the Pillars of Heracles, an island larger than Libya and Asia combined; from it travellers could in those days reach the other islands, and from them the whole opposite continent which surrounds

* Lee reads 'ocean'. See page 30.

what can truly be called the ocean [25a]. For the sea within the strait we were talking about is like a lake with a narrow entrance; the outer ocean is the real ocean and the land which entirely surrounds it is properly termed continent. On this island of Atlantis had arisen a powerful and remarkable dynasty of kings, who ruled the whole island, and many other islands as well and parts of the continent; in addition it controlled, within the strait, Libya up to the borders of Egypt and Europe as far as Tyrrhenia [25b]. This dynasty, gathering its whole power together, attempted to enslave, at a single stroke, your country and ours and all the territory within the strait. It was then, Solon, that the power and courage and strength of your city became clear for all men to see [25c]. Her bravery and military skill were outstanding; she led an alliance of the Greeks, and then when they deserted her and she was forced to fight alone, after running into direst peril, she overcame the invaders and celebrated a victory; she rescued those not yet enslaved from the slavery threatening them, and she generously freed all others living within the Pillars of Heracles. At a later time there were earthquakes and floods of extraordinary violence, and in a single dreadful day and night all your fighting men were swallowed up by the earth, and the island of Atlantis was similarly swallowed up by the sea and vanished [25d]; this is why the sea in that area is to this day impassable to navigation, which is hindered by mud just below the surface, the remains of the sunken island.'

That is, in brief, Socrates, the story which Critias told when he was an old man, and which he had heard from Solon [25e]. When you were describing your society and its inhabitants yesterday, I was reminded of this story and noticed with astonishment how closely, by some miraculous chance, your account coincided with Solon's [26a]. I was not willing to say so at once, for after so long a time my memory was imperfect; I decided therefore that I must first rehearse the whole story to myself before telling it. That was why I was so quick to agree to your conditions yesterday, thinking that I was pretty well placed to deal with what is always the most serious difficulty in such matters, how to find a suitable story on which to base what one wants to say [26b]. And so, as Hermocrates said, as soon as we left here yesterday I started telling the story to the others as I remembered it, and when I got back I managed to recall pretty well all of it by thinking it over during the night. It is amazing, as is often said, how what we learn as children sticks in the memory. I'm not at all sure whether I could remember again all I heard yesterday; yet I should be surprised if any detail of this story I heard so long ago has escaped me [26c]. I listened to it then with a child's intense delight, and the old man was glad to answer my innumerable questions, so that the details have been indelibly branded on my memory. What is more, I have told the whole story to the others early this morning, so that they might be as well placed as I am for the day's discussion.

And now, to come to the point, I am ready to tell the story, Socrates, not only in outline but in detail, as I heard it. We will transfer the imaginary citizens and city which you described yesterday to the real world, and say that your city is the city of my story and your citizens those historical ancestors of ours whom the priest described [26d]. They will fit exactly, and there will be no disharmony if we speak as if they really were the men who lived at that time. We will divide the work between us and try to fulfil your instructions to the best of our ability. So tell us, Socrates, do you think this story will suit our purpose, or must we look for another instead? [26e]

SOCRATES: What better choice could there be, Critias? Your story is particularly well suited to the present festival of the Goddess, with whom it is connected, and it is a great point in its favour that it is not a fiction but true history. Where shall we find an alternative if we abandon it? No, you must tell it and good luck to you; and I can take it easy and listen to your reply to my narrative of yesterday.

From the **Critias**

CRITIAS: We must first remind ourselves that in all 9000 years have elapsed since the declaration of war between those who lived outside and all those who lived inside the Pillars of Heracles [108e]. This is the war whose course I am to trace. The leadership and conduct of the war were on the one side in the hands of our city, on the other in the hands of the kings of Atlantis. At the time, as we said, Atlantis was an island larger than Libya and Asia put together, though it was subsequently overwhelmed by earthquakes and is [now] the source of the impenetrable mud which prevents the free passage of those who sail [to the sea beyond] [109a].* The course of our narrative as it unfolds will give particulars about the various barbarian and Greek nations of the day; but we must begin with an account of the resources and constitutions of the Athenians and their antagonists in the war, giving precedence to the Athenians.

Once upon a time the gods divided up the Earth between them – not in the course of a quarrel [109b]; for it would be quite wrong to think that the gods do not know what is appropriate to them, or that, knowing it, they would want to annex what properly belongs to others. Each gladly received his just allocation, and settled his territories; and having done so they proceeded to look after us, their creatures and children, as shepherds look after their flocks [109c]. They did not use physical means of control, like shepherds who direct their flock with blows, but brought their influence to bear on the creature's most sensitive part, using persuasion as a steersman uses the helm to direct the mind as they saw fit and so guide the whole mortal creature. The various gods, then, administered the various regions which had been allotted to them. But Hephaestus and Athene, who shared as brother and sister a common character, and pursued the same ends in their love of knowledge and skill, were allotted this land of ours as their joint sphere and as a suitable and natural home for excellence and wisdom [109d]. They produced a native race of good men and gave them suitable political arrangements. Their names have been preserved but what they did has been forgotten because of the destruction of their successors and the long lapse of time. For as we said before,† the survivors of this destruction were an unlettered mountain race who had just heard the names of the rulers of the land but knew little of their achievements [109e]. They were glad enough to give their names to their own children, but they knew nothing of the virtues and institutions of their predecessors, except for a few hazy reports [110a]; for many generations they and their children were short of bare necessities, and their minds and thoughts were occupied with providing for them, to the neglect of earlier history and tradition. For an interest in the past and historical research come only when communities have leisure and when men are already provided with the necessities of life. That is how the names but not the achievements of these early generations come to be preserved [110b]. My evidence is this, that Cecrops, Ereetheus, Erichthonios, Erusichthon and most of the other names recorded before Theseus, occurred, according to Solon, in the narrative of the priests about this war; and the same is true of the women's names. What is more, as men and women in those days both took part in military exercises, so the figure and image of the goddess, following this custom, was in full armour, as a sign that whenever animals are grouped into male and female it is natural for each sex to be able to practise its appropriate excellence in the community. [110c]

---

* 'out of the straits into the open sea', Lee.

† See *Ti.* 236.

In those days most classes of citizen were concerned with manufacture and agriculture. The military class lived apart, having been from the beginning separated from the others by godlike men [110d]. They were provided with what was necessary for their maintenance and training, they had no private property but regarded their possession as common to all, they did not look to the rest of the citizens for anything beyond their basic maintenance; in fact they followed in all things the regime we laid down yesterday when we were talking about our hypothetical Guardians. And indeed what we said then about our territory is true and plausible enough; for in those days its boundaries were drawn at the Isthmus, and on the mainland side at the Cithaeron and Parnes ranges coming down to the sea between Oropus on the right and the Asopus river on the left [110e]. And the soil was more fertile than that of any other country and so could maintain a large army exempt from the calls of agricultural labour. As evidence of this fertility we can point to the fact that the remnant of it still left is a match for any soil in the world for the variety of its harvests and pasture. And in those days quantity matched quality [111a]. What proof then can we offer that it is fair to call it now a mere remnant of what it once was? It runs out like a long peninsula from the mainland into the sea, and the sea basin round it is very deep. So the result of the many great floods that have taken place in the last 9000 years (the time that has elapsed since then) is that the soil washed away from the high land in these periodical catastrophes forms no alluvial deposit of consequence as in other places, but is carried out and lost in the deeps [111b]. You are left (as with little islands) with something rather like the skeleton of a body wasted by disease; the rich, soft soil has all run away leaving the land nothing but skin and bone. But in those days the damage had not taken place, the hills had high crests, the rocky plain of Phelleus was covered with rich soil, and the mountains were covered by thick woods, of which there are some traces today [111c]. For some mountains which today will only support bees produced not so long ago trees which when cut provided roof beams for huge buildings whose roofs are still standing.* And there were a lot of tall cultivated trees which bore unlimited quantities of fodder for beasts [111d]. The soil benefited from an annual rainfall which did not run to waste off the bare earth as it does today, but was absorbed in large quantities and stored in retentive layers of clay, so that what was drunk down by the higher regions flowed downwards into the valleys and appeared everywhere in a multitude of rivers and springs. And the shrines which still survive at these former springs are proof of the truth of our present account of the country [111e].

This, then, was the general nature of the country, and it was cultivated with the skill you would expect from a class of genuine full-time agriculturalists with good natural talents and high standards, who had an excellent soil, an abundant water supply and a well-balanced climate. The layout of the city in those days was as follows. The Acropolis was different from what it is now [112a]. Today it is quite bare of soil which was all washed away in one appalling night of flood, by a combination of earthquakes and the third terrible deluge before that of Deucalion. Before that, in earlier days, it extended to the Eridanus and Ilisus, it included the Pnyx and was bounded on the opposite side by the Lycabettos; it was covered with soil and for the most part level [112b]. Outside, on its immediate slopes, lived the craftsmen and the agricultural workers who worked in the neighbourhood. Higher up the military class lived by itself round the temple of Athena and Hephaestus, surrounded by a single wall like the garden of a single house. On the northern side they built their common dwelling-houses and winter mess-rooms, and

---

* The reading is uncertain but the sense is fairly clear.

everything else required by their communal life in the way of buildings and temples [112c]. They had no gold or silver, and never used them for any purpose, but aimed at a balance between extravagance and meanness in the houses they built, in which they and their descendants grew old and which they handed on unchanged to succeeding generations who resembled themselves. In the summer they abandoned their gardens and gymnasia and mess-rooms and used the southern side of the Acropolis instead [112d]. There was a single spring in the area of the present Acropolis, which was subsequently choked by the earthquakes and survives only in a few small trickles in the vicinity; in those days there was an ample supply of good water both in winter and summer. This was how they lived; and they acted as Guardians of their own citizens, and were voluntarily recognized as leaders of the rest of Greece. They kept the number of those of military age, men and women, so far as possible, always constant at about twenty thousand [112e].

This then was the sort of people they were and this the way in which they administered their own affairs and those of Greece; their reputation and name stood higher than any other in Europe or Asia for qualities both of body and character. I will now go on to reveal to you, as friends,* if I can still remember what I was told when I was a child, the nature and origin of their antagonists in the war.

Before I begin, a brief word of explanation, in case you are surprised at hearing foreigners so often referred to by Greek names [113a]. The reason is this. Solon intended to use the story in his own poem. And when, on inquiring about the significance of the names, he learned that the Egyptians had translated the originals into their own language, he went through the reverse process, and as he learned the meaning of a name wrote it down in Greek [113b]. My father had his manuscript, which is now in my possession, and I studied it often as a child. So if you hear names like those we use here, don't be surprised; I have given you the reason.

The story is a long one and it begins like this. We have already mentioned how the gods distributed the whole earth between them in larger or smaller shares and then established shrines and sacrifices for themselves [113c]. Poseidon's share was the island of Atlantis and he settled the children borne to him by a mortal woman in a particular district of it. At the centre of the island, near the sea, was a plain, said to be the most beautiful and fertile of all plains, and near the middle of this plain about fifty stades inland a hill of no great size. Here there lived one of the original earth-born inhabitants called Evenor, with his wife Leucippe [113d]. She was just of marriageable age when her father and mother died, and Poseidon was attracted by her and had intercourse with her, and fortified the hill where she lived [smoothing it over and]† enclosing it with concentric rings of sea and land. There were two rings of land and three of sea, [which looked as if they had been measured with compasses],‡ with the island at their centre and equidistant from each other, making the place inaccessible to man (for there were still no ships or sailing in those days) [113e]. He equipped the central island with godlike lavishness; he made two springs flow, one of hot and one of cold water, and caused the earth to grow abundant produce of every kind. He begot five pairs of male twins, brought them up, and divided the island of Atlantis into ten parts which he distributed between them [114a]. He allotted the elder of the eldest pair of twins his mother's home district and the land surrounding it, the biggest and best allocation, and made him King over the others; the others he made governors, each of a populous and large territory. He gave them all names. The eldest, the King, he gave a name from which the whole island

* A reference to a Greek proverb, 'friends share things in common'.

† Omitted by Lee.

‡ 'like earthwheels', Lee.

and surrounding ocean took their designation of 'Atlantic', deriving it from Atlas the first King [114b]. His twin, to whom was allocated the furthest part of the island towards the Pillars of Heracles and facing the district now called Gadira, was called in Greek Eumelus but in his own language Gadirus, which is presumably the origin of the present name. Of the second pair he called one Ampheres and the other Euaemon. The elder of the third pair was called Mneseus, the younger Autochthon, the elder of the fourth Elasippus, the younger Mestor; the name given to the elder of the fifth pair was Azaes, to the younger Diaprepes [114c]. They and their descendants for many generations governed their own territories and many other islands in the ocean and, as has already been said, also controlled the populations this side of the straits as far as Egypt and Tyrrhenia [114d]. Atlas had a long and distinguished line of descendants, eldest son succeeding eldest son and maintaining the succession unbroken for many generations; their wealth was greater than that possessed by any previous dynasty of kings or likely to be accumulated by any later, and both in the city and countryside they were provided with everything they could require. Because of the extent of their power they received many imports, but for most of their needs the island itself provided [114e]. It had mineral resources from which were mined both solid materials and metals, including one metal which survives today only in name, but was then mined in quantities in a number of localities in the island, orichalc, in those days the most valuable metal except gold. There was a plentiful supply of timber for structural purposes, and every kind of animal domesticated and wild, among them numerous elephants. For there was plenty of grazing for this largest and most voracious of beasts, as well as for all creatures whose habitat is marsh, swamp and river, mountain or plain [115a]. Besides all this, the earth bore freely all the aromatic substances it bears today, roots, herbs, bushes and gums exuded by flowers or fruit. There were cultivated crops, cereals which provide our staple diet, and pulse (to use its generic name) which we need in addition to feed us [115b]; there were the fruits of trees, hard to store but providing the drink and food and oil which give us pleasure and relaxation and which we serve after supper as a welcome refreshment to the weary when appetite is satisfied - all these were produced by that sacred island, then still beneath the sun, in wonderful quality and profusion.

This then was the island's natural endowment, and the inhabitants proceeded to build temples, palaces, harbours and docks, and to organize the country as a whole in the following manner [115c]. Their first work was to bridge the rings of water round [the ancient metropolis]* so forming a road to and from their palace. This palace they proceeded to build at once in the place where the god and their ancestors had lived, and each successive king added to its beauties, doing his best to surpass his predecessors, until they had made a residence who size and beauty were astonishing to see [115d]. They began by digging a canal three plethra wide, a hundred feet deep and fifty stades† long from the sea to the outermost ring, thus making it accessible from the sea like a harbour; and they made the entrance to it large enough to admit the largest ships [115e]. At the bridges they made channels through the rings of land which separated those of water, large enough to admit the passage of a single trireme, and roofed over to make an underground tunnel; for the rims of the rings were of some height above sea-level. The largest of the rings, to which there was access from the sea, was three stades in breadth and the ring of land within it the same. Of the second pair the ring of water was two stades in breadth, and the ring of land again equal to it, while the ring of water running immediately round the central island was a stade across. The diameter of the island on which the palace was situated was five stades [116a]. It and the rings and the bridges (which were a plethrum broad) were enclosed by a stone wall all round, with towers and gates guarding the bridges on either side, where they crossed the water. The stone for

* Lee reads 'their mother's original home'.

† (Greek) feet = 1 plethrum, 6 plethra = 1 stade = 185 metres (approximately).

them, which was white, black and [red]*they cut out of the central island and the outer
and inner rings of land, and in the process excavated pairs of hollow docks with roofs of
rock [116b]. Some of their buildings were of a single colour, in others they mixed
different coloured stone to divert the eye and afford them appropriate pleasure [116c].
And they covered the whole circuit of the outermost wall with [amber laid in oil]†, they
fused tin over the inner wall and orichalc gleaming like fire over the wall of the acropolis
itself.

The construction of the palace within the acropolis was as follows. In the centre was a
shrine sacred to Poseidon and Cleito, surrounded by a golden [barrier]‡ through which
entry was forbidden, as it was the place where the family of the ten kings was conceived
and begotten; and there year by year seasonal offerings were made from the ten
provinces to each one of them [116d]. There was a temple of Poseidon himself, a stade in
length, three plethra wide and proportionate in height, though somewhat outlandish in
appearance. The outside of it was covered all over with silver, except for the figures on
the pediment which were covered with gold. Inside, the roof was ivory picked out with
gold, silver and orichalc, and all the walls, pillars and floor were covered with orichalc
[116e]. It contained gold statues of the god standing in a chariot drawn by six winged
horses, so tall that his head touched the roof, and round him, riding on dolphins, a
hundred Nereids (that being the accepted number of them at the time), as well as many
other statues dedicated by private persons. Round the temple were statues of the original
ten kings and their wives, and many others dedicated by kings and private persons
belonging to the city and its dominions [117a]. There was an altar of a size and
workmanship to match that of the building and a palace equally worthy of the greatness
of the empire and the magnificence of its temples. The two springs, cold and hot,
provided an unlimited supply of water for appropriate purposes, remarkable for its
agreeable quality and excellence; and this they made available by surrounding it with
suitable buildings and plantations, leading some of it into basins in the open air and
some of it into covered hot baths for winter use. [117b]. Here separate accommodation
was provided for royalty and for commoners, and, again, for women, for horses and for
other beasts of burden, appropriately equipped in each case. The outflow they led into
the grove of Poseidon, which (because of the goodness of the soil) was full of trees of
marvellous beauty and height, and also channelled it to the outer ring-islands by
aqueducts at the bridges. On each of these ring-islands they had built many temples for
different gods, and many gardens and areas for exercise, some for men and some for
horses [117c]. On the middle of the larger island in particular there was a special course
for horse-racing; its width was a stade and its length that of a complete circuit of the
island, which was reserved for it. Round it on both sides were barracks for the main body
of the king's bodyguard [117d]. A more select body of the more trustworthy were
stationed on the smaller island ring nearer the citadel, and the most trustworthy of all
had quarters assigned to them in the citadel and were attached to the king's person.

Finally, there were dockyards full of triremes and their equipment, all in good
shape.

So much then for the arrangement of the royal residence and its environs [117e].
Beyond the three outer harbours there was a wall, beginning at the sea and running right
round in a circle, at a uniform distance of fifty stades from the large canal to the sea. This
wall was densely built up all round with houses and the canal and large harbour were
crowded with vast numbers of merchant ships from all quarters, from which rose a
constant din of shouting and noise day and night.

* 'yellow', Lee.
† 'a veneer of bronze', Lee.
‡ 'wall', Lee.

I have given you a pretty complete account of what was told me about the city and its original buildings; I must now try to recall the nature and organization of the rest of the country [118a]. To begin with the region as a whole was said to be high above the level of the sea, from which it rose precipitously; the city was surrounded by a uniformly flat plain, which was in turn enclosed by mountains which came right down to the sea. This plain was rectangular in shape, measuring 3000 stades in length and at its midpoint 2000 stades in breadth from the coast. This whole area of the island faced south, and was sheltered from the north winds [118b]. The mountains which surrounded it were celebrated as being more numerous, higher and more beautiful than any which exist today; and in them were numerous villages and a wealthy population, as well as rivers and lakes and meadows, which provided ample pasture for all kinds of domesticated and wild animals, and a plentiful variety of woodland to supply abundant timber for every king of manufacture.

Over a long period of time the work of a number of kings had effected certain modifications in the natural features of the plain [118c]. It was naturally a long, regular rectangle; and any defects in its shape were corrected by means of a ditch dug round it. The depth and breadth and length of this may sound incredible for an artificial structure when compared with others of a similar kind, but I must give them as I heard them. The depth was a plethrum, the width a stade, and the length, since it was dug right round the plain, was 10,000 stades. The rivers which flowed down from the mountains emptied into it, and it made a complete circuit of the plain, running round to the city from both directions, and there discharging into the sea [118d]. Channels about 100 feet broad were cut from the ditch's landward limb straight across the plain, at a distance of 100 stades from each other, till they ran into it on its seaward side. They cut cross channels between them and also to the city, and used the whole complex to float timber down from the mountains and transport seasonal produce by boat [118e]. They had two harvests a year, a winter one for which they relied on rainfall and a summer one for which the channels, fed by the rivers, provided irrigation.

The distribution of manpower was as follows: each allotment of land was under obligation to furnish one leader of a military detachment [119a]. Each allotment was ten square stades in size and there were in all 60,000 allotments; there was an unlimited supply of men in the mountains and other parts of the country and they were assigned by district and village to the leaders of the allotments. The leader was bound to provide a sixth part of the equipment of a war chariot, up to a total complement of 10,000, with two horses and riders; and in addition a pair of horses without a chariot, a charioteer to drive them and a combatant with light shield to ride with him, two hoplites, two archers and two slingers, three light-armed stone throwers and three javelin men, and four sailors as part of the complement of 1200 ships [119b]. Such were the military dispositions of the royal city; those of the other nine varied in detail and it would take too long to describe them.

Their arrangements for the distribution of authority and office were the following [119c]. Each of the ten kings had absolute power, in his own region and city, over persons and in general over laws, and could punish or execute at will. But [their rule and their community]* were governed by the injunctions of Poseidon, enshrined in the law and engraved by the first kings on an orichalc pillar in the temple of Poseidon in the middle of the island [119d]. Here they assembled alternately every fifth and sixth year (thereby showing equal respect to both odd and even numbers), consulted on matters of mutual interest and inquired into and gave judgement on any wrong committed by any of them. And before any prospective judgement they exchanged mutual pledges in the following ceremony. There were in the temple of Poseidon bulls roaming at large [119e]. The ten

* 'the distribution of power between them and their mutual relations', Lee.

kings, after praying to the god that they might secure a sacrifice that would please him, entered alone and started a hunt for a bull, using clubs and nooses but no metal weapon; and when they caught him they cut his throat over the top of the pillar so that the blood flowed over the inscription. And on the pillar there was engraved, in addition to the laws, an oath invoking awful curses on those who disobeyed it [120a]. When they had finished the ritual of sacrifice and were consecrating the limbs of the bull, they mixed a bowl of wine and dropped in a clot of blood for each of them, before cleansing the pillar and burning the rest of the blood. After this they drew wine from the bowl in golden cups, poured a libation over the fire and swore an oath to give judgement in accordance with the laws written on the pillar, to punish any past offences, never knowingly in future to transgress what was written, and finally neither to give nor obey orders unless they were in accordance with the laws of their father [120b]. Each one of them swore this oath on his own behalf and that of his descendants, and after drinking dedicated his cup to the god's temple. There followed an interval for supper and necessary business, and then when darkness fell and the sacrificial fire had died down they all put on the most splendid dark blue ceremonial robes and sat on the ground by the embers of the sacrificial fire, in the dark, all glimmer of fire in the sanctuary being extinguished [120c]. And thus they gave and submitted to judgement on any complaints of wrong made against them; and afterwards, when it was light, wrote the terms of the judgement on gold plates which they dedicated together with their robes as a record. And among many other special laws governing the privileges of the kings the most important were that they should never make war on each other, but come to each other's help if any of them were threatened with a dissolution of the power of the royal house in his state; in that case, they should follow the custom of their predecessors and consult mutually about policy for war and other matters, recognizing the suzerainty of the house of Atlas [120d]. But the King of that house should have no authority to put any of his fellows to death without the consent of a majority of the ten.

This was the nature and extent of the power which existed then in those parts of the world and which god brought to attack our country. His reason, so the story goes, was this [120e]. For many generations, so long as the divine element in their nature survived, they obeyed the laws and loved the divine to which they were akin. They retained a certain greatness of mind, and treated the vagaries of fortune and one another with wisdom and forbearance, as they reckoned that qualities of character were far more important than their present prosperity [121a]. So they bore the burden of their wealth and possessions lightly, and did not let their high standard of living intoxicate them or make them lose their self-control, but saw soberly and clearly that all these things flourish only on a soil of common goodwill and individual character, and if pursued too eagerly and overvalued destroy themselves and morality with them. So long as these principles and their divine nature remained unimpaired the prosperity which we have described continued to grow.

But when the divine element in them became weakened by frequent admixture with mortal stock, and their human traits became predominant, they ceased to be able to carry their prosperity with moderation [121b]. To the perceptive eye the depth of their degeneration was clear enough, but to those whose judgement of true happiness is defective they seemed, in their pursuit of unbridled ambition and power, to be at the height of their fame and fortune [121c]. And the god of gods, Zeus, who reigns by law, and whose eye can see such things, when he perceived the wretched state of this admirable stock decided to punish them and reduce them to order by discipline.

He accordingly summoned all the gods to his own most glorious abode, which stands at the centre of the universe and looks out over the whole realm of change, and when they had assembled addressed them as follows: . . .

BIBLIOGRAPHY

Adam of Bremen (c. 1075). *History of the Archbishops of Hamburg-Bremen*, transl. with an introduction and notes by F. Tschan. New York: Columbia University Press, 1959.

Aeschines (389–314 BC). *The Speeches of Aeschines,* with English transl. by C.D. Adams, Loeb Classical Library. London, 1919.

Ahrens, C. 1966. *Die Vorgeschichte des Kreises Pinneberg und der Insel Helgoland.* Neumünster.

Ahrens, C. 1967. 'Drei Kernbeile von Helgoland', *Die Heimat,* 10.

Alcaeus (c. 600 BC), in *Lyra Graeca,* vol. 1, ed. and transl. by J.M. Edmonds. Loeb Classical Library. London, 1928.

Alcuin (730–804). *Vita Willibrordi.* Translation in V.C.H. Talbot, *Anglo-Saxon Missionaries in Germany.* London, 1954.

Almgren, O. 1934. *Nordische Felszeichnungen als religöse Urkunden.* Frankfurt.

Alexander, M. 1966. *The Earliest English Poems.* Harmondsworth: Penguin.

Altfried, Bishop of Münster (d. 849). *Vita Liudgeri,* ed. W. Diekamp, in *Geschichtsquellen des Bistums Münster,* 4.

Andersson, J.G. 1914. 'Floran i Norrland', *S.T.V. Jahrbuch,* 15 ff.

Andrée, K. 1937. *Der Bernstein und seine Bedeutung in Natur- und Geisteswelt.* Königsberg.

Andrée, K. 1942. 'Miozäner Bernstein im Westbaltikum und an der Nordsee? Abalus, die Glaesarien oder Elektriden und der Eridanus der Alten', in *Petermanns geographische Mitteilungen,* 173 ff.

Andrée, K. 1951. Der Bernstein, das Bernsteinland und sein Leben', *Kosmós.*

Andrée, K. 1952. 'Gedanken zu Kants geologischen Anschauungen und ihre Auswirkungen auf die heutige Geologie', *Jahrbuch der Albertus Magnus Universität zu Königsberg,* vol. 2.

Apollodorus (2nd century BC). *The Library,* with transl. by Sir James Frazer. Loeb Classical Library. London, 1921.

Apollonius Rhodus (c. 295 BC–after 247 BC). *Argonautica.* Transl. as *The Voyage of Argo,* by E.V. Rieu, 2nd ed. Harmondsworth: Penguin, 1971.

Arago, D.F. 1854–7. *Astronomie Populaire.* Paris.

Aristophanes (c. 450–c. 385 BC). *Plays,* transl. P. Dickinson. Oxford, 1970.

Artemidorus Daldianus (late 2nd century AD). *Oneirocritica,* German transl. by F.S. Kraus. 1884.

Atkinson, R.J.C. 1959. *Stonehenge and Avebury and Neighbouring Monuments,* London.

d'Aulaire, E. 1975. *Bernstein, Juwelen aus dem Meer.* Stuttgart.

Avienus, Rufus Festus (4th century AD). *Ora Maritima,* with German transl. by D. Stichtenoth. Darmstadt, 1968.

Bachhofer, L. 1937, in *Welt als Geschichte,* vol. 3, p. 279. Quoted in Paret 1948, p. 144.

Baltzer, L. 1919. *Hällristningnar fran Bohuslän.* Göteborg.

Baranski, A. 1903. *Die Urgeschichte Nordeuropas nach ägyptischen Quellen.* Lemburg.

Bartholomäus, K. 1976. *Astronomische Betrachtung zur Reiseroute des Odysseus.* Düsseldorf.

Baumgärtel, E. 1926. 'Dolmen und Mastaba', *Der Alte Orient,* Beiheft 6.

Baumgärtel, E. 1953. *The Cave of Manaccora, Monte Gargano.* Papers of the British School at Rome, No. 21.

Bechtel, F. 1964. *Lexilogus zu Homer.* Darmstadt.

Becksmann, E. 1933. 'Dithmarschens Geestrand'. In *Handbuch der Landschaft Dithmarschen.* Heide.

Behn, F. 1920. *Italische Altertümer in vorhellenischer Zeit.* Mainz.

Behn, F. *Vor- und Frühgeshichte.* Wiesbaden.

Bellamy, H. 1949. *Moons, Myths, and Man.* 2nd ed. London: Faber & Faber.

Berger, H. 1960. *Bericht über das Erdbeben am 21.5.1960 in Chile.* Puerto Montt.

Bernabò Brea, L. 1954. *La Sicilia Prehistórica y sus Relationes con Oriente y con la Península Ibérica.* Madrid.

Bernabò Brea, L. 1957. *Sicily before the Greeks,* transl. C.M. Preston & L. Guido. London: Thames & Hudson.

Berve, H. 1942. *Das neue Bild der Antike,* Bd. 1, 'Hellas'. Leipzig.

Berve, H. 1951. *Griechische Geschichte.* Freiburg.

Bessmertny, A. 1932. *Das Atlantisrätsel.* Leipzig.

Bilabel, F. 1927. *Geschichte Vorderasins und Ägyptens vom 16/11. Jahrhundert.* Heidelberg.

Biollay, E. 1961. *Die Einbrüche der Nordvölker in Ägypten.* Sion. Atlantisbericht'. Lecture delivered in Hamburg.

Biollay, E. 1961. *Die Einbrüche der Nordvölker in Ägypten.* Sion.

Biollay, E. 1963. 'Der Atlantisbericht, die geographischen und kulturellen Angaben'. Lecture delivered in Hamburg.

Bittel, K., and Naumann, R. 1934. *Prähistorische Forschungen in Kleinasien.*

Bittel, K., and Naumann, R. 1952. *Boghazköi-Hattusa: Ergebnisse der Ausgrabungen des Deutschen archäologischen. Instituts und der Deutschen Orientgesellschaft in den Jahren 1931-1939.* Bd. 1.

Bolton, W. 1891. 'Über Kupfererzvorkommen auf Helgoland'. *Dingelers naturwissenschaftliche-technische Zeitschrift,* Jg. 2.

Borchardt, P. 1927. 'Platons Insel Atlantis' (various articles), *Petermanns Geographische Mitteilungen.*

Bradford, E. 1963. *Ulysses Found.* London: Hodder & Stoughton.

Bragin, A.P. 1938. *The Shadow of Atlantis.* London.

Brandenstein, W. 1951. *Atlantis, Grösse und Untergang eines geheimnisvollen Inselreiches.* Vienna.

Braune, W. and Ebbinghaus, A. 1962. *Althochdeutsches Lesebuch,* 14th ed. Tübingen.

Breasted, C. 1943. *Pioneer to the past: The Story of James Henry Breasted.* New York: Scribner, 1943; London: Herbert Jenkins, 1947.

Breasted, J.H. 1906-7. *Ancient Records of Egypt.* Chicago: University of Chicago Press. Reprint—New York: Russell & Russell, 1962.

Breasted, J.H. 1929-54. *Earlier Historical Records of Ramses III.* Chicago.

Breasted, J.H. 1954. *Geschichte Ägyptens.* Vienna.

Breusing, A. 1889. *Die Irrfahrten des Odysseus.* Bremen.

Brögger, A.W. 1937. *Arkeologie og Historie.* Oslo.

Brohm. 1907. *Helgoland in Geschichte und Sage.* Cuxhaven-Helgoland.

Broholm, H.C. 1943. *Danmarks Bronzealder.* Copenhagen.

Broholm, H.C. 1953a. *Danske Oldsager.* Copenhagen.

Broholm, H.C. 1953b. *Studier over den yngre Bronzealder i Danmark.* Copenhagen.

Bröndsted, J. 1960-2. *Nordische Vorzeit.* Neumünster.

Broneer, O. 1939. 'A Mycenaean fountain on the Athenian Acropolis', *Hesperia,* vol. 8, No. 4, p. 317-429.

Broneer, O. 1948. 'What happened at Athens', *American Journal of Archaeology,* p. 111-14.

Bühler, J. 1947. *Die Kultur der Antike und die Grundlegung der abendländischen Kultur.* Stuttgart.

Bülow, K. von. 1933. 'Wie unsere Heimat wohnlich wurde', *Kosmos,* Beiheft.

Bülow, K. von. 1935. 'Helgoland', *Kosmos,* 32.

Burchardt, M. 1912. 'Zwei Bronzeschwerter aus Ägypten', *Zeitschrift für ägyptische Sprache und Altertumskunde,* 50.

Burr, V. 'Neon Katalogos', Klio, Beiheft 9; reprinted Aalen 1961.

Busch, A. 1936. 'Neue Gesichtspunkte zur Kartographie des mittelalterlichen Nordfrieslands', *Jahrbuch des nordfries. Vereines.*

Camerer, J.F. 1756. *Sechs Schreiben von einigen Merkwürdigkeiten der Holsteinischen Gegenden.* Leipzig.

Camerer, J.F. 1762. *Vermischte historisch-politische Nachrichten,* Tl. 2. Flensburg.

Capelle, W. 1937. *Das alte Germanien: Die Nachrichten der griechischen und römischen Schriftsteller.* Jena.

Carson, R. 1956. *The Sea Around Us.* Harmondsworth: Penguin.

Carstens, G. 1965a. 'Zur Lage der Insel Farria', *Nordfries. Jahrbuch.*

Carstens, G. 1965b. 'Über den Verfasser des Chronikon Eiderostadense vulgare', *Nordfries. Jahrbuch,* p. 55-8.

Catling, H.W. 1956. 'Bronze cut and thrust swords in the eastern Mediterranean', *Proceedings of the Prehistoric Society.*

Ceram, C.W. 1952. *Gods, Graves and Scholars.* London. 2nd ed. London: Gollancz 1971.

Ceram, C. W. 1956. *Narrow Pass, Black Mountain.* London.

Chadwick, J. 1967. *The Decipherment of Linear B*, 2nd ed. London: Cambridge University Press.

Childe, G. 1950. *Prehistoric Migrations in Europe*. Oslo.

Childe, G. 1956. *Prehistoric Communities of the British Isles*. London.

Childe, G. 1957. *The Dawn of European Civilization*, 6th ed. London: Routledge.

Christ, W. 1886. 'Platonische Studien', *Abhandlungen der phil. hist. Klasse der Bayr. Akademie der W.*

Claudian (Claudius Claudianus) (died c. AD 404). *In Rufinum*, ed. L. Jeep. Leipzig: Teubner, 1876.

Clemen, C. 1934. *Altgermanische Religionsgeschichte*. Bonn.

Clement of Alexandria (AD c. 150–c. 214). *Exhortation to the Greeks* [etc.], with tr. by G.W. Butterworth. Loeb Classical Library. London, 1919.

Cles-Reden, S. von. 1960. *Die Spur der Zyklopen, Werden und Vergehen einer Weltreligion*. Cologne. Translation – *The Realm of the Great Goddess*, transl. E. Mosbacher. London: Thames & Hudson, 1962.

Conze, A. 1870. 'Zur Geschichte der Anfänge der griech. Kunst', *Sitzungsberichte der Kaiserl. Akad. d. W.* Vienna.

Cordeyro, A. 1717. *Historia Insulana*. Lisbon.

Cosmas Indicopleustes (6th century AD). *Topographia* ('The Christian topography'), ed. E.O. Winstedt. Cambridge, 1909.

Cowen, J.D. 1951. *The Earliest Bronze Swords in Britain and their Origins on the Continent of Europe*. Cambridge.

Cowen, J.D. *Bronze Swords of Northern Europe*. Cambridge.

Curtius, L. 1925. *Die antike Kunst*. Potsdam.

Damascius the Syrian (c. AD 480–c. 550). *Das Leben des Philosophen Isidoros*, transl. R. Asmus. Leipzig, 1911.

Danckwerth, C. 1652. *Newe Landesbeschreibung der zwei Herzogthümer Schleswich und Holstein*. Husum.

Decken, F. von der. 1826. *Philosophisch-historisch-geographische Untersuchungen über die insel Helgoland oder Heiligland und ihre Bewohner* Hanover.

Delff, C. 1934. 'Nordfrieslands Werden und Vergehen', *Nordelbingen* (Flensburg), Bd. 10.

Delff, C. 1936. 'Wo sind die Bernstein-Nordseeinseln des Altertums geblieben?', *Jahrbuch des Heimatbundes Nordfriesland*, 23.

Denton, G., and Porter, S. 'Neoglaciation', *Scientific American*, vol. 22, No. 6. p. 101.

Desborough, V.R. 1964. *The Last Mycenaeans and Their Successors*. London: Oxford University Press.

Desborough, V.R. 1972. *The Greek Dark Ages*. London.

Dethlefson, D. 1904. 'Die Entdeckung des germanischen Nordens im Altertum'. In *Quellen und Vorschungen zur alten Geschichte und Geographie*, ed. W. Sieglin. Berlin.

Diller, H. 1953. *Der Atlantisbericht ein Platonischer Mythos*. Kiel.

Diodorus Siculus (fl. 60–30 BC). Text with English transl. by C.H. Oldfather *et al.* Loeb Classical Library. London 1936–67.

Dionysius Exiguus (first half of 6th century AD). *Liber de Paschate*. In J-P. Migne (ed.), *Patrologiae Cursus Completus*, t. 67, p. 454–507. Paris, 1848.

Diplomatarium Danicum, vol. 1 and 2. Copenhagen 1963.

Dirlmeier, F. 1940a. 'Die Pelasgermauer der Athener Akropolis'. In *Kleine Kostbarkeiten*, ed. J.O. Plassmann. Berlin.

Dirlmeier, F. 1940b. 'Apollon, Gott und Erzieher des hellenischen Adels', *Archiv für Religionswissenschaft*, 36, 2.

Donnelly, I. *Atlantis: The Ante-diluvian World*, ed. E. Sykes. London: Sidgwick & Jackson, 1970.

Drerup, E. 1903. *Die Anfänge der hellenischen Kultur: Homer*. Munich.

Drerup, E. 1915. *Homer*. Mainz.

Ebert, M. 1924–32. *Reallexikon der Vorgeschichte*. Bd. 1–15. Berlin.

Edda (Poetic Edda). *Edda, Die Lieder des Codex Regius nebst verwandten Denkmälern*. ed. G. Neckel. Heidelberg, 1914. German translation by F. Genzmer. Jena, 1934.

Edda (Prose Edda). See Snorri Sturluson.

Edgerton, W. F., and Wilson, J. 1936. *Historical Records of Ramses II: The Texts in Medinet Habu*. Chicago: University of Chicago Press.

Eggers, J.K. 1968. *Gudrunforschung und Nordfriesland*.

Eisler, R. 1928. 'Die "Seevölker"-Namen in den altorientalischen Quellen', *Caucasica* (Leipzig).

Ermann, A. 1923a. *Die Literatur der Ägypter*. Leipzig. Translation – *The Literature of the Ancient Egyptians*, transl. A.M. Blackman. London, 1927; *The Ancient Egyptians: A Sourcebook of Their Writings*. New York: Harper & Row, 1966.

Erman, A. 1923b. *Die Reise des Wen-amun.* Leipzig. Translation of the Wen-amun papyrus.

Eudoxus of Cnidos (c. 408–355 BC). Ed. F. Lasserre. Berlin, 1966.

Euhemerus of Messene (c. 300 BC). *Hiera Anagraphe.* In F. Jacoby (ed.), *Fragmente der griechischen Historiker,* T1. 1A. Leiden: E.J. Brill, 1968.

Euripides (c. 484–406? BC). *Hippolytus,* transl. P. Vellacott. In *Three Plays,* rev. ed. Harmondsworth: Penguin, 1974.

Evans, Sir Arthur. 1921–36. *The Palace of Minos.* London: Macmillan.

Faulkner, R.O. 1969. *The Ancient Egyptian Pyramid Texts.* Oxford: Clarendon Press.

Février, J.G. 1949. 'L'ancienne marine phénicienne', *La Nouvelle Clio,* 1/2, p. 128–43.

Fick, A. 1915. 'Die Kriegszüge nördlicher Völker unter den Pharaonen Menephtah und Ramses III. *Zeitschrift für vergleichende Sprachforschung,* 47.

Filip, J. 1936-7. *Die Urnenfelder und die Anfänge der Eisenzeit in Böhmen.* Prague.

Fimmen, D. 1921. *Die kretisch-mykenische Kultur.* Leipzig.

Florin, St. 1943. 'Die älteste Bauernkultur des schwedischen Mätartales', *Forschungen und Fortschritte.*

Földes-Papp, K. 1975. *Vom Felzbild zum Alphabet.* Bayreuth.

Forchhammer, E. 1837. 'Über dauernde Niveauveränderungen und Spuren von Überflutungen an der Westküste des Herzogtums Schleswig', *Neues Staatsbürgerliches Magazin* (Schleswig), 6.

Forchhammer, E. 1884. 'Om en stor Vandflod der har truffet Danmark i meget gammel Tid'. In *Dansk Folkekalender for 1844,* Copenhagen.

Förstemann, E.W. 1966-7. *Altdeutsches Namenbuch,* ed. H. Jellinghaus. Munich; Hildsheim.

Fouqué, F. 1879. *Santorin et ses Éruptions.* Paris.

Freuchen, P. 1958. *Knaurs Buch der sieben Meere,* transl. F. Bolle. Munich; Zurich: Droemer.

Freuchen, P., and Loth, D. 1958. Translation of *Peter Freuchen's Book of the Seven Seas.* London: Jonathan Cape, 1958.

Franke, A. 1972. 'Zum Wahrheitsgehalt der beiden platonischen Atlantisberichte', *Mannus,* 38, 4, p. 267–86.

Franke, A. 1976. 'Auf der Spuren der Atlantisforscher', *Mannus.*

Fuchs, S. 1939. 'Zur Frage der Indogermanisierung Griechenlands', *Neue Jahrbücher für Antike und deutsche Bildung,* 2.

Furtwängler, A. 1900. *Die antike Gemmen.* Leipzig; Berlin.

Furtwängler, A. 1965. *Briefe.* Stuttgart.

Galanopoulos, A.G. 1958. 'Zur Bestimmung des Alters der Santorin-Kaldera', *Annales géologiques des Pays helléniques,* 9.

Galanopoulos, A.G. 1963a. 'Die Deukalonische Flucht aus geologischer Sicht', *Das Altertum,* 9.

Galanopoulos, A.G. 1963b. 'On mapping of seismic activity in Greece', *Annali di Geofisica,* 16.

Galanopoulos, A.G. 1964. 'Die ägyptischen Plagen und der Auszug Israels aus geologischer Sicht', *Das Altertum,* 10.

Gall, A. Freiherr von. 1926. *Basileia tou Theou.* Heidelberg.

Gams, H., and Nordhagen, G. 1923. *Postglaziale Klimaänderungen und Erdkrustenbewegungen in Mitteleuropa.* Munich.

Gaucher, G., and Mohe, J-P. 1972. *Typologie des Objets de l'Age du Bronze en France.* Paris.

Geer, Ebba Hult de. 1936. 'Jahresringe und Jahrestemperatur', *Geographische Annalen* (Stockholm), 18.

Gardiner, A. 1908-9. *Admonitions of an Egyptian Sage.* Leipzig.

Gessmann, A. 1935. *Neuland in Österreich.* Vienna.

Ginzberg, L. 1946-7. *Legends of the Jews.* Philadelphia.

Golenischef. 1876. 'Die Weissagungen des Nefer-Rehu, (Nfr-rwm)' *Ägypt. Zeitschrift,* 14.

Golther, W. 1895. *Handbuch der germanischen Mythologie,* Leipzig.

Gordon, D.H. 1953. 'Swords, rapiers and horse-riders', *Antiquity.*

Goyon, G. 1936. 'Les Travaux de Chou et les Tribulations de Geb d'après le naos 2248 d'Ismailia', *Kemi, Revue de Philologie et Archéologie égyptienne.*

Grant, E. 1936. 'The Philistines', *Journal of Biblical Literature,* 55.

Grapow, H., *Ausgewählte inschriftliche Quellen zur Geschichte, Sprache und Kunst der sog. Mittelmeervölker, A. Ägyptische Quellen.* Undated.

Griffith, F.L. 1890. *The Antiquities of Tell el Yahû diyeh, and Miscellaneous Work in Lower Egypt during the Years 1887-1888.* Egypt Exploration Fund Memoir 7, London: Trübner & Co.

Grimm, W. 1857. 'Die Sage vom Polyphem', *Abhandlungen der Königl. Akad. d. W. Berlin.*

Gripp, K. 1933. *Geologie von Hamburg und seiner näheren Umgebung*. Hamburg.

Gripp, K. 1936. 'Die Enstehung der Nordsee', *Das Meer* (Berlin), 5.

Gripp, K. 1941. *Eider und Elbe, ein erdgeschichtlicher Vergleich*. Neumünster.

Gripp, K. 1964. *Erdgeschichte von Schleswig-Holstein*.

Grove, P. 1961. *Danmarks Daap*. Copenhagen.

Günther, H.F.K. 1956. *Lebensgeschichte des hellenischen Volkes*. Pähl.

Gutenbrunner, S. 1939. 'Germanische Frühzeit in den Berichten der Antike'. In *Handbücherei der Deutschkunde*, 3. Halle.

Gutenbrunner, S. 1949. *Schleswig-Holsteins älteste Literatur*. Kiel.

Gutenbrunner, S. 1952. *Völker und Stämme Südostschleswigs im frühen Mittelalter*.

Haarnagel, W. 1941. 'Die Hebung III nach Schütte und ihr Ausmass'. In *Probleme der Küstensenkung im südl. Nordseegebiet*, Bd. 2. Hildesheim.

Haarnagel, W. 1950. 'Das Alluvium an der deutschen Nordseeküste'. In *Schriftenreihe der niedersächsischen Landesstelle für Marschen- und Wurtenforschung*, Bd. 4. Hildesheim.

Haarnagel, W. 1951. *Das deutsche Küstengebiet der Nordsee im Wandel der letzten 10,000 Jahre*. Wilhelmshaven.

Haarnagel, W. 1953. 'Wurtengrabungen und Küstensenkung'. Lecture delivered in Oldenburg December 1953.

Hall, H.R.H. 1922. *The Peoples of the Sea*. Bibliothèque de l'École des Hautes Études 1922.

Hampe, R. 1956. 'Die homerische Welt im Lichte der neuesten Ausgrabungen', *Gymnasium* (Heidelberg), 63, 1–2.

Hampel, J. 1890. *Altertümer der Bronzezeit in Ungarn*. Budapest.

Handelmann, H. 1882. *Die amtlichen Ausgrabungen auf Sylt 1873, 1877 und 1880*. Kiel.

Hansen, C.P. 1865. *Das schleswigse Wattenmeer und die friesischen Inseln*. Glogau.

Harms, M. 1954. *Vom Untergang von Atlantis zum Untergang des Abendlandes*. Lübeck.

Hartung, G. 1860. *Die Azoren, mit Atlas*. Leipzig.

Hauer, W. 1940. *Urkunden und Gestalten der germanisch-deutschen Glaubensgeschichte*. Stuttgart.

Haupt, R. 1930–1. 'Rolande in Nordelbingen', *Nordelbingen*, 8.

Hawkins, G.S. 1965. *Stonehenge Decoded*. Garden City, NY: Doubleday. London: Souvenir Press, 1966; Fontana, 1970.

Heck, H. 1936a. 'Küstensenkungen und Erdgeschichte Nordfrieslands', *Nordfriesischen Jahrbüchern*.

Heck, H. 1936b. 'Die nordfriesische neuzeitliche Küstensenkung al Folge diluvialer Tektonik', *Jahrbuch d. Preuss. Geolog. L. A.*, 57.

v. Hedemann-Heespen. 1926. *Schleswig-Holstein in der Neuzeit*.

Heimreich, A. 1666. *Nordfresische Chronika*. Schleswig.

Heine-Geldern, R. von 1928. 'Die Megalithen Südostasiens und ihre Bedeutung für die Erklärung der Megalithfrage in Europa und Polynesien', *Anthropos*, 23.

Helck, W. 1962. *Die Beziehungen Ägyptens und Vorderasiens im 3. und 2. Jahrtausend v. Chr. Wiesbaden.*

Hennig, R. 1925. *Von rätselhaften Ländern und versunkenen Städten der Geschichte*. Munich.

Hennig, R. 1934. *Die Geographie des homerischen Epos*. Leipzig.

Hennig, R. 1936. *Von rätselhaften Ländern*. Munich.

Hennig, R. 1941a. 'Eridanos', *Germanien*, 25, 2.

Hennig, R. 1941b. 'Abalus, die Bernsteinsinsel der Antike', in *Geographischer Anzieger*.

Hennig, R. 1942. 'Der Rhein als Bernsteinweg des Altertums', *Petermanns geographische Mitteilungen*.

Hennig, R. 1949a. 'War Helgoland die Bernsteininsel und das friesische Fositesland?' *Die Heimat*, (Neumünster).

Hennig, R. 1949b. *Wo lag das Paradies?* Berlin.

Hennig, R. 1950. *Rätselfragen der Kulturgeschichte und Geographie*. Berlin.

Herbig, R. 1940. 'Philister und Dorier', *Jahrbuch des Deutschen Archäologischen Institutes*, Vo. LV, 1940.

Herbig, R. 1941. 'Philister und Dorier', *Forschungen und Fortschritte*, 17, 1/2.

Herm, G. 1973. *Die Phönizier*. Düsseldorf; Vienna.

Herodotus (c. 484–c. 420 BC). *The Histories*, transl. A. De Selincourt. Harmondsworth: Penguin, 1954.

Herrmann, A. 1936. *Katastrophen, Naturgewalten und Menschenschicksale*. Berlin.

Herrmann, P. 1952. *Sieben vorbei und Acht verweht*. Hamburg. Translation—*Conquest by Man*, transl. M. Bullock. London: Hamish Hamilton, 1954.

Herrmann, P. 1928. *Altdeutscher Kultbräuche*.

Hesiod (c. 750 BC). [Works], transl. R. Lattimore, Ann Arbor: University of Michigan Press, 1959.

Heurtley, W.A., 'Prehistoric sites in Western Macedonia and the Dorian invasion'. *British School at Athens*, 28, p. 158–94.

Heurtley, W.A. 1939. *Prehistoric Macedonia*. Cambridge.

Hicks, J. 1974. *Die ersten Reiche*, transl. J. Abel. Amsterdam: Time-Life International.

Hitzig, H. 1845. *Urgeschichte und Mythologie der Philister*. Leipzig.

Hoffmann, H. 1935. 'Zur Siedlungsgeschichte der jüngeren Bronzezeit'. *Nordelbingen*, 11.

Hoffmann, H. 1938. *Die Gräber der jüngeren Bronzezeit in Schleswig-Holstein*, Neumünster.

Höfler, O. 1934. *Kultische Geheimbünde der Germanen*. Frankfurt.

Holmberg, U. 1927. *Finno-Ugric, Siberian*. Mythology of all Races, 4. Boston.

Hölscher, W. 1937. 'Libyer und Ägypter'. In *Beiträge zur Ethnologie und Geschichte libyscher Völkerschaften nach altägyptischen Quellen*, Glückstadt.

Homer (8th century BC?). *The Odyssey*, transl. E.V. Rieu. Harmondsworth: Penguin, 1946.

Homer. *The Iliad*, transl. E.V. Rieu. Harmondsworth: Penguin, 1950.

Hopfner, T. 1925. 'Orient und Griechische Philosophie', *Beihefte zum Alten Orient* (Leipzig), 4.

Hrouda, B. 1964. 'Die Einwanderung der Philister in Palästina'. In *Festschrift für Moortgat*, p. 126 ff. Berlin.

Hsü, Kennet J. 1976. 'Als das Mittelmeer eine Wüste war'. In *Mannheimer Forum*, ed. H. v. Ditfurth, Mannheim.

Hülle, W. 1966/7. 'Die Megalithkultur im westlichen Mittelmeerraum', *Die Karawane* (Ludwigsburg), 3.

Hülle, W. 1967. *Steinmale der Bretagne*. Ludwigsburg: Die Karawane-Verlag.

Huth, O. 1939. 'Der Feuerkult der Germanen', *Archiv für Religionswissenschaft*, 36.

Huth, O. 1943. 'Der Glasberg des Volksmärchens', *Germanien*, 11/2.

Huth, O. 1950. 'Marchen und Megalithreligion', *Paideuma*, 5, 1/2.

Huth, O. 1953a. 'Der Germanische Königshügel'. Unpublished MS.

Huth, O. 1953b. 'Der Heidenkönig im dreifachen Sarg'. Unpublished MS.

Huth, O. 1953c. 'Atlantis, Utopie oder Wirklichkeit', *Universitas*, (Stuttgart) Nov. 1953.

Huth, O. 1955. 'Der Glasberg', *Symbolon*, 2. 1955.

Isidore of Seville (7th century AD). *Geschichte der Gothen, Vandalen und Sueven*. In *Die Geschichtschreiber der Deutschen Vorzeit*, ed. G.H. Pertz. Bd. 10. 1910.

Jacoby, F. (ed.). 1954–64. *Fragmente der griechischen Historiker*. Leiden: E.J. Brill.

Jacoby, G. 1953. 'Helgoland bei Johannes Meyer und Adam von Bremen', *Die Küste, Archiv f. Forschung u. Technik an der Nord- und Ostsee*, Jg. 1953, H. 1, p. 95–129.

Jankuhn, H. 1937. *Die Wehranlagen der Wikingerzeit zwischen Schlei und Treene*. Neumünster.

Jax, K. 1929. 'Odysseusmotive in der Sage des Nordens', *Bayr. Blätter für das Gymnasialschulwesen*, 65.

Jensen, C. *Vom Dünenstrand der Nordsee und vom Wattenmeer*. Schleswig, [c. 1900].

Jensen, C. 1927. *Die nordfriesischen Inseln*. Lübeck.

Jensen, C. 1930. 'Ist der Bernsteinfluss Eridanos die Eider?' *Die Heimat* (Neumünster).

Jonas of Bobbio (7th century AD). *Vita Wulframni*. In G.H. Pertz (ed.). *Monumenta Germaniae Historica*. 1826–.

Jonas, F. 1944. 'Von der Heide zur Marsch'. In *Repertorium Novarum Regni Vegetabilis*, ed. F. Fedde. Berlin.

Jung, E. 1939. *Germanische Götter und Helden in christlicher Zeit*. Munich.

Kahl-Furthmann, G. 1967. *Wann Lebte Homer?* Meisenheim am Glan.

Kahl-Furthman, G. 1956. *Kalevala*. Transl. W.F. Kirby. Everyman's Library. London.

Karageorghis Vassos. 1968. *Zypern* Munich; Geneva; Paris.

Karsten, T.E. 1932. *Germanische Minderheitsprobleme*. Helsinki.

Kehnscherper, G. 1963. *Wanderwege der Nord- und Seevölker*, Tl. 1. Hamburg.

Kehnscherper, G. 1964. 'Santorin'. Thesis. Leipzig.

Kehnscherper, G. 1969. *Wanderwege der Nord- und Seevölker*, Tl. 2. Ottendorf.

Kehnscherper, G. 1972. *. . . und die Sonne verfinsterte sich*. Halle Saale.

Kehnscherper, G. 1973. *Kreta, Mykene, Santorin*. Leipzig; Jena.

Kehnscherper, G. 'Ansiedlung der Nord- und Seevölker nach der verlorenen Schlacht im Nildelta'. Unpublished MS lent to the author.

Kersten, K. 'Zur älteren nordischen Bronzezeit', *Veröffentlichungen der Schleswig-Holsteiner Universitätsgesellschaft*, 3, 3. [c. 1935].

Kersten, K., and la Baume, P. 1958. *Vorgeschichte der nordfriesischen Inseln*. Neumünster.

Kimmig, W. 1964. 'Seevölkerbewegung und Urnenfelderkultur'. In *Studien aus Alteuropa*, Tl. 1, p. 220-83.

Kircher, A. 1665. *Mundus subterraneus.*

Kirsten, E., and Kraiker, W. 1956. *Griechenlandkunde.* Heidelberg.

Kitto, H.D.F. 1957. *The Greeks*, rev. ed. Harmondsworth: Penguin.

Kleemann, G. 1962. *Schwert und Urne.* Stuttgart: Kosmos-Verlag.

Kleemann, S. 1962. *Ausgrabungen in Deutschland.*

Knötel, A.F.-R. 1893. *Atlantis und das Volk der Atlanten.* Leipzig.

Koehn, H. 1954. *Die nordfriesischen Inseln.* Hamburg.

König, E. 1919. *Kommentar zur Genesis.*

Kossack, G. 1954. 'Studien zum Symbolgut der Urnenfelder- und Hallstatt-zeit Mitteleuropas', *Röm.-German. Forschungen*, 20.

Kossack, G., Harck, O., and Reichstein, J. 'Zehn Jahre Siedlungsforschung auf Sylt'. In *Berichte d. Röm.-Germ. Kommission* 55. Tl. 2.

Kossack, G., Harck, O., and Reichstein, J. 1975. 'Siedlungsform und Umwelt, Grabungen in Archsum auf Sylt'. In *Ausgrabungen in Deutschland*, Bd. 2. Mainz: Röm.-Germ. Zentralmuseum.

Kossinna, G. 1928. 'Ursprung und Verbreitung der Germanen in vor- und frühgeschichtlicher Zeit', *Mannus*, 20.

Kossinna, G. 1931. 'Anfänge der Eisengewinnung und Eisenverarbeitung', *Mannus*, 25.

Kossinna, G. 1933. *Die Deutsche Vorgeschichte.* Leipzig.

Köster, A. 1923. *Das Antike Seewesen.* Berlin.

Köster, A. 1924. 'Schiffahrt und Handelsverkehr im östlichen Mittelmeer im 3. und 2. Jahrtausend', *Der Alte Orient* (Leipzig), Beiheft 1.

Krahe, H. 1949. *Die Indogermanisierung Griechenlands und Italiens.* Heidelberg.

Kraiker, W. 1938. 'Die Einwanderung der Nordstämme in Griechenland', *Die Rasse*, 5.

Kraiker, W. 1939. 'Nordische Einwanderung in Griechenland', *Die Antike*, 15, p. 195-230.

Krause, E. 1891. *Tuiskoland.* Glogau.

Krause, E. 1893. *Die Trojaburgen Nordeuropas.* Glogau.

Krause, W. 1937. *Die Runenschriften im älteren Futhark*, Halle/Saale.

Krause, W. 1941. *Die Herkunft der Germanen.*

Kretschmer, P. 1951. 'Der Name des Elefanten', *Anzeiger der phil.-hist. Klasse der Österr. Akad.d. W.*, Nr. 21.

Krogmann, M. 1952. 'Wie der Hummer nach Helgoland kam'. In *Helgoland ruft.* Hamburg.

Krüger, W. 1938. 'Die Küstensenkung an der Jade', *Der Bauingenieur*, 19.

Kübler, K. 1942. 'Kerameikos, Ergebnisse der Ausgrabungen der Frühzeit'. In *Berve*, 1942.

Kühn, H. 1938. 'Das Problem der Chronologie in der Vorgeschichte', *Forschungen und Fortschritte*, 14.

Kummer, B. 1935. *Midgards Untergang.* (2nd ed. 1972.)

Kummer, B. 1950. *Brünhild und Ragnarök.* Lübeck.

Kummer, B. 1953. 'Atlantis zwischen Kanzel und Katheder', *Der Quell* (Munich), p. 1032-40.

Kummer, B. 1954. 'Der Altantissreit', and 'Das Atlantisrätsel'. In *Forschungsfragen unserer Zeit.* Munich.

Kummer, B. 1961a. *Völuspa, die Schau einer Seherin.* Zeven.

Kummer, B. 1961b. *Die Lieder der Codex Regius und verwandte Denkmäler.* Zeven.

Kummer, B. 1962. *Vermächtnis eines Glaubenweschsels.* Zeven.

Kutzleb, H. 1940. *Steinbeil und Hünengrab*, 4th ed. Hamburg.

La Baume, W. 1924. 'Bernstein'. In *Eberts Reallexikon der Vorgeschichte*, Bd. 1.

Lappenberg, J.M. 1830. *Über den ehemaligen Umfang und die alte Geschichte Helgolands.* Hamburg.

Lartéguy, J. 1964. *Alexander der Grosse.* Wiesbaden.

Laur, W. 1949a. 'Germanische Heiligtümer im Herzogtum Schleswig im Spiegel der Ortsnamen und Ortssagen'. Dissertation. Kiel.

Laur, W. 1949b. 'Fositesland', *Jahrbuch des nordfries. Vereins*, 27.

Laur, W. 1951. 'Fositesland und die Bernsteininsel', *Zeitschr. der Ges. f. schlesw.-holst. Geschichte*, 74/5.

Lehmann, U. 1954. 'Der Grenzhorizont', *Naturwissenschaftl. Rundschau*, H. 12.

Leithäuser, J.G. 1964. *Entfesselte Elemente.* Husum.

Leipoldt, J., and Morenz, S. 1953. *Heilige Schriften.* Leipzig.

Lesky, A. 1947. *Thalatta.* Vienna.

Libby, W.F. 1952. *Radiocarbon Dating*. Chicago. (2nd ed. 1955.)

Lippens, P. 1974. 'Atlantis-Steine', *Husumer Nachrichten*, 18 September 1974.

Lissner, I. 1973. *Die Rätsel der grossen Kulturen*. Stuttgart.

Livy (Titus Livius Patavinus) (59 BC–AD 17). *History of Rome*. Transl. Rev. Canon Roberts. Everyman's Library. London, 1912–24.

Logbuch. Ludwigsburg: Karawane-Verlag.

Lübbing, H. 1928. *Friesische Stammeskunde, Friesische Sagen von Texel bis Sylt*. Jena.

Luce, J.V. 1969. *The End of Atlantis*. London: Thames & Hudson. Translation *Atlantis, Legende und Wirklichkeit*. Bergisch-Gladbach, 1969.

Luce, J.V. 1975. *Homer and the Heroic Age*. London: Thames & Hudson.

Lüdemann, H. 1939. *Sparta, Lebensordnung und Schicksal*. Leipzig; Berlin.

Ludwig, E. 1932. *Schliemann*. Berlin.

Maack, P.H.K. von. 1869. *Urgeschichte des schleswig-holsteinischen Landes*. Kiel.

Mager, F. 1927a. *Der Abbruch der Insel Sylt durch die Nordsee*. Veröffentlichungen der Schlesw.-Holst. Universitätsgesellschaft, 8. Breslau.

Mager, F. 1927b. *'Die Entwicklungsgeschichte der Insel Sylt in historischer Zeit'*, *Nordelbingen* (Flensburg), 6, p. 189 ff.

Maisel, A.Q. 1961. *'Die Steinkreise von Stonehenge'*, *Das Beste*, November 1961.

Malten, L. 1925. 'Elysion und Rhadamantys', *Jahrb. d. Kaiserl. Archäol. Institute*, 40.

Maréchal, J.R. 1962. *Zur Frühgeschichte der Metallurgie*. Lammersdorf.

Maréchal, J.R. 1959a. 'Causes et effets de l'esprit colonisateur des Scandinaves', *Annales de Normandie*, December 1959.

Maréchal, J.R. 1959b. 'État actuel des analyses spectrographiques des objets protohistoriques en cuivre et en bronze', *Revue des Sociétés de Haute Normandie Préhistoire-Archéologie*, 14.

Marinatos, S. 1939. 'The volcanic destruction of Minoan Crete', *Antiquity*, 13, p. 425–39.

Marinatos, S. 1950. ['On the myth of Atlantis'] (in Greek), *Kretika Chronika*, 2, p. 195–213.

Marinatos, S. 1959. *Kreta, Thera, und das mykenische Hellas*. Munich.

Marinatos, S. 1968. *Excavations at Thera*. Athens.

Marinatos, S. 1971. *Some Words about the Legend of Atlantis*. Athens.

Marinos, G., and Melidonis, M. 1959–61. ['The height of the waves caused by the prehistoric eruption of Santorin'] (in Greek), *Greek Geology*, 4, p. 210 ff.

Matthes, W. 1969. *Eiszeitkunst im Nordseeraum*. Otterndorf.

Matz, F. 1958. 'Die Katastrophe der mykenischen Kultur im Lichte der neuesten Forschungen'. In *Vorträge auf dem archäolog. Kongress in Neapel*.

Matz, F. 1964. *Kreta und früheres Griechenland*. Baden-Baden.

Matz, F. 1965. *Kreta, Mykene, Troja*. Stuttgart.

Matzen, H. 1907. *Forelaesninger over den Danske Retshistorie*, I. Copenhagen.

Mavor, J.W. 1973. *Voyage to Atlantis*. London: Fontana (First publ. 1969.) Translation—*Reise nach Atlantis*. Vienna; Munich; Zürich, 1969.

Maxwell-Hyslop, K.R. 1965. *Notes on Some Distinctive Bronzes from Populonia, Etruria*. London.

Mayer, M. 1925. 'Rhodier, Chalkidice und die Odyssee', *Jahrbuch des Deutschen Archäol. Institutes*, 40.

Meillet, A. 1908. *Les Dialectes Indo-européens*. Paris.

Meillet, A., and Cohen, M. 1952. *Les Langues du Monde*. Paris.

Meinhold, J. 1918. 'Indogermanen in Kanaan', *Beihefte z. Zeitschrift für alttestamentliche Wissenschaften*, p. 331 ff.

Mela, Pomponius (1st century AD). *De Chorographia*, ed. C.Frick. Leipzig: Teubner, 1880. German transl. H. Philipp 1918, and extracts in Capelle 1937.

Meyer, E. 1906. *Die Israeliten und ihre Nachbarstämme*. Halle.

Meyer, E. 1926. *Geschichte des Altertums*. Stuttgart.

Meyn, L. 1864. *Zur Geographie der Insel Helgoland*. Kiel.

Meyn, L. 1872. 'Der Bernstein der norddeutschen Ebene . . .' *Zeitschr. d. Deutschen Geolog. Ges.* (Königsberg).

'Meyniana', *Veröffentlichungen aus dem Geologischen Institut der Universität Kiel*, 1 (1952). Journal named after L. Meyn.

Milojcic, V. 1948/9. 'Die Dorische Wanderung im Lichte der vorgeschichtlichen Funde'. *Archäol. Anzeiger*.

Milojcic, V. 1955. 'Einige mitteleuropäische 'Fremdlinge' auf Kreta', *Jahrbuch des Röm.-Germ.*

Zentralmuseums in Mainz.

Mitchel, H. 1955. 'Oreichalkos', *Classical Review*, n.s.

Miltner, F. 1934. 'Die Dorische Wanderung', *Klio* (Leipzig), 47.

Möller, G. 1920/1. 'Die Ägypter und ihre lybischen Nachbarn', *Zeitschrift für Ethnologie.*

Mogk, E. 1906. *Germanische Mythologie.* Berlin.

Montelius, O. 1899. *Der Orient und Europa, Einfluss der orientalischen Kultur bis zur Mitte des letzten Jahrtausends vor Chr. Geb.* Stockholm.

Montelius, O. 1911. 'Über die Herkunft des Bernsteins in vorgeschichtlicher Zeit', *Prähist. Zeitschrift*, 2.

Moscati, S. 1968. *The World of the Phoenecians*, transl. A. Hamilton. London: Weidenfeld & Nicolson.

Mozsolics, A. 1957. 'Archäol. Beriträge zur Geschichter der Grossen Wanderung', *Acta Archaeologicae Hungariae.*

Much, R. 'Balder', *Zeitschrift für das Altertum*, 61.

Much, R. 1937. *Die Germania des Tacitus*, with commentary by R. Much. Heidelberg.

Muchau, H. 1908. 'Das dreitausendjährige Alter der nordisch-germanischen Schiffahrt', *Die Flotte*, 11, 1/2.

Muck, O. 1954. *Atlantis gefunden.* Stuttgart. Reissue—*Alles über Atlantis.* Düsseldorf; Vienna. 1976. Translation—*The Secret of Atlantis.* London: Collins. 1978.

Müllenhoff, K. 1870. *Deutsche Altertumskunde.* Berlin.

Müller, F. 1917–38. *Das Wasserwesen an der schleswig-holsteinischen Nordseeküste*, ed. O. Fischer.

Müller, G. 1925. *Zeugnisse germanischer Religion.* Munich.

Müller, H. 1844. *Das nordische Griechentum und die urgeschichtliche Bedeutung des nordwestlichen Europas.* Würzburg.

Müller, O. *Geschichte der hellenischen Stämme*, Bd. 1, 'Dorier'.

Müller, R. 1936. *Himmelskundliche Ortung auf nordisch-germanisch Boden.* Leipzig.

Müller, R. 1970. *Der Himmel über den Menschen der Steinzeit.* Berlin; New York; Heidelberg.

Müller, S. 1897. *Nordische Altertumskunde*, Bd. 1 and 3. Strasbourg.

Müller, W. 1962. 'Der Ablauf der holozänen Meerestransgression an der südlichen Nordseeküste', *Eiszeitalter und Gegenwart*, (Öhringen/Württemberg) 13.

Müller-Karpe, H. 1962. 'Die spätbronzezeitliche Bewaffnung in Mitteleuropa und Griechenland', *Germania*, 40.

Muus, R. 1932. *Nordfriesische Sagen.* Niebüll.

Nagel, G. 1932. 'Marsch, Donn und Klev in Süderdithmarschen' *Nordelbingen* (Flensburg).

National Academy of Sciences. 1968. *Report on the Alaska Earthquake of 1964.*

Naville, E. 1885. *The Store-City of Pithom and the Route of the Exodus.*

Neckel, G. 1908. *Beiträge zur Eddaforschung.*

Neckel, G. 1910. *Die Überlieferungen vom Gotte Balder.* Dortmund.

Neckel, G. 1918. 'Studien zu den germanischen Dichtungen vom Weltuntergang', *Sitz. Ber. d. Heidelb. Akad. d. W.*

Neckel, G. 1921. 'Die Götter auf dem goldenen Horn', *Zeitschrift für das deutschen Altertum.* (Berlin), 58.

Neckel, G. 1925. 'Die jüngere Edda', *Thule* (Jena), 20.

Neitzel, N. 1969. 'Bernstein an der schleswig-holsteinischen Westküste', *Schleswig-Holstein Keil*, February, April 1969.

Neokorus (Pastor in Busum 1590–1624). *Geschichte Dithmarschens von Karl dem Gr. bis in 15 Jahrh.* ed. in 2 vol. by Dahlmann. Kiel, 1827.

Nerman, B. 1958. *Hur Gamal är Völuspa?* Ark.

Neubert, M. 1920. *Die Dorische Wanderung.* Stuttgart.

Nielsen. 1873. *Liber Census Dania.* Copenhagen.

Nilsson, M.P. Visiting lecture at the University of Berlin, 15 November 1937.

Ninkovitch, D., and Heezen, B.C. 1965. 'Santorini tephra'. In *Submarine Geology and Geophysics, Proceedings of the 17th Symposium of the Colston Research Society.* Bristol.

Nissen, T. 1925. 'Die älteste erhaltenen Verse über die Nordsee', *Nordelbingen* (Flensburg), 4.

Nordén, A. 1926. *Kiviksgraven och andra forminnesplatser.* Stockholm.

Nordén, A. 1933. *Ord och Bild.* Stockholm.

Nordén, A. 1939. 'Die Schiffbaukunst der Bronzezeit', *Mannus*, 31, 3.

Norden, E. 1920. *Die Germanische Urgeschichte in Tacitus' Germania*, Leipzig.

Norden, E. 1934. *Altgermanien.* Leipzig.

Oetker, F. 1855. *Helgoland.* Berlin.

Olrik, A. 1922. *Ragnarök.* Berlin.

Olshausen, O. 1890. Über den Bernsteinshandel der cimbrischen Halbinsel und seins Beziehungen zu den Goldfunden', *Verh. d. Berliner Ges. f. Anthropol., Ethnologie und Urgeschichte.*

Olshausen, O. 1893. 'Zur Vorgeschichte Helgolands', *Verh. d. Berliner Ges. f. Anthropol., Ethnologie und Urgeschichte.*

Oppeln-Bronikowski, F. von. 1931. *Archäologische Entdeckungen des 20. Jhs.* Berlin.

Orosius, Paulus (5th century AD). *Seven Books of History against the Pagans,* transl. by I.W. Raymond. New York, 1936.

Orpheus. *Argonautica,* ed. H. Müller. Würzburg, 1844.

Otten, H. 1963a. 'Das Ende der Hethiterreiches, Zypern und die Seevölker', typescript of lecture delivered at Kiel University, 8 February 1963.

Otten, H. 1963b. 'Neue Quellen zum Ausklang des Hethitischen Reiches', *Mitt. d. Deutschen Orientgesellschaft,* 94.

Otto, H., and Witter, W. 1952. *Handbuch der ältesten vorgeschichtlichen Metallurgie in Mitteleuropa.* Leipzig. 1952.

Otto, H. 1948. 'Über die um 2000 v. Chr. Geb. in Europa benützten Kupferlegicrungen', *Forschungen und Forstschritte,* 24.

Otto, H. 1949. 'Typologische und technologische Bronzezeit', *Forschungen und Fortschritte,* 25.

Otto, W.F. 1947. *Die Götter Griechenlands.* Frankfurt am Main. Translation—*The Homeric Gods,* transl. M. Hadas. London, 1955.

Ovid (Publius Ovidius Naso) (43 B–AD 17 or 18). *The Metamorphoses of Ovid,* transl. Mary M. Innes. Harmondsworth: Penguin, 1955.

Oxenstiernà, Eric Graf. 1957. *Die Nordgermanen.* Stuttgart. Translation—*The World of the Norsemen.* London, 1967.

Packross, J. 1952. *Helgoland ruft.* Hamburg.

Palmer, L.R. 1960. 'The Truth about Knossos', *The Observer,* 3 July 1960.

Palmer, L.R. 1962. *Mycenaeans and Minoans.* New York.

Panten, A. 1976. Article on J. Heimreich's *Nordfriesische Chronik,* 15 April 1976.

Paret, O. 1948. *Das neue Bild der Vorgeschichte.* Stuttgart.

Pastor, W. 1906. *Deutsche Vorzeit.* Weimar.

Patek, E. 1957. 'Lausitzer Keramik in Ungarn'. In I. Folny, *Régészeti Füzelek,* 4.

Patek, E. 1961. 'Die Siedlung und das Gräberfeld von Neszmély', *Acta Archaeologicae Hungariae,* 13.

Patek, E. 1962. 'Die Urnenfelderkultur von Dunántuloa'. Dissertation. Budapest.

Pauly, A.F., and Wissowa, G. 1912. *Real-enzyklopädie d. klassischen Altertumswissenschaft.* Stuttgart.

Pausanias (c. AD 150). *Description of Greece,* with transl. by W.H.S Jones. Loeb Classical Library. London, 1918–35.

Pettersson, H. 1948. *Atlantis und Atlantik.* Göteborg; Vienna.

Pettersson, H. 1949. 'Geochronology of the deep ocean', *Tellus,* 1.

Pettersson, H. 1950–9. *Reports of the Swedish Deep Sea Expedition, 1947/8,* Göteborg.

Pettersson, H. 1954. *Über unerforschte Tiefen.* Munich.

Petrejus, J. (died 1603). *Annalen.*

Pfanmüller, H.W. 1970a. *Platons Atlantisbericht, 'Untergang' und 'Schlammeer'.* Neustat an der Aisch.

Pfanmüller, H.W. 1970b. Review of Mavor (q.v.) in *Mannus,* 36, 1, p. 63–76.

Pfeiff, K.A. 1943. *Apollon,* Frankfurt.

Pfeilstücker, S. 1936. *Spätantikes und german. Kunstgut in frühangelsächsicher Kunst.*

Pherekydes (5th century BC). *Genealogia.* Only fragments survive. In Jacoby, No. 3.

Pindar (518–438 BC). *Pythian Odes,* ed. E. Snell, Leipzig: Teubner, 1959. German translation by L. Wolde. 1940. English translation by O. Lattimore. Chicago, 1947.

Planck, M. 1948. *Wissenschaftl. Selbstbiographie.* Leipzig. Translation—*Scientific Autobiography.* London, 1950.

Plassmann, J.O. 1939. 'Wintersonnenwende in der Symbolik des Kivik-Grabes', *Germanien,* (Jena), 11.

Platon, N. 1966. *Crète.* Geneva.

Pliny (Gaius Plinius Secundus, AD 23–79). *Natural History,* with English transl. Loeb Classical Library. London, 1938–62.

Plischke, H. 1957. 'Das Notfeuer', *Kosmos,* 8, p. 409ff.

Plutarch (AD c. 46–c. 127). *Lives*, transl. B. Perrin. Loeb Classical Library. London, 1914–26.
Plutarch. *De Iside et Osiride*, ed. and transl. J. Gwyn Griffiths. Cardiff: University of Wales Press, 1970.
Pokorny, J. 1938. 'Zur Urgeschichte der Kelten und Illyrier', *Zeitschrift für kelt. Philol.* (Halle). Quoted in Scherer 1968, p. 186.
Posidonius (c. 135–c. 50 BC). Fragments in Jacoby, No. 87.
Pratje, O. 1923. 'Geologischer Führer für Helgoland', *Sammlg. geolog. Führer* (Berlin), 23, p. 9 ff.
Pratje, O. 1937. 'Das Werden der Nordsee', *Bremer Beiträge zur Naturwissenschaft*, 4, 1937, p. 63–94.
Pratje, O. 1949. 'Die Stadien der Entwicklung der Insel Helgoland', *Erdkunde* (Bonn), 1, p. 323 ff.
Pratje, O. 1950. 'Helgoland', *Universitas*, 5, 8.
Pratje, O. 1951. 'Die Deutung der Steingründe in der Nordsee als Moränen', *Deutsche Hydrogr. Zeitschrift*, 4, 3.
Pratje, O. 1952. 'Aufbau und Werden der Insel Helgoland'. In *Packross* 1952.
Pratje, O. 1953. 'Das veränderte Helgoland', *Helgoland und die Helgoländer*.
Preller, L. 1881. *Die griechische Heldensage*, Bd. 3. Berlin.
Preller, L., and Preller, R.C. 1884–91. *Griechische Mythologie*. Berlin.
Prigge, H. 1974. *Farbiges Helgoland.* Hamburg.
Proclus (AD 410–485). In *Platonis Timaeum Commentaria*, ed. E. Diehl. Leipzig: Teubner, 1903-6.
Procopius (born c. AD 500). *De Bello Gothico*, ed. and transl. H.B. Dewing, Loeb Classical Library. London, 1914–40.
Pytheas of Massilia (Pytheas of Marseille, c. 350 BC). Fragments preserved in various Greek and Latin authors, collected in: H.J. Mette. *Pytheas von Massilia.* Berlin, 1952; and D. Stichtenoth, *Pytheas von Marseille.* Weimar, 1959.
Quiring, L. 1948. 'Die Entdeckung des Ozeans durch ägyptische und phönizische Goldsucher', *Petermanns geographische Mitteilungen.*
Radermacher, L. 1903. *Das Jenseits im Mythus der Hellenen.* Bonn.
Radermacher, L. 1915. 'Erzählungen der Odyssee', *Sitz. ber. d. Akad. d. W., Wien, Phil.-hist. Klasse B* 178.
Radermacher, L. 1938. 'Nordische und Hellenische Sage', *Forschungen und Fortschritte.*
Ragnar Lodbrok's Saga. In *The Saga of the Volsungs, the Saga of Ragnar Lodbrok, together with the Lay of Kraka*, transl. M. Schlauch, London 1930.
Ramskou, T. 1970. 'Et dansk Stonehenge?' *Nationalmuseets Arbejdsmark.*
Rantzau, H. (1526–1598). 1590. *Descriptio Chersonesi Cimbricae.* Husum.
Reche, O. 1936. 'Die Entstehung der nordischen Rasse und Indogermanenfrage'. In *Germanen und Indogermanen, Festschrift für H. Hirt.*
Reck, H. 1936a. *Der Werdegang eines Inselvulkans und sein Ausbruch 1925–28*, Bd. 1–3. Berlin.
Reck, H. 1936b. *Die Geologie der Ringinseln und der Caldera von Santorin.* Berlin.
Redslob, G.M. 1855. *Thule, phönizische Handelswege nach dem Norden, insbesondere nach dem Bernsteinlande.* Leipzig.
Reinert, H. 1963. 'Pfahlbauforschung unter Wasser', *Vorzeit*, 11, 3/4.
Reinerth, *Vorgeschichte der deutschen Stämme*, vol. 1, Bibliogr. Inst. Leipzig.
Reiskius, J. 1696. *Kurtze sowohl historische Untersuchungen des beym alter Teutschen gebräuchlichen Heidnischen Nodfyrs.* Frankfurt.
Reiss, W., and Stübel, A. 1868. *Geschichte und Beschreibung der vulkanischen Ausbrüche bei Santorin.* Heidelberg.
Renfrew, C. 1970. 'New configurations in Old World archaeology', *Süss, World Archaeology.* 2, p. 199 ff.
Renfrew, C. 1971. 'Carbon 14 and the prehistory of Europe', *Scientific American*, October 1971.
Reuter, O.S. 1921. *Das Rätsel der Edda.* Bad Berka.
Reuter, O.S. 1934. *Germanische Himmelskunde.* Munich.
Reyna, G.S. 1956. *Los Grabados rupestres del Arquilo de los Paryneros.* Oviedo.
Richardson, H. 1926. 'The myth of ER', *Classical Quarterly*, 20, p. 118 ff.
Richthofen, B. von. 1939. 'Urnenfelder', *Mitt. d. Anthroph. Ges. Wien*, 49.
Richthofen, B. von. 1970. 'Zur Herkunft der Germanen und Indogermanen', *Mannus*, 36, 1.
Richthofen, K. von. 1840. *Altfriesische Rechtsquellen.* Berlin.
Richthofen, K. von. 1882. *Untersuchungen zur friesischen Rechtsgeschichte.* Berlin.
Rietschel, S. 1907. 'Untersuchungen zur Geschichte der germanischen Hundertschaft', *Zeitschrift d. Savignystiftung für Rechtsgeschichte.*

Riis, P.J. 1948. *Hama, La Cimetière à Crémation*. Copenhagen.
Robert, C. 1921. *Die griechischen Heldensagen*. Berlin.
Rodenwaldt, G. 1947. 'Europäische Züge der kretischen Kunst', *Forschungen und Fortschritte*.
Roeder, G. 1919 *Urkunden zur Religion des alten Ägypten*. Breslau.
Roscher, W.H. 1884. *Lexikon der griech. und röm. Mythologie*. Leipzig.
Rössler, O. 1941.   Die Weltsäule im Glauben und Gebrauch der Kanarier', *Archiv für
    Religionswissenschaft*, 37.
Rudolf of Fulda (died AD 865). *Translatio Alexandrini*. German transl. by B. Richter, in Watten-
    bach, *Geschichtsschreiber der Vorzeit*, 21, 3rd ed. 1940.
Rudolf of Fulda. *Fuldaer Annalen*. In *Geschichtsschreiber der Vorzeit*, 21, 3rd ed. 1940.
Runge, H. 1942. *Bernstein in Ostpreussen*. Königsberg.
Sach, A. 1896-9. *Das Herzogtum Schleswig in seiner ethnographischen Entwicklung*, 1 and 2. Halle.
Sax, Peter. 1631. *Eyderstedtische Landesbeschreibung*.
Sax, Peter. 1636. *Neue Beschreibung des ganzen Nordfriedlands*.
Sax, Peter. 1637. *Beschreibung Helgolands*.
Saxo Grammaticus (1150-1220). *Gesta Danorum*, 16 books, ed. P. Herrmann. 1901. The first 9
    transl. O. Elton. London, 1894.
Schachermeyr, F. 1929. *Etruskische Frühgeschichte*. Berlin; Leipzig.
Schachermeyr, F. 1936. 'Wanderung und Ausbreitung der Indogermanen im Mittelmeergebiet',
    In *Festschrift für H. Hirt*. Heidelberg.
Schachermeyr, F. 1944a. *Indogermanen und Orient*. Stuttgart.
Schachermeyr, F. 1944b. 'Dritter Bericht über die Neufunde und Neuerscheinungen der ägäischen
    und griechischen Frühzeit', *Klio*, 36.
Schachermeyr, F. 1944c. *Die Minoische Kultur des alten Kreta*. Stuttgart.
Schachermeyr, F. 1950. *Poseidon und die Entstehung des griechischen Götterglaubens*. Bern.
Schachermeyr, F. 1957. 'Die "Seevölker" im Orient'. In *Mnemes Charin, Gedenkshrift für Paul
    Kretschmer*, Bd. 3.
Schachermeyr, F. 1962. 'Forschungsbericht zur ägäischen Frühzeit 1957-60', *Archäol. Anzeige*, 2.
Schadewaldt, W. 1942. 'Homer und sein Jahrhundert'. In Berve 1942.
Schaeffer, C. 1948. *Stratigraphie Comparée et Chronologie de l'Asie Occidentale, IIIe et IIe millénaires*.
    Oxford.
Schaeffer, C. 1952. 'Philistine remains in Cyprus,' *Illustrated London News*, 27 August 1949. *Enkomi-
    Alasia*. Paris.
Schaeffer, C. 1955. *Ugaritica*. Paris.
Schaeffer, C. 1957. 'Götter der Nord- und Inselvölker auf Zypern', *Archiv für Orientforschung*, 21,
    59-69.
Scharff, A., and Moortgat, A. 1962. *Ägypten und Vorderasien um Altertum*. Munich.
Schefold, K. 1949. *Orient, Hellas und Rom in der archäol. Forschung seit 1939*. Bern.
Schellenberg, G. 1925. 'Die schleswig-holsteinischen Moore', *Nordelbingen*, p. 225-58.
Scherer, A. 1968. *Die Urheimat der Indogermanen*. Darmstadt.
Schilling, H. 1940. *Germanische Urgeschichte*. Leipzig.
Schlabow, K. 1943. 'Die 3500 - jährige germanische Hutmacherkunst durch einen neuen Fund auf
    deutschem Boden bestätigt', *Forschungen und Fortschritte*.
Schlabow, K. 1951. 'Der thorsberger Prachtmantel, der Schlüssel zum altgermanischen Webstuhl'.
    In *Festschrift für G. Schwantes*. Neumünster.
Schlosser, W. 1975/6. 'Sterne und Steine, urtümliche Formen der Astronomie und Zeitbestim-
    mung', *Mannheimer Forum*.
Schmid, W. 1940. 'Der Übergang von der Bronzezeit zur Eisenzeit, dargestellt an steirischen
    Funden', *Das Joanneum* (Graz).
Schmidt, H. 1939a. 'Funde im Moor unter Klei auf der Insel Sylt', *Die Heimat*, 49, p. 48-51.
Schmidt, H. 1939b. 'Jungsteinzeitliche Funde im nordfriesischen Wattenmeer', *Die Heimat*, 49,
    p. 251 ff.
Schmidt, H. 1940. 'Vorgeschichtliche Grabhügel unter den Dünen der Insel Sylt', *Geol. d. Meere u.
    Binnengewässer*, 4.
Schmidt-Thomé, P. 1937. 'Der tektonische Bau und die morphologische Gestaltung von
    Helgoland', *Abhandlungen des geologischen staatsinstitutes in Hamburg*.
Schmidt-Thomé, P. 1939. 'Geologische Betrachtungen zu einer Tiefenlinienkarte der Umgebung
    von Helgoland', *Geol. d. Meere u. Binnengewässer*, 3, p. 61-9.

Schminke, H.U. 1971. *Dateirung von Holzstücken aus der Lava von Gran Canaria durch das Mineral. Inst. der Universität Bochum.*

Schneider, H. 1918. 'Die Felszeichnungen von Bohuslän, das Grab von Kivik, die Goldhörner von Gallehus und der Silberkessel von Gundestrup als Denkmäler der vorgeschichtlichen Sonnenreligion', *Veröffentl. d. Provinzialmuseums zu Halle*, 1, 2.

Schneider, H. (ed.). 1938. *Germanische Altertumskunde.* Munich.

Schneidermann, H. 1954. *Wissenschaft missbraucht? Kritik an den sog. 'Diskussionen' veranstaltet von K. Gripp in Schleswig und Kiel.*

Schoo, J. 1936/7. 'Vulkanische und seismische Aktivität des Ägäischen Meeresbeckens im Spiegel der griech. Mythologie', *Mnemosyne.*

Schott, C. 1950. 'Die Westküste Schleswig-Holsteins', *Schriften des geographischen Institutes der Universität Kiel*, 13, 4.

Schreiter, R. 1932. 'Kupfererz im Buntsandstein von Helgoland', *Zeitschrift d. Deutschen Geolog. Ges.*, 84.

Schröder, F.R. 1924. 'Germanentum und Hellenismus, Untersuchungen zur germanischen Religionsgeschichte', *German. Bibliothek* (Heidelberg).

Schröder, F.R. 1929. *Altgermanische Kulturprobleme.* Leipzig.

Schröder, O. 1905. 'Hyperboreer', *Archiv für Religionswissenschaft*, 7.

Schubart, H. 1958. 'Nordische Bronzezeit in der DDR', *Ausgrabungen und Funde*, 3.

Schuchhardt, C. 1916. *Atlas vorgeschichtl. Befestigungen in Niedersachscen.* Hanover.

Schuchhardt, C. 1928. *Vorgeschichte Deutschlands.* Munich. 2nd ed. 1934.

Schuchhardt, C. 1935. 'Alte Sagenzüge in den homerischen Epen', *Archäol. Sitzbericht d. Akad. Berlin, phil.-hist. Klasse.*

Schuchhardt, C. 1936. 'Der germanische Mantel und das illyrische Röckchen', *Sitzber. d. Preuss. Akad. d. W., phil.-hist. Klasse*, 15.

Schuchhardt, C. 1939. *Vorgeschichte von Deutschland.* Munich; Berlin.

Schuchhardt, C. 1941. *Alteuropa*, 4th ed. Berlin.

Schulten, A. 1939. 'Atlantis', *Rhein. Museum für Philologie*, 88, 4.

Schulten, A. 1948. 'Das Rätsel Atlantis und seine Lösung', *Deutsche Zeitung für Spanien*, 30.

Schulten, A. 1950. *Tartessos, Beitrag zur ältesten Geschichte des Westens*, 2nd ed. Hamburg.

Schulten, A. 1953. Interview. *Kristall*, 21.

Schultze, E. 1938. 'Die Seeschiffahrt der Philister', *Internationales Archiv für Ethnographie* (Leiden), 30.

Schwantes, G. 1939. *Die Vorgeschichte von Schleswig-Holstein.* Neumünster.

Schwantes, G. 1952. *Aus Deutschlands Urgeschichte*, 4th ed. Stuttgart.

Schwantes, G. 1958. *Die Urgeschichte*, Tl. 1. Neumünster.

Schwarzbach, M. 1961. *Das Klima der Vorzeit.* Stuttgart. Translation—*Climates of the Past*, transl. F. Muir. London, 1963.

Schweitzer, B. 1922. *Herakles, Aufsätze z. griech. Rel. und Sagengeschichte.*

Schwerin, C. von. 1907. 'Die altgermanische Hundertschaft', *Untersuchungen zur deutschen Staats und Rechtsgeschichte* (Breslau), 90.

Seger, H. 1936. 'Vorgeschichtsforschungen und Indogermanenproblem'. In *Festschrift für H. Hirt.* Heidelberg.

Seitz, F. 1953. *Die Irminsul im Relief der Externsteine.* Pähl.

Seneca the Elder (Marcellus Annaeus Seneca, 55 BC–AD 40?). *Suasoriae.* In *Declamations* ed. and transl. M. Winterbottom. Loeb Classical Library. London, 1974.

Sethe, K. 1928. 'Altägyptische Vorstellungen vom Lauf der Sonne', *Sitzber. d. Preuss. Akad. d. W.*, 22.

Sethe, K. 1908–22. *Übersetzung und Kommentar zu den altägypt. Pyramidentexten.* Leipzig.

Siebs, B., and Wohlenberg, E. 1963. *Helgoland und die Helgoländer.* Kiel.

Siebs, T. 1909. 'Der Gott Fosite und sein Land', *Beiträge zur Geschichte der deutschen Sprache und Literatur*, 35.

Siecke, E. 1909. *Götterattribute und sogennante Symbole.*

Snorri Sturluson (1179–1241). *Die jüngere Edda*, transl. G. Neckel and F. Niedner. Jena, 1925.

Solinus, Gaius Julius (3rd century AD), *Collectanea rerum memorabilium*, ed. T. Mommsen, 1895.

Spanuth, J. 1953. *Das enträtselte Atlantis.* Stuttgart. Translation—*Atlantis, the Mystery Unravelled.* London 1956.

Spanuth, J. 1955. *Und doch: Atlantis enträtselt!* Stuttgart. Reprint—Tübingen, 1976.

Spanuth, J. 1965. *Atlantis*. Tübingen, 1965.
Spanuth, J. 1968. 'Der Vulkane Thera-Santorin in der Forschung der letzten Jahre', *Deutsche Hochschullehrer-Zeitung* (Tübingen), 2.
Spanuth, J. 1969. 'Widerlegung der Fälschungen von C. Schott . . .', *Erdkunde* (Bonn), 23, 1.
Spanuth, J. 1970. 'Lag Atlantis in der Ägäis?' (Review of German translations of Mavor and Luce 1969) *Deutsche Hochschullehrerzeitung*, 1.
Spanuth, J. 1971. 'Widerlegung der Fälschungen von W. Wetzel . . .', *Nordfries. Jahrbuch.*
Spanuth, J. 1972. 'Rätsel um Atlantis', *Deutschland in Geschichte und Gegenwart*, November, 1972.
Spanuth, J. 1976. 'Alles über Atlantis?' (Review of 1976 reissue of Muck 1954), *Deutschland in Geschichte und Gegenwart.*
Splieth, W. 1900. 'Die Bernsteingewinnung an der schleswig-holsteinischen Westküste, *Mitt. d. Anthropolog. Vereines* (Kiel).
Sprockhoff, F. 1927. 'Über den Rundschild in der Bronzezeit in Europa', *Mitteilungen d. Anthropolog. Ges. zu Wien*, 57.
Sprockhoff, F. 1930. *Zur Handelsgeschichte der Bronzezeit*. Berlin.
Sprockhoff, F. 1931. *Die germanische Griffzungenschwerter*. Berlin.
Sprockhoff, F. 1936. 'Zur Entstenung der Germanen'. In *Festschrift für H. Hirt*. Heidelberg.
Sprockhoff, F. 1938. 'Die nordische Megalithkultur'. In *Handbuch der Vorgeschichte Deutschlands*, Bd. 3. Berlin; Leipzig.
Sprockhoff, F. 1942. 'Niedersachsens Bedeutung für die Bronzezeit Westeuropas'. In *31. Ber. d. Röm.-Germ. Kommission des Dtsch. Archäolog. Institutes*. Berlin.
Sprockhoff, F. 1945. '. . . und Zeugen von einem grossen Geschlecht'. Oslo: Germanische Leitstelle Norwegen.
Sprockhoff, F. 1950. 'Chronologische Skizze'. In *Reinecke-Festschrift*. Mainz.
Sprockhoff, F. 1954. 'Nordische Bronzezeit un frühes Griechentum', *Jahrbuch des Röm.-Germ. Zentralmuseums* (Mainz).
Sprockhoff, F. 1961. 'Eine mykenische Bronzetasse von Dohnsen', *Germania*, 39, 1/2.
Stadelmann, R. 1968. 'Die Abwehr der Seevölker unter Ramses III.', *Saeculum*, 19, 2/3.
Staehelin, F. 1956. 'Die Philister', In *Reden und Vorträge*. Basel.
Stechow, E. 1950. 'Die Santorin-Katastrophe und "Ägyptische Finsternis"', *Forschungen und Fortschritte*, 26, 13/14.
Steenstrup, J. 1874. *Studier over Kong Valdemars Jordebog*. Copenhagen.
Steiner, R. 1928. *Unserer atlantischen Vorfahren*. Berlin. Translation—*Cosmic Memory, Atlantis and Lemuria*, transl. K.Zimmer. Blauvelt, NY: Multimedia Publishing Corp., 1959.
Steinert, H. 1970. 'Mikrofossilien bestätigen die Kontinentaltrift', in: *Frankfurter Allgemeine Zeitung*, 13 June 1970.
Steinert, H. 1971. '"Re-entry", ein neuer Erfolg . . .', *Frankfurter Allgemeine Zeitung*, 19 January 1971.
Steinert, H. 1976a. *Minisender orten die Zugwege der Aale ins Sargassomeer.*
Steinert, H. 1976b. 'Wenn Beben über die Erde springen', *Die Welt*, 20 May 1976.
Stemann, C. 1871. *Den Danske Retshistorie indtil Christian V's Lov*. Copenhagen.
Stephan, W. 1930. 'Die älteste Karte von Helgoland', *Zeitschrift der Gesellschaft für schleswig-holsteinische Geschichte*, 60.
Stichtenoth, D. 1955. 'Farria vel Heiligland', *Zeitschrift für schleswig-holsteinische Geschichte*, 59, p. 184-95.
Stichtenoth, D. 1955/6. 'Abalus und die Nerthusinsel', *Zeitschrift für Deutsches Altertum* (Wiesbaden).
Stichtenoth, D. 1959. *Pytheas von Massilien, die Fragmente übersetzt und erlautert*, Weimar. Also in *Das Altertum*, 7, 3 (1961).
Stichtenoth, D. 1968. *Ora Maritima des Avienus*. Darmstadt.
Strabo (64 or 63 BC–after AD 21). *Geography*, ed. and transl. J. Sterett. Loeb Classical Library. London, 1917-32.
Ströbel, R. 1940. 'England und der Kontinent in vor- un frühgeschichtlicher Zeit', *Germanenerbe*, 5, 11/12.
Stubbings, F.H. 1947. 'Mycenaean pottery from the Levant', *Annual of the British School at Athens*, 42.
Stumpfl, R. 1936. *Kultspiele der Germanen als Ursprung des mittelalterlichen Dramas*. Berlin.
Suball, L. 1958. *Die Neuentdeckung der Erde*. Vienna; Munich.
Suda or Suidas (AD 536-582). Ancient encyclopedist, quoted many authors whose works are

otherwise lost.

Sues, H.E. 1958. 'Die Methode der Radiokohlenstoffdatierung und ihre Bedeutung für die prähistorische Forschung'. In *Beitrag zum 5. Internat. Kongress für Vor- und Frühgeschichte, Hamburg 1958,* ed. G. Bersu. Berlin. 1961.

Sues, H.E. 1964. 'Die Eichung der Radiokarbonuhr', *Bild der Wissenschaft,* February 1964.

Sulze, H. 1958. 'Die Zimmermannsarbeit der mykenischen Bauten', *Minoica,* (East Berlin).

Swan, D.A. 1971. 'C14 und die Vorgeschichte Europas', *Mannus,* 37, 4, p. 48–53.

Tacitus, Cornelius (born c. AD 55). *Germania.* In *The Agricola and the Germania,* transl. H. Mattingly, rev. S.A. Handford. Harmondsworth: Penguin, 1970.

Thom, A. 1967. *Megalithic Sites in Britain.* Oxford.

Thom, A. 1971. *Megalithic Lunar Observatories.* Oxford.

Thomas, E.B. (ed.). 1956. *Archäologische Funde in Ungarn.* Budapest.

Thomas, H.L. 1969. 'Some problems in chronology', *World Archaeology.*

Thorarinsson, S. 1944. 'Tefrokronologiska studier pa Island', *Geogr. Ann.* 25, p. 1 ff.

Tièche, E. 1945. 'Atlas als Personifikation der Weltachse', *Museum Helveticum,* 2, 2, p. 65–86.

Trier, J. 1941. 'Irminsul', *Westfäl. Forschungen* (Münster), 4, 3.

Trogmayer, O. 1963. 'Beiträge zur Spätbronzezeit des südlichen Teiles der ungarischen Tiefebene', *Acta Archaeologicae Hungariae,* 15.

Ukert, F.A. 1838. 'Über das Elektron und die mit demselben verknüpften Sagen', *Zeitschrift für Altertumswissenschaft,* p. 425 ff.

Ukert, F.A. 1816–46. *Geographie der Griechen und Römer von der frühesten Zeit bis Ptolemäus,* Bd. 1–3. Weimar.

Usener, H. 1899. *Die Sintflutsagen.* Bonn.

Velikovsky, I. 1950. *Worlds in Collision.* London.

Velikovsky, I. 1952–77. *Ages in Chaos,* vol. 1–4. London.

Ventris, M., and Chadwick, J. 1956. *Documents in Mycenaean Greek.* London: Cambridge University Press.

Vietta, E. 1972. *Zauberland Kreta.* Vienna.

Virgil (Publius Vergilius Maro, 70–19 BC). *The Aeneid,* transl. W.F. Jackson Knight. Harmondsworth: Penguin, 1956.

Vitalis, G. 1930. 'Die Entwicklung der Sage von der Rückkehr der Herakliden'. Dissertation. Greifswald.

Vonessen, F. 1969. 'G. Kahl-Furthmanns Homer-Buch und das Problem der Philologie', *Zeitschrift für Philosophische Forschung,* 23.

Vorland, Zeitschrift für Vorgeschichte (Hamburg) 1973–.

Vosseler M. 1959. *Vorwort zu Ovids Metamorphosen.* Munich.

Wace, A.J.B. 1940. *Mycenae, an Archaeological History and Guide.* Princeton.

Wahle, E. 1924–32. 'Wirtschaft'. In *Eberts Reallexikon.*

Wainwright, G.A. 1932. 'Letopolis', *Journal of Egyptian Archaeology,* 18.

Waldemar II, King of Denmark, '*Jordebog*'. See also Steenstrup 1874 and Nielsen 1873.

Wasmund, E. 1937. 'Der unterseeische Rücken von Südstrand zwischen Helgoland und Eiderstedt', *Geologie der Meere und Binnengewässer,* 1.

Weber, F. 1905. 'Spuren des Menschen der Bronzezeit in den Hochalpen', *Korrespondenzblatt der Deutsche Anthopolog. Ges.*

Webster, T.B.L. 1964. *From Mycenae to Homer,* 2nd ed. London.

Weigelt, G. 1858. *Die nordfriesische Inseln vormals und jetzt.* Hamburg.

Weinhold, K. 1944. *Altnordisches Leben.* Stuttgart.

Welcker, F.G. 1833. 'Die Homerische Phäaken und die Inseln der Seligen', *Rhein. Museum,* 1. Also in *Kleine Schriften.* Bonn, 1845.

Werner, J. 1950. 'Mykenae-Siebenbürgen-Skandinavien'. In *Atti del I Congresso di Preistoria e Protoistoria Mediterranea.* Florence.

Wernick, R. 1974. *Steinerne Zeugen früher Kulturen.* Amsterdam: Time-Life International.

Westphalen, E.J. 1739–45. *Monumenta inedita rerum Germanicum praecipue Cimbricarum et Mega lihensium.* Leipzig.

Wetzel, W. 1925. 'Die Mineralien Schleswig-Holsteins', *Nordelbingen,* 4.

Wetzel, W. 1939. 'Miozäner Bernstein im Westbaltikum', *Zeitschrift der Deutsche Geolog. Ges.,* 91, p. 815 ff.

Wiebel, J. 1842. *Die Insel Helgoland nach ihre Grösse in Vorzeit und Gegenwart.* Hamburg.

Wiesner, J. 1939. *Fahren und Reiten in Alteuropa und im Alten Orient.* Leipzig.

Wiesner, J. 1941. 'Indogermanen in der Fruhzeit des Mittelmeerraumes und des vorderen Orients', *Neue Jahrbücher für Antike und deutsche Bildung,* 5/6.

Wiesner, J. 1943. 'Vor- und Frühzeit der Mittelmeerländer', *Sammlung Göschen.* (Berlin), 1149/1150.

Wiesner, J. 1949. 'Italien und die grosse Wanderung', *Die Welt als Geschichte,* 8.

Wide, S. 1910. 'Griechische und römische Religion'. In *Einleitung in die Altertumswissenschaften,* p. 191 ff.

Wilamowitz-Möllendorf, U. von. 1914. 'Die Phäaken', *Internationale Monatsschrift für Kunst und Technik* (Berlin), 8.

Wilamowitz-Möllendorf, U. von. 1916. *Ilias und Homer.* Berlin.

Wilamowitz-Möllendorf, U. von. 1920. *Platon.* Berlin.

Wilamowitz-Möllendorf, U. von. 1931. *Der Glaube der Hellenen.* Berlin.

Wildvang, D. 1911. *Eine prähistorische Katastrophe. . . .* Emden-Borkum. 1911.

Wildvang, D. 1938. 'Die Geologie Ostfrieslands', *Abhandl. d. Preuss. Geolog. Landesanstalt.*

Willkomm, H. 1969. 'Absolute Altersbestimmung mit der C14-Methode', *Naturwissenschaft,* 55, p. 415–18.

Wilthum, W. 1953. *Glacialgeologische Untersuchungen in den Alpen.* Vienna.

Windberg, F. 1933. 'Die Geschichte der Unterems', *Ann. Hydrographie.*

Wirth, F. 1938. Der nordische Charakter des Griechentums, *Mannus,* 3, p. 222 f. .

Wirth, W. 1966. 'Die Volute, Symbol einer kultischen Weltordnungsidee', *Antios* (Stuttgart), 7, 5.

Witter, W. 1941. 'Die Philister und das Eisen', *Forschungen und Fortschritte,* p. 223 ff.

Witter, W. 1942. 'Über die Herkunft des Eisens', *Mannus,* 24, 1/2.

Witter, W. 1948a. *Über die Herkunft des Kupfers in der ältesten Metallzeit Mitteleuropas.* Halle.

Witter, W. 1948b. *Über die Herkunft der kupfernen Flachbeile in Mittel- und Nordeuropa.* Halle.

Woebcken, C. 1932. *Das Land der Friesen und seine Geschichte.* Oldenburg.

Wölfel, D. 1940. 'Die Kanarischen Inseln und ihre Ureinwohner'. In *Quellen und Forschungen zur Geschichte der Geographie und Völkerkunde,* 4. Leipzig.

Wölfel, D. 1942. 'Die Hauptprobleme Weissafrikas', *Archiv für Anthropologie,* 27, 3/4, p. 89 ff.

Wölfel, D. 1950. 'Die Kanarischen Inseln, die westafrikanischen Hochkulturen und das Mittelmeer'. In *Paideuma,* Bd. 4. Bamberg.

Wölfel, D. 1958. 'Rätsellhafte Inschriften auf den Atlantischen Inseln, Zeugnisse der Steinzeit-Wikinger', *Die Umschau* (Frankfurt) 8.

Wölfel, D. 1976. 'Eine Felsgravierung eines neolithisch-bronzezeitlichen Schriftstypus u.a. aus der Archäologie der Kanarischen Inseln'. In *Afrikanische Studien.* Berlin.

Wolff, W., and Heck, H.L. 1923. *Erdgeschichte und Bodenaufbau Schleswig-Holsteins,* 2nd ed.

Wolff, W. 1936. 'Das Felsen-Eiland Helgoland und seine . . . . Verwandten', *Geistige Arbeit,* 4, 6.

Wolff, W. 1939. 'Worauf beruht die Küstenertränkung an der Nordsee?' *Forschungen und Fortschritte,* 15, 9.

Wreszinski. *Atlas zur altägyptischen Kulturgeschichte.* Gotha.

Wundt, W. 1939. 'Klimaänderungen in der Nacheiszeit', *Forschungen und Fortschritte,* 15, 19

Zanot, M. 1976. *Die Welt ging dreimal unter'.* Vienna; Hamburg.

INDEX

Abalus (Abalonia) (Basileia), 51, 54-6, 69, 88, 232, 250, 253

Abaris, 257

Achaeans, the, 38, 74, 104, 184, 195, 215, 243

Acropolis, Athens, 15, 17-19; 'Cyclopean' wall, 17, 18, 184, 186, 187, 199; spring, 18, 19, 256, 272; destruction by earthquake, 18-19, 159; floods, 175, 177

Adalbert, Archbishop, 44, 56

Adam of Bremen, 46, 47, 56, 63, 113

Aegaeus, god of the Eridanus, 230, 252

Aeschines, 78

Aesir (pillars of the world), 92, 144, 145, 201, 207, 208, 210

Ahrens, C., 50-1, 56, 58, 69, 118, 141, 146, 254

Al-Arish, shrine of, 148, 165

Alaska: tsunami, 168; earthquakes, 170; movement of glaciers, 176

Albinovanus Pedo, 63, 100, 243

Ålborg, 45, 192

Alcaeus, 75

Alcinuous, King of the Phaeacians, 219, 221, 234, 235, 237, 241, 242, 253

Alexander the Great, 16, 17, 35, 75, 100

Alexander, M, 235

Almería, 114

Alps, 171, 176, 181, 255; remains of burnt trees, 153, 154

Altheir, F. 79, 192

Amasis (I'ahmases II), King of Egypt, 13, 21, 267

Amber, 47-56, 64, 91, 108-9, 118, 143, 219, 243, 250, 253, 256, 260; in Eidenstadt area, 48, 51; great value, 48-50; route and trade, 51-3, 69, 98, 118, 181, 183-8, 216, 222, 227, 252; cessation of trade, 52; Asgard and amber, 209-12

Ambrones, the 99, 191, 192

Ammurapi, King of Ugarit, 152

Amor (Amurru) and the Amorites, 26, 188, 193, 196, 260

Amrum island, 69, 192

Anat, the star, 147, 152, 178

Anatolians, the, and amber, 49

Andersson, J.G., 68, 154

Andrée, K. 47, 48, 50, 51, 54, 55, 92

Anglii, the, 260, 261

Anglo-Saxons, the, 262

Antequera, Megalithic centre, 128

Apollo, 75-6, 87, 88, 112, 252, 257

Apollodorus, 30, 54, 99, 168

Apollonius Rhodius, 49, 185, 217, 224, 230, 234, 243, 250, 252, 253

Apulia, 191

Aquae Sextiae (Aix-en-Provence), battle of, 191-2, 223

Arago, D.F., 166

Archsum, grave-mounds, 174

Argonauts, the, 233, 252, 253

Aristodemus, 185

Aristophanes, 248

Artemidorus, 100

Asgard, 88, 201, 202, 204, 205, 208, 234, 242, 260; its situation, 208-12

Ashdod, 106, 198

Ashqelon, 198

Assur, 49, 152, 154

Assyria and the Assyrians, 80, 81, 92, 96, 256; and amber, 49

Astronomy, Megalithic knowledge of, 136, 138-41

Athens and the Athenians, 14-19, 87, 187, 188, 192, 199, 210, 222, 267, 268, 270; Temple of Athene and Hephaestus, 15, 18; resistance to the Atlanteans, 17, 21, 179, 186, 187, 247; earthquake, 159; tsunami, 168; floods, 175 *see also* Acropolis

Atkinson, R.J.C., 134

Atlantic, explanation of name, 29-30

Atlantis: date of narrative, 15-22; seafaring people, 16; and the Greeks, 16-17, 21, 179; conquest of Libya, 17, 179; use of cavalry, 21; home of the Atlanteans, 26-38; and the Atlantic Sea, 29; site of the royal island, 39-65; the sea of mud, 61-3; social organization, 70; Plato's use of term, 72; rule of the kings, 73; ceremonial robes, 74-5 'troy town', 91, 104, 106; and elephants, 119, 121-2; theories about its situation, 122, 245-54; ten realms of the kings, 122-33; 'com-

293